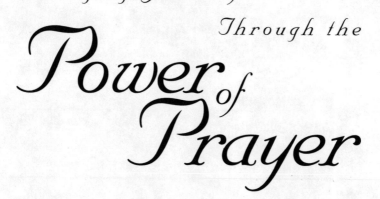

Changing Your Life
Through the
Power of
Prayer

# Changing Your Life Through the Power of Prayer

### Three Bestselling Works Complete in One Volume

## WHAT HAPPENS WHEN WOMEN PRAY

## LORD, CHANGE ME

## GAINING THROUGH LOSING

## Evelyn Christenson

*Assisted by Viola Blake*

Inspirational Press • New York

Previously published in three volumes:


WHAT HAPPENS WHEN WOMEN PRAY,
copyright © 1975 by SP Publications, Inc.
LORD, CHANGE ME!,
copyright © 1977 by SP Publications, Inc.
GAINING THROUGH LOSING,
copyright © 1980 by SP Publications, Inc.

First Inspirational Press edition published in 1993.

Inspirational Press
A division of BBS Publishing Corporation
386 Park Avenue South
New York, NY 10016

Inspirational Press is a registered trademark of BBS Publishing Corporation.


Published by arrangement with Chariot Victor Publishing,
a division of Cook Communications Ministries.

Library of Congress Catalog Card Number: 92-76115
ISBN: 0-88486-081-7

Printed in the United States of America.

# Scripture Quotation Sources

# Contents

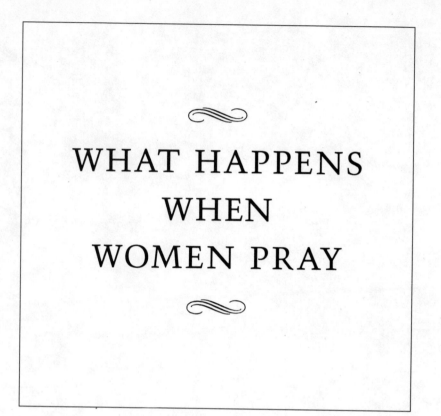

# WHAT HAPPENS
# WHEN
# WOMEN PRAY

# Contents

# Introduction

IN 1968 I was the national women's chairman for the Baptist General Conference's involvement in the Crusade of the Americas. My task was to lead the women of my own church, Temple Baptist, in Rockford, Ill. to discover through six months of experimentation "What Happens When Women Pray." Such exciting and life-changing results were experienced from the actual praying and the methods of prayer we worked out that I began sharing them at retreats, workshops, church meetings, and conferences from coast to coast and in Canada.

In January 1972 after moving to St. Paul, Minn., where my husband had joined the staff of Bethel College, I began six-week, and later five-week prayer seminars in this area. Since then we have added one-day seminars for which the material is consolidated and presented in three sessions of about two hours each. These have worked best for out-of-state seminars.

A steering committee made up of representatives from most of the churches of a given geographic area organizes and sponsors the seminars. Many times participants from over 100 different churches, both Protestant and Catholic, have attended.

Early in 1974 we opened the seminars to men and young people in addition to women. This has proved worthwhile as whole families have learned to pray together. Pastors take the material back to their churches to be used in prayer meetings, prayer weeks, and Sunday School classes. The results are exciting.

Rev. James Rehnberg describes what happened in his church in Thousand Oaks, Calif. as follows: "Our Board of Trustees had called in representatives of two fund-raising organizations for we needed to raise $226,000 to build an addition to our church. After listening to both presentations and tentatively deciding which procedure to use, I asked for 15 minutes. I quickly briefed my board on your 6S method of short, simple prayers. I reminded them that, according to Psalm 66:18, if we regard iniquity in our hearts, God will not hear us. Giving them specific instructions to pray confessing the sins in their lives before asking for God's guidance as to how to raise the money, I divided them into six small groups and sent them off to pray in different rooms of the house. After just 15 minutes of praying they came back together and unanimously voted what God had told each of them separately: *Don't use a fund-raising company. Borrow the money from the members of your own church.* Immediately we raised not $226,000 but $250,000—over and above what we needed—without even going to the local bank!"

After hearing the methods of prayer we developed, someone invariably asks, "Is this material in print?"

My answer has always been the same: "I have committed this completely to God. If He wants this in a book, He will open the doors." Then, enlisting their prayer support, I would ask them to pray specifically, *if it were God's will,* that He would open doors. So people across the United States and Canada have prayed about this book since 1968.

The preparation of the material has been a series of answers from God—from the taping of the seminar sessions, to the transcribing of the tapes, to the writing of the manuscript. God has placed on the heart of Viola Blake the conviction that it was His will for her to assist in the writing of the book.

Every step of the prayer seminars and every step in the preparation of this book has been prayed through by my Advisory Board and telephone prayer chains, with explicit instructions to pray *only for God's will.* We did not plan, or make contacts or phone calls—we only prayed.

Since we have no way of knowing who you are or what your needs may be as you read this book, our Advisory Board and prayer chains are continuing to pray daily that God will show you the next step in prayer that is *His will for you.*

*Evelyn Christenson*

# 1

## *Prayer Is the Answer*

---

*"The effectual fervent prayer of a righteous [person] availeth much."*
James 5:16

"LORD, HELP! HOW do I motivate eight gripers?" Here they were, on a cold January morning, sitting around my dining room table—the favored ones, those who had been chosen to learn to pray. I thought they would be enthusiastic about the idea. Weren't they all "spiritual life chairmen" of women's circles at church? Instead, they sat there griping.

Earlier, in the fall of 1967, the national committee of our denomination had asked me to do a project for the Crusade of the Americas. "Working with women in your own church, would you discover in a six-month period what happens when women pray?"

I had replied, "I'll take that little task."

It had sounded so simple in 1967. But on New Year's morning I awakened with a jolt: "It's 1968, and I have to find out what happens when women pray!" I didn't have a single thought in my head. I didn't know how to start. I didn't know with whom I should start. What would you have done? I panicked.

But as I was lying there I said, "Lord, please help. I feel negative. Everything is black. It's dark and it's cold and it's everything it shouldn't be. What shall I do? Show me."

Suddenly, just as if a horizontal door opened over my head, God was speaking to me, though there was no audible voice. He said, "Evelyn, if you're going to find out what happens when women pray, you are going to have to learn to use this door, the door of access to Me. This is the door of prayer. You, Evelyn, are going to have to learn to use it more effectively."

I simply said, "Thank You, Lord. Now I know just what to do."

That week I called together those eight spiritual life chairmen of the women's circles in the church where my husband was pastor. I thought, "This will really do it. These women will all be excited about learning to pray; they will be the steering committee."

Instead they griped. "I'm the spiritual life chairman of my circle," one said, "but all the president lets me do is close in prayer."

Another remarked, "My president lets me pray for the food, and that's it."

They went on and on. Evidently they didn't know what I was talking about. That's when I silently cried to the Lord for help. He answered, "OK, Evelyn, back way up and tell them about yourself."

"You know," I began, "I want to tell you something about your pastor's wife. I never teach a Sunday School class, never lead neighborhood Bible study, never speak anywhere without calling on my two strong prayer partners. The three of us pray earnestly that God will enable me to speak."

"Not you," they said. "Not our pastor's wife. You don't have any needs."

"Your pastor's wife needs prayer," I insisted; "she knows very well that she can fall flat on her face if there isn't prayer support."

I still wasn't getting through to these eight women. I had to back up some more. "In 1961, six months after I had major surgery, I was scheduled to speak at just one session of a retreat. I thought that after six months I'd be flying high, but I wasn't. A series of infections had slowed my recovery. From that standpoint, to accept the engagement was a foolish thing for me to do, but after making me comfortable in the car, my husband drove me to the conference grounds.

"All during the dinner hour I didn't say a word. I knew that if I talked then I wouldn't have enough strength to address the ladies afterward. By 10 P.M. I still hadn't been called on to speak (you know how women's retreats go on and on). Weak and trembling I searched out the chairman and said, 'Joyce, forget the whole thing. I don't have enough strength left to speak. I can't say one word.'

"Joyce Ankerberg replied, 'Just a minute, Evelyn.' She went to summon a very mature 'pray-er' whom she knew. The three of us found a little room with bunks in it, and we got down on our knees. Those two women prayed until I had enough strength to go out there and speak. At the end of the meeting we had a fireside service of rededication, and only 10 of the 400 women present did not rededicate their lives to Christ."

I had at last convinced my eight women that their pastor's wife depended 100 percent on prayer when she went out to minister for Christ. Slowly, they began to pray.

"Oh, Lord, show me."

"Lord, cleanse me."

"Lord, use me." That was all they prayed that first time, but it was a beginning.

## CONVERSION AT THE COUNTRY CLUB

Gradually, as they learned simple methods of praying effectively, God began to encourage these former gripers with beautiful answers to prayer. The first exciting result was a dramatic conversion. I had been teaching a weekly neighborhood Bible study specifically designed to introduce women to Christ, but nothing was happening. I said to the eight women, who were now praying every Tuesday morning, "I have a problem. Let's zero in on one person in that Bible study group. I know that Marion doesn't know Christ as her personal Saviour." That morning we prayed, and we prayed.

Then I told them, "I'm taking Marion to lunch." Right away they volunteered to pray while we were at lunch, and through the afternoon. As they were leaving, one said, "I'm going to pray that you take her to a place where you can really talk."

Each woman took a similar specific request home with her, and I drove on to Marion's house. When I got there she said, "Let me drive." So with my little Bible under my arm I got into her big white Cadillac convertible and we drove to her country club. Have you ever led anyone to the Lord in a country club? I hadn't, and I wasn't at all sure what was going to happen next.

Knowing that Marion's husband owned much of the stock in that country club, the host "bowed and scraped" and asked, "Wouldn't you like this nice secluded table here in the corner?" It was just the right spot for conversation. We talked and talked while the waitress kept bringing us coffee. I finally said, "You know, Marion, I think it's time we stop talking and go out to the car and pray."

What had we been talking about all afternoon? Marion had been picking my brains about Jesus. "How do you accept Jesus into your life?" / "What is it like to have Jesus in your heart?" / "What's it like living with Him?" So many

12

questions. But at 3:20 Marion jumped up from her chair and together we went out to the parking lot, sat in that big white Cadillac, and Marion bowed her head and prayed, "O God, forgive all my sins; and Jesus, please come in to be my Saviour." Marion had found Christ.

Another exciting part of this story unfolded on the following Thursday morning when the dear black woman who helped me clean once a week opened my front door with the immediate question, "What happened on Tuesday?"

"Why, Mary, what do you mean, 'What happened on Tuesday?'"

She explained, "Well, the Lord said on Sunday, 'Now, Mary, you fast and pray,' so I didn't eat; I just prayed from Sunday until Tuesday afternoon. Then in the middle of the afternoon the Lord said to me, 'It's OK, Mary, you can eat now.' What happened on Tuesday afternoon?"

I said, "Mary, would you believe that at 3:20 on Tuesday afternoon, Marion accepted Christ?"

Mary was huge, and she put those big arms around me, and I put my arms almost around Mary, and we stood there and cried, for she and I had prayed together for Marion by name for many months.

## PRAYERS, NOT PLANS OR PROGRAMS

We learned that things could happen when we didn't plan at all but just prayed. A long distance call came to our church after one of the Sunday morning services. It was Arthur Blessit calling from California. "May I use your church building for a meeting on Tuesday night?" he asked. "You won't have to do a thing. I just want to reach some hippies for Christ."

My husband said, "Fine, you may use our church."

Arthur arrived on Tuesday morning. There had been no time to advertise the meeting in local newspapers or in other churches. The only means of communication had been the

13

hippie "underground" method. But Tuesday morning was our prayer time. The entire kitchen area of the church was "wall to wall" with women who had only one prayer—that somehow the hippies of the area would hear there was to be a meeting for them in our church that night.

As we were praying, our church secretary, Carolyn, came flying downstairs and interrupted our prayer with, "The religion editor of the newspaper came to interview Art Blessit; now they're on their knees praying!" The religion editor received Christ. Art Blessit's meeting had front-page coverage that evening. How else would you get newspaper advertising in such a short time?

We had 1,100 hippies in our church that night. They had come from as far away as Chicago—90 miles—by thumb, by motorcycle, by car. Some were on hard drugs. These characters, and I mean characters, came en masse to the service. When Art gave the invitation that night over 100 of them accepted Christ. As the Christians came forward to find a place to pray with these young people, there wasn't a closet, or a hallway, or a side room anywhere in the church where people weren't already praying!

My husband is a very organized man. In fact, he is now teaching a course in management in a seminary. But the next Sunday he laid aside his already prepared sermon and announced, "I can speak on only one subject this morning: 'What Happens When You Don't Plan, You Just Pray!'"

## PRAY FIRST, PLAN AFTERWARD

God expects us to be orderly. He expects us to manage our time, to discipline ourselves, to prepare well-planned programs, but if we could learn to pray first and plan afterward how different would be our homes, our churches, our Christian women's clubs, our Bible studies, whatever we are doing for Christ. Maybe, just maybe, we are planning in one direction and God's will is in another direction. God might say, "Hold everything! Turn around and go this way. This is My will for you, not that way."

Even if we are plugged into God's will and know we're going in the right direction, we may be going at a snail's pace. God says, "Look, you see only a tenth of what I have for you. There are nine-tenths that you're not seeing, that you don't know anything about."

God wants us to make ourselves available to Him, and to say before we start to plan, "Lord, tell me what You want me to do, where You want me to go, how You want me to do it." Then our omnipotent God, with all the abundance of heaven at His disposal, will pour out His power upon us. Instead of following our tiny, tiny plans, God wants to open heaven and flood us. It's exciting.

In our early days of learning to pray, the best source of requests was the Christian Education department of our church. Gail, our children's worker, came up with a fantastic idea after she witnessed some miraculous answers to prayer. Her suggestion, "Let's pray first and plan afterwards," became the slogan for our church. During Vacation Bible School that year we set up a prayer room and collected requests along with attendance sheets. Then teachers and helpers spent their break times in prayer.

An urgent request came from one department. Not one child had received Christ though the school had been in session for a week and a half. That Wednesday morning we zeroed in on that request. The same teacher was giving the same kind of Bible story, but what a difference prayer made. I stepped into the department to see 23 hands raised to receive Christ. The spiritual ceiling of our church went straight up!

## NO DRY EYES

The original notes I made for my report at our national conference in 1968 reveal what happened in six months as we were learning to pray:

15

January—the gripe session, "Cleanse me." / "Use me." / "Forgive me." / "Show me." That was all.

February—eagerness had replaced complaining. They were excited. They were actually seeing the worth of themselves in prayer.

March—great joy and much sharing of answered prayer. They were talking about changes in their own lives due to praying.

April—there were no dry eyes as we were experientially learning what effectual, fervent prayer really is. '

May—we were claiming victory over Satan as our specific prayers were answered in specific ways. We were learning that Satan gets busy when we actually pray, not when we study about prayer or even memorize Bible verses about prayer. But the exciting thing is that in prayer we gain victory over Satan.

June—by popular demand we opened our prayer meetings to all of our church women. In just six months we had learned that "the effectual, fervent prayer" of a righteous person avails much—not plans or programs, but effectual, fervent *prayer*.

Recently, an occult high priest was quoted in our local newspaper. He said that the churches of America had given up the supernatural. They don't deal in the supernatural; they just deal in plans and programs and social action. He said that every human being is created with a supernatural vacuum, and since Christians aren't doing anything in the realm of the supernatural, he feels that witchcraft is a reasonable substitute for Christianity.

Can we still have the supernatural in our churches? I think we can, for effectual, fervent prayer is capable of producing supernatural results.

The women of a 4,000-member church learned this in a two-session prayer seminar. A week later the wife of one of the four pastors told me, "The most amazing thing happened when we learned to pray: the Holy Spirit just went 'whoosh' through our church! I didn't tell you before, but we were just about to split. Our Christian Ed department was deteriorating Sunday by Sunday, and members were pulling out. When nothing else worked, we decided to try prayer. Problems were solved and walls between the factions started to crumble."

I met her a year later and asked, "How is it going in your church?"

Her answer, "It's still going great."

## UNITY IN THE COMMUNITY

The "availeth much" of prayer was apparent, but there was more to come. One of the surprises was the terrific unity we found in communities where people learned to pray together. *Caution:* this refers to the body of Christ praying together, not just church members.

Last year I met the pastor of the host church where our first prayer seminar was held. He said to me, "Ev, you know our daughter was killed in a tragic accident last month, and an amazing thing happened at her funeral. There were priests and pastors and lay people from every single church in the area." And then he added, "This never would have happened if the women had not learned to pray together."

Was it because they met for a series of six meetings? No. It was because they had learned the unifying dimension of prayer.

Marcella, wife of the mayor of a northern Minnesota town, had a fantastic vision of what God can do when women pray. One day she called and said, "Evelyn, I'm concerned about our town. There are lots of Christians here, but we all go our own directions. We compete rather than work together for the cause of Christ. Could you come for a rally?"

One of the miracles at that rally was that there were representatives from every single church present. After the meeting a woman came to me and said, "I'm chairman of the women's committee here, and I know why this rally was a success."

"OK," I said, "you tell me."

"Well, Marcella told us last May, 'If Evelyn's coming for a rally, she expects you to be praying. Now get on the ball.' So we did and we have prayed in an organized fashion every other week from May to October."

I was still shaking hands with the women when a beautiful blond girl stepped up to me and asked, "Why am I here?"

I sort of blinked and replied, "Don't you know why you're here?"

"No, I don't know why I'm here. I've never been in this church before, but this afternoon a very peculiar thing happened to me. All at once it was as if an irresistible force was urging me to come to this meeting tonight; I thought I'd better come. Why am I here?"

I looked at her and asked, "Honey, do you know Christ as your Saviour?"

She replied, "No, I don't."

Then I asked, "Would you like to?"

She said, "Yes, I would like to."

After I finished shaking hands we went downstairs and prayed together, and there she accepted Christ as her personal Saviour.

Marcella envisioned something more for the Christian women of her town—a retreat. Several months later the women who had begun to feel their marvelous unity in Christ came to the retreat. One was the same little blond I had prayed with before. "I now know what that irresistible force was," she said. "It was God's power. My husband has been a Christian for many years, and God has been calling him into full-time service, but I wasn't even a Christian. Now I'm going to be a pastor's wife. My husband has enrolled in seminary. What a horrible pastor's wife I would have made, not even knowing Jesus as my Saviour."

18

As we were leaving the retreat one woman remarked to me, "I think we ought to call this the 'red nose session.' Just look around at all the tears and all the red noses!" It was true. Women who formerly had crossed the street to keep from speaking to each other were now throbbing in one accord, in unity, loving each other in Christ. Something really had happened there. An irresistible force had been at work, as a result of prayer.

One day my husband walked out of the sanctuary of our church and encountered our custodian fairly dripping with perspiration. He was a giant of a Christian, but was gradually losing his ability to think and work effectively because of hardening of the arteries. As my husband saw him struggling with the vacuum cleaner he looked down, and there lying on the floor was the plug. The dear man had vacuumed the whole auditorium and didn't have the plug in the outlet!

Isn't that what happens to many of us? We work, we pull, we struggle, and we plan until we're utterly exhausted, but we have forgotten to plug in to the source of power. And that source of power is prayer—the "effectual, fervent prayer" of a righteous person that avails much.

**For You to Pray:**
"Dear God, teach me to plug in to Your power. Amen."

19

# 2

## *It Doesn't Take So Long*

---

*"If I regard iniquity in my heart, the Lord will not hear me."* Psalm
*66:18*

"HOW'S IT GOING, 'Mrs. Chris'?" My very good friend,
Steve, one of our church boys, always asked me that ques-
tion when he came home for an occasional weekend from
Harvard School of Business.

Some days I answered, "Oh, is it ever going great. We just
learned this kind of prayer and look what's happening. It's
going just great!"

Then, when he would come home other times and ask
how things were going, I would have a different answer.
"Oh, did we fall on our faces this week! It was a mess. I
don't know who suggested the method of prayer we tried
this time, but it sure didn't work."

Finally Steve, with his youthful fervor, was getting a little
exasperated hearing of the struggles we were having as we
were learning to pray effectively. I'll never forget the day
he and I met down by the piano in the front of the sanctuary. He stood there with his hands on his hips, and look-

ing straight at me, asked, *"'Mrs. Chris,' why does it take so long?"*

I said, "Steve, I don't know. I wish I did. I'm sure it's not God's fault. This is all experimentation; it's trial and error for us. We're just learning. I really don't know why it's taking us so long."

Steve is now one of the vice-presidents of an international Christian organization, and last spring while he was teaching a management course in Atlanta, I sent him a message via one of our officers. I asked her to please tell Steve that "it doesn't take so long anymore."

Several weeks later when Steve visited us at our cottage on the shores of Lake Michigan, he said, "You know, when Jan gave me your message, 'It doesn't take so long anymore,' I had to scratch my head and wonder, *What is Ev saying to me?* Then I remembered my question back in 1968."

As I stood cooking the breakfast eggs in the cottage kitchen that next morning, I explained to Steve how and why it doesn't take so long anymore. It went something like the following.

## EFFECTIVE FERVENT PRAYER IN ONLY SIX WEEKS

Our first prayer seminar was held in White Bear Lake, Minn. with 20 different churches represented. It was a six-week seminar, and the women were practicing simple, sometimes hesitant, audible praying. At the fifth session, one of the women shared with us that the occult had been invited into a local high school. Witches, with all their garb and paraphernalia, were instructing the students, including her daughter, in the ways of witchcraft. Of the 250 women present, many had children in that high school.

Fervent prayer really began then for those students and their teachers. In fact, women were praying so earnestly in their groups that I had to step to the microphone and tell them to conclude their praying because the baby-sitters had to go home! God had given them an urgent reason for learning to pray quickly.

God also gave them answers to their prayers. A group of Christian parents went to school officials about the matter, and, as a result, Christian speakers were given equal time to expose the errors of the occult.

Something else was stirring in that first prayer seminar. It came from a group of women from a liturgical church who sat in the second row. I could always count on them to be in the same place each week. What an inspiration they were. At the third session one of them came to me and said, "Mrs. Christenson, we want you to know that after just two weeks of praying we are already in 'April praying.'"

I had to scratch my head and think, "April praying, April praying?" Oh yes, I recalled having told the group that in 1968 it had taken us from January to April to get to our "No dry eyes," as we were experientially learning what effectual, fervent prayer really was. I said, "Tell me about your 'April praying.'"

She went on, "After the very first session, all of us from our church went home, and we promised each other that though we couldn't meet together every single day, we would pray for our church every morning at 9 o'clock. In just two weeks we are seeing fantastic things happen; we are already in 'April praying.'"

A couple of weeks later they brought me a copy of their church bulletin. One of the women said, "Look what our minister has written!"

I read, "If all these wonderful things happen to women who learn to pray, let's start praying as families."

The minister even began to preach a series of sermons on prayer because that little group practiced what they had learned the very first week.

This is what's exciting to me about the prayer seminars. There is always a nucleus of people, both men and women, from all denominations going back and turning their churches upside down.

I said to Steve, "It took only two weeks for that group from that church to learn to pray. No, it doesn't take so long anymore."

## SIX MONTHS, SIX WEEKS, SIX HOURS

One day a district leader of the Young Life Campaigners came to me with a question, "Do you think you could teach our Campaigners to pray in six hours? We're planning to meet at a college, but there's going to be a wedding there at 4 o'clock, so we have to be out of the building by 3."

I blinked, and thought, *Six hours! Six weeks is one thing; six months is how long it took us at first; but now this group is asking for only six hours!* I said, "I don't know if I can, but I'll try."

We met together at 9 o'clock in the morning. By 11 A.M. those teenagers, many of whom were disenchanted with the established church, had pushed back their chairs and were kneeling on the floor in little circles fervently praying. I felt tears spring to my eyes at that sight—after only two hours.

Recently, in Fargo, N. D. we had our first one-day seminar. I had to tell the ladies that I wasn't sure it would work, but we plunged in, breaking just once for mid-morning coffee. Then, following lunch, we had an all-afternoon session. At the end of the day, the chairman said to me, "Evelyn, the most exciting thing to me has been to hear this fervent prayer so soon by 100% of the people who have just learned to pray today." How long does it take? It doesn't take so long.

## RELEASED TO PRAY FOR OTHERS

I want to share with you one other six-week session that took place way back in the fall of 1964 when my two prayer partners, Lorna and Signe, and I began to pray together.

Everything seemed to be going great in our church. In four years our membership had almost doubled, a building program was in progress, and we had a full schedule of activities to meet the needs of our congregation. Yet, the three of us sensed that there was a missing dimension. We decided to meet once a week to pray for our church—a very noble idea, we thought.

We agreed at the start to base our praying on a verse of Scripture (a good rule to follow), and right away God gave us Psalm 66:18: "If I regard iniquity in my heart, the Lord will not hear me."

"Lord, what do You mean?" we asked. "We're going to pray for our church." But He continued to apply the pressure gently: "If *I* regard iniquity in *my* heart, the Lord will not hear *me*." Wow! I, the pastor's wife? Lorna and Signe? Uh, huh.

God didn't release us to pray for other needs until we had cleaned up our own lives by confessing *our* sins. It took us, oh, so long. We prayed and prayed, and God kept bringing sins and sins to our minds. As our first prayer meeting came to a close, we thought, *Phew! We got that one over with; next week we can start praying for the needs of the church.*" But when we met the following week, we still couldn't get beyond Psalm 66:18! This was a new concept to us. God kept bringing our wrong priorities, thoughts, reactions, and attitudes to our minds. It took the three of us six weeks—six whole weeks—to get out of Psalm 66:18 and into effectual, fervent praying. I see one of those prayer partners occasionally, and we still shake our heads at that one!

You don't have that many things to be cleaned up in your life, do you? But I did, as a pastor's wife. The other day someone asked me, "What kinds of sins do pastors' wives commit, or is that too personal?"

Not knowing how to answer her offhand, I decided to compile a list, from memory, of the many sins we confessed then. Two days later Signe stopped in the Twin Cities en route back to her home from California. "Sig, what specific sins do you remember from those six weeks of Psalm 66:18 back in 1964?" I asked.

"The main one I remember," she replied immediately, "was our superior attitude concerning our spiritual status as compared to others and the idea that we should pray *for* them. God showed us that attitude was sin." (I added that one to the two-page list I had jotted down in answer to the question!)

What other sins had we confessed?

*Divided motives.* All of us were very involved in serving Christ, thinking our reasons were all for His glory. But God showed us how much there was of ego, self-fulfillment, self-satisfaction, and desire to build up our own worth in the eyes of our fellow church members.

*Pretense.* One said it was the first time in her life she was really honest before God. People had her on a spiritual pedestal; and she didn't dare admit, even to her family, that she wasn't as spiritual as everybody told her she was. Then she confessed to God a bad attitude toward one member of her family that no one could have dreamed was there.

*Pride.* How surprised I was when God exposed as sin the feeling of "look what I've done" that would come over me as I passed the mimeographed copies of *my* lesson outline to the members of my adult Sunday School class. I was never satisfied in the preparation of my lesson until I had exhausted the resources in my husband's library, put the volumes of notes in outline form, typed stencils, and run off copies for all.

No, none of us had been practicing any of the "dirty dozen" sins, but God exposed one by one the "little Christian sins" that Peter could have been referring to when he wrote, "For the eyes of the Lord are over the righteous, and His ears are open unto their prayers; but the face of the Lord is against them that do evil" (1 Peter 3:12).

THE POWER OF PRAYER

## A PREREQUISITE TO ANSWERED PRAYER

The three of us learned in a very practical way that there are prerequisites to effective intercessory prayer. There is one word we didn't touch on in the first chapter when we cited: "The effectual, fervent prayer of a righteous person availeth much." Did you catch what we missed? "The effectual fervent prayer" of what kind of person! A *righteous* person. It is his prayer, and only his, that availeth much.

If we are living in sin and liking it, if we are keeping it there, finding that it feels kind of good, if we're regarding—nurturing, patting that little sin along—God does not hear us.

The Prophet Isaiah gives a powerful description of someone in this plight, "Listen now! The Lord isn't too weak to save you. And He isn't getting deaf! He can hear you when you call! But the trouble is that your sins have cut you off from God. Because of sin He has turned His face away from you and will not listen anymore" (Isa. 59:1–2, LB).

Do you wonder why your prayers aren't answered? We're going to learn many reasons why they are not in the chapters that follow, but here is the first one: sin (or sins) in your life. It is "the effectual, fervent prayer of a *righteous* person that availeth much." If your prayers aren't availing much, this may be the reason. Maybe it isn't. Maybe you're long past this. But I find that when I think I'm past this one, all at once a little pride pops up, and I have to confess it quickly, get it out, and then go on.

Your problem may not be *sins*, but *sin*. And this is a very important point. When our Lord was talking to His disciples just before His crucifixion, He told them that He was going to send the Comforter, the Holy Spirit, who would convict *the world* (those who were not Christ's followers) "of sin, because they believe not on Me" (John 16:9). This is the sin that will keep God from hearing intercessory

26

prayer—the sin of not believing in Christ as your personal saviour. If this is your sin, the only prayer from you that God promises to hear is one of repentance and faith as you invite Christ into your life.

After we become Christians we commit sins. What do we do with them? Do we live with them? The answer is that we get rid of them. God gives Christians the formula through John, "If *we* confess our sins, He is faithful and just to forgive us *our sins,* and to cleanse us from all unrighteousness" (1 John 1:9). This is written to Christians, and tells us how we may be cleansed and ready for an effectual intercessory prayer life.

Even little sins can muddy up our communication system. We try to get through to God and there's something in the way. It may be an attitude, a spoken word. God wants these things cleared up. He doesn't want anything between Him and us. If there is, it's our fault, not His, when His ears are closed to our prayers.

Back in 1968, one dear woman objected to this. She said, "I don't like this one bit, this cleaning up of my life before I can be a good, strong, powerful intercessory pray-er."

Another said, "Not me. I have pre-school twin boys, and no matter how much I clean up my life before I start for this prayer meeting, by the time I reach here with them in the car, there's some attitude I have to get cleaned up before I can pray for others."

I found out later that the one who objected so strenuously was harboring a grave sin in her life. She didn't like this process, but it's very definite in God's Word. This, then, is the first prerequisite—nothing between God and ourselves when we approach intercessory prayer.

How long does it take? It really doesn't take so long.

**For You to Pray:**
    "Dear Father, bring to my mind that sin or sins keeping You from hearing my intercessory prayers.

"I confess whatever You have brought to my mind as sin.

"Thank You, Lord, for cleansing me as You promised in 1 John 1:9 and qualifying me for effectual, intercessory prayer."

# 3

## *Praying in One Accord*

---

*"These all continued with one accord in prayer and supplication, with the women, and Mary the mother of Jesus, and with His brethren."* Acts 1:14

"Ev, THIS IS a completely different church from what it was when we left. Why?"

To the returned missionary who asked this question, I replied, "The answer is simple. We have learned to pray in the four years that you and your husband have been in Ethiopia." Then I went on and shared with her how it all started in 1968, the experimentation with prayer techniques, and the method we finally came up with in those days—the small group method of prayer which we call "Praying in One Accord." We found this in God's Word, in the Book of Acts:

And when He had spoken these things, while they beheld, He was taken up; and a cloud received Him out of their sight. . . . Then returned they unto Jerusalem from the mount called Olivet, which is from Jerusalem a sabbath day's journey. And when they were come in, they went up into an upper room, where abode both

Peter, and James, and John, and Andrew, Philip, and Thomas, Bartholomew, and Matthew, James the son of Alpheus, and Simon Zelotes, and Judas the brother of James. *These all continued with one accord in prayer and supplication,* with the women, and Mary the mother of Jesus and with His brethren" (Acts 1:9, 12–14).

It was a new and exciting experience for us to discover that women were included at this significant time, in the life of the Early Church. Among them was Mary, the mother of Jesus. In this final reference to her in the New Testament, she is on her face before God, praying with the disciples, the brethren, and the other women. Wouldn't you like to have been with them in that upper room? What do you suppose they were praying about? We can't answer that question, but we do know that their hearts were throbbing together as they were praying in one accord.

Jesus, their Lord, had just left Planet Earth. He had gone from their sight, yet the 120 gathered in the upper room had the privilege of sensing His presence in their midst. Only a short while before, He had told His disciples, "For where two or three are gathered together in My name, there am I in the midst of them" (Matt. 18:20). Jesus was speaking of those who gather together *in His name,* not of just any group of people who meet together on earth. It is only to His followers that He gives the promise of His presence. Small group praying, the method of praying in one accord, is based on the eligibility to pray in the name of Jesus, it pertains only to the followers of Christ.

## LORD, TEACH US TO PRAY

We can learn something else from the upper room prayers. They were putting into practice what Jesus had taught them about prayer when He was on earth. His disciples must have felt a tremendous lack in their own lives as they saw the beautiful example of the prayer life of their Lord.

30

In their need they cried, "Lord, teach us to pray" (Luke 11:1).

Today earnest followers of the Lord sense their need just as the disciples did. It's amazing that we can knock on doors, get on the telephone, invite people to our prayer groups, only to find that when we meet together we do not know how to pray. I was one of 11 chairmen who formed 5,000 prayer groups for a Billy Graham Crusade held in our area. Later, I will describe how I got involved in that. In any case, we heard afterward that fantastic things had happened in some of those prayer groups where women had prayed for five consecutive weeks before and during the crusade. But hundreds of women have said to me, "We did everything you told us to do. We knocked on doors, we called our neighbors. We did all these things, but we didn't know what to do when we got together. We didn't know how to pray."

Jesus' response to His disciples and to us is simple, yet so beautiful: "When you pray, say, 'Our Father who art in heaven. . . .'" You recognize that don't you? It's the beginning of what we sometimes call "The Lord's Prayer." What is prayer? *Prayer, real prayer, is simply conversation with God, our Father.* Jesus didn't say, "Now, when you pray, say, 'My Father.'" No, He used the plural, "Our Father." He is your Father, my Father, Jesus' Father—"Our Father, who art in heaven." It's so simple. Just conversation with God.

## CHANGES

When people start praying together on this basis—in one accord, to our Father in heaven, in the name of Jesus—and practice praying together, things begin to change. Our lives change, our families change, our churches change, our communities change. Changes take place not when we study about prayer, not when we talk about it, not even when we

31

memorize beautiful Scripture verses on prayer; it is when *we actually pray* that things begin to happen. And we don't suffer from the "paralysis of analysis." We are not paralyzed by analyzing prayer, but we take the problems at hand and pray about them.

A newspaper reporter recently asked me in an interview, "Would you mind telling me how much you charge for these prayer seminars?"

I replied, "We don't charge anything."

"Well, then, will you tell me why you do it? If you don't charge what is your reason for spending all this time and effort?"

I had to stop and think a minute. Then I said, "The reason I teach people to pray is that I have seen so many changed lives as a result of prayer. This is what makes it so exciting. We learn not *about* prayer, but *to* pray, to converse with our Father who is in heaven."

One day I received an invitation from the women of another church in our hometown to come over and teach them to pray. I said I would. A few days later, as we drove along the main street in her little red Volkswagen, the woman who picked me up took her eyes off the road and looking straight at me asked, "Do you care if our pastor comes this afternoon?"

I was quiet for a minute because I have a "thing" about this. I thought, "Who am I to be teaching pastors?"

Noticing my hesitancy, she went on to assure me, "He really wants to come."

I said, "OK, if he really wants to come, you tell him it's all right." So the pastor sat way back in one corner of the room while the women of his church, many of whom had never prayed out loud before, learned our six little S's of prayer. Afterward we broke into smaller groups, and I know that 100% of those women prayed that day.

A week later at a Sunday School dinner meeting, I was sitting one place away from the speaker, who was the assistant pastor of that same church. During the meal he leaned over and loudly announced to me, "Say, do you know you turned our church upside down?"

I asked, "What happened?"

He replied, "Well, ever since our pastor heard the women praying, and learned how all this prayer works, he won't let us have a single meeting unless we pray. We can't even have a book review in our church unless we pray about it!" He didn't seem too happy about the whole thing.

"I didn't turn your church upside down," I replied. "But it's very possible that God did."

Recently a pastor greeted me at the door when I arrived to speak to the women of his church. "I'm so glad finally to see what you look like. A woman is here today who attended the prayer seminar in downtown Minneapolis. She bought a set of your tapes, and has been a little missionary circulating them among the women's circles for the last 11 months. Each circle has had its own mini-prayer seminar, with the women learning to pray. I can see such a difference in their lives."

## NOT FOR WOMEN ONLY

One night in the fall of 1969 my husband bounced in from a deacon board meeting with a message for me: "Will you please ask the women if they will take our annual Prayer Week the first week in January?"

Right away I shot back the answer. I didn't stop to pray. I didn't ask God what He thought about it at all. I just said to Chris, "You tell your deacon board, 'No.' God has called me to teach women." But I wasn't really being honest with God.

My husband trotted back to the board and told them, "No, there's no way they're going to teach the whole church how to pray."

The board said, "You go back to your wife and tell her that we have been watching and we feel that the women have discovered a method of prayer that works, and we would like them to teach it to the whole church."

By this time my husband was becoming like a Ping Pong ball being batted back and forth between two paddles—the deacon board and me. When Chris returned with the same request, I realized that I had been hasty in my reply the first time.

I said, "OK, I'll take it to the women."

Their response was also negative.

Again I agreed, but suggested that at this point we pray about it. After fervent prayer we concluded that this request was really God's way of speaking to us. We consented to take Prayer Week for 1970 on one condition—that it be held the second week in January, the first being preparation week. The board agreed. That first week we trained prayer group leaders representing every department of the church— the choir, the deacon board, the trustee board, and the Sunday School. They all came to learn the ground rules for effective praying.

In the week of prayer that followed, we discovered that we had about five times as many people participating as we ever had in the past. There were boys and girls, men and women—preschoolers to "golden agers"—from every area of our church life, all learning to *pray in one accord*. I don't know of one person who didn't pray, but I'll stay on the side of caution and say that of all those who attended, 95% actively participated in verbal prayer. Now, that's a lot of people praying, and there were some very definite answers that gave us great encouragement.

I recall, particularly, how thrilled the members of the Junior Department were after I had taught them our method of praying in one accord on the Sunday morning during Prayer Week. They came up with two urgent needs along with their other prayer requests: "We need a superintendent and a piano player in our department." That morning the Juniors with their teachers divided into small groups and

prayed specifically that God would send them these workers. I cringed a little inside. What if God didn't answer their
prayer?

On the following Wednesday, one of the church's busi-
nessmen came to Gail, our children's worker, and said,
"The Lord has laid it on my heart to be superintendent of
the Junior Department, and my wife would like to play the
piano for the juniors if she can be replaced in her present
department."

Meanwhile God had been working in the college-age class
also. On the same Sunday of Prayer Week, along with specific prayer, they were offering themselves to God for service in the church. A student nurse wrote on her card, "I
am available to play the piano where I'm needed." Gail
assigned the student nurse to replace the wife in the other
department, and the following Sunday the juniors almost
exploded with excitement as they were presented their new
superintendent and pianist. God had really answered their
prayers!

## IN ONE ACCORD

We, as women of the church, had simply shared the
method that God had given to us from the Bible, the
method of praying in one accord in small groups. How is
this achieved? *Simply by praying about only one subject
at a time with one person praying aloud while the others
in the group are praying silently on the same subject.* In
this way everyone is praying together (in one accord) instead
of planning other prayers in advance.

Have you ever been in a group when someone is praying a long prayer? And have you found that you were
not really praying along with that person? Instead you
were mulling over in your mind all the things you were
going to pray about when your turn came? I have, and
my thoughts have run like this, "Lord, now bring to my

mind . . . "/"Oh, I don't want to forget that one!"/"Say, that's a good request"/"Thank You, Lord, for reminding me of that one." Then I have gone back and reviewed the prayer subjects on my fingers. Next, I've wondered what my introductory statement should be, or how I should conclude my prayer. While someone else has been praying, I have been planning my own long prayer in advance instead of praying silently on the same subject with the person who is praying audibly. That's *not* praying in one accord.

You see, if everyone in a group is praying in one accord with the person who is praying aloud, the number of prayers ascending to heaven are multiplied by the number who are praying silently. How much more power there is in prayer when the participants are praying in one accord!

**For You to Pray:**
"Father, teach me to pray in one accord with other people, sharing **their** burdens, joys, and petitions."

# 4

## *The Method—Six S's*

*"But when ye pray, use not vain repetitions, as the heathen do; for they think that they shall be heard for their much speaking. Be not ye therefore like unto them, for your Father knoweth what things ye have need of, before ye ask Him." Matthew 6:7–8*

"WELL, I SUPPOSE you all know how to pray. I won't fit into this group." With that remark, Betty, my neighbor, joined the three of us meeting in a home on our block to pray for the coming Billy Graham Crusade. There she was, apparently wanting to take part, but scared to death to pray aloud, even with only three other women present.

There are thousands of people just like Betty. They are all over the country—in neighborhood prayer groups, in midweek services, and in special prayer sessions—and they are not praying audibly for only one reason: *they don't know how.*

We have found in our prayer seminars that about 50% of those participating have never prayed aloud before. They come from a great variety of churches, Protestant and Catholic, but talking with God in the presence of others is a very real problem to them.

My response to my neighbor, Betty, was, "Oh, yes, you certainly will fit into this group. It's really not difficult. After we hear the prayer requests, we all are going to pray just one simple sentence on each one. And we did. The three of us, who had prayed for years, prayed one simple sentence following the request, and so did Betty! In fact, as we concluded that session, she had prayed four times, audibly. What happens when we put ourselves on the level of the most inexperienced pray-ers? Many of them hear their own voices in prayer for the first time.

The rules we applied that morning were the ones our women devised in 1968 to implement our method of praying in one accord—praying about only one subject at a time, with one person praying aloud while the others in the group are praying silently on the same subject. There are *six S's*, six simple rules to follow, whether one is a participant or a prayer group leader, a seasoned pray-er or a shy and untrained one. These six rules serve as effective tools to help a prayer group get started, to encourage newcomers, and to motivate timid people to pray aloud. But a prayer group doesn't have to stay with these elementary rules. It's exciting to know that the participants can go on and graduate into effective, fervent, spontaneous praying.

Suppose your present prayer group is not going very well with no one wanting to join or perhaps not coming back after trying it once. Or, suppose you would like to start a prayer group in your church or in your neighborhood. You may find that these *six S's* are just what you need to encourage 100% participation.

## 1. SUBJECT BY SUBJECT

The first "S" is *Subject by Subject*—praying in one accord about only one subject at a time. As one person prays out loud, the rest pray silently on the same subject, *not planning their own prayers in advance*. This assures complete concentration and fervent prayer on one request at a time. Also, in this way no one is deprived of the privilege of praying for the request before going on to another.

You may be accustomed to praying around the world, mentioning every person you know, every missionary in many different countries. And you may be tempted to pray this way as a prayer group leader. But your part is only to announce one subject for prayer at a time, and then to pray a short sentence prayer yourself. Sometimes it's a good idea to have a list ready and to say, "Right now we are going to pray one simple sentence about so and so." Then, as the leader, pray one simple sentence and wait for others to pray audibly on the same subject before going to the next request. Because the participants will have to "shift mental gears" before going on to another subject, it's a good idea to pause between subjects. Then the group will be prepared to pray again.

As the participants learn to pray in one accord, subject by subject, prayer gains momentum and becomes more spontaneous. When this happens, the leader may simply lead out in prayer on a subject rather than announcing it. When those in our groups become proficient in this method, their spiritual pulses will be throbbing together in such a way that each one will begin to sense the direction of the Holy Spirit when it is time to start a new subject. Everyone in the group will then have the freedom to initiate a new topic for prayer. It may take a while, but this is our goal. They won't have to have a leader anymore!

I remember the first time I tried this with my group in 1968. I had always come to the prayer meeting with a written list of requests at which I would peek with one eye. That day I told God I was going to hide the list and trust Him completely to bring to the minds of the pray-ers those things He wanted us to remember in prayer. Checking the list after we finished praying, I was delighted and amazed to find that He had reminded someone to pray about every single request I had written down!

When praying subject by subject, everyone is free to pray audibly in turn. But whether praying audibly or silently, all are praying in one accord on the same subject, not planning their own prayers in advance, and multiplying the power of all the prayers that are ascending simultaneously to God's throne.

## 2. SHORT PRAYERS

*Short Prayers*, the second handle, are the secret of the success of small group prayer. Just one, or only a few sentences from each person on each subject allows time for all to pray if they wish. No one should be forced to pray aloud, but let prayer be something spontaneous, something a person wants to do, even if it's only to hear her own voice in prayer.

As leaders we are responsible to see that the prayers are short. How are we going to do this? Superimpose our wills on our groups and say, "Look everybody, let's pray short prayers"? No, but at first *we* will have to back way up and start praying just one simple sentence ourselves in order to get the shy, untrained ones to pray. We make the rest of the group more comfortable by the kind of praying we do. Might it be that God is much more interested in the short statement of a new pray-er who has never prayed audibly before than He is in an elaborate prayer uttered by one who has had years of practice? It may be that we, veteran pray-ers, mature pray-ers, are inhibiting the shy ones. Some of us may even have an idea that God hears us for our "much praying."

Christ had something to say about this when He was teaching His disciples to pray. He said, "But when ye pray, use not vain repetitions, as the heathen do; for they think that they shall be heard for their much speaking. Be not ye therefore like unto them, for your Father knoweth what things ye have need of, before ye ask Him" (Matt. 6:7–8).

Do we think we're going to be heard because we give an introduction, three points, and a conclusion to everything we pray about? God knows all we need, and all we have to do is to lay our requests before Him. Just think of all the requests that go unremembered when someone dominates the group with lengthy prayers on one, two, or even three subjects!

Now, there are times when long, involved prayers are very much in order. If you are asked to lead in prayer at a meeting and respond by praying one simple sentence, you will probably jar the whole group! Long prayers are appropriate at the right time and in the right place, but that time is not when the shy and untrained are learning to pray.

### 3. SIMPLE PRAYERS

The third "S" is *Simple Prayers*. Those who have never prayed before will find it possible to utter one *simple* sentence from the heart when the leaders and other participants avoid using complicated phrases and a special prayer vocabulary. When we leave our high-sounding theological expressions at home in our prayer closets and make our short prayers simple ones, then the new pray-ers will feel comfortable about praying one simple, uncomplicated prayer themselves, and will be more apt to return the following week.

Though he didn't know it at the time, I learned a valuable lesson from one of our church leaders during our Prayer Week in 1970. He was an Irishman with a beautiful accent and a rich vocabulary. Whenever he prayed aloud our hearts soared heavenward. But we had a problem. When he finished praying nobody else dared to follow him! Why, I wouldn't be "caught dead" praying after he had just uttered his long, beautiful prayer, couched in lofty theological phrases. I can remember even my husband hesitating a bit to close in prayer after this man had prayed so eloquently.

As we approached that 1970 Prayer Week, I wondered what was going to happen in a group he would be leading. I soon found out, for one night he and I were leading our respective groups in areas separated only by a plastic curtain. As I presented the prayer requests to my group, I found it difficult to concentrate because I was so curious to learn what was happening on the other side of the curtain. Have you ever had your ear attuned in one direction while your voice was aimed in another?

I heard him open his prayer group with just one simple sentence. Astounded, I listened. But he didn't say another word. Soon, one by one, all the people in his group prayed their own simple sentences. Then he prayed another sentence on the next subject and stopped. Once again each one prayed. I was acquainted with everyone in his group, and I knew that many of them had never prayed aloud before; but that night every single person in his circle prayed aloud. What happens when we are willing to put ourselves temporarily on the level of those who don't know how to pray? We encourage them to pray with us.

Back in 1968 when we were practicing and experimenting with all these methods, eventually a whole room in our church was filled with women praying; but Eva, a woman who lived next door, declared that she would not join the others in prayer. She said she had never prayed out loud in a group and she never would.

I knew that Eva's family had a very fine devotional life. She was a great Christian. This wasn't her problem, but praying aloud with others was. She would shake her finger at me in other meetings and say, "Don't you ever call on me to pray; don't you ever call on me."

I assured her that we never call on anybody to pray, but still she didn't come to our prayer meetings. As we drove up to the church, we would see the curtains part as she peeked out the window, but that's as close as Eva got. Then one day, without explanation, she joined us. She came every week after that, but never prayed out loud.

As the summer rolled around, we moved our meetings to one of the parks in town. It was at one of those park sessions that I had a distinct impression from God that Eva was going to pray that day. But as I led the group in prayer, mentioning one request after another, she didn't utter a word. Though it was past time for us to start home, I kept adding requests and waiting for her. Suddenly, Eva began to pray. She forgot all the rules she ever learned. It was like Niagara Falls breaking loose! That day Eva prayed around the world.

When we had Prayer Week in January 1970, one of the groups praying was made up of all men, including the pastor and the chairman of the church board, except Eva. Again my ear was attuned in another direction. Guess who prayed *first* in that group? Eva! She has said to me since, "Ev, if I can do it, *anybody* can."

## 4. SPECIFIC PRAYER REQUESTS

Handle number four is *Specific Prayer Requests.* Specific requests listed and specific answers noted are a great encouragement to continuing and expanded prayer. Use a notebook or file folder for this.

If our groups start falling apart, and they may, or if people suddenly aren't interested, the best way to get things going again is to encourage them by showing specific answers to their specific requests. When there's a lag, whip out that little book in which requests and answers are recorded and point out how God has used the prayer group to change circumstances and individuals. Spend time in prayer *praising God* for His specific answers. Then watch as new life floods your prayer group!

As the specific answers to their prayers pile up, you will begin to see the pray-ers change as well. By keeping records, the individuals who are praying start to see *the worth of themselves in prayer,* and this is important.

*Date* your specific requests and date the answers. God is not controlled by time as we human beings are. He is only *aware* of time. He places his answers down on Planet Earth when He knows best. Therefore, if we keep track of *time—*

how long God takes to answer our prayers—we're going to learn some tremendous spiritual lessons about how God operates. As weeks and months and years come and go, we will see that His timing is always perfect.

We will also learn some *whys* when we keep track of how He answers. It may be that we are not ready for some answers. My two prayer partners and I prayed every week for two solid years before I had my first neighborhood Bible study. I wasn't ready and God knew I wasn't. If we keep a record of the specific timing of our requests and God's answers, then we can look back and see many of the reasons for His delays and His withholdings.

God may answer our prayers not only at a time when we least expect, but He may answer in a *way* we don't expect. We will be astounded at *how* God answers prayer. He may answer in a way that is completely opposite to the way we think He should. He knows what is best for us, and He never makes a mistake.

Our women experienced this great joy in praying specifically in May 1968, when we were preparing for a mother-daughter banquet. Ruth Johnson of "Back to the Bible Broadcast," a "daughter" of our church, was to be the speaker. We set up a prayer room and asked the women who came to the church to work (cook, set tables, or decorate) to spend some time, equal time if they could, in the prayer room, praying specifically for Ruth Johnson. What a great moving of God there was at the banquet that night!

On the following Sunday, with my little notebook in hand (I always recorded the results of our prayer experimentation), I said to Ruth, "Please be very careful how you answer me because we zeroed in on you in prayer, and I want a very honest answer. This will be reported to our national conference in June. Will you tell me what happened, if anything did happen, on Friday night when you spoke at our banquet."

Ruth drew a deep breath and tears came to her eyes. "Ev," she said, "the last time I was in this church it was to bury my mother. It all came back to me last Friday as I was on my way here. After I got to the church, I couldn't even bring myself to open the door. I kept thinking of my mother, and then I thought of my former Sunday School teachers who were going to be at the banquet. You know, I used to be 'naughty little Ruthie' to those teachers, and I had a feeling that they were all going to be looking at me and thinking, *There's that "naughty little Ruthie" again.* Evelyn, I could not walk through that door. But suddenly, I felt a great sense of strength and freedom. I can't explain it, but there was complete release and I walked in. It was just fantastic. My voice has gone around the world via radio for 30 years, but never in all those years have I felt such freedom and such power as I experienced when I sang and spoke last Friday night."

Not long afterward Ruth's missionary brother came home from India. He came to me and said, "Evie, what did you do to my sister?"

I replied, "We didn't do anything to your sister."

He said, "Oh, yes you did. Since the women prayed, my sister has been a completely different woman."

Now I thought Ruth was a fantastic Christian before that time, but I learned something. It was that we don't limit our praying to the down-and-outer, or to someone we think is dying or experiencing great tragedy. We also need to pray for those who are ministering, who don't appear to have any needs. What did we do? We only prayed—specifically. And God worked.

## 5. SILENT PERIODS

The next "S" is *Silent Periods.* Silent periods between prayers are a privilege and a blessing. Don't panic when there's a lull—just listen! This is an added dimension to our definition of prayer in chapter 3. Prayer is a *two-way* conversation with God.

Today silence is almost a lost art. After a few seconds pass without audible prayer, someone usually feels compelled to clear his throat, shuffle his feet, or nervously finger a song book. Somehow we think we have to talk *at* God all of the time, but there are marvellous things that God wants to say to us. He has answers to our questions, secrets He wants to share, yet we bombard Him with our "much praying." We forget that God is on His throne in heaven just waiting to say something great to us, if we would only give Him a chance. How frustrated He must be (if God can become frustrated) when He has something so wonderful to tell you and me, and we aren't quiet long enough to listen to what He has to say.

One day I asked my son about a girl who lives near us, and he said, "Oh, I guess she's fine, Mom, if she'd ever keep still so we could find out."

"What do you mean?" I asked.

"Well on the school bus that girl talks every single minute. She might be a real great girl, but she doesn't shut up long enough for us to find out."

Has God ever said that about me? Has He ever said it about you? Have we learned to keep still long enough for God to say something to us? It is in the *silence* that our communication becomes two-way.

The first time I practiced the six "S" method at a retreat was 1969. It was evening, and as the women finished praying in their small groups of four, I dismissed them to go out to a point near the water. "Just one rule," I said, "please don't talk while you are walking out to the point." There had been fervent prayer in their groups, and I wanted them to keep their hearts open to God's voice.

We had planned that the KTIS radio trio would come to the point by boat and, at a given signal, sing to the women on shore. But the signal somehow failed, and they waited and waited, not knowing when to start their song. The leader of the testimony meeting kept putting more wood on the fire and thinking, "I *have* to say something." But each time she thought it, God said, "Keep still, Mary." In fact, Mary told me later, "You know very well, Evelyn, that God said, 'Mary, shut up!'"

Twenty minutes went by with about 500 women sitting in absolute silence at the water's edge. Now and then we could hear soft crying. Then from the boat totally obscured by the darkness, came the beautiful strains of "Take my life and let it be, consecrated Lord to Thee." The common theme that ran through the testimonies that night was:

"God spoke to me not so much in the songs or in the message, *but in the silence.*"

## 6. SMALL GROUPS

*Small Groups*, the sixth "S," are usually best for newcomers, as well as for the shy or untrained. For some, it would take great courage to stand before a group of 100 people, or even 25 people, and raise their voices in prayer for the first time. But in smaller groups they can gain confidence in praying audibly.

In our seminars when there are several hundred participants in one room, we divide into small groups of four or five. This is quickly accomplished by standing and having every other row turn back, each two rows of people facing each other. We then just draw apart in groups of four, two from each row. How my heart thrilled at one of our prayer seminars in a large church recently when almost 200 small groups of people in the same room lifted their voices earnestly to God.

Yesterday, when one of my original prayer partners called me long distance, we chatted about the joy and the privilege of being just two or three in a little group. "Ev," she recalled, "when we started praying, just the three of us, that was the turning point in my spiritual life."

Whatever we do, we must never underestimate the value of a small group praying, for Christ promised that *where two or three of His followers are gathered together in His name, He will be in their midst* (see Matt. 18:20). What an opportunity it provides to practice the presence of Christ in our midst!

Do you remember in the account of the stoning of Stephen that he lifted up his eyes and "saw the glory of God, and Jesus standing on the right hand of God"? (Acts 7:55) The right hand of God is the place of authority and honor. Christ is still at the right hand of God today, interceding for us, but we also have His promise that He will be *with* us—where even two or three are gathered together. Now, we want to be very careful that we do not take Christ off His throne, that we do not play games with Him in prayer. He is in heaven, but *His* presence is in the midst of those who gather together in His name.

Christ helped the disciples and those who knew Him very intimately here on earth to understand this. G. Campbell Morgan, in his message "Rekindled Fire," emphasizes the importance of our Lord's vanishing and appearing after His resurrection. He explains that the disciples and His friends were learning the lesson that Christ was with them, even when they did not see Him with their physical eyes. These followers of Jesus were practicing His presence even though they could not see Him. After He had vanished from their sight for the last time at His ascension, He was in their midst in the upper room, and they knew it.

**For You to Pray:**

"Dear Father: Please give me the privilege of being aware of the presence of Jesus, my Saviour, in a prayer group. Teach me to help others to pray. Teach me to listen to You speaking to me in the silent periods."

# 5

## *How to Pray in God's Will*

---

*"And this is the confidence that we have in Him, that, if we ask any-thing according to His will, He heareth us. And if we know that He hear us, whatsoever we ask, we know that we have the petitions that we desired of Him." 1 John 5:14–15*

ON THE MORNING following Lindon Karo's funeral, I posed some searching questions to those attending our prayer seminar. "What do you think went wrong? Why did this tremendous pastor, only 32 years old, die of cancer? Thousands of prayers were offered for him. Forty people in his church had covenanted to fast and pray one day a week for him. I don't think I attended a meeting anywhere dur-ing that period, but that we were all praying. Why weren't those prayers answered? What went wrong? Why did we bury Lindon Karo yesterday?"

When I reached this point in the seminar, a steering com-mittee member (wanting to be helpful) waved her hand from the back of the church, and said, "Yes, Evelyn, and Lindon Karo's mother-in-law and sister-in-law are here with us today."

Wow! I stopped for a second and pondered, *Do I go on? Do I insult these people by teaching a lesson on how to pray in God's will? What do I do about these loved ones*

49

*who buried their son-in-law and brother-in-law just yes-terday?* What would you have done? I felt God was telling me to go ahead and teach the lesson.

When the session was over, those two very beautiful Christian women came to me and said, "Please don't worry about today's lesson. Many months ago we as a family com-mitted the whole matter of Lindon's illness to the Lord. We prayed, 'Only Your will, God, whatever it is.' We did not ask for healing only; we prayed that God's will be done in our loved one's life."

Have you come to the place where you can pray, "Only God's will"? Do you know that you are in absolute oneness with the will of God? Have you come to that place?

We read in 1 John 5:14–15 about a prerequisite to effec-tive praying. "And this is the confidence that we have in Him, that, if we ask anything according to His will, He heareth us. And if we know that He hear us, whatsoever we ask, we know that we have the petitions that we desired of Him." Did you catch the prerequisite? How can we have confidence in anything we ask? It is by praying *according to His will.* And what is confidence in prayer? It is knowing absolutely and irrevocably that we have what-ever we have asked.

## "IF IT BE THY WILL, AMEN"

What do we mean when we use the expression "praying in God's will"? Is it simply tacking on the end of a prayer the phrase we use perhaps more frequently than any other? You know how it goes. We ask God for a whole string of things, then we piously add, ". . . if it be Thy will, Lord. Amen." Or it may be that we ask God for something we know is not good for us. Let's say, for example, that we ask for a bushel of Hershey bars! God knows very well (and so do we) that if we ate a bushel of Hershey bars we'd die of indigestion, but many times we ask Him for something just as ridiculous and tack on "if it be Thy will," just to get ourselves off the hook. This is not what it means to pray in God's will.

## THE PRAYING PERSON—
## NOT THE PRAYER REQUEST

Berkeley Mickelsen, professor of New Testament Greek in a nearby seminary, said to me one day, "Evelyn, I hope that when you're teaching all those women to pray in God's will that you are teaching them that it is the person praying, and not the prayer request, that changes."

I said, "Berkeley, that's the whole gist of our lesson on God's will."

Praying in God's will is not easy, yet it's very simple. It involves a commitment of every single thing that comes into our lives to God and His perfect will. And it's exciting to live in complete oneness with the will of God. It is never dull or static because it is not a one-time, once-for-all commitment. It is something we have to work at constantly, moment by moment.

This is expressed in a beautiful definition of the word "effectual" as it is found in James 5:16. According to Vine's *Expository Dictionary of New Testament Words*, it means "The effect produced in the praying person, bringing him into line with the will of God." It is the pray-er who changes, rather than the prayer. Praying "in the will of God" means, then, *being* conformed to the will of God as we pray. Wouldn't it be great if we could always *be conformed to the will of God* (with all known sin confessed), so that we would never pray outside the will of God? The effectual pray-er, then, is a person who is completely committed to God's will for answers, and not to his own will.

After our women had been praying for a few months back in 1968, my husband exclaimed one day, "Wow, if God doesn't answer a single one of your prayers, what He's doing *in* the people who are praying will be worth it all."

What God does in the lives of people who are praying, in bringing them in line with His will, is one of His miracles here on Planet Earth. The turning point in our Prayer Seminars is the session where people in prayer commit their whole lives to God's perfect will. This happened to a college teacher, who sent me this note recently:

On February 26 my sister invited me to attend your prayer seminar. I thought, *A prayer seminar! What good will it do! I have prayed and prayed, and it hasn't done any good.* But I went.

You see, I have been a Christian all of my life. I was raised in a wonderful Christian home and reared in an atmosphere of loving and trusting Jesus. But, suddenly, I was faced with very severe testing of my faith. My husband's construction company folded, leaving a large sum of debts which we were 50% responsible for. Because of this, we had to sell our home and liquidate our assets. Also, I was not well, and our little two-year-old son had just undergone surgery.

Then, the Scripture that was to change my life and my prayers, 1 John 5:14–15, "and this is the confidence. . . ." Up to that point I had not prayed for His will. I could only see what I wanted to happen.

Evelyn asked us to stand at the end of the session and form our prayer groups of four. She told us to ask God for the *one* thing we wanted most from Him. I remember saying aloud in my little circle of four Christian sisters, "Lord, I want Your perfect will for me and my family."

That was it! I was to learn later that was what was keeping my prayers from being answered. I had never asked God for His will.

Now, I felt entirely free. I felt the whole load lift, as if the responsibility to straighten up the messy things was not mine.

Now it is nine months since that time, and I cannot begin to tell you of the peace I have in my heart. My husband's business debts are not all cleared up as yet, but God is moving. The burden is lifted. My health has improved tremendously. In fact, I got a teaching position at Bethel College this fall, a position that just seemed to come right out of heaven itself. I was not applying or seeking such a position, but was asked to join the staff. Praise God! He can "do exceeding abundantly above all that we ask or think" (Eph. 3:20)

## ON EARTH, AS IT IS IN HEAVEN

For us to pray, "Lord, I want Your will down here on earth," is a tremendous prayer. Wouldn't it be fantastic if we could pray that prayer for Washington, D.C. today? If we could by our praying get God's will done in Moscow, or in the Middle East? While there is a sense in which we can pray that God's will be done in these places, they are not within our direct sphere of influence, are they? But there is a spot on earth, a sphere of influence that belongs only to you. It has been given to you by our heavenly Father. And it's possible for you to bring about God's complete will in your sphere of influence here on earth.

The disciples whom Jesus taught to pray: "Our Father . . . Thy will be done on earth as it is in heaven," knew they couldn't change the whole Roman Empire, but they also knew it was possible for them to change the spheres of influence which were theirs, which had been given to them by God. And they did. God changes circumstances and people when we in a very personal way pray that His will be done in the sphere of influence which is ours.

The Lord's prayer really comes into focus right where we are when we pray, "Thy will be done on earth as it is in heaven." Is there anything contrary to God's will in heaven? No! Think of what would happen if every Christian really brought God's will to the little sphere that is his, with nothing contrary to God's perfect will! How different would be our nation, our cities, our churches, our homes.

## THE EXAMPLE OF CHRIST

The supreme example of praying in the will of God is that of Christ praying in the garden of Gethsemane on the night before He was to die on the cross for our sins. Our Lord, in His humanity, did not want to suffer. He prayed, "Father, if Thou be willing, remove this cup from me; nevertheless not my will, but Thine, be done" (Luke 22:42). Then, after much agony of Spirit, He said, "Father, I am willing for Your will."

Have you come to the place in your life where you can say, "Lord, not my will, but Thine be done? No matter how much it hurts, how difficult the task, how high the mountain You've given me to climb, it doesn't make any difference, dear Lord, I am willing"?

When we visited the Holy Land a few years ago, I sat alone under one of those old, gnarled olive trees in the garden of Gethsemane, and read in Luke's Gospel the account of all my Jesus went through the night before He died, before He took upon Himself the sin of the world, including mine; when He sweat as it were great drops of blood there in the garden. With my heart absolutely breaking, I wrote in the margin of my Bible, "Lord, please, only Your will in my life, only Your will!" We don't have to sit under an ancient olive tree in His land to come to that place, but right where we are today we can say to Christ, "Lord, not my will, only Yours be done."

When we reach the place where we're really on our faces before God, does He as an "ogre" sitting up in heaven say, "Good, I have another doormat on which to wipe My feet"? Is that what He says? Do we become doormats for God to wipe His feet on when we say, "Lord, I'm willing for Your will"? Oh, no. What happened to Christ the day after He said this to His heavenly Father? He became the *Redeemer of mankind!* He became your Saviour and my Saviour.

Mary, too, had a tremendous privilege because she was willing for God's will in her life. Do you recall her response at the time of the Annunciation? When the angel came to her and said that God had chosen her to be the mother of the Saviour, Mary immediately responded, "Behold, the handmaid of the Lord; be it according to thy word."

Do you think it was easy for Mary to say yes to the will of God, to being pregnant out of wedlock? When it meant vulnerability to misunderstanding, to ridicule? When it could mean possible rejection by her fiance or even being stoned to death? It was not easy for Mary, but because she was willing for God's will, she was greatly blessed by Him. She was given the great privilege of bearing the Son who became our Redeemer.

## OPEN DOORS

What happens to Evelyn when she is on her face before God and says, "OK, Lord, I don't know what You want. That's a big mountain, that's difficult surgery, these are hard things in my life, but, Lord, no matter what it is, I want Your perfect will"? At that point does God become an ogre and take advantage of my commitment? No, at that point He starts to open doors, and fantastic things begin to happen—even prayer seminars—when I just make myself available to Him.

One day our campus pastor inquired, "Ev, how did you ever get all those prayer seminars started, anyway?"

I shrugged, "They just sort of grew, like Topsy." He looked at me, wondering at what I was saying. I went on, "You know, we really didn't plan them. They just happened. In every single step, the constant prayer of steering committees, prayer chains, and our advisory board has been,

'Lord, Your will.' Then we wait to see what His will is. We never even make contacts asking to hold a seminar, and it is so thrilling to watch God work when we let Him."

One day a young woman who had traveled almost 100 miles round trip each day to attend a Minneapolis prayer seminar asked me, "What is the procedure to get you to come to our town for a prayer seminar?"

I replied, "Pray about it, and if it is God's will, we'll come."

"Oh, three of us have been praying for several months," she replied, "and we believe God is saying we should have it."

"That's good enough for me," I said. "I'll come."

I better understood her insistence on having a seminar in her town when she handed me this note:

"Dear Evelyn: Since being in your prayer seminar at Elim Lutheran Church my life has been changed through accepting Christ. Also, my four-year-old daughter and nine-year-old son have asked Jesus into their lives. Now my husband wants me to work on him. Thank you."

God rewarded her eagerness when 30 women found Christ in "her" seminar. It was God's will!

In fact, the Bible study on prayer for all the churches in White Bear Lake, Minnesota, that automatically turned into our first prayer seminar, came into being because God took over. The chairman and I, frustrated at not being able to work my schedule into all the fall events of that area, finally in tears just prayed together, "All right, Lord, only *Your* will. Whatever *You* want this Bible study, work it out." And God timed it perfectly. He knew all along when prayer would be needed in that town. He knew that the next February, witches and occult personnel would be in one of the high schools, so He planned for those 250 women to be "praying in one accord" just at the right time.

What has turned into this whole prayer ministry in my life started in November 1967, when I was asked to work on the prayer experiment with our church women, as described in chapter 1. I hesitated at first, not knowing for certain whether to make the commitment. But one day while I was reading God's Word, a phrase in Revelation, "Behold, I have set before thee an open door," stood out as if it were in bold print. God said, "Evelyn, I have set before *you* an open door." I closed my Bible, said, "Lord, I'm willing," and went to the phone and dialed long distance to Chicago. I said excitedly to the executive secretary of our National Women's Board, "How can I say no when God has just put before me an open door in Revelation 3:8?"

Has God put before you an open door? Are you hesitating, perhaps rebelling, or holding back because of fear, when God is challenging, "Look, here's an open door, wouldn't you like to walk through it for Me? This is My will for you."

Oh, answer Him, "Lord, here I am. There is no friction between my will and Yours. Whatever You have for me, I know that You will give me enough strength, enough grace. I know You will give me all that I need, so Lord, here I am ready to do Your will."

"Try it. You'll like it!" It's amazing what happens when we step out.

## MEN TOO?

Sometimes I seem to need a little help from other people in going through the doors God is opening for me. "I don't think God is hung up on you teaching men to pray, but I think you are," a professional Christian counselor chided as we chatted at a Christmas party. I suddenly realized that I was so hung up that I was praying, "God, Your will," but didn't have the courage to accept it.

My prayer chains had been praying for several months about frequent requests from men to attend prayer seminars. Then I learned that, while I was planning to give a three-minute speech the next Sunday encouraging attendance at our up-coming seminar, the host church was planning for me to present *the* morning message. I was panicking, just *knowing* it never could be God's will for me to do *that!*

Suddenly, as we were together praying, a prayer chain member prayed, "Lord, we're sick and tired of praying this request. We're going to put out a fleece. The way the men accept Evelyn next Sunday morning will be our answer as to whether she opens the prayer seminars to men or not." I nearly fainted as she prayed. *I* never would have dared talk to God like that.

The next Saturday I received a call from a woman in one of St. Paul's suburbs. "I've met with some of our deacons (we're between pastors), and we want an evening prayer seminar in our church that is open to men, women, and young people. We definitely feel it is God's will."

"I'll give you my answer on Monday," I stalled, not daring to tell her I had to see how the "fleece" came out the next day!

With fear and trembling I shared "What Happens when We Pray" with that Sunday congregation. After the service the knuckles on my right hand were white from all those men shaking hands and thanking me. Nine days later we started our first prayer seminar for women *and men.* Sometimes I need a little pushing to go through doors God is opening. Do you?

## IF YOU WANT ME, LORD

One Friday afternoon during our first prayer seminar, I asked my small telephone prayer chain of 10 members to pray that God would keep my schedule in balance speaking against the occult and on prayer. That night, in one of those deep devotional times that come periodically in many of our lives, I prayed, "Lord, I don't know what it is, but I want Your will, just Your will." And I meant it. Then, out of the blue it seemed (but I'm sure it was God-inspired), I heard myself promising God that I would be involved in two areas if He wanted me to. One was the Billy Graham Crusade which was to be held that coming summer; the other was a national women's prayer movement.

The very next morning my telephone rang. It was Myrl Glockner. She said, "Evelyn, we've never met, but I just felt I had to call and ask if you will be one of eleven committee members to get 5,000 prayer groups going for the Billy Graham Crusade. Do you want time to pray about it?"

I was stunned, "Myrl," I stammered, "I don't need time to pray. How can I say no when just last night I said so completely, 'Lord, Your will, if You want me to be involved in the Billy Graham Crusade.'"

On the following Tuesday, after I had completed a prayer seminar session, a woman came down the aisle of the church waving a paper and calling, "Evelyn, I have a message here for you from Vonette Bright of the Great Commission Prayer Crusade. She would like you to become involved in the program."

Friday, Saturday, and Tuesday. There it was—God's opening of two doors when I told Him I was willing for His will for me with those two organizations. It's a very exciting thing. Don't say, "I want it my way, Lord," but, "Lord, Your way. Whatever You have for me, I'm Yours. You just take me, open any door, lead me in any direction." You will be astounded at what God will do. You will be panting, trying to keep up with the opportunities. Phone calls will come from people you didn't even know existed. Who inspired that person to call and ask you to go here or there to minister? Nobody— but God.

**For You to Pray:**

"O God, I want only Your will in my life. Open the doors You have for me, and give me the courage and faith to go through them."

# 6

# *God Never Makes a Mistake*

*"Wherefore let them that suffer according to the will of God commit the keeping of their souls to Him in well doing, as unto a faithful Creator." 1 Peter 4:19*

IN ORDER TO pray effectively in God's will, you may have to get a new view of God—a God who never makes a mistake. Our daughter Jan was still in high school when a friend of hers was in a serious automobile accident just before Labor Day. Not knowing whether Rick was dead or alive, she went down to the courthouse to see his demolished car that had been placed on the lawn by city officials to serve as a gruesome reminder to weekend travelers.

I was standing at the kitchen sink doing dishes when Jan came in trembling. Describing the car, she wondered how they ever pried Rick out of that crushed front seat. Suddenly she said, "But, Mom, God never makes a mistake!" And turning on her heel, she flew upstairs sobbing, and threw herself across her bed.

It was a few years later while she was in college that Jan came home because our family was going through a crisis. Once again she stepped into that same kitchen, and after we had wept together, she backed off, raised her finger at me and said, "Now, Mom, don't *you* forget, God makes no mistakes."

## AN OMNISCIENT FATHER

Is your God an all-wise Father, who knows the end from the beginning, who knows all the causes and all the outcomes, and who never makes a mistake? We may pray for something that seems very good to us, but God knows the "what ifs" in our lives. He knows the calamities that might occur if He answered our prayers in the way we think best. He also knows about all our difficult situations and wants to turn them into something tremendously good.

This view of God as an omniscient Father comes into focus very clearly as the years pass. One of the advantages of growing older is that we can look back and see that God has not made a single mistake in our lives. Maybe we'll have to get to heaven before we understand some things, but it's exciting to recognize as the years come and go that everything has worked together for good if we have really loved Him. When we keep a record of what is happening to us, it isn't long before we realize that the difficult things are there for a reason, and God is making no mistakes.

## MAKE REQUESTS—DON'T DICTATE ANSWERS

When we first started a telephone prayer chain in our church, I, as chairman, soon learned that it was a full-time job. With 66 pray-ers signing up and averaging four, five, sometimes six prayer requests per day, it became more than I, as a pastor's wife, had time to handle, so I turned over the chairmanship to another woman. When Elmy took over I said to her, "You're going to have a problem. Some people will be calling to give you *answers* instead of requests. When they ask you to pray that such and such will happen, tell them kindly, 'We do not pray answers, we pray requests.'"

Do you see the difference? When we pray answers we're demanding that God do something and telling Him we want it done now—"just the way we want it, Lord." When we're bringing our requests to Him, we're saying, "Lord, here's the need" (the circumstance, the person, whatever it may be); then we ask Him to answer according to His omniscient will.

Even with pure motives, it's easy to pray answers rather than requests. One woman on a prayer chain to which I belong is a returned missionary to Africa. After she and her family came back to the States, they all wished they were back on the field, so they started to pray, "Lord, send us back to Africa." They even reapplied for the position they had vacated.

One day I received a telephone call from this dear lady. She was sobbing. "Ev, we just received word from our mission board that the position we held is filled, and we can't go back. Oh, Ev, we prayed and prayed that God would send us back to Africa."

What could I say about her praying that beautiful, noble "answer" to God? "Honey," I comforted, "you prayed the wrong prayer. If God had wanted you back on your mission station, He could have kept that position open until your letter arrived. It must not have been His will."

## A PAWN IN GOD'S HANDS?

I was discussing this with a faculty wife one day, and she said, "Look, Girl, I'd feel like a pawn in God's hand if I ever prayed that way."

I thought for a minute. *Wow! Maybe so.* Then I said to her, "You know, maybe the greatest privilege in the whole world would be for Evelyn to be a pawn in the hands of God, who never makes a mistake. Just think, I'd never have to 'trial and error' anything. I'd never fall on my face (which I do very frequently). If God were in control of my every action, I would never do anything wrong. What a privilege to be a pawn in God's hands!

But God hasn't quite chosen to do things that way, has He? God has given Evelyn a free will, and He has given you a free will. He has given us the privilege of saying, "All right, Lord, I'm free. I have a free will, but I want to do what You know is not a mistake in my life." Then, it isn't God pushing Evelyn, is it?

I'm not being a pawn on a chessboard if I say willingly, "Lord, I really don't know what the best approach would be, where I should go, when I should start." With my free will I can say, "Now, Lord, You know all the 'what ifs' and all the outcomes. So, Lord, in my free will, you just use me to bring about your perfect will on Planet Earth."

## ARE YOU ASKING AMISS?

How can we be sure that we are not asking amiss? James writes, "Ye ask, and receive not, because ye ask amiss, that ye may consume it upon your lusts" (James 4:3). Let's never insult God by saying, "O Lord, that other woman's husband looks just a little bit good to me. Is it OK if I just sit at his feet—in my imagination? There won't be anything physical about our relationship, Lord." Let's not ever ask whether that can be God's will. We know what His will is, and He says, "Be ye holy for I am holy."

Perhaps we say, "Lord, *look* at that new car, that new house," or "Wow! Look at her wardrobe, Lord, look at it! Is it OK if I'm just a little bit jealous?" Now, we don't really ask God such questions, but we often rationalize our feelings and attitudes in an attempt to justify them, don't we?

It may be that we're a little bit touchy. We whimper and complain, "Lord, she rubs me the wrong way. Look at what she did. I really don't like her very well. Could that be Your will, Lord?" No. God's Word says, "Love does not demand its own way. It is not irritable or touchy" (1 Cor. 13:5, LB). So one sure way of not asking amiss is to know God's Word, the Bible. If God calls it sin, don't insult Him by asking about it.

But the Bible isn't all negative. We find in God's Word what we *can* do and what we *ought* to do. Responding to the positive commands of God's word is another prerequisite to answered prayer based on obedience: "If ye abide in Me, and My words abide in you, ye shall ask what ye will, and it shall be done unto you" (John 15:7). There is nothing in God's Word that is contrary to God's will, is there? If we find it in His Word, we can believe it, we can live it, and we can act upon it.

At this point you may be asking, do we dare to pray for somebody's salvation? Is it God's will? Peter tells us, "The Lord is . . . not willing that any should perish" (2 Peter 3:9). We are to pray for those outside the body of Christ, but we must not forget that the person for whom we are praying has a free will, just as you and I have. God never superimposes His will upon anyone, but the timing and the sovereignty are His. Pray, yes. It is God's will that we pray that everyone will be saved. In answer to our prayers, the Holy Spirit faithfully woos, but we are to leave the results with God.

There is one more way we can be sure we don't ask amiss. God's Word tells us we believers have two Intercessors— Christ at the right hand of God and the Holy Spirit dwelling in us. The Holy Spirit takes our prayers *when we don't know what we should pray for as we ought* and brings them to the Father *"according to the will of* God" (Rom. 8:26– 27). At those times when we cannot even put the deep yearnings of our hearts into words, we can rest assured that the Holy Spirit is interceding for us before the Throne of God according to the Father's will.

## WHEN GOD SAYS NO

Is it ever good when God says no? I had a meaningful no answer when we first moved to St. Paul. I was asked to be the vice-president of a large hospital auxiliary. I knew nothing about the two hospitals they served, but was assured it was a "you-won't-have-to-do-a-thing" job.

I immediately called back home to the prayer chains I had just left, asking them to pray God's will. Soon the answer came from them and from others I had asked to pray: "God is saying no." And He was telling me no also.

When I told the committee what God had said, I almost felt the eyebrows being raised in surprise. I could not understand either why God would say no to such a great job when I was lonely with nothing to do in my new town.

A couple of weeks later, I found out why. The auxiliary's president was transferred with her husband out of state. Within two weeks, I would have been president of an organization that ran coffee shops and gift shops, and supervised volunteers and student candy stripers in two large hospitals. In addition, the whole work was needing to be reorganized through the hospital administrators and lawyers—a process which is being completed only now, four years later. What a mess I would have made of that gigantic job!

"O dear God," I prayed, "thank You for knowing the 'what ifs' and for keeping me from falling on my face in this my new hometown."

## IS SUFFERING EVER GOD'S WILL?

One year in our neighborhood Bible study we discovered a verse of Scripture which had a great impact on all of our lives. I knew the concept was scriptural, but I had never noticed it in God's Word before. "Wherefore let them that suffer according to the will of God commit the keeping of their souls to Him in well doing, as unto a faithful Creator" (1 Peter 4:19) .

*Those who suffer according to God's will*—is that in the Bible? Yes, it is. And almost everyone in our group that year was suffering. Of course, they weren't suffering because they were in the Bible study group (I hope!). They were suffering in their bodies and in their spirits in various ways, but they began to see tremendous things take place. Whenever a problem arose with a crisis-impact, God gave us a specific answer immediately, in His Word, and we received strength, grace, peace, maturity in Christ—whatever was needed.

The husband of one woman in that group had a peculiar fungus growing under his skull, and his only hope for survival was in the administration of a drug that had side effects on the mind and personality. He became an entirely different person. As a result he divorced his wife and turned his back on his whole family. Recently, I had lunch with this woman. She's still radiant in Christ.

Another member's husband had contracted syphilis and had to name all his partners, a whole string of them. That woman found strength in the Word of God. Two daughters of one woman, both teenagers, were pregnant out of wedlock, as was one teenage daughter of another woman. About the least that happened to anybody was major surgery or breast cancer!

Can suffering be God's will? Yes, we all saw it come into focus in First Peter. If you're suffering read that epistle. It's tremendous. We, as Christians, aren't promised that we'll be free from suffering. Sometimes we suffer simply because we have frail, human bodies, but if we're committed to the God who doesn't ever make a mistake, we can have the assurance that He has permitted our suffering and *has a specific reason for it.*

I have no way of knowing whether you are suffering as you read this chapter, but if you are, while you are, can you truly pray, "Lord, I still want Your will. Amen"? It means taking every facet, every area of our lives, and turning them over to the Lord. It's easy to pray, "Lord, how I love Your will" when we're on the mountaintop. But there are other times when we can only pray, "O Lord, I'm in the valley and it hurts. But, Lord, my answer is yes. I know that Your will is right, and I'm willing to conform to Your will no matter what it is."

## ALL THINGS FOR GOOD

Way back in our college days, I faced a crisis when I lost my third pregnancy. I had already had a miscarriage, then a full-term stillborn, and now another miscarriage. "Lord, Lord, why all of this?" my heart cried.

It was just after World War II, and we had returned to college after Chris had promised God in a burning bomber over Berlin that he would become a preacher after the war was over. Then God allowed us to lose this third baby. Was He turning His back and letting us suffer?

No, not at all. God gave me at that time Romans 8:28, "And we know that all things work together for good to those that love God." I loved God and Chris loved Him, and God had His reasons for not allowing those three babies to live.

What all of God's reasons were, I may never know short of eternity. But one thing God seemed to tell me was, "Do you think that you and Chris could have gone through seven more years of schooling if you had had those three babies? Your dad had become an invalid and Chris' dad had died leaving two younger children. Could you have had the courage and the financial support to face seven more years of schooling with three babies to care for?"

Did God make a mistake? No. Not at all. Romans 8:28 has been our family's life verse ever since. We know that *all* things, absolutely everything, work together for our good. This was the omniscient God who never makes a mistake dealing in the lives of those who loved Him.

Despite my earlier miscarriages, Jan came along normally, and then, when we were in our first pastorate, it seemed God was giving us a second healthy child. But Judy lived to be only seven months old. And all the pain came back again. "Lord, how come? Haven't I suffered enough? Haven't I learned?"

When God took Judy, He spoke to me so clearly from the 12th chapter of Hebrews. "For they [our earthly fathers] verily for a few days chastened us after their own pleasure; but He [God] *for our profit,* that we might be partakers of His holiness" (v. 10). God said, "Look, Evelyn, this is for your profit. If you're going to be a pastor's wife, you will have to understand some of these things." I wish I could write of all the ways that God through the years has used that experience for my profit ass I've stood with heartbroken parents by tiny caskets or hospital cribs.

Ultimately God did permit us to raise three happy, healthy children, Jan, Nancy, and Kurt. And He had things to teach us through each of them, as well as through those we lost.

Do we ever arrive? My mother-in-law once said to me, "Oh Evelyn, I'm over 70 and I still haven't arrived." No, we never arrive, but God is doing something. He's making us what He wants us to be. It's in the suffering, and it's in the hard things that He wants us to say, "Lord, you never make a mistake. I want only your will."

When I was speaking about this at an After Five Club near my home, three young women came to speak to me. I learned that one of them was going blind, one had just lost her two-year-old son in an accident, and the other was facing serious hip surgery within the next few days. As they spoke to me individually, each said that Romans 8:28 had come into focus for her that night. And each added, "I am now willing for God's will, whatever it may be."

## THE OTHER HALF OF GOD'S WILL

Are you willing for God's will? In the previous chapter I wrote about the open door and the excitement. That's half of it, but the other half is being willing for God's will no matter how hard it is. At one of our church circle meetings, our spiritual life chairman, whose only sister was dying of cancer, said while leading our devotions, "I have struggled for months and months. Now I can finally tell you that if God takes my sister or lets her live, I am willing for God's will."

Her words completely broke us. We forgot everything on the agenda and started to pray. There were women there with very serious problems. A young, pregnant mother who had lost her only other child to crib death syndrome the preceding March could say, "I'm willing for God's will in this pregnancy." Another lady suffering from Hodgkins disease could say the same. Each of those women prayed and meant it, "Lord, I'm willing for Your will!" Then they immediately went to intercessory prayer for me while I spoke at the church where the youth pastor later said to me, "You turned our church upside down!" If you and I want to be powerful intercessory pray-ers, we must be willing for God's will not only in the things for which we are praying—that's only half of it. The other half is *being willing for God's will in our own personal lives.*

## HOT FIRES

At Lindon Karo's funeral, my 14-year-old niece was sobbing out her heartbreak; she loved her pastor dearly. As I put my arms around her, I said, "Carla, God must have something very, very great for you if He's giving you this hot a fire so early in life." What did I mean? I meant that God has a way of making us greater persons by the "hot fires" which are preparing us for what is ahead. This is a beautiful concept. David understood it. He said, "Thou hast enlarged me when I was in distress" (Ps. 4:1). The word *enlarged* means "prepared for the task ahead."

Our Jan learned this when she was in the ninth grade. Her friend, Dave, was a fantastic boy, an A student, president of the student council, as well as class president. He was captain of the basketball team, and had singlehandedly pitched the local pony league baseball team to the world championship. His poetry had been published nationally— everything was going for him with two exceptions: Dave was not a Christian, and he had leukemia. But he didn't know about the leukemia and neither did Jan.

In the spring of that year, our local churches sponsored a gigantic youth rally with Dave Wilkerson as the speaker. At first Jan was timid about inviting Dave, but she finally worked up courage. On the evening of the rally, Chris and I took the car and drove them down to the armory. My husband sat close enough to Dave to hear him pray as he slipped to his knees at the end of the service: "Dear God, forgive all my sins and, Jesus, come into my heart as my Lord and Saviour."

Dave had no idea at that time that he was soon to enter into battle with a deadly killer—leukemia. By the time the junior high yearbooks came out, Dave knew he was very sick, but hardly realized how near the end was. He wrote in Jan's yearbook: "Dear Jan, Thank you for introducing me to Christ. You'll never know what He means to me now, and what He will in the future."

Two weeks later, Dave's "future with Christ" was a reality. Early on the day he died, I was sitting alone in my purple chair in the living room. Sensing that something was wrong, Jan got out of bed, came downstairs and asked, "Where's Dad?"

I said, "He's at Dave's house, Honey."

She said, "Dave's gone, isn't he?"

I replied, "Yes."

For a little while we sat and cried together in that little purple chair. I said, "Honey, God is making you finer gold." She had heard that many times in our home. We talked about Romans 8:28, and Job's assurance that "When He hath tried me, I shall come forth as gold" (Job 23:10) . That morning I said to Jan what I recently repeated to Carla at Lindon Karo's funeral, "Honey, God must have something great in mind for you to give you all this 'fire' at your age." Then Jan sobbed, "Oh, Mother, what if I hadn't invited him to hear Dave Wilkerson preach?"

Dave's funeral was the largest that had ever been held in our city. Hundreds of teenagers, teachers, and school officials were present at the mortuary. As my husband stood up to speak, he said, "I can almost hear the basketball bouncing in heaven today."

Then he told all those people what Dave had said just before he died. He had raised himself from his bed and asked, "Where am I?"

His mother had replied, "Dave, you're in Billings Hospital in Chicago and you're very, very sick. But all the doctors and nurses are here."

Then Dave had said, "Oh, no. Where I am it's all green and beautiful." And then he had died.

My husband could tell all those teenagers and the others that Dave was with his Christ in a future that was only two weeks away when he had written about it in Jan's yearbook.

Suffering can be according to God's will. Are you willing—even if suffering is to be a part of your future?

## COMMITTED TO HIS WILL

At our seminar session on this subject we invite participants at prayer time to commit their lives to God's perfect will. On a Wednesday morning, following such a session, one woman who attended committed her whole life, everything she held dear, to God's will. That very weekend her husband was killed in a motorboat accident! On the following Wednesday, one of the seminar members came with a message from this widow. "Please tell Evelyn that God prepared me for this experience when I committed my life to Him for His will last Wednesday."

Several months later at a prayer leaders workshop, with tears in her eyes, she told us that she could really see God's will in this tragedy because one of her daughters who had turned away from Christ and left home had come back to Him, and was now taking her Daddy's place in leading the smaller children in Bible reading and prayer each day.

After prayer time in a seminar the following February, a young woman whose husband was a seminary student said to me, "I cannot pray for God's will in my life. I cannot do it."

When I asked why, she replied, "I prayed and prayed and prayed for a baby. Then I became pregnant and was so excited, because I knew it was an answer to prayer. I knew God had given us that baby! But last December I had a miscarriage—and now I don't have my baby."

I said, "God doesn't make mistakes. He gave you the child for just the few months that you carried it. God has accomplished His purpose for that baby's life."

The young woman thought for a moment, and said, "Now I can pray for God's will." We bowed our heads and she prayed, "Lord, whatever it is, I want only Your will in my life."

Again, following a seminar session on God's will, a young man who had undergone surgery for a brain tumor about five years previously struggled up the aisle with the help of two canes, and asked if he could say something. We all thought he was going to ask for prayer for healing or make some other request. But, supported on either side by his "new" mother and myself, he leaned toward the microphone and said, "I just want to thank God for these seminars and for the privilege of being here. You know, my mother died while I was still in a coma after my accident." (He called his brain tumor his accident.) Then he added, "If all these things hadn't happened to me, I would not have come to live with this new mother who is a Christian. She has introduced me to Jesus, and I have received Him as my Saviour. If I hadn't had my accident, I would never have come to know Jesus." Then he said, "I'm willing for anything that God's will has for me." And he stood there, not even able to support himself, but willing for God's will.

## THE PLACE OF PRAISE

We may reach the place suddenly, or it may take us years to realize that God isn't making a mistake in our lives. But then we are at the point where we can praise Him. A new Christian in my Bible study called me one day and said, "'Mrs. Chris,' I think I found a wrong translation in the Bible. It's there in the first chapter of James, verses two to four. Isn't it wrong when it says, 'Count it all joy when you fall into various trials'?"

I smiled over the phone and said, "No, Honey, it's not wrong. This is the place you reach when after years and years of trials and difficulties, you see that all has been working out for your good, and that God's will is perfect. You see that He has made no mistakes. He knew all of the 'what ifs' in your life. When you finally recognize this, even *during* the trials, it's possible to have joy, deep down joy."

And Philippians 4:6 comes into focus at this point: "Be careful [anxious] for nothing; but in everything, by prayer and supplication with *thanksgiving*, let your requests be made known unto God." It is a privilege to see God being glorified in our lives. We are to give thanks always, knowing that we have a God who never makes a mistake. And if we are going to be effectual intercessory pray-ers, praying in the will of God, it's not something we tack on to the end of our prayers. It's a commitment to God's will, a way of life. It's being willing for His will in the things for which we are praying and in our personal lives. And it's "Giving thanks always for *all* things unto God and the Father in the name of our Lord Jesus Christ" (Eph. 5:20). As I said earlier, it's easier said than done—but the rewards are fantastic!

**For You to Do:**

Bow your head, close your eyes, and **think** of the most important thing in the world to you. (It may be health, a loved one, a job, finances, schooling, etc.)

Now **pray**: "Father, I want only Your will in this thing that is most important in the whole world to me."

Now in prayer **thank** God for however He chooses to answer, knowing it is according to His perfect will.

Please don't pray the following prayer unless you really mean it. "Father, I want Your will in **every area** of my life including my job, my home, my health, my children, my loved ones, and my service for You. Amen."

# 7

## The Space
## Dimension of Prayer—
## Where We Pray

*"But thou, when thou prayest, enter into thy **closet**, and when thou hast shut thy door, pray to thy Father which is in secret; and thy Father which seeth in secret shall reward thee openly."* Matthew 6:6

MY OLD GREEN chair has long since been reupholstered, but years ago, when it was brand new, it became the quiet place to which I would steal very early in the morning to spend time alone with God. It was on my knees at that old chair that I would pour out the inmost groanings of my heart—for only God to hear. Groanings much too personal to be heard by any other. My tears stained its cushion as I knelt interceding for a loved one. It was there I was filled with awe and adoration for Him and all He is—the "heaven of heavens cannot contain Thee" (1 Kings 8:27).

It was there on my knees with my open Bible that God taught me to wait on Him for every point in a series of messages. It was there with my head buried in my hands that I begged God for wisdom for a certain message that I was to give. Not getting any answers, I reached for the morning newspaper, laid it on the seat of the chair, and read in the headlines that Russia had sent Sputnik I into outer space. Then God said, "It isn't who can *conquer* outer space that counts, but He who *created* it and by whom it consists" (see Col. 1:16–17). I had my message!

## PRIVATE PRAYER—PUBLIC PRAYING

Do you have a secret place for private prayer, a certain corner, a particular chair, or a room set apart where you can spend time alone with God? A "closet" where you daily *shut the door* to pray to your Father in secret? The group concept of prayer is important, and we do need to pray *with* one another, "not forsaking the assembling of ourselves together" (see Heb. 10:25). But the drawing apart to pray in secret is perhaps the most vital type of prayer in which we engage. It is also an indicator of the kind of prayer group participant we really are, for *it is our private praying, that determines the quality and validity of our public praying.*

Though we are never to be critical of the prayers of others, we can often recognize in our prayer groups those who have spent time in private closet prayer and the others who have come perhaps to do the only praying that they have done all week. Some struggle and strain to sound pious, but it's obvious that they haven't experienced the deeper dimension of closet prayer.

Have you ever seen a bright blue iceberg? In Alaska recently I stared in awe at a mountain lake filled with beautiful blue icebergs that had broken off Portage Glacier. Immediately my mind went back to an article I had read in a *Family Tie* magazine that compared our secret praying to an iceberg. The "absolutely no boating" sign reminded me that eight-ninths of the bulk of an iceberg is below the waterline—out of sight. Only one-ninth is visible above the surface. The next day at our prayer seminar in Anchorage I explained how prayer should be like those icebergs, with about one-ninth showing in our public group praying and eight-ninths out of sight in our secret closets.

## OTHER CLOSETS

I can almost hear you saying, "I can't spend great periods of my time in a closet." No, neither can I, but I have found another kind of closet praying. It's just drawing apart to God wherever I am—at the kitchen sink, at a desk, or even in a room filled with people.

"You must have tremendous power of concentration," someone said.

No, I've just learned to draw apart from people to God. Practicing this at a California retreat with 525 people packed in a room that barely held 500, we found, though touching elbows physically, that we could each draw apart mentally to God. This, too, is closet praying, though it is no substitute for drawing apart to that one spot, at that one time of the day, when we really spend time with God and His Word.

One of my very favorite "closets" is my car. As I draw apart, you may be sure I don't take my hands off the wheel, fold them, and kneel. To shut my eyes would be even worse!

One morning last week, as I was getting ready to leave for an all-day prayer seminar 50 miles away, everything went wrong. My husband called from California asking me to find out when certain professors should be met at the San Francisco airport, and to give the information to his secretary so he could call her after I had gone. I couldn't find the professors; I couldn't find the secretary after frantically dialing all the possible numbers.

Then my son called from school: "Mom, I forgot all my books; could you bring them over?" I did, and was completely out of time when I left his school only to run into such a long detour that I could hardly find my way back to the freeway.

As I finally emerged on the right road, I cried to God, "O Lord, take over! Remove from me all this tension and frustration. Flow through me with Your peace and power. Make me what You want me to be by the time I arrive at the prayer seminar." And He did! My car had become my prayer closet.

Even a plane seat can be a prayer closet. For two years I had been praying with a friend about her sister who did not know Christ. Every time my friend wrote to her sis, she'd call asking me to pray for God to work in her heart as she received the letter. One day my plane had a 10-minute layover in a Midwestern city with no time to disembark. I looked out over that city and thought, *That's where my friend's sister lives!* Suddenly there descended from God a heavy, overwhelming burden to pray for her. I sat in that plane in the very depths of intercessory prayer. Two days later my elated friend called to say, "I just received a letter from my sis, and she accepted Christ!" When? The exact day God had said in that plane, "Evelyn, pray."

## WHICH POSTURE?

Just as our "momentary" closet praying requires no particular place, neither does it require a certain prayer posture. In one of our seminars a man announced to me after the first session that he would not be back. "You're not praying scripturally," he said. When I asked him to please explain, he said, "You're not 'holding up holy hands.'" He could see only this one position to be used at all times even though I pointed out to him that there are many postures of prayer mentioned in the Word of God.

Jesus, when He was praying in the garden of Gethsemane, set for us the example of *kneeling* in prayer: "And He was withdrawn from them about a stone's cast, and kneeled down, and prayed" (Luke 22:41). At the tomb of Lazarus, while standing, "Jesus *lifted up His eyes*, and said, 'Father, I thank Thee that Thou hast heard Me'" (John 11:41). Paul wrote, "I will therefore that men pray everywhere, *lifting up holy hands*, without wrath and doubting" (1 Tim. 2:8).

My husband can recall circumstances in which men experienced such grief and anguish that they have lain prostrate on the floor of his study. One was a dad who had just learned that his teenage daughter was pregnant out of wedlock. He cast himself to the floor, weeping, and my husband had to take him in his arms and gently lift him up.

King Solomon, in the Old Testament, *prostrated himself before the Lord* when he prayed in the temple. His father, David, communed with God upon his bed (Ps. 4:4). Whatever our posture, whatever the place, the ears of our God are open to our cry (see Ps. 34:15).

## HOLY PLACES

God does not dwell in temples made with hands. Even so, some spots have been used as closets for prayer by so many that they seem to be holy places. Have you ever stepped into a room and felt God there? My husband and I were looking over the grounds at a Midwestern retreat center last fall. We stepped into an old chapel—and I felt God's presence immediately. "Hon, please go on without me for a few minutes," I said. I knelt at that altar—not talking or praying, but just *feeling* God so powerfully there.

Another time I arrived at Bethel Seminary in St. Paul to speak at a women's retreat just as the planning committee stepped out of the Eric Frykenberg Prayer Tower, where they had been praying for our meetings. Their eyes were wide with wonder and amazement. "We felt Jesus in there!"

"Yes," I replied "that is one of those places where I always feel a particular sense of the presence of Christ." That little circular room has no windows, no furniture—but it is filled with the thousands of prayers uttered by students and faculty of that seminary—and His presence!

79

Christ recognized the need for spending time alone with God. What a tremendous example Chris's prayer life was to His followers and to us. Though the disciples were Jesus' very closest friends, He knew there were times He had to pray in secret to His heavenly Father. So Christ, though He taught His disciples the concept of group prayer, as we have learned in previous chapters, also knew the importance of this private closet praying. Even though He himself was God incarnate, He thought it necessary to withdraw to a mountain to pray all night alone before the important task of choosing the 12 apostles. If He—why not us?

**For You to Pray:**

"Lord, give me the joy of secret closet praying. Keep me faithful to shut the door every day and spend time with You and Your Word in secret. Teach me to draw apart alone with You, no matter where I am or with whom."

# 8
## The Time
## Dimension of Prayer—
## When We Pray

*"Pray without ceasing."* 1 Thessalonians 5:17

DID YOU EVER sit in a room before a glowing fire with someone you love? Did you talk every minute? Or did you feel compelled every now and then to clear your throat and say, "Now dear, I think I'll say something to you." Then with a bright introduction, did you proceed with a formal speech? Of course not. When you're with a person you love, there need not be a bit of conversation in order for you to experience real communication. If you feel like saying something, you do; if not, you don't, but the line of communication is always open.

Praying without ceasing is like that. How? It's simply turning the dial of our communication system with God to *on*, making possible a two-way conversation with Him at any time. When that communication line is open, we can say whatever we want to Him, and He in turn can say anything He wishes to us. Yes, it's possible to "pray without ceasing" 24 hours a day.

81

When we leave our daily closet praying, do we walk out and slam the door, saying, "That's it for today. Same time tomorrow, Lord, same station"? That isn't what the Holy Spirit meant when He inspired Paul to write, "Pray without ceasing" (1 Thes. 5:17). Nor is it what Christ meant when He taught His disciples, "Men ought always to pray, and not to faint" (Luke 18:1).

After Paul lists the armor with which we are to resist Satan, he goes on to say, "Praying *always* with all prayer and supplication in the Spirit" (Eph. 6:18). The source of strength in our battle with the enemy is "praying always." But when the line of communication with God closes, wham—the fiery darts of Satan strike! But that need not be the case. Let's break down the day and see how the communication system between us and God can be open all 24 hours.

## A LARK OR AN OWL?

How do you start your day? Are you a "lark" or an "owl"? "Larks" twitter and sing in the morning, but by the end of the day they're not doing too well; they have slowed down considerably. "Owls" take a little longer to get going in the morning. You know—"Right now I don't love anybody, but when I start loving again, you'll be first on the list." But owls gain momentum as the night progresses.

We're divided at our house. I'm a "lark" and my husband is definitely an "owl." When we pray together at night and Chris prays on and on, I sometimes have to say, "Hurry up, Chris; you're losing me." But in the morning it's a different story. Chris groans and pulls the covers up tighter when I shake him to tell him some great gem that I've just gotten from the Lord.

Because our individual, inbuilt clocks function differently, I've learned that there are no spiritual "brownie points" for being a "lark." Is it possible our heavenly Father created some of us to be "larks" and some to be "owls" so He would have somebody on the alert all 24 hours of the day?

I used to say, and I'm sure it was with pride, "I'm creative in the morning. That is my creative time." Then I realized, *Ev, you're not creative in the morning; you've just learned to listen to God in the wee hours.*

When I'm asked, "How do you get all those messages ready? How can you possibly write so many?" I have to reply, "I don't write messages, but I keep a little notebook on my bedstand at all times. Then lying there communing with my heavenly Father early in the morning, I just jot down whatever He says to me."

When I awaken, I say, "Lord, here I am. What do You want to say to me?" I usually think they should be ideas for immediate needs, but frequently He gives thoughts for retreats and messages months away. I write them down and keep them in file folders. Then when I put those papers in outline form, it's astounding to learn that God has given me every single thought I'll ever need—in time!

It's a very exciting procedure to wait upon God early in the morning while the mind is fresh, before anyone else comes upon the scene, or before the "tyranny of the urgent" rushes in. Have you learned to say in the morning, "Lord, here I am. You tell me what You want me to know today, what You want me to do"? Have you asked Him, "Is there someone You want me to call? What do You have in mind for me today?" You'll be amazed at His answers!

One morning as I was lying in bed talking to the Lord, I said, as I frequently do, "OK, Lord whom would You have me call on the phone today?" The answer came as if it were in lights, "Mona."

"But Lord, I don't know Mona. I met her at a band concert, and at a PTA meeting—and that's it."

I waited until the kids left for school; then I went to the phone and said, "Lord, You're going to have to tell me what to say to Mona—I don't know."

I really felt a little silly about calling her, but I dialed and said, "Good morning, Mona. This is Evelyn Christenson from down the street." That's all I said. And Mona started to cry. She told me that the day before, she and her husband had been told by the doctors that their son, Dave (our Jan's friend), had leukemia and would never recover. My obedience gave me the opportunity to at least build a bridge to Mona and to comfort her in her distress.

One morning, after my daughter had asked me to pray for a girl who was feuding with her parents, I said, "Lord, if You want me to talk to her, have her call or come over." At 2 o'clock in the afternoon I answered my doorbell, and there she stood with a suitcase in her hand. "Hi, I've come to move in with you for a while."

It had been one of those unbelievably hectic days, and I glanced heavenward and sighed, "Lord, I didn't mean that *literally*."

I used to think that if one were an "owl," talking with God in the morning wasn't necessary. But one day, as I was reading Psalm 5, I saw something for the first time. I said to Chris, "Hey, it's really scriptural to talk to God first thing in the morning." In all the times I had read that psalm, it had never really hit me before. "Give ear to my words, O Lord, consider my meditation. Hearken unto the voice of my cry, my King, and my God: for unto Thee will I pray. My voice shalt Thou hear in the morning, O Lord; in the morning will I direct my prayer unto Thee, and will look up" (Ps. 5:1–3).

It doesn't say hours of prayer time are necessary, but at least we must say good morning to the Lord and give Him our day. So whether you are a "lark" or an "owl," God's Word says early in the morning, before the "tyranny of the urgent," before breakfast, before the school busses, before anyone says a word to you, "Early in the morning, Lord, I will look up, and pray unto You."

## PRAYER BEFORE SCHOOL

After breakfast, it's time for the children to start off to school. Since our first child was in kindergarten, we have made a practice in our home of praying individually with each of our children just as they left for school. This to me has been a very precious experience. It's been more than a time to pray! We have been able to put our arms around our children, assuring them of the security of their home, and then to send them out into the big, often overwhelming world with God watching over them, whatever they will face that day.

Every once in a while I'm told by my son, "Hurry up, Mom, make it short. The school bus is coming," and out the door he goes! Sometimes it's only one or two sentences. But meeting God with our family before we separate is a very vital part of our day.

## THE DAY PROGRESSES

I have a great time with the Lord in the morning. As God and I communicate with one another, He tells me what He wants me to do, and I say, "OK, Lord." There are no problems. There aren't any people around to bother me. There are no bad reactions for me to contend with. You know, I could really be a tremendous Christian if I could stay in my "closet" with God. But I can't stay there all day. I can't even remain sheltered with members of my own family, those who love me. I have to get out and meet people—and occasionally my early morning relationship with God suddenly falls apart!

I'm a "people person," and I really like almost everybody I meet. But once in a while somebody makes me bristle, and I retaliate. There are other occasions when I just look at someone and think, "Oh, brother!"

How do I solve the problem? I've learned what I call my

*SOS prayer.* I say, "Help, Lord." (But not out loud!) "Lord, give me the attitude *You* want me to have toward that person."

Perhaps you can imagine what it's like for a wife and mother to prepare to go out-of-town for a speaking engagement. You get all the laundry done, matching the socks with the shirts. Then you stock the refrigerator with enough food for all the days you'll be gone, outline each of your messages, try to get yourself and your clothes ready, and do the last-minute shopping. It's really hectic! In addition, you have to get "prayed up." You just can't go without spiritual preparation, so you spend extra time with the Lord. Finally you settle into the plane seat, review your notes once more, and pray.

Things had gone that way before I arrived in an eastern city for a retreat a few years ago. As I was being introduced to the ladies, a pastor's wife who was sitting next to me leaned over and gibed, almost sneering, "Do you really like these little women's meetings?"

Wow! After all I'd gone through to get there! Besides, I didn't think that meeting was so little—about 200 women were there from several states. And I was all primed and ready to share what the Lord had given me for them. Do you know what I did? I bristled!

Now, I didn't have time to say a long prayer. I had only seconds left before speaking. As I walked to the platform, I silently pleaded with the Lord. *"Help, SOS,* give me the attitude You want me to have toward that pastor's wife." And do you know, all the bristle disappeared. Because God knew I didn't have a lot of time to get this cleaned up, He answered my SOS prayer just like *that!* What would have happened if I had started out bristling at that audience? It would have "pulled the rug" right out from under the whole retreat.

One of the prayer requests presented at a faculty wives' prayer meeting I attended several months ago involved a serious financial problem. On the day before, the promise of a large gift of money for the new campus had been withdrawn, and we were going to pray about it.

As we were drinking coffee and chatting before the start of the prayer meeting, a woman came in whom I had never met. I didn't know who she was, but I looked down my spiritual nose and thought, *My word, she's the "squarest" woman I've ever seen in my life.* And the more she talked the more "square" I thought she was.

Then the Lord began to reprove me: "Evelyn, that's sin." Do you remember our first prerequisite to answered prayer? "If I regard iniquity in my heart, the Lord will not hear me"? I suddenly realized that I was about to spend my morning in prayer for these financial needs with sin in *my* heart! Another SOS prayer flew to heaven, "Lord, please, give me the attitude You want me to have toward that woman, whoever she is."

You know, when we pray that prayer, we never ask amiss. God knows what attitude He wants to give us. When we look at Christ's life, we can see that sometimes His perfect attitude was love, sometimes it was righteous indignation, sometimes patience, sometimes discipline, sometimes compassion. That day God gave me a surprise.

Guess who prayed first at that prayer meeting? She did. And as she started to pray, I suddenly realized that this woman had a dimension to her prayer life that I knew nothing about. She said, "Thank You, Lord, that that money didn't come through yesterday." And I blinked. She went on, "Now, Lord, You have given us the *privilege* of being on our faces before You this morning with a desperate need. Lord, what a privilege this is. Thank You, Lord. And thank You that today the school's president has the privilege of being on his face before You with this need. Thank You that the whole staff has this tremendous need, and thank You that they have the privilege of being on their faces before You."

I felt two inches high.

When I learned who this woman was, I discovered some other things. She had an intercessory prayer life that was never less than two hours a day. She used a prayer list that was pages and pages long, containing the names of the people for whom she prays daily. And *I* had looked at *her* and thought, *Wow, is she "square!"*

I had a trying experience when I was teaching wives during a pastors' conference. We had gone over the material on praying in God's will, and were going to have a spiritual exercise by taking partners with whom we would share and pray. My partner was a young pastor's wife. We took our chairs to a corner as we were supposed to, and got all ready for the spiritual exercise, when suddenly she looked me right in the eye and said, "I hate you."

Do you think I smiled and said, "Oh, I just love you"? Not on your life. I said, "I guess we had better not do our exercise; we'd better just talk. Tell me why you hate me."

But as I was talking outwardly, inwardly I was praying, "SOS, Lord. Help me to have the attitude You want me to have toward this person." And God gave me the ability to sit there calmly without becoming angry and retaliating. "Would you like to tell me why you hate me?" I asked.

She said, "OK, I'll tell you. My husband has been interviewed by the pulpit committee seeking a pastor for your former church." She went on, "I didn't know who you were when I came to this meeting. I had never seen you before, had never heard one of your tapes, but I knew you were the wife of the former pastor of that church." Then she exploded, "You're everything I don't want to be and can't be in a pastor's wife, so I hate you. Look at that dress you're wearing," she said. "I'm a sweatshirt and jeans girl myself."

I was at a loss as to where to start, but God seemed to be saying to share deeply with her out of my heart. I told her of the hard things I had talked about in my message that morning, things that had happened *during* my time at that church. I even told her of a very personal trial I never mention in public, and how those wonderful people prayed for me—just as they would pray for her if she were their pastor's wife. It wasn't long before the two of us were in tears, clasping hands, and praying together.

As we parted, she said, "As my husband and I drive home this afternoon, I want to tell him about how I feel now. Will you pray for me?"

I said I would, but she didn't wait until afternoon. At lunch her husband came flying across the dining room and asked, "What did you do to my wife?"

I told him I didn't do anything to his wife, but I wanted to know what happened.

He said, "You know, God is calling me to leave the church I'm now serving, and my wife has been saying, 'Absolutely not. I don't care where you're called. I won't go.' But she just came to me and said, 'Honey, wherever God leads you, I'll go along.' What did you do?"

What had I done? I had prayed, "SOS, Lord. Give me the right attitude toward this woman." And immediately He had given me an understanding attitude toward a young pastor's wife who didn't want to leave her rural community and her sweatshirt and jeans.

Not long ago a woman stopped me in a church and said, "We just called a new pastor." Guess who it was? That same young man! Then she went on, "Do you know why we called him? He's a great guy, but we were very impressed with his wife. She was so eager to have her husband where God wanted him to be, and she was undergirding his ministry like we've never seen any pastor's wife do before." I smiled and breathed a thank-you to God for that little sweatshirt-and-jeans girl who only a year before had said, "I hate you."

When we say to God, "Give me the attitude You want me to have toward that person," immediately these amazing attitudes come, the ones He wants us to have. We don't have to reach for the pill bottle. I had one toddler who I said was not just an *"Anacin* headache kid," she was a *"Vanquish* headache kid." She could paint the back fence and her hair and everything else faster than I could get out there to grab the paint can! What do we do? We pray, "Lord, right now, give me the attitude You want me to have toward that person in my family, toward that person I meet on the street, even toward the one who looks at me and says, 'I hate you.'" All day long if people rub us the wrong way, we can have the communication system open between us and God. We just pray, "SOS *Lord*. Give me the attitude *You* want me to have." It works all day long, the whole 24 hours.

## BEAR YE ONE ANOTHER'S BURDENS
## —ALL THE TIME

How about your family? Is it as easy for your children to say, "Mom, I'm having a math test at 10:30, please pray," as it is for them to ask you for $2.50 for lunch money? Do your children know that your communication system with God is always open?

One morning while she was still in high school, one of our daughters was so frightened about an up-coming important interview that I found her sick to her stomach in the bathroom. I helped her out the front door and promised to pray. Soon the phone rang. "Mother, it went great," she exclaimed, then softly, "I could *feel* you praying, Mom."

Our married daughter's father-in-law had just had open-heart surgery. Suddenly the "Red Alert" was flashed over the hospital intercom. Jan ran to a phone, dialed our number, and, with the sounds of running hospital personnel in the background, said, "Mother, Skip's dad's heart has stopped."

*My* heart stood still. I felt so helpless and so far away. "What can I do?"

There was a long pause, and then she said, "Just pray, Mother, just pray," and hung up.

I did pray, and her father-in-law revived and God gave him four more years to live. But the point is that Jan knew she could depend on me to pray about her concerns, any time, any place.

This family prayer support works two ways. After finishing a retreat at Mt. Hermon in California, I phoned home long distance. My then 10-year-old son answered with, "How did it go, Mom?"

"Oh, Kurt, it went just great."

"Well," he said with pride in his voice, "how could you miss with my whole pastor's Saturday class praying for you?"

Do you have someone who will pray for you and for whom you will pray? If you don't know where to start with all these prayer suggestions, find one person with whom you can share the secret problems and needs of your life. Someone who cares and who will never, never divulge your secrets. Then fulfill the law of Christ by "bearing one another's burdens" (see Gal. 6:2).

## THE NIGHTWATCH

Are you one of these people whom God can awaken in the middle of the night to pray for one of His needs down here on Planet Earth? "But I need my sleep," you say. So did I, or at least I thought I did. For many years I was strictly hung up on sleeping pills. I thought I had to have eight solid hours of sleep or I'd never make it the next day. Then one summer day, I very undramatically tossed those pills into the toilet, flushed it, and said, "Lord, I'm not going to worry if I'm awake at night, because if You awaken me, there's a reason for it. I'll just ask You, 'For whom should I be praying?'"

God knows when I'm finished praying and ready to go back to sleep. And somehow there's no frustration and I never miss the sleep when God needs me to pray. It's a very beautiful, exciting thing.

One night the Lord awoke me and said, "Pray for Jacque" (a long-time prayer partner). At that time she was in San Francisco, and I learned later that she was going through a very deep spiritual battle, seemingly surrounded by forces of Satan. A letter Jacque wrote to me the next morning confirmed the reason God had awakened me. As I prayed in St. Paul, great peace had flooded her in San Francisco. *If at night you can't sleep, don't count sheep—talk to the Shepherd!*

Another time I was driving on the freeway in the state of Wisconsin very late on a Saturday night. It hadn't occurred to me that my gas tank might be a little bit hungry since I wasn't. All at once, *putt, putt, putt.* I was out of gas! I pulled off to the side of the road and opened the trunk (I knew that if I opened the hood, other motorists approaching from behind would see that there was a woman alone in a car).

As each set of headlights appeared behind me, I prayed, "Lord, if there's anybody in that car with whom I won't be safe, keep them going, Lord, keep them going." I sat there for 15 minutes, and every set of headlights shot right by. Nobody stopped.

Then I saw a blinking red light and heard the sound of a siren behind me. For the first time in my life I was happy and excited to hear that sound! The state trooper got out of his car and said, "You know, Lady, that you're in danger out here alone on the freeway this late at night, don't you?"

I said, "Yes, sir, I know it."

He told me that it would take about five minutes to transfer some gas from his patrol car to mine, and invited me to sit in the squad car. I noticed that he was trembling, and needed desperately to talk to someone.

He said, "I just came from an accident. A pregnant mother fell asleep, and her car veered off to the right and struck a cement culvert. I looked at the car with the right one-third sheared off and thought, *Oh, oh, this is going to be one of those messy ones.* But the first thing I saw was a little two-year-old girl walking around with just one pulled tendon in her leg. What really unnerved me, though, was that a Mrs. Beasley doll that was placed between the mother and daughter was decapitated by a piece of metal that came through the windshield, but the two of them were unharmed." He turned to me and asked, "Do you believe in God?"

I said, "Yes."

Then with deep emotion he said, "Do you think God was riding in the back seat of that car?"

I replied, "I think He may very well have been." Then I added, "Do you know that you're an answer to prayer, too?"

He said, "Me? I'm an answer to prayer?"

Then I told him how I had prayed about every single pair of lights approaching my car that night.

This is only a part of the story, and we must go back to Jacque for the end of it. "Evelyn, why did I feel an overwhelming urgency to pray for you last night? We were having a birthday party and I couldn't pray right then. But again God said, 'Jacque, pray for Evelyn.' So I gathered up the birthday wrappings, excused myself to take them out, and stood by the garbage cans, and prayed." Then she told me the exact time. Can you guess what time it was? Yes, it was exactly the time I had run out of gas on that freeway!

Is your communication system so open to God that you are available to pray any time of the day or night? When God sees a need down here on Planet Earth, can He say to you, "Wake up, wake up, I need you to pray for somebody"? Or are you like I was at one time, thinking you need eight hours of sleep or you'll collapse the next day? Are you one of those with whom God can trust His burdens?

# 9

## The Vertical
## Dimension of Prayer—
## to Whom We Pray

*"Draw nigh to God, and He will draw nigh to you." James 4:8*

AN OFTEN OVERLOOKED but very important part of prayer is the drawing nigh to God. Before we are ready to start our intercessory prayers, we need to *wait* before God until we know we have established communication with Him. This is a time of silence when we are shutting out every other thought and distraction around us. There is no talking *to* God, just a complete mental drawing to Him; and then, as He promised, *He will draw nigh to us.*

### DRAWING NIGH TAKES TIME

Drawing apart to God is important in groups as well as in private praying. It may be easier to do in our closets; but because of the hectic rush to arrive at a prayer meeting on time or because of the chatting after we've arrived, it is a must to pause for the seconds or minutes it takes to withdraw from all this and draw nigh to God. Often there seems to be embarrassment in a group if someone doesn't start praying audibly right away as we go to prayer—ready or not.

I remember way back in the "green chair" days struggling and struggling to draw nigh to God. I can recall how I would strain and wonder where He was. And it seemed as if my prayers were only reaching the ceiling. But through the years God has taught me many things—and I'm not in the struggling stage any more.

One thing I learned when I found it impossible to establish meaningful communication with God was that it wasn't His fault, it was mine. He is the same yesterday, today, and forever, but I am not. I let sins creep in that break my fellowship with Him, and frequently I must search my heart and confess those sins that are blocking communication between us.

I also learned the simple process of envisioning my God when approaching Him in prayer. The joy that floods my whole being as I find myself visualizing all God is—all His love, all His power, all His concern for me—defies description. What greater privilege could there be for a human being than to actually *draw nigh* to the omnipotent, omniscient God, high and lifted up on His throne in glory? This to me is the most precious part of my prayer time.

## BE SURE IT'S GOD

Why do you suppose Christ taught His disciples, and us in turn, to pray, "Our Father who art in heaven"? Have you ever thought of that? Our God, capital *G*, is the only God in heaven, but there are other gods. "Thou shalt have no other gods before Me" (Ex. 20:3). If there were no other gods, our God would not have given Moses this commandment.

"The god of this world [age]" is a title Paul gives Satan (see 2 Cor. 4:4). In the explosion of the occult that is sweeping our nation, we are finding that even Christians—real Christians—are getting answers that are not from God.

Christ spent one-fourth of His recorded ministry dealing with the enemy, and this is a warning to us to be constantly alert that we open our minds, not to Satan, but to God who is in heaven.

In a question and answer period following a lecture on the dangers of the occult at a church youth meeting, a man counselor raised his hand and asked, "Why is it that when I pray I get more answers from Satan than I do from God?"

I didn't want to belittle that man before the students for whom he was responsible, but I had no choice. I looked at him, and I said as kindly as I could, "Sir, if you are getting more answers from Satan than you are from God, there's something drastically wrong with your prayer life."

Is it possible for even sincere Christians to unwittingly open themselves to suggestions from the enemy?

I know of five different pastors who claimed a voice said to them, "Divorce your wife," and each one promptly did. They said they thought it was the Lord speaking to them. But it was not surprising to learn that in every instance another woman was involved.

While flying over Canada, one pastor said to another, "I now know there is a life after death and I am preaching it from my pulpit."

"How do you know?" asked the surprised pastor sitting beside him.

"Because my stillborn baby is communicating with me. I wasn't sure before, but I know now there is life after death!"

When I speak on the occult, I find to my horror that even Christian youth are experimenting with all sorts of occult practices. As I ask them what they do at slumber parties, their response is frightening. Many have crossed the thin line between parlor games and the occult. They are hearing voices during their séances, experiencing supernatural power, and getting answers in uncanny ways from Ouija boards.

After I had talked with one group of teenagers in a fine local church, a mother came to me and said, "I want to tell you that those kids had a Ouija board burning. My daughter is the ringleader of that junior high group in our church, and she came home from your meeting and said, 'Mother, playing with Ouija boards and all that stuff is an abomination to God. It says so in Deuteronomy 18.'" Yes, getting supernatural answers through any form of divination or mediums is not drawing nigh to God—and is forbidden by Him (see Deut. 18:9–14).

Halloween parties, too, seem to be changing in character these days. A friend of mine was having her hair done the week after Halloween. Her hairdresser said that every one of her customers who discussed attending any halloween party said it turned out to be an attempt to draw nigh to spiritual beings other than God. What ever happened to bobbing for apples?

## MEDITATION CAN BE DANGEROUS

Putting oneself into a state of passivity is a very dangerous spiritual exercise in which even true Christians are engaging. To open our minds and allow ourselves to be receptive to all the thoughts and suggestions which enter is a perilous business. We may think we are drawing nigh to God—but zing! There's Satan, and we are listening to *his* voice.

At a prayer seminar, a woman stepped up to me and said, "Do you know that I taught yoga and gave it up?"

I said, "Tell me, why did you give it up?"

"Well," she replied, "I suddenly realized that there I was in that room meditating with Buddhists, with Hindus, with people involved in every religion you can imagine. Sure, you sit there and you meditate and you get a feeling of peace and strength; but I've learned that I get all the peace and strength I need from the Lord Jesus Christ, and I don't need

98

yoga meditation. And God told me it's a sin for me to be meditating with those others who do not know the true God in heaven."

Oh how foolish to put ourselves in such a vulnerable position! It does make a difference with whom we attempt to draw nigh to God. "What communion hath light with darkness?" (2 Cor. 6:14)

Transcendental Meditation is a guise that Satan frequently uses today to infiltrate minds. It is being taught in many of our schools, libraries, YMCAs, YWCAs, and even in some churches.

While the president of a local women's club and I were driving home together some 70 miles from a meeting, our conversation shifted to communicating. "You know," she said, "I communicate in the middle of the night. Do you?"

"Oh, yes, I communicate in the middle of the night," I replied.

She went on, "I know 'It' is out there, because I communicate with 'It'."

I quickly changed the pronoun and said, "I know 'He' is out there. My God is out there."

She went on, "I don't know what it is I'm communicating with, but I know *something* is out there. Why don't you come to one of our meditation meetings? You can tell us how you communicate in the middle of the night, and we can tell you how we do." By that time I had an ill feeling in the pit of my stomach. I couldn't get out of that car fast enough!

Prayer is always directed from the pray-er up to God— who is in heaven. This is the vertical dimension of prayer. In the next chapter you will see how this dimension becomes a triangle when God reaches back down to earth with the answers to our prayers.

In Hebrews 11:6 we read that the faith that pleases God is two-faceted: (1) believing that He is and (2) that He is a rewarder of them that diligently seek Him. I wonder if

Christians before the occult explosion really knew the full meaning of this. Have we concentrated so much on the fact that He is a rewarder that we have lost sight of *who* our God is—holy, high, and lifted up? We must draw nigh to *this* God—and then He will draw nigh to us.

Moses drew nigh to God in reality when he "rose up early in the morning, and went up unto Mount Sinai" (Ex. 34:4, 29–35). Do you remember what happened when he came down? The children of Israel were afraid to come near him because the skin of his face shone! He had to put a veil over his face, it was so radiant. Wouldn't it be great if we could so draw nigh to God that we would become radiant? So draw nigh that others could tell by our very countenance that we had been with God? That we had learned the secret of His presence? That before bombarding Him with our requests, we had taken time to enter into His fellowship?

**For You to Do:**

Before starting to pray, in absolute silence practice drawing nigh to God.

This may involve confessing some sin which God brings to your mind. If so, confess it, so that there is nothing between you and God in heaven.

**Now draw nigh to Him.** Wait in silence until you feel God is there.

**Now pray,** thanking God for who He is—whatever you want to say in adoration and praise for who He is—this God to whom you have just drawn nigh.

**Now pray at least one request for some other** person's need.

# 10

## The Horizontal Dimension
## of Prayer—Results

*"But without faith it is impossible to please Him: for he that cometh to God must believe that He is, and that He is the rewarder of them that diligently seek Him." Hebrews 11:6*

WITH THE STUDY of the horizontal dimension of prayer, we now reach full circle. We have said that we cannot pray effectively when there is sin in our lives. We have described how to pray in God's will so that our prayers will be answered. We have spoken of the need to draw nigh to God, and to bask in the sunshine of His love because He never makes a mistake.

For what purpose have we taught about these prerequisites to prayer? Primarily, that we might become powerful, intercessory pray-ers. We are now back to the theme verse of chapter one, "The effectual fervent prayer of a righteous man *availeth much"* (James 5:16).

*The horizontal dimension of prayer is the visible result of our effective praying here on Planet Earth.* But there can never be a horizontal dimension of prayer unless there is first the vertical dimension—that drawing nigh to God. The two are inseparable, standing as it were at the opposite points of the base of a triangle, with God at the top. The pray-er petitions God the Father, who receives the prayer, sifts it out according to His will, then reaches down to change people and circumstances on earth. *The results we humans see represent the horizontal dimension of prayer.*

## UNITY

In chapter one I gave many illustrations to show what happens when women pray. Each was a visible result, on the horizontal level, of prayer that had ascended to God the Father, who in turn acted upon an individual or a set of circumstances here on earth. I also mentioned the tremendous unity that was experienced as members of the body of Christ prayed together. It is still happening.

Following the day of humiliation, fasting, and prayer for our country on April 30, 1974, I received telephone calls from several prayer seminar members. One woman said, "It was just beautiful in our group."

Another exclaimed, "Guess what? We finally got off the ground for the first time, really off the ground, and we're going to meet next month again, just as we did on April 30."

Another said, "We had the most beautiful experience. I helped our pastor organize the prayer meetings in our church. We used the six S's and prayed in groups of four. It was a fantastic experience."

What else happened to many of us that day? We sensed deeply the humiliation for which we had prayed. With the continuing exposure of the Watergate affair, we knew that God was bringing us as individuals and our nation as a whole to the place of humiliation. And we felt a tremendous unity not as we studied together, or talked, or met as committee members, but as we prayed together. One definite horizontal result of prayer, then, is unity—in the church, in the home, and in the community.

## PRAYER TRANSCENDS MILES

Do you have loved ones who live a great distance from you? Perhaps a son or a daughter who is away at school? Between my mother and me lies the entire state of Wisconsin, and beyond that the vastness of Lake Michigan. Yet in prayer we both sense a oneness that transcends the miles that separate us. God is not limited to space, as we are. He is able to reach down and give the unifying sense of His presence not only to people sitting beside us in the room but to individuals who are separated by continents. We proved this by an experiment in 1965.

After I had been praying with my two prayer partners Lorna and Sig every Thursday afternoon for almost a year, my husband and I went overseas to visit the mission fields. Before leaving we noted when we were scheduled to land in Addis Ababa, Ethiopia (where Sig's daughter Shirlee and her son-in-law Cliff were stationed). Our arrival would be just prior to the corresponding time that Lorna and Sig would be meeting for prayer in Rockford, though there would be an eight-hour difference on the clock. We calculated that if all the planes were on schedule and if everything went according to plan, we would be in Addis Ababa to pray with Sig's daughter and her husband at exactly the same time Sig was praying with Lorna in Rockford.

Having slept only two out of four nights en route, we arrived in Addis Ababa exhausted, but on schedule. All the guests went to bed except me. After the house was quiet, Cliff, Shirl, and I went to prayer in the living room. We had prayed for a short while when suddenly each of us had an overwhelming sense that no miles separated us and the two prayer partners back in Rockford. It was just as if they were right there praying with us. God had transcended all the miles across half the continent of the United States, the entire Atlantic ocean, and most of the continent of Africa, and given to us a sense of oneness in His Spirit through prayer.

After we returned home, I was anxious to learn what had happened in Rockford that Thursday afternoon. Had they felt that oneness that transcends the miles? Sig said to me then, and she has repeated it over and over since, "Ev, I have never in all my years as a Christian been so aware of God and His power, so aware of His reality, as I was when I sensed that tremendous unity we had in Him, even though we were separated by thousands of miles." This, too, is the horizontal dimension of prayer, linking the pray-ers through our omnipresent God.

## WE HAD NEVER MET

Closely related to the transcendence of miles is the bond created by prayer even among people who have never met. In 1968 one of the ladies in our prayer chain went to another state to purchase a poodle from a woman we knew only as Joy. Joy had had major surgery involving the insertion of a plastic esophagus, and was having an extremely difficult pregnancy. It was no wonder that our prayer-chain member came back and said, "Let's pray for Joy." We started, and week after week, month after month, we prayed for her.

One day, after Joy delivered her baby, she told her husband that it was only because those women down there in Rockford were praying that she had the strength and the courage to get through her pregnancy. And that was not all—this dear woman accepted Christ as her personal Saviour, and became the best missionary we ever had! Everyone who came to buy a poodle heard that she had found Christ, and was told about the women many miles away who had prayed and prayed for her physical and spiritual needs. I haven't met Joy to this day. It isn't likely that I will, for I don't think I'll ever buy a poodle. But God answered anyway!

On our prayer-chain lists are many whom we have never met, but God knows who they are and where they are. He knows their needs. All we do is pray our requests—we don't pray answers—and God with the mighty arm of His power reaches down to anyone anywhere on Planet Earth with His answer.

## GOD IS THE REWARDER

Much happens when we pray. And answers come as we pray in faith believing. As I mentioned in the previous chapter, "But without faith it is impossible to please Him: for he that cometh to God must believe that He is, and that He is a rewarder of them that diligently seek Him" (Heb. 11:6). We come first of all believing that He is, and then believing unequivocally that "He is a *rewarder* of them who diligently seek Him."

As we pray believingly, we see a fourth result in the horizontal dimension of prayer—*it is great in its working.* We are not dropping our prayers into a bottomless barrel. How do we know? One way is by the specific answers to specific requests.

We began to experience great answers to prayer early in our prayer ministry. At the very first seminar in White Bear Lake, a woman handed me a request for our intercessory prayer time. It was for her sister to receive Christ. She said, "We've tried everything we know. We've talked to her; we've taken her to meetings where she's spurned invitation after invitation to receive Him. Please pray." Though they did not even know her name, 250 women zeroed in on that unsaved sister.

The next week the woman who had requested prayer stopped me before the seminar. "Do you know what? I took my sister to a Christian Women's luncheon right after the seminar last week, and she accepted Christ within two hours of your praying!" Those 250 pray-ers gave great praise during prayer time that day.

One morning we missed one of our prayer seminar steering committee members. Someone said, "She's taking her mother, who has TB, to the hospital."

Another woman suggested immediately, "Let's stop right now and pray."

To that another steering committee member added, "But that isn't her mother's greatest need. Neither her mother nor her father knows Christ as Saviour."

Instead of doing much planning that morning, we spent most of the time praying for the mother and father of our committee member. A couple of weeks after the seminar was over, still another member of the steering committee stopped me on the street and asked, "Ev, did you hear the good news? Do you know that within two weeks after the steering committee prayed, both the mother and father found Christ?" In just two weeks! "The effectual fervent prayer of a righteous man availeth much" (James 5:16).

At a recent seminar session we prayed very definitely that a certain woman would find Christ. That very night she received Him as her Saviour. In the same week we had another answer. A mother was called out of one of our seminars because her little boy had injured his leg at school and couldn't step on his foot. We promised to pray during the intercessory prayer time. When he was told that all those women had prayed for him, he said, "Then I must be OK." He threw away the ice pack, and went riding off on his bicycle!

God gave us a beautiful answer to prayer last year. We had learned that a young woman of 23 with two children had a cancerous growth on her brain. It was the type that had spread like the tentacles of an octopus, and her doctors gave her only a few weeks to live. All of us in the seminar went to prayer for this young mother, not just praying that she would be healed, but that God's will would be done in her life. In this instance God chose to heal this young woman. A few weeks later, we learned that the tumor was shrinking rapidly and that there was not a sign of a cancerous cell in her whole body. The doctors had given her a normal life expectancy!

What happens when we pray? Things do happen. We do not drop our intercessory prayers into a bottomless barrel. We send them up to a heavenly Father, who in His time, in His way, according to His will, answers them down here on Planet Earth.

## REQUESTS CHANGE

We see something else taking place in the horizontal dimension of prayer—we begin to see changes in our prayer requests. In 1968, when our prayer experimentation started, several in our denomination were trained in Washington, D.C. for the Crusade of the Americas. We returned to our homes all excited over the prospects of prayer and evangelism. I said to my husband, "We're going to pray for a year and then we're going to evangelize for a year."

He grinned and announced, "It'll never work."

Jolted, I asked, "Why not?"

He replied, "You show me somebody who's praying and I'll show you somebody who's evangelizing. A praying church is an evangelizing church."

He was right! Our objective had been to pray in 1968, and to evangelize in 1969. But when the time came for my report to our national committee in June, 1969, I had to say, "The transition has already taken place."

We found that people who prayed automatically evangelized; they naturally shared their Christ with somebody else. With prayer chains praying for each of them, we developed 35 evangelism Bible studies in our church, in homes, offices, and in a high school, among women, couples, and young people. A Bible study group entirely composed of hippies was studying regularly as a result of Art Blessit's meeting that year. New converts had already become hosts, hostesses, and teachers for their evangelism Bible studies. We had participated in the distribution of Gospels to every home in our city.

In my 1969 report, I said, "We are seeing our total church program becoming increasingly evangelistic, not superimposed by programs, but from within the hearts of the workers. . . . Our local church has been the greatest recipient of the blessings because we, as the pilot church, have put into practice the [prayer] ideas of the committee before they were passed on as being workable."

Are you concerned about outreach in your own life? In your church? When you have a praying life and a praying church, I guarantee you will have a life and a church with a vital outreach, because as we learn to pray, our prayer requests change.

It's interesting to go back and look at the careful notes I made in those months in 1968 when we first started to pray. I notice particularly that one had to have a broken leg or something equally serious to be included on our prayer lists! If we could see the need with our physical eyes—if it needed a bandage or a cast—we gave the request to our prayer chain. Otherwise it didn't get very much attention.

Gradually, though, things changed. As our spiritual eyes began to open, we saw spiritual needs and added these to our lists. God in heaven is concerned about physical needs. He expects us not only to pray about them but to put feet to our prayers, to bring in that casserole, or to help in any other way we can. But we aren't to stop there. We need to ask God to open our spiritual eyes that we might see the spiritual needs around us, especially in the lives of people who need to be transformed by Christ. This is the greatest need of every person on Planet Earth. But how can we share these prayer requests with others?

## PRAYER PARTNERS

After a banquet at which I had shared the horizontal blessings of a prayer ministry, a woman came to me with tears in her eyes. She said, "I'm overwhelmed; there's so much to remember. Where do I start?"

I told her that beyond her own personal praying, the place to start intercessory prayer is with *one prayer partner.* This is the best way I know. Find someone with whom you can share big things and little things. When you hurt or have a headache, when some little thing goes wrong or when the whole world collapses around you, have one person you can trust absolutely, and upon whom you can call at any time. Find someone who will not betray your confidence, someone who is always ready to say whenever you give her a call, "I'll pray right now." Then, as you pray together, start praying for what God wants you to do for your church, family, and those in need. And then be open to those God would have pray with you.

## CHURCH LISTS

As your intercessory prayer develops on the horizontal level through private praying and prayer partners and prayer groups, we can proceed to church lists. One church in which we held a seminar encourages members of the congregation to fill out a form early in the Sunday morning service. It reads, "During our prayer time this morning, I would like my brothers and sisters in Christ to pray for . . . ." Following several blank spaces there is room for the signature of the person making the requests. These sheets are collected, and the pastor remembers the specific requests in his morning prayer.

The members of another congregation place their prayer requests on registration cards during the morning service. Later in the day these requests, along with items for praise, are listed on sheets which are distributed in the evening service. These are beautiful examples of members of the body of Christ praying for one another and bearing one another's burdens as members of Christ's family.

## PRAYER CALENDARS

Prayer calendars represent another method of systematic prayer on the horizontal level. Usually two categories are covered—people and events. An individual may have a particular need on a certain day, or there may be a public meeting or an evangelistic effort which demands definite prayer. These requests may be on a local or a national level.

In 1968, in a circle of less than 30 women, we placed our names on a prayer calendar. Each woman prayed for a different woman each day so every person in that circle was prayed for daily. It was exciting. We heard women say, "I could feel you praying; my life was different when I knew that I was being supported and undergirded specifically by somebody in my circle."

There can be any number of variations in prayer calendars. Include missionaries, your pastor and church staff, youth ministries, and special projects. It is a great spiritual exercise.

Yes, when we started experimenting with all these methods of intercessory prayer in 1968, I wondered if anything would happen, if there would be any horizontal results. I'm not wondering any more. I know that the effectual, fervent prayer of a righteous person does avail much, and I know it from experience.

**For You to Pray:**
1. Ask God to give you the next step He has for you in prayer—a prayer partner (ask for a specific name), a

group He wants you to join or start, or a new method of prayer for your church, group, family, or club.

2. Wait in silence for Him to speak.
3. Promise Him you will start **immediately** whatever He is telling you to do.

# 11

## *Forgiven as We Forgive*

---

*"And forgive us our sins, just as we have forgiven those who have sinned against us." Matthew 6:12, LB*

A HORIZONTAL DIMENSION of prayer that Christ taught is frequently overlooked by those seeking a deeper prayer life. And it relates to the thing that is *most apt to break up your prayer group*—your relationship with the other people who are in that group!

In the Lord's Prayer we read, "And forgive us our sins *as* we forgive those who sin against us" (Matt. 6:12). Your Bible translation may say debts or transgressions, but both have the same literal meaning: sins. Now, this is the Lord Jesus Himself teaching the disciples, and us in turn, how to pray. If you want to keep your prayer group intact, practice this principle.

That word *as* is a conditional word meaning "to the extent that"—to the extent that I forgive others, I'm asking God to forgive me.

Christ explained it like this in the two verses which follow the Lord's Prayer: "For if ye forgive men their trespasses, your heavenly Father will also forgive you; but if ye forgive not men their trespasses, neither will your Father forgive your trespasses" (Matt. 6:14–15).

Do you remember our first prerequisite to answered prayer in chapter two, "If I regard iniquity in my heart, the Lord will not hear me"? ( Ps. 66:18) Christ says that if we don't forgive others, our heavenly Father will not forgive us. If He does not, our sins will keep Him from hearing our intercessory prayers. They will be of no avail.

So, unless we keep our relationships with other people clear, we cannot be effective intercessory pray-ers. Now, let's remember one more thing from chapter two: God always hears the penitent sinner's prayer as he confesses his sins and seeks Christ as his Saviour. God also hears the plea for forgiveness of sins by the one who is already a Christian. But for us to refuse to forgive others is itself a sin. We can't be right with God and effective intercessors if we harbor the sin of an unforgiving spirit—even though we may have confessed all *other* known sins. This is a very difficult lesson for some to learn, but it is very important.

At another time while teaching His disciples to pray in faith, Jesus admonished them in rather strong words, "Listen to Me! You can pray for anything, and if you believe, you have it; it's yours! But—when you are praying, first forgive anyone you are holding a grudge against, so that your Father in heaven will forgive you your sins too" (Mark 11:24–25, LB).

## DEALING WITH THOSE WHO CAUSE GRIEF

I want to share with you the way this truth was brought into focus for me in the summer of 1972. I was all set to speak at a prayer breakfast for vacationers and women from several churches in Michigan. It was possible that some people present would not know Christ, so I first made a telephone call to the spiritual life chairman of a local prayer chain and gave her my request. She jotted it down, dated it, and indicated that she would be happy to take care of the whole thing. Still feeling the need for special prayer, I called another local chain and then dialed long distance back to my former prayer chain in Rockford for their support.

When I got back home, I called the prayer chains to send through praise for God's blessing at the prayer breakfast. The spiritual life chairman to whom I spoke during my first call was very quiet for a minute. Then she said, "Um, we didn't pray."

I exclaimed, "You didn't pray!"

"No," she replied, "one of the members said, 'We don't pray for speakers on this prayer chain.'"

I was stunned, and I gathered that this woman was seeing prayer needs only with her physical eyes, not with her spiritual eyes, for this was a spiritual need. This person who had enough authority to prevent a prayer from going through an entire prayer chain stopped it dead—and no one received the request.

How did I react? Just like a human being. I admit it was wrong, but I was very grieved for several days. And my spiritual life? I can only explain it by saying it became just like straw. If you want your prayer group to fall apart, to become like straw, just become grieved with another person in the same way I did.

Soon after this incident, Chris and I took a vacation 9,000 feet up in the Rockies. It should have been a beautiful time of fellowship with God, but I couldn't get through to Him in prayer. My Bible reading was meaningless; my whole spiritual life still felt just like straw. I was grating away on the inside and feeling perfectly miserable.

Finally, by Thursday of that week, I had had it. At 5 A.M. I grabbed my Bible, went out under those gorgeous pine trees, knelt by an old pine log, and cried out to God, "Show me what's wrong with my life. I can't get through to You."

I leafed through the pages of my Bible, but found nothing that suited my need. Then in desperation I turned another page, and my eyes fell on the words right at the bottom of a page, "If any have caused grief." *Why, Lord, that's what's wrong with me,* I thought. *I've been grieved.* Then God spoke to me: "Why don't you read on." I read on—and, wow, what I discovered was a *formula* to remedy my ailment.

I remember the exact page in my King James Version, it was 1253, where God met me. This prescription was for me as an individual, and it's also for you as an individual, and for your prayer group as well. It will keep your prayer group and your prayer chain intact. The Scripture passage is 2 Corinthians 2:5–11

"*But if any have caused grief . . .*" (v. 5). Yes, this woman had caused me grief all right! Though I was innocent, I was still grieved—and miserable.

"*Sufficient to such a person is this punishment, which was inflicted by the many*" (v. 6). I suddenly realized that she was being shunned not only by me, but by others who had learned of her refusal to let my prayer request be put on the prayer chain. The news had gotten around.

"*So that contrariwise ye ought rather to forgive . . .*" (v. 7). I saw that I had to forgive. You see, God wasn't hearing my prayers. I had asked Him for forgiveness, but I hadn't forgiven the person who had grieved me. So I prayed, "Father, give me the strength to forgive this person." He did, and I forgave her at that point.

"*And comfort . . .*" (v. 7). I was shocked, I knew that word comfort meant encouragement plus alleviation of grief. "But, Lord," I said, "*I'm* the one who's been grieved. I'm supposed to alleviate *her* grief? Lord, you have something turned around."

"No," He said, "you are supposed to comfort, encourage, and alleviate the grief 'lest perhaps such a one should be swallowed up with overmuch sorrow'" (v. 7).

"Lord, do you mean that the person who has grieved me

might have a reason for acting that way? Maybe feels threatened? Maybe is struggling?"

I could hear Him say, "Right."

If someone is grieving us, how many of us take the wrong attitude? Though we may not say it in so many words, by our manner we are saying, "I know you're drowning, but I'll just take my foot and push you under to be sure you go down and drown right." Aren't we guilty of this? But God's word says we are to get underneath, alleviate, and lift! Then, after we do that, we are to:

"*Confirm your love toward him*" (v. 8). I began to see that I had no love. Oh, I might have had a little supply of the ordinary love that one has for the members of her church—you know the kind I mean. But it wasn't any special love—there was none of that. In fact, it might have been something just the opposite right then. I'm not sure what I felt, but I know it wasn't deep Christian love.

Then I had to pray, "Lord, give me the love You want me to have for this person." And kneeling by that old pine log, I suddenly had a tremendous sense of God's love being poured upon me. There it was—and I loved her.

But there was a new problem: how to "confirm it." I couldn't get myself to write a letter, but when I reached home I was still convinced that I had to confirm my love to her.

The woman who had grieved me attended the same church I did. (Chris is now Assistant Vice President of Bethel College and is not in the pastorate, so we were attending as members, not as pastor and wife.) On the first Sunday morning we were back in church, I spied her sitting on the opposite side of the sanctuary from me. I didn't hear one word the pastor said as I kept praying, "Lord, if You want me to confirm this love, You have to put her right where I'm going to run into her. I'm not going to make a fool of myself and run over to her."

You know how that kind of prayer goes. Maybe I didn't get quite that hard-nosed, but that's what I was saying to

God: "I'm not going to make a fool of myself. You're going to have to put her in my path." And so help me! At the close of the service I opened the big double doors at the back of the sanctuary and almost knocked her down! There she was!

And what did I have to do? I put my arms around her and said only one thing, "I just want you to know I love you." And the tears started to roll.

She said, "And I just want you to know that my husband and I are praying for your Bible study."

She "knew" and I "knew." We got together and really worked it out a few days later.

*"That I might know the proof of you . . ."* (v. 9). Why did I have to go to her? "That I might know the proof of you"—you the member of the prayer group who has been grieved, the innocent member of the prayer group, who is responsible to forgive and to go and confirm his or her love so that God will know how big a person you are—not the one who did the grieving, but the innocent one who was grieved.

*"Lest Satan should get an advantage of us"* (v. 11). This is the most frightening thing of all. There is nothing the enemy would rather do than to see our prayer groups broken up by our failure to forgive and confirm love. Let's never be guilty of allowing him to "get his foot in the door," for we are not ignorant of his devices.


## THIS IS FOR EVERYBODY

I had taught a Sunday School class on this subject of forgiveness, and following the morning service that day, a leading layman who had been in the class said to me, "I just want you to know that two men in our church got together after Sunday School and resolved something that had been between them for many years, and should have been handled long ago."

A man who attended one of our seminars had loaned a relative $70, even though he could hardly spare the money. He shared his feelings with me after our session on forgiving others. "Evelyn," he said, "I just told God that I now forgive the one who borrowed that money a couple of years ago and has not even mentioned it to me since. I was becoming more and more bitter in my heart, and I now know that I have to go and confirm my love to that relative. So, after I get home tonight, I'm going to dig out that little promissory note for the $70 and write on it 'Paid in full,' and put it right in the mail."

**For You to Do:**

Ask God to bring to your mind that person who has grieved you and whom you have not forgiven.

Pray and ask God to forgive you for the sin of not forgiving that person.

Now forgive that person, asking God to give you the strength and ability if you need to.

Now ask God for as much love as He wants you to have for that person who grieved you.

Next ask God how you should confirm your love to that person.

Wait in silence for His answer.

Pray, promising God that you will do whatever He has told you.

Go do it!

# 12

## *Telephone Prayer Chains*

---

*"Be careful for nothing; but in everything by prayer and supplication with thanksgiving let your requests be made known unto God." Philippians 4:6*

WHAT I MISSED most when I moved from Rockford, Ill. in the fall of 1970 was the 115 women who prayed for me on the telephone prayer chains. Every time I spoke, every time I was sick, every time there was a need in my family, these women prayed. I, of course, was not the only one for whom they interceded. There were hundreds of others whose physical and spiritual needs were brought before God.

For a long time after we moved to Minnesota, I kept a hot line going to Rockford with requests for the prayer chains. There were pray-ers in my new home area, but I hadn't found them yet. I no longer need to dial Rockford as often for there are many active prayer chains in our area now!

You don't have to be told that I believe strongly in prayer chains. They are very close to my heart since I depend almost entirely on the answers God gives when they go to prayer, and I act accordingly. When everyone is praying

119

simultaneously for the same requests, there is really tremendous power in prayer. I know that great changes have taken place in my life because the prayer chains have prayed for me.

## POWER OVER THE ENEMY

When I first started to speak against the occult, for example, I began to experience some horrible inner feelings. At times after speaking I was so filled with resentment and anger that I actually wanted to kick my car! Members of my family remarked that I was a different person when I spoke on that subject. Why was this so? Because I was intruding in Satan's realm. Then I took the advice of one of the leading Christian authorities on the subject of the occult, and formed a 10-member prayer chain from among the strongest pray-ers I knew.

The very next time I went out to speak on this subject, all those negative feelings had disappeared. Since that prayer chain was activated, I have had nothing but a victorious experience each time I have spoken against the occult.

## PERSONAL NEEDS

Before leaving for meetings in another state, I asked several prayer chains to be praying at the exact hour when I would be appearing on a TV talk show. After I completed one speaking engagement at a Christian Women's Club luncheon, I was whisked crosstown to the TV studio to take part in the second half-hour of the program. Arriving during the commercial between the two segments of the hour, I was not aware that a well-known false evangelist from Korea had just preceded me on the program. Had I known this, I would have been completely unnerved. Instead I chatted enthusiastically on the subject of prayer—how, when, and where God answers. Friends who watched both half-hours of that talk show told me the astounding difference there was between them. God had guarded me—because of all those simultaneous prayers.

I have a file folder bulging with recorded prayer requests and answers that were handled through our Rockford prayer chains. As I reviewed these in preparation for the writing of this book, I was overwhelmed at the number of times my name appears—on an average of four times a week! There are requests for my speaking engagements, for physical strength, and for help at times when I was ministering for Christ. Here's one example: "April 14: Pray for strength for Evelyn. She has the flu, and is scheduled to speak at Janesville tonight. The ladies want to learn about prayer chains and how to pray effectively."

"April 15: Evelyn made the meeting. She had great praise. Many ladies were touched and eager to be changed." It was always understood that they were to pray that God would make me well enough to go if it was His will that I be there.

You may feel that you could not have such a prominent place in the prayer concerns of a large group. Perhaps that is true. I have a wonderful privilege to be prayed for so much. Nevertheless, you can reap great benefits by finding just one or two prayer partners and praying regularly for and with one another. But remember, my prayer chains started with just eight members. Why don't you start one?

## A TEACHING INSTRUMENT FOR THE FAMILY

One exceptional thing about prayer chains is what they do for your home. If you want to really teach prayer to your children, I know of no better way than prayer-chain procedures.

As the children hear Mother calling through the prayer requests, and then watch as she bows her head immediately after putting down the receiver, they know that Mother believes in prayer. When the answer comes through they can hear her say, "Oh, that's great!" They watch her as she dials the next person on the prayer chain, and they listen as she says, "Praise God. He answered our prayer." They take note of her joy as she bows her head and thanks God for answering.

As prayer-chain calls come into the home, the children and other members of the family can observe the progress of prayer, taking note of specific requests, specific answers, God's timing, and the flow of praise.

For our family this has been one of the greatest teaching instruments through all the years of bringing up our children. They believe so much in prayer chains that both our daughters, when they were out of town, have spent their own money to call long distance with requests. Now our son, Kurt, the only child still living at home, every once in awhile comes out with, "I think it's time to call the prayer chain!"

Once while Kurt and I were painting the ceiling of our sun porch, the telephone rang, but I wasn't in any particular hurry to answer—you know how it is—being up a ladder and with the paint dripping down my arms! Our daughter Nancy picked up the kitchen phone, and in a few seconds she called in, "Never mind, Mother, it's *just* another answer to prayer."

Nancy herself was a subject for prayer on her wedding day. The note from my file reads: "June 8—6:30 P.M. Chris called the prayer chain with a specific request: 'Pray for Nancy who is vomiting and has diarrhea. Pray for God's divine healing as she will be married at 7:30 tonight.'"

The entry on June 9 reads: "Praise the Lord. Nancy was a bit queasy in the tummy, but came through in fine shape for the wedding!"

In Rockford we had an amusing illustration of the way children are impressed by the prayer chains. Our children's worker, Gail, was teaching prayer to a group of fifth- and sixth-graders. While meeting one Saturday, Gail said to the

122

youngsters, "Would you please pray for the pastor's wife? She's speaking in Chicago today."

Just then a little boy raised his hand and said, "Never mind. You know that thing, that prayer chain thing? They've already prayed. It's all done."

Prayer chains provide a wonderful method of teaching complete confidence in answered prayer, and in the God who answers prayer. Let your children hear these specific answers that are reported over your telephone. It will do something for your entire family.

Not only mothers, but whole families are involved in the ministry of prayer chains. I remember one Sunday in Rockford a well-known Gospel singer and his family were visiting his parents. He is paralyzed from the waist down, and on that particular day his urinary tract had stopped functioning. By 6 P.M. the family was quite alarmed and had called the hospital emergency room.

As they were ready to leave for the hospital, his mom said, "Let's try the prayer chain first." At 6:20, when everybody was scurrying around getting ready for the evening church service, the prayer chains were activated. The request could not have come at a better time; everybody was home. Members of whole families stopped what they were doing and prayed for him. Later his mother said, "A very amazing thing happened. While the prayer chains were praying, suddenly, it was just as though an electric shock whizzed right through our house, and through my son's body. We didn't have to take him to the hospital because his whole system started to function normally once again."

## CHURCH FAMILIES, TOO

Another beautiful illustration of family involvement was the result of a request dated Sunday, March 23: "Please pray for Becky. She has started labor pains. The baby is not due for seven or eight weeks." (Becky is the one mentioned in an earlier chapter whose only child was lost through a crib death.) That morning, before Sunday School, 120 homes received this specific request through the prayer chains. Mothers, fathers, and children all stopped to pray.

Later, the burden was shared in every department of the Sunday School; the whole church family joined in prayer for Becky. The notation made on Monday, March 24, reads: "Pray for Becky, and especially for her 3 lb., 8 oz. daughter." On Tuesday, March 25, the request was urgent: "Becky's baby has developed lung complications. Pray that God's strength will sustain Becky and Eddie, that the God who never makes a mistake will do what is best." God worked in a wonderful way.

Becky and I belonged to the same circle in our church. Every month she brought that healthy, happy little "answer to prayer" to our meetings and set her on a blanket in the middle of the floor—what a precious reminder of God's ability to answer prayer!

## FELT IN HOSPITALS

Many prayer-chain requests are for those who are confined in hospitals. I have one note in my folder which reads: "Alice went to see Inez, who remarked, 'Your friends must be really praying. God was so near to me, and I'm not afraid anymore.' Her tests show a malignancy, and the nurses and her roommates can't understand the change in her attitude. She tells them God did it, and she's not afraid anymore."

There was also praise from Florence: "I'm so thankful God took me through this last experience. I was never more conscious that He was near. Each day I felt upheld by your prayers." As we received thank-you notes and telephone calls from patients for whom we prayed, most of them said, "I could feel you praying."

## IN BIBLE STUDY GROUPS

Some of the most exciting answers to our prayer-chain praying have come out of Bible study groups. There was Lynn, for example. She had threatened to break up our meeting the first time she attended one of my Bible studies. She stood on her head, showing us how *she* had learned to meditate in her search for answers to life. Our prayer chains were already praying for her, and Lynn found Christ when she attended the Bible study the second time. After receiving Him she said to me, "I want to be on the prayer chain that prayed for me." Immediately she requested prayer for her friend, Sandy, to find Christ. Then came the day when she called, full of excitement, "Sandy just accepted Christ!" After a long pause, she said, "Now I'll have to find somebody else to put on the prayer chain."

Do you believe that thoroughly in prayer, in answers to prayer? Lynn does.

Among my notes, I have a request dated March 19, pertaining to Friendship Bible Coffees: "Lee would like us to pray for the seven Bible studies this morning and others this afternoon. Pray especially that the Holy Spirit will convict of the need for salvation." The answer: "Four found Christ that day!" One of the requests our prayer chains honored everyday was to pray specifically for those attending the Bible studies.

## SEMINARS

Recently I received a call from the chairman of one of our previous prayer seminars. It illustrates the way prayer chains grow out of these sessions. She said, "This is the week you're going to teach prayer chains in your present five-week seminar, isn't it?" I told her it was. Then she went on, "Well, I'm leaving for California, but I want you to know what we have done in our area. We have just started six prayer chains, and we have almost enough people to form a seventh. We have three morning chains, an evening chain, and an emergency chain that operates around the clock. Both men and women take part in this one. And we average three to nine requests per day on those prayer chains."

I then asked, "What's happening?"

She answered, "We're taking requests for physical and spiritual problems, from those who are having difficulties in their homes, and we're seeing things cleared up with beautiful answers to prayer. This is the most exciting thing that has come out of our prayer seminar. We're finding a unity among people from all the different churches that are represented on our prayer chains, and we feel this is a real service to the Lord."

The woman who was chairman of our retreat at Forest Home in California wrote, "Prayer chains are springing up all around now—men's, women's, and even children's prayer chains!" Prayer chains are not just for women. It's exciting to see everyone in a church involved—the pastor, members of the various boards, the Sunday School— everybody. A host pastor at one of our prayer seminars started an all-men's prayer chain with a challenge to the men in one of his church groups. "You know," he said, "there are certain things I cannot give to women to pray about. I need some men volunteers." He got them—one hundred percent!

A national youth speaker called me long distance and said, "I just listened to your prayer tapes while I was driving from Michigan to Pennsylvania. Now I feel that I wouldn't dare go through these 14 speaking engagements where I'll be bringing messages against the occult without prayer." We prayed, and when I next heard from him, he wrote, "I could feel you praying and I never before had such freedom, such attentiveness, and discipline in the schools where I spoke."

## THE CHAIRMAN

In Rockford we had 10 prayer chains with 10 or so persons on each chain. Because we wanted to have as many people as possible praying simultaneously, our chairman, after receiving the calls and recording the requests verbatim, called person number one on all 10 of the prayer chains, and in 15 minutes 115 people were praying.

Incoming prayer requests may come from any source, but it's important that only the bare essentials be communicated in the request. A discerning chairman will sense when something is too personal, and will ask, "Have you checked with the person for whom you're requesting prayer?" As I look over the recorded requests in my folder I am amazed at the spiritual insight of our chairman and the careful wording she used in the prayer requests. For years she had helped me with housework in the parsonage, and we had spent many hours there in prayer together. But there came the day when after much surgery, she could no longer do housework and felt that God was calling her to be our prayer-chain chairman.

When she accepted the position, she stood up in our women's meeting and said, "I thank God for all the pain and the surgery, for He has shown me that there's something much greater that I can do for Evelyn than ironing and baking cookies."

## NO GOSSIPING

A testimony by one of our prayer recipients attests to the strong commitment of our prayer-chain members. It happened that the woman who was my Bible study hostess for three years had a daughter who had left home and strayed far from Christ. Through her broken marriage, a divorce, and her remarriage, our prayer chains kept praying for this dear girl, and then for her new mate.

One day, while they were traveling in the East, this couple stepped out of their car, knelt in a parking lot, and without any human intervention, both accepted Christ as their personal Saviour. When they came back to our church in Rockford, the husband gave a testimony during a Sunday morning service. He said, "My wife and I owe our eternal salvation to the prayer chains of this church."

After they had gone away to study at a Christian college, the wife, as she related her experience to a group of faculty wives, said, "The thing that really astounded me after I came back home was that not one person of the 115 on those telephone prayer chains gossiped. They all knew I had been married and divorced, and that this was my second husband, but no one else knew about it."

That is the way it should be.

It's possible that some may find it difficult to keep juicy information confidential. If such is the case, they could call the chairman and say, "I would like my name removed from the prayer chains." This hasn't happened yet in our experience, but someday it might!

We have found that it is a great source of strength for prayer-chain members to sign the list of rules governing chain procedures at one time, while they are all together. In this way it is not a commitment to a person, or to a prayer-chain chairman, but it is a commitment to God.

Our basic rules are few and simple. Members promise to pray *immediately* when receiving requests by telephone. They also promise to pass on the request immediately to the next person in the prayer chain. They are not to delete anything or add anything to the request. And they are to keep it confidential—no gossiping.

## THE STRONGEST LINK

Ordinary chains are as weak as their weakest link, but a prayer chain is as strong as its strongest link. Why is this so? Because every single link in a prayer chain, every member, is united from here on earth to God the Father in heaven. All, the weak and the strong, are praying simultaneously to God the Father, and we see the dramatic, exciting results here on Planet Earth.

In January 1968, we started with eight gripers, and in just a few months we had 66 pray-ers. From March to December, these 66 pray-ers prayed for 508 requests which multiplied to 33,528 prayers to God the Father, who sent back as many answers. Multiply your prayers on a chain and watch exciting things happen!

## A CHAIN REACTION

Prayer chains have a peculiar and wonderful way of linking people together. We found this out when our Jan made a long distance telephone call from college to our prayer chairman in Rockford—325 miles away. The chain reaction started with her request on Tuesday, May 12, 1970: "Pray for God to be with and help a professor [Jan's chemistry teacher] at Bethel, whose wife has a serious back problem. She was to have had immediate surgery, but they just found out that she is pregnant. She has to be in bed much of the time and cannot take many pain pills as it might hurt the baby." Periodically after that we prayed for Sharon.

Two years later, after moving from Rockford, I was having my first Bible study class in St. Paul, when a young mother with a toddler in tow introduced herself to me in the church parking lot: "I'm Sharon," she said.

"Are you *the* Sharon for whom our prayer chains prayed when our Jan was so concerned about her chemistry professor's wife?" I asked.

As she grinned and nodded, her girlfriend spoke up, "Oh, Sharon, *that's why* you had such an easy delivery!"

Not long after that I was almost 2,000 miles away teaching the Six S's and telephone prayer chains at a women's retreat at Forest Home in California. I read some illustrations of prayer-chain requests directly from the bulging file folder—my most powerful teaching tool! As I read the request Jan had phoned in from Bethel in 1970, a woman sitting in the back of the auditorium waved her hand to get my attention. She said, "I have an urgent request from Sharon's mother-in-law. She just found out today that Sharon's husband's brother has an extremely serious brain tumor." God gave to that roomful of women a tremendous sense of urgency as we broke into groups of four to practice and experience the reality of "praying in one accord."

Returning to St. Paul, I immediately placed this pressing request with the faculty wives' prayer chain which we had recently started. Through the long, difficult illness and death of his brother, we continued to pray for this professor's need. And now, who do you think has been the telephone prayer chairman of this faculty wives' prayer chain for the past two years? Yes, Sharon.

Sharon was also one of those chosen to be on my first personal prayer chain in the Twin Cities. The chain is still active, and this last year the other members and I prayed for Sharon through another difficult pregnancy, through the baby's late arrival (timed to be after the brother's out-of-state funeral), and the new baby's surgery. And we continued to pray about Sharon's back problem—for which we started prayer four and one-half years earlier in Rockford! In December 1974, Sharon had that surgery, and mother and baby are now doing beautifully.

Yes, telephone prayer chains (as all forms of prayer) have a unique way of joining the human links together on a horizontal plane here on earth. But the marvel of it is that each individual is directly connected to the source of power of the whole universe, who is up in heaven—God Himself!

"Lord, teach me to pray! Amen."

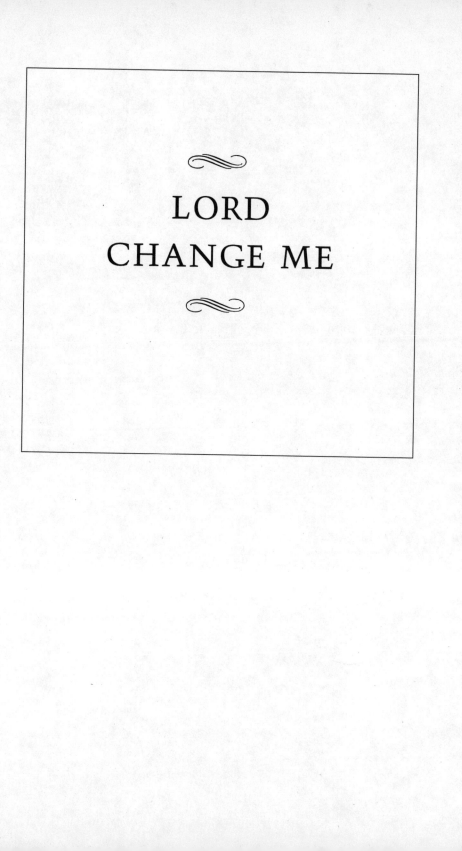

# LORD
# CHANGE ME

# Contents

To my dear husband, Chris, for wanting God's will for me rather than his own, and for his patience and love during the long hours of producing this book.

&

To my dear children, Jan, Nancy, and Kurt, who have given to me the privilege of motherhood, without which many of these lessons could never have been learned.

# Introduction

WHEN I FINISHED the *What Happens When Women Pray* project of the first six months of 1968, I thought it was time to relax. The job was done. But God had other plans. Before I left the conference at which I reported the outcome of that experimentation in prayer, God had begun a new process in me. I came home, not to look on the things which were behind, but to press on in another personal project, this time praying, "Lord, change me—not my husband, not my children—just me!"

I struggled alone with God for 14 months, allowing Him to change me. And all during this time He was clearly putting the emphasis for changing on ME, not anybody else.

God used the seven methods I have outlined in chapters two through eight of this book to teach me how He wanted me to change and how He would provide the direction and the means for my changing. These methods have been used successfully for Christian education retreats, teacher training sessions, church prayer weeks, women's retreats, Sunday School classes, and Bible studies.

135

This process of waiting on God brought forth the theme, *Lord, Change Me,* spontaneously and unplanned at a retreat I was conducting 14 months after He began teaching it to me. Then the theme gathered momentum as I began sharing it at retreats, conferences, and studies around the United States and Canada.

But I discovered one danger in this process. I had to make sure I was being changed by the Lord and not by the other three possible sources of wisdom James lists in verse 15 of his third chapter. The last four chapters of this book (SECTION III) deal with the subtle or deliberate ways our thinking is influenced by other people, our own sensual selves, demons, or by God. And what we think eventually produces our life-styles. We can tell the source of our instruction by what this wisdom produces in our lives—how we are changed. And this is an ongoing process of becoming more like Christ—until we see Him face-to-face.

*Evelyn Christenson*

# Section I
# ME

---

# 1
## *Why Me?*

---

"LORD, I WILL never speak again—never—if this is the price my husband has to pay for my being a public speaker." And I wept as I prayed, "Lord, I want You to change me into the kind of wife *You* want me to be."

I had crept out of bed at 5:30 A.M. to seek the Lord in my private "prayer closet" by my old green chair. And as the minutes ticked into hours, I stayed on my knees struggling.

Why was I telling God I would never speak again? Was I disappointed, disillusioned, tired out? Oh, no—just the opposite. Flooding over me as I agonized with God was the enormity of what I was promising. I was willing to give up a way of life to which I was sure He had called me: my weekly women's neighborhood Bible study, the large adult Sunday School class—one of the greatest joys of my life—I had been teaching for almost twelve years, and my busy banquet-speaking schedule. Then my mind turned to all the retreats in the United States and Canada, where I had seen God work in such quiet, yet powerful, ways. I thought of

the Vacation Bible Schools, teacher-training classes, conferences, conventions—the list parading through my mind
seemed endless. But I prayed, "Yes, Lord, *all!*"

My husband Chris missed me, and suddenly I was aware
of his footsteps on the stairs. He paused halfway down and
asked, "May I join you?" I looked up at him and sobbed,
"Chris, I'm not praying for *you*, I'm praying for *me!* I'm
praying that the Lord will change *me.*" (The Lord may have
had some changing to do in Chris' life, but that was not
*my* concern that morning. That was between the Lord and
Chris.)

## WHY ME, LORD?

But why did I need to be changed? Hadn't I cried over my
sins all one Sunday afternoon when I was only nine years
old? I had heard Evangelist Harry McCormick Lintz preach
in church that morning in Muskegon, Michigan, and I
thought the evening service would never come—and then
that it would never end—so eager was I to respond to his
invitation to those who wanted to invite Jesus into their
hearts. I almost ran down the aisle, then opened my heart
completely to Jesus, as our Sunday School superintendent
knelt beside me and carefully explained from the Scriptures
how I could become a Christian.

And hadn't I really made Him *Lord* in addition to Saviour that Sunday? Yes, I had. From that day on I had grown
steadily—sometimes in little baby steps and at other times
in giant steps of faith—but always I had wanted and sought
His will. Hadn't I even spent months praying about my first
and only boyfriend until I was positive he was the one God
wanted me to marry? And hadn't Chris and I, as engaged
students at Moody Bible Institute, spent our free moments
poring over Walter A. Maier's *For Better Not for Worse*, the
Christian classic in those days for brides and grooms who
wanted a Christ-centered marriage? And hadn't I, in agree-

140

ment with my husband, sought only God's will as we struggled to find His spot for us in full-time Christian service, and later as we served Him as pastor and wife for 16 years? Yes, I had.

And in that last pastorate hadn't I spent six miserable weeks confessing sins to God with Lorna and Signe, my two prayer partners, before He released us to pursue our goal—prayer for our church? Hadn't God given us three years of deep intercessory prayer? And hadn't He done a Herculean job *in* and *on* and *through* us as the women of our church experimented in prayer in 1968?

## SO, THEN WHY ME?

My personal agony that early morning by my old green chair was precipitated by what had happened at our denomination's annual conference in Davenport the week before. It was June 1968, and I was flying high. Earlier, in the fall of 1967, the national committee of our denomination had asked me to do a project for the Crusade of the Americas: "Working with women in your own church, would you discover in a six-month period *what happens when women pray?*" I had accepted the challenge with enthusiasm. Now I had a fantastic report to give to the 600 women attending the opening banquet of our conference. Women from all over the United States and Canada, as well as foreign missionaries, would hear the results of our six-month experiment. Just before the banquet started, a man carrying what looked like a movie camera arrived and said to me, "Wave your arms and make believe you're speaking." As I complied, our national director, sitting at my right, whispered laughingly out of the corner of her mouth, "Psst. I think that's a TV camera!" And I was horrified to discover that she was right!

Early the next morning the jabs started—not at me, but at my husband—from fellow pastors and friends. "Hey, I saw

141

THE POWER OF PRAYER

your wife on television last night." "How does it feel to be the husband of Mrs. Christenson?" One pastor remarked to Chris, as he glanced at the shocking pink dress I was wearing, "I saw your wife on TV. Wow! It wasn't in technicolor, though." To my horror, the local TV station had chosen the segment showing my pseudospeech to represent our entire national conference on its news telecast. All week long Chris had borne the brunt of this cruel teasing. It became so embarrassing that I was the most crushed wife you could possibly imagine when we left the conference. I arrived home in Rockford, brokenhearted and puzzled. That is what had brought me to my knees beside my old green chair.

## WHY NOT VICTORY DAY?

All through breakfast that same morning, the first Tuesday in July, and while dressing for our women's weekly prayer meeting at Alpine Park, I kept dabbing away the tears. Even as I drove to the park I kept telling myself, "This is victory day, and we are going to have a victory celebration." But the tears persisted—not tears of joy, but tears of brokenness.

Eagerly the pray-ers gathered, waiting expectantly to hear what had happened in Davenport. These were the women with whom I had experimented in prayer the previous six months. These were the women, their ranks now multiplied, who had pled daily with God during the whole week I was in Davenport, that He would undergird me and that what they had experienced would spread to other women.

I felt strongly that these women waiting at Alpine Park deserved to know that after I shared what had happened in those six months when *they* prayed, every one of the 600 women present at the banquet stood to her feet and promised God that she would go home and start proving that God does answer "when women pray." They deserved to learn the outcome of their praying as they arbitrarily picked out one of the conference speakers to zero in on in prayer. I wanted to tell them that after he had spoken I had followed him into the wing of the platform area and asked, "Rev. Hanstad, would you tell me how it was preaching out there today? You see, our ladies in Rockford picked you from among all the conference speakers as a special subject of prayer for many days. Did it make a difference?" He drew a quick breath and said, "Oh, I've never had such *freedom*. I'm usually so uptight and nervous when I speak before all my peers and those administrators, but today it was different. I felt so free; there was no tension at all."

These women who had prayed for me so faithfully while I was in Davenport also deserved to know that I had awakened on the morning of the banquet with a burning sore throat and a throbbing, stuffy head. I had been too sick to pray for myself. All I could do was mumble weakly from my bed. "Oh, God, tell somebody to pray; tell somebody to pray." And without knowing of my condition, these women who were waiting in the park had prayed all that day for me. They deserved to know that God had heard and answered their prayers, for after I had crawled out of bed to get ready for the banquet that evening, still unable to talk out loud or breathe freely, a miracle had happened. I had bent over to brush my teeth, and, when I raised my head, I was well. My voice was normal, my head was clear, the sore throat and miserable aching had disappeared.

I had planned the victory speech they deserved. Their six-month job was done. But God had further plans. He was leading us up the next rung of the spiritual ladder. He had already started the process in me, bringing me down to the depths of despair that I might rise to something higher. He had some more changing to do in me. So, instead of the victory speech, I told them the whole story of what had transpired earlier that morning by my old green chair.

Trying to hide my stubborn tears, I shared the pain of my experience with the women. They all wept with me. We were feeling an unexpected and different kind of victory. I remember Katy praying that morning, "Lord, I don't care what it is, take it from me so that I can serve You effectively. Lord, I don't care what it is." Now, Katy is a sharp gal. Her husband is a tennis champion, and they have two beautiful children. She is one of those women you watch to find out what the styles are going to be next year. But Katy wept along with the rest of us that morning as we prayed, "Lord, change me." Our hearts were all echoing her prayer, "O God, take away anything—so that You can really use me." Katy desperately wanted God to be first in her life.

But a strange thing happened. Following that meeting, and for over a year afterward, we never used the phrase, "Lord, change me." It was to go underground, to emerge 14 months later.

## A NEW PROCESS

God didn't take me up on my offer to give up my speaking and teaching, but He did begin that day to answer my prayer, "Lord, change me." He already had the next step in my spiritual maturity planned and ready for me. He started that morning to teach me a great principle which began a process in my life that is still at work. I have discovered through the years that surprising things happen when I pray, "Lord, change *me*—don't change my husband, don't change my children, don't change my pastor, change *me*!" This doesn't mean that I approve or even condone everything they do, but rather that I concentrate on how *I* handle my actions and reactions. More and more the fact comes into focus that they, and not I, are responsible before God for their actions. But I am responsible for the changes that need to be made in *me*.

This concept became the process whereby Evelyn was to become more Christlike, conformed to *His* image, as stated in Romans 8:29, "For whom He did foreknow, He also did predestinate *to be conformed to the image of His Son."* And since being Christlike is my goal, I must expect this process to continue throughout my life and end only "when He shall appear" and I shall be "like Him" (1 John 3:2).

Although it was to be 14 months before the "Lord,-change-me" concept was to become an actuality, the process had started. God had launched me personally on a 14-month gestation period. The "birth" would not take place until over a year later. This was the process of facing the reality of *my* need to change—again and again and again.

The struggle was like a hot iron inside me. That's the only way I can describe it. And it took 14 solid months of turning to the only adequate, worthy Source of change—God Himself—and of searching His Word and allowing Him to make changes in my life, not in anybody else's.

"O God," I kept praying, "don't change anybody else, not my husband, not my children, just change ME!"

## ME AGAIN?

That same month, June 1968, I had some more changes to make. (What a horrible month that was!) I discovered something new about myself—because my daughter told me!

At the dinner table one evening Jan, our just-turned-18 eldest, abruptly announced, "Mother, I don't ever want to hear your philosophy again. Do you know that the tone of your voice actually changes when you start giving your philosophy? I know what's coming every single time."

*"Me* again?" I pushed my chair from the table, flew up to my bedroom and threw myself, sobbing, on my bed.

What was God teaching me *this* time? Jan always had been an independent first child, determinedly doing her own thing—following the encyclopedia's instructions for formal table settings while still in second grade; conquering the world of reading in sixth grade by winning our denomination's national reading contest. Her "I-can-do-it-myself,-Mother" personality had been there from birth, but always under mother's guidance. So what was happening to her now? What had legally becoming an adult at her eighteenth birthday done to her?

Then, agonizing in my soul, I prayed, "Lord, don't change Jan. I know she's a teenager who needs to find her way in the world. Just change me! Lord, make me the kind of mother You want me to be. O God, I know she's growing up. Show me, please, how You want me to change!"

Then began in earnest what was to stretch into 14 months of soul-searching for me.

## WITHOUT A WORD

As I looked in the Bible for direction, God gave me a *principle* from 1 Peter 3:1–2 that guided my "changing" and carried me through those difficult 14 months. At that time the emphasis for me from God was that others were to *observe my* chaste and reverent behavior. "So that some . . . may be won *without a word*" (RSV).

Although this verse speaks specifically of the husband-wife relationship, I was to find that the "without-a-word" principle also worked with mothers and daughters. I determined not to impose my philosophy on Jan again. No more "preachy" mother!

Keeping my advice to myself, especially with my personality, wasn't easy. And Jan even enrolled at my alma mater as a freshman that fall! Oh, how I could have helped her by telling her just how to do everything. After all, hadn't I spent seven years with her daddy on that campus (and with her as a little baby)? And hadn't I, as secretary to the president, typed the disciplinary letters to parents and worked with the details of scholarships and college administration? But I restrained myself from offering my help. She didn't want it. Her independent attitude prevailed. She had to find out who *she* was—by herself.

I've learned since that that time wasn't easy for Jan either. She has confided to me that frequently, those first few weeks, she would sit in her dorm, bite her lip and blink hard to keep back the tears—determined not to call home every time she felt lonely—determined to become independent—determined to make her own decisions in college. And at the same time I was sitting home just as determined—blinking back my tears—determined to let her find her own philosophy of life, to find her own way in the world.

When the first child turns 18 and decides to cut the apron strings, parents (especially mothers) almost bleed to death. Their wounds seem to be much deeper than those of the children, and heal so much more slowly. Letting go of Jan was one of the most devastating things that had ever happened to me. How I thank God for five years of preparation before our next child became of age. I didn't bleed nearly so much, for I had had five years to change my "smotherhood" to "motherhood." And Nancy could walk with much more confidence in the field which Jan had plowed as virgin soil those many years before.

## IT WORKS

By February following that horrible June, my then eight months of silence about my philosophy was starting to bring results, although I honestly wasn't looking for them. I was only concentrating on the Lord changing me. That He might in turn be changing my daughter hadn't occurred to me. Our first visit to her college was for Founder's Week. As we sat conversing at dinner with Jan and the boy she was then dating, I sat in stunned silence as she carefully, deliberately kept saying to him, "My mother thinks this about that. And

147

she thinks this about that." The other part of those verses in 1 Peter 3 was proving to be true, "That some . . . *may be won* . . . when they [observe] your reverent and chaste behavior" (3:1–2, RSV). But this wasn't the time to say anything.

Multiplying my prayers for her, I entrusted Jan to God and kept my "hands off" policy going those 14 months. Without mentioning to anybody what I was doing, I silently stayed in God's Word, wept and prayed, "Lord, don't change Chris, don't change Jan, don't change my other children, don't change the people in my church, don't change anybody else—but, Lord, change Evelyn."

I recently checked with Jan about this, and she said, "Oh, Mom, you really never did open your mouth to me once with any of your philosophy for all those months. You never did."

Now eight years later, I have just had the shock of my life. A doctor's wife from our church greeted me one Sunday morning and said, "I was chatting with your Jan at our Christian Medical Society's retreat, and she told me that she gets her philosophy of life from her mother." And it was Jan herself who had said to me just days before that, "Mother, your next book has to be, must be, *Lord, Change Me.*"

But the most surprising and thrilling thing to come out of those 14 agonizing months of keeping my mouth closed and letting God change me was a birthday card the next year from my Jan. It was signed: "To my mother—who says so much in her silence."

I had learned the first step in becoming more Christlike—*admitting* that I was the one who needed changing, and in silence *living* my life before others.

The struggle paid off in many ways, but one of the most gratifying was when Nancy, our middle child, came home from her part-time job four years later, burst into the living room and said, "Mother, I found you in the Bible! I was

just reading my *Living Bible* and found you in Titus 2:7."
Tears came to my eyes as she read it to me. "And here
you yourself must be an example to them of good deeds of
every kind. Let everything you do reflect your love of the
truth and the fact that you are in dead earnest about it."

I cried in my heart, "O God, have I really *lived* in front
of Nancy an 'example . . . of good deeds . . . love of truth
. . . and . . . in dead earnest'? Are there really those who are
being won, not with my words but by observing me?"

# Section II
# CHANGE

# 2

## *Lord,*
## *How Do I Change?*

---

"LORD, I WANT to change. But how do I discover *Your* 'chaste and reverent' behavior, mentioned in 1 Peter 3:1–2? Especially since I've been trying so hard for so long? Is there more, Lord? How should I go about becoming what You want me to be now?"

### LET HIM ASK OF GOD

When I asked God these questions, He showed me that *He* gives answers. All I needed to do was ask: "If any of you lack wisdom, let him ask of God, that giveth to all men liberally, and upbraideth not; and it shall be given him" (James 1:5). One definition of wisdom is "that endowment of heart and mind which is needed for the right *conduct of life.*" Wisdom is not just philosophic speculation or intellectual knowledge, but a practical, applied life-style. It is not only knowing something in your head, but applying it to your life so that it becomes a part of you.

153

## IF ANY LACK WISDOM

In 1966 God had taught me the *process* of seeking wisdom from His Word. I had been given my first denominational assignment—to bring four messages to women's and girls' work directors from our 18 districts in the United States and Canada on the theme, "God's Word for a New Age." I was to prove that the Bible was an adequate guide for this new age—an age of exploding knowledge, with technical libraries becoming obsolete every six months, and with a whole new world being conquered in outer space.

Trying to come up with the material for my messages, I drew a blank month after month. Finally, on July 8, 1966, I panicked, realizing I had only two months left to find the solution to this mind-boggling challenge. So, at 5:30 one morning, I sought my green chair "prayer closet," fell on my knees, and begged God to give me the answer. I prayed and pleaded for over an hour—but no answer came. In desperation I reached for my Bible, opened it to where I was reading devotionally, and started to read Psalm 25.

Suddenly one little four-letter word in the fifth verse almost jumped off the page at me. It seemed to be in very black bold type. W-A-I-T. "Lead me in Thy truth, and teach me: for Thou art the God of my salvation; on Thee do I *wait* all the day."

"O Lord," I cried, "I'll take You at Your Word. I'll trust You. I won't read any books on the subject. I'll just stay in *Your* Book and let You tell me what I should teach those women."

Then every day for the next six weeks I read the Scriptures, not consecutively in one book, but at random. And each time God stopped me (as He had at the word *wait*), I would jot down the specific thought on a separate piece of paper. When I finished this process during our vacation at the cottage on Lake Michigan that summer, God had a surprise for me. I looked at the hopeless pile of random notes and announced to the family that I needed to use the dining room table to divide these into some semblance of order.

As I read through these disconnected, scattered thoughts gleaned from my Bible reading, I realized that they were logically dividing themselves into four specific subjects. And I no longer had one large pile but four smaller piles of paper. With mounting enthusiasm and curiosity, I reread each grouping and discovered that these random notes fell into a natural outline form. (They reminded me of my college freshman English class where we learned to make notations from our research on index cards.) In almost a state of shock I, who had always thought of myself as the "commentary kid," looked at the four piles of notes in outline form for the four messages which would prove that God's Word is an adequate guide for our sophisticated, proud minds. Wow! The Bible was alive—sufficient for our new age!

The process of obtaining wisdom from God was indelibly impressed on my mind. For six weeks He had been carefully guiding and directing my "random" reading, speaking specifically to the subject through scattered Scriptures.

## WHO GIVETH TO "ALL" MEN LIBERALLY

God had another surprise for me in this process of seeking wisdom from His Word. After giving these four messages at the Regional Chairmen's Conference in Chicago and sharing them at a retreat in the foothills of Mount Rainier in Washington, I taught them at the annual fall "Learning for Serving" seminar at our church. Soon afterward a visiting college president was our guest speaker on a Sunday morning.

After the service my phone began to ring. "Did you recognize your outline this morning, Evelyn?"

"That was not *my* outline," I assured the caller. "I know that man never heard a word I ever taught. That was *his* outline, not mine."

God had taught both of us the same truths from His Word! I don't know the method God used to give our guest speaker his message, but it overwhelmed me that identical instructions had been given to both of us.

The following January I kept my radio tuned to Moody Bible Institute's annual Founder's Week broadcasts while doing my housework. Day after day I listened in stunned silence as two nationally known speakers used the same points and illustrations God had given me in that random reading the previous summer for my "God's Word for a New Age" project. Finally I pressed the "off" buttons of the washer and dryer, ran into the dining room and dropped my head in my arms at the table. "O God," I sobbed, "You gave *me* the same information out of Your Word that You gave those two great men of God with earned Ph.D. degrees! *Me*—a nobody!"

## READ UNTIL

Two years later, in June 1968, God offered me a new project which originated with my oldest daughter's criticism, described in the last chapter. This time I was to let God *change me through His Word* while I kept my philosophy to myself. Most mothers go through a time of deep introspection when their children leave the nest. Now I had joined their ranks. I too reevaluated myself—soon to be out of a job just as I was becoming experienced at being a mother.

I set out in earnest using the process God had taught me, allowing Him to tell me *how* He wanted me to change. Staying in the Scripture for instruction, I would read only *until* He spoke. Then I would stop to pray about what He had said, analyze His reason for stopping me at that particular point, discover the need He knew I had, and then determine what I could do to change. I underlined hundreds of verses during those 14 months, but I'll share here only a few that were the most meaningful to me.

As I read in the Psalms, day by day, starting in June 1968, God gave me the *source* of wisdom that would effect changes in my life. First, He gave me Psalm 1:2, "But his delight is in the law of the Lord; and in His law doth he meditate day and night." In the margin of my Bible by that verse I wrote: "24 hours" and "all undergraduates, no alumni." I was to meditate in His law day and night, and not consider myself as having graduated from God's school of learning and changing. There was still more for me to learn.

*How I was to approach this process* was shown to me in Psalm 25: "The meek will He guide in judgment; and the meek will He teach His way" (v. 9), and "What man is he that feareth the Lord? Him shall He teach in the way that He shall choose" (v. 12). Coming to God humbly and meekly, admitting that *I* needed to be changed, was a new, emerging thought to me in those days.

Then underlined heavily in my Bible was *the promise of authoritative direction from God* for me in Psalm 32:8: "I will instruct thee and teach thee in the way which thou shalt go; I will guide thee with Mine eye." There was no question about it, God was going to instruct me and He was going to guide me in my quest for instruction as to *how* I was to change.

As God spoke to me forcefully out of the 139th Psalm, the idea of Scripture being profitable for reproof (2 Tim. 3:16) became evident. "Search me, O God, and know my heart; try me, and know my thoughts; and see if there be any wicked way in me, and lead me in the way everlasting" (vv. 23–24). God had to show me through His Word what displeased Him and what needed to be changed in me. In the margin I penciled, "Prayer: 'Lord, change me.'"

Then, as I read until God spoke from the Book of Proverbs during those 14 months, He gave me much instruction about *obtaining wisdom:* "Yea, if thou *criest* after knowledge, and *liftest up thy voice* for understanding; if thou

157

*seekest* her as silver, and *searchest* for her as for hid treasures; then shalt thou understand the fear of the Lord, and find the knowledge of God. For the Lord giveth wisdom; out of His mouth cometh knowledge and understanding" (Prov. 2:3–6, italics mine). Once again God was impressing upon me the truth that "the fear of the Lord is the beginning of wisdom" (Prov. 9:10). And that wisdom was to be found in His Word.

## TRANSFORMED—BY THE RENEWING OF YOUR MIND

Some specific points on *how* I could change began emerging during those 14 months as I searched the Scriptures. I remember rising early in the morning in a Fort Lauderdale condominium, struggling with what God meant when He had given me Romans 12:2 the month before: "But be not conformed to this world: but be ye *transformed* by the renewing of your mind, that ye may prove what is that good, and acceptable, and perfect, will of God."

On December 29, 1969, I wrote in the margin of my Bible, "Transformed—same word as Christ's transfiguration." Did God want me changed as dramatically as Christ was on the Mount of Transfiguration when His face shone as the sun and His raiment was white as the light? Then I wrote, "Changed—from worm to butterfly." I almost felt like the surprised worm I had seen on a poster. Watching a butterfly soar overhead, the worm was saying, "Who, *me* change?" Then I wrote in the margin of my Bible beside Romans 12:2, "Pronouns—does God want *me*?" The pronouns were so very, very personal. I circled them. No mistaking it. God wasn't talking to my husband, my children—but to me. Then the abrupt note in my Bible said, "Spiritual maturity—period." Yes, that's what all that changing was about—to be mature in Him. Like Him. Proving what is His good and acceptable and perfect will—for me.

God also told me how I *didn't* have to change. Although I felt no inner compulsion to give up my teaching and speaking after I had told God I would that previous June, it was such a thrill to get the confirmation directly from Him. As I was reading in Ephesians 6, I blinked in surprise and then tears of relief swelled in my eyes as He stopped me at: "And for me, that utterance may be given unto me, that I may open my mouth boldly, to make known the mystery of the Gospel, for which I am an ambassador in bonds; that therein I may speak boldly, as I ought to speak" (vv. 19–20). This was one of the greatest things God taught me those 14 months. He told me to continue speaking and teaching even though I was willing to give it all up if it was going to hurt my husband. My final affirmation to this came last fall from my husband himself when he said to me, "Honey, I'm your greatest fan."

God continued to show me how to change. On February 18, 1969, I read Galatians 2:20: "I am crucified with Christ; nevertheless I live; yet not I, but Christ liveth in me; and the life which I now live in the flesh I live by the faith of the Son of God, who loved me and gave Himself for me." Then, in my Bible, I wrote, "Ego moves to the side—Christ center of me." The *how* to change was becoming obvious. I was to let Christ live in me, transforming me into the likeness of Himself.

There were many specific instructions, but Philippians 2:3, with the notation, "Humility—April, 1969," was so meaningful to me at that time: "Let nothing be done through strife or vainglory; but in lowliness of mind let each esteem other better than themselves."

God even showed me some affirmation of the learning in silence through my 11-year-old Kurt as we were reading together that January. "Isn't it amazing how much you can learn when you don't argue?" he commented on Philippians 2:14: "Do all things without murmurings and disputings." Renewing my mind!

159

God seemed to reassure me through one verse of Scripture in my struggle to become changed, more Christlike. In February I had a heavy speaking schedule and was utterly exhausted at a retreat in Mount Hermon, California. I fervently prayed for God to change me before the Saturday night banquet. Two days later, after an almost miraculous rejuvenation for the banquet, I marked this in my Bible: "Being confident of this very thing, that He who hath begun a good work in you will perform it until the day of Jesus Christ" (Phil. 1:6).

A verse I would only be able to understand later prompted me to write "me" in the margin beside it on February 1, 1969. Like Paul, would I be a more effective servant of Jesus after this? Would my ministry for Christ be more effective because of the experiences of these 14 months? "But I would ye should understand, brethren, that the things which happened unto *me* have fallen out rather unto the furtherance of the Gospel" (Phil. 1:12).

## PRECEPT UPON PRECEPT

Then God gave some more specific instructions about His method of teaching me those 14 months. On March 23, 1969, He showed me emphatically that He was the Teacher. "But the anointing which ye have received of Him abideth in you, and ye need not that any man teach you but as the same anointing teacheth you of all things, and is truth, and is no lie, and even as it hath taught you, ye shall abide in Him" (1 John 2:27). "Whom shall He teach knowledge? And whom shall He make to understand doctrine? Them that are weaned from the milk, and drawn from the breasts. *For precept must be upon precept, precept upon precept; line upon line, line upon line; here a little, and there a little*" (Isa. 28:9–10, italics mine).

That was it. Through hundreds of verses God spoke directly to me during that time. He had piled precept upon precept and line upon line, showing me what needed to be changed, and how to depend completely upon Him for wisdom to change. This maturing was for those who were weaned from milk, those who were growing up—by the renewing of the mind!

## AND UPBRAIDETH NOT

Never once in those 14 months did God scold me for asking for more wisdom. Over and over again He reassured me that He wanted to give me all the wisdom I needed. The gift of wisdom is the only gift promised to *all* who ask for it. The other gifts are given by the three Persons of the Trinity as They please to distribute them.

In 1 Corinthians 12:8–11 we read that the Holy Spirit divides gifts to every man as He wills. Romans 12:3–6 shows us that "God hath dealt to every man the measure of faith . . . having then gifts differing according to the grace that is given to us." Then, in Ephesians 4:7 and 11, we read, "But unto every one of us is given grace according to the measure of the gift of Christ . . . and He gave some, apostles; some, prophets; and some, evangelists; and some, pastors and teachers." Thus Christ, too, gave people of differing gifts to the churches as He desired. But the gift of wisdom is different. Every believer can ask for and receive, the precious gift of wisdom for making changes in his life. He is given a renewed mind to know the perfect will of God.

## CHANGED—THROUGH MY SPIRITUAL DIARY

But receiving wisdom for my life from His Word has not been confined to those 14 months. Recently I did a project in preparation for an assigned retreat theme of "God's Living Word." To prove to myself—and those at the retreat —that the Bible had been alive in my own life, I dug out the three Bibles from which I had read devotionally since I was 18 years old. I went through those Bibles, systematically and laboriously, and recorded in three columns (one for each Bible) the most significant underlined, and usually dated, Scriptures. As I pored over these three Bibles for a month I had a surprise. I could tell from the passage I had underlined whether I had been in victory or defeat, joy or depression, death, birth, surgery, illness, open doors, challenge, or closed doors. And as the evidence piled up, I slowly began to realize that God had *always* given *specific answers for specific needs at specific times.*

As column after column on page after page filled up on the legal pad I was using, something overwhelmingly significant came into focus. I had in three Bibles a *spiritual diary of my life* from the time I was 18! For all of those years God had been instructing me specifically out of His Word. The process that came into focus as "Lord, change me" that June, 1968, actually had been an unrecognized goal of my life since I had graduated from high school in 1940.

May I share a few of the verses that are most precious to me, selected from the thousands underlined and usually dated in those three Bibles?

At our first pastorate in the fall of 1953 God spoke definitely to me the day the doctors told us our baby, Judy, could not live. I remember taking her to the hospital, coming home with aching, empty arms and a horrible rebellion in my heart—stubbornly hanging on to my right to keep her. I struggled alone in my bedroom for hours over a statement our former pastor had made, "God must love Harold and Evelyn a lot to give them all that sorrow." As I thought about the Scripture he was referring to in Hebrews 12:6, "For whom the Lord loveth He chasteneth," I became more and more angry at the man for saying such a terrible thing.

But as I fought with God in my solitude, He seemed to be saying to me, "Read on." So I opened my Bible and read to Hebrews 12:10 where it says that our earthly fathers "chastened us after their own pleasure; but He [God] for our profit." God seemed to be whispering to me that, if I was going to be a pastor's wife, I would have to understand some of these things. I would need compassion when I was called upon to stand beside a crib in a hospital or by a little casket. I could only be all He wanted me to be as a pastor's wife as I experienced this chastening. Then verse 11 explained it all: "Now no chastening for the present seemeth to be joyous, but grievous; nevertheless *afterward* it yieldeth the peaceable fruit of righteousness unto them which *are exercised* thereby" (italics mine).

I felt my stubborn will go limp within me—at the same moment my tense, rebelling body crumpled on the bed beside which I was kneeling. I had surrendered to His will, whatever that might be. And at that point God changed me. My battle was over. My rebellion ceased. From that point on there was no struggle, although there were two more months of watching Judy slowly burn out. I was filled with grief on the day she died—but there was no rebellion. He had prepared me for those difficult days—but even more so for all the years ahead. God had changed me by *exercising* me with chastening. But it was all for my profit—so that I could be a "partaker of His holiness." And that "peaceable fruit of righteousness" did come at last.

In 1973 I was quite shaken when a pastor's wife accused me publicly of leaving out a theologically important point in a message. Checking the tape of the message later, and finding that I really *had* said it, didn't ease the embarrassment. But God had the answer for me. The next morning as I read Psalm 19 one word stood out in the 14th verse— "Thy." "Let the words of my mouth, and the meditation of my heart, be acceptable in Thy sight, O Lord, my strength, and my Redeemer."

In the margin of the Bible I wrote, "In *Thy* sight, not in people's sight." And then I prayed, asking the Lord to remove all the negative thoughts I had had the night before. I asked Him to forgive me and "make EVERY thought and ALL my words acceptable to YOU, LORD!" Immediately I sensed His affirmation, His OK on that message. The desire to defend my innocence melted. God had changed me!

It was pouring rain as I started for an out-of-state retreat in April 1973. Three miles from home a truck, a compact car, and Evelyn stopped for a red light, but the car behind me didn't. Crunch. And all four vehicles accordioned into one. I recovered from the jolt to my back but evidently not from the jolt to my nervous system, for as I drove during the following week I kept my eyes as much on the rearview mirror as I did on the road ahead of me! And the next weekend I was to drive to a northern Minnesota retreat. I couldn't. I felt nothing but apprehension and fear at the possibility of being hit from behind. And the theme for the retreat was to be J-O-Y! But just before I was to drive to the retreat, God gave the answer as I was reading in the Psalms. A smile spread over my face as I read: "But let all those who put their trust in Thee rejoice; let them ever shout for *joy*, because Thou defendest them; let them also that love Thy name be joyful in Thee" (Ps. 5:11). Immediately I saw my problem—failing to trust Him! At that moment He exchanged my fear for His—yes, literally—His joy. The apprehension disappeared, and I drove, a changed woman, to that J-O-Y retreat, really experiencing what I was to preach.

My spiritual barometer for years has been 1 John 1:4: "These things [are written] that your joy may be full." I can always measure the amount of time I'm spending in the Scriptures by how much joy (not superficial happiness, but deep down abiding joy) I have. When I find a lack of joy in my life, the first thing I check is how much time I'm spending in God's Word!

I'll never forget speaking at a convention where our schedule included breakfast, morning coffee and rolls, lunch, afternoon coffee and rolls, dinner, evening snack with sweet rolls! I had a badly sprained ankle at the time and was forced to go to my room to elevate it several times during each day. My car driver and I took that time to read the Bible together, practicing the "until He speaks" process.

One afternoon Luke 4:4 took on a completely new meaning: "Man [or woman] shall not live by bread alone, but by every word of God." I actually found myself thanking God for my sprained ankle so I could exchange some of the sweet rolls for the Bread of Life. I wrote in the margin of my Bible: "Plenty of time for coffee and rolls, but not enough time for God's Word alone."

I'm convinced that God has a sense of humor. In 1965 our church experienced a great moving of God, and every Sunday for four months I had the privilege of praying with at least one, and frequently with many, who came to find Christ as their Saviour. It was exciting. But suddenly I had pain in my middle and was hospitalized for tests. A "No Water" sign was hung on the end of my bed, and by early morning the real or imagined desperation for water had set in. In my discomfort I prayed, "God, please give me something to read in my Bible that's just for me, right now." And Psalm 63 popped into my head, although I didn't have the foggiest idea what it was about. I grabbed my Bible, turned to the Psalm and read: "Oh, God, Thou art my God; early will I seek Thee." So far so good. It was 5:30 in the morning.

As I read on in that first verse, I cried, "Lord, is this a joke?" "My soul thirsteth for Thee, my flesh longeth for Thee in a dry and thirsty land, where no water is."

Then I saw in verse 2 what God was really trying to say to me: "To see Thy power and Thy glory, so as I have seen Thee in the sanctuary." God showed me that my real problem was not the lack of water, but in not wanting to miss seeing Him move in the sanctuary. My real rebellion was at being put on a shelf in the midst of the action!

When the tests were over I remembered smiling bravely as my doctor told me that I would have to have surgery right away. I nodded and smiled until he disappeared out the door, and then burst into tears. Reaching for my Bible, I prayed, "Oh, God, give me something for *right now!*" Immediately Romans 12:1 flashed into my mind, and I turned to it, "I beseech you, therefore brethren, by the mercies of God, that ye present your bodies a living sacrifice, holy, acceptable unto God, which is your reasonable service."

Now I had His answer. I had given Him so completely my spirit—my mind, my emotions, my energy. All that I was, I thought. But *I had never given Him my body!*

Surgery and days of recuperation came and went, but I was still kicking at being left on a shelf when so much was going on in "the sanctuary." Not until the next Sunday when I tuned into a pastor friend's radio program did I obey God's instruction to me. I was still kicking because *my* body was in a hospital bed instead of at church that morning. But a little poem he read, "Gaining Through Losing," struck a responsive chord, and I gave God my body—once and for all. (I knew the verb tense of "gave" was a once-for-all and not continuous action.)

Gradually my attitude toward my health changed. Illness didn't disappear completely (although its diminishing frequency has been rather amazing), but my *attitude* toward it changed. I relaxed. I felt somewhat like the pastor who called his banker saying *our* car is in the ditch. Through the years I have learned to say, "God, *our* body is sick."

God changed me from an overprotective guardian of my body to one who entrusts that body to Him. What a great way to live! No friction, no hassle. Whenever I don't feel well, I just say, "Lord, if You want me to be well enough to do the job for You that's coming up, thank You. But if not, just teach me what You have for me to learn while I'm on a shelf." This obedience to His specific instruction has done more than anything else in my life to take the pressure off and change my whole outlook on life.

One of the favorite things we do during our vacation in Michigan around August 12 is to lie on the beach at midnight and watch the fantastic display of shooting stars. The summer our Kurt was seven I read an article in the *Reader's Digest* about a father who got his seven-year-old boy up in the middle of the night to see the shooting stars because, he reasoned, there were some things more important than sleep. So, when the exhibition was at its peak, we decided it was time for Kurt to join the rest of the family on the beach. The excitement and the "oh's" and "ah's" mounted with each display of God's celestial fireworks.

But the real excitement came the next morning when, as a family, we read at the breakfast table Psalm 33, and especially the fifth to ninth verses: "The earth is full of the goodness of the Lord. By the word of the Lord were the heavens made; and all the host of them by the breath of His mouth. . . . Let all the inhabitants of the world stand in awe of Him, for He spake, and it was done." I found myself not only excited over an astronomical wonder, but changed into a mother awed at God's timing and selection of our daily reading—overawed that He wanted to tell us that He only had to speak and all this was done!

The beach at Lake Michigan is also my favorite place to read God's Word and let Him speak to me. Every day while we are on vacation I rise early and, weather permitting, take my Bible down to the edge of the lake and read until He speaks. One morning I read such a great Psalm about our God that I found myself skipping down the beach instead of doing my usual hiking. God had changed an ordinary, run-of-the-mill vacation day into one of exhilaration and exploding joy, joy that could not be contained in ordinary steps. The thrill that sent my body soaring like the eagle's burst out in impromptu songs of praise as I adored Him for who He is and praised Him for what He is. Changed by a psalm? Yes, changed!

Thirty-six years of underlining answers for actual situations have proven to me that the Bible truly is a *living* Book. "For the Word of God is living and active," Hebrews 4:12 (NASB) tells us. Yes, it is alive. It has answers in the midst of our knowledge explosion today—or tomorrow—on this planet and in outer space. And precept upon precept as I let it renew my mind and my attitudes, I am changed. Changed into what is His perfect will for me to be.

## TREASURE

I packed those three Bibles in my tote bag to show at that retreat where I was to speak on "God's Living Word." As I headed for the plane in Minneapolis, the security guard started systematically to check my carry-on luggage. When he pulled out the first Bible he gave me a "that's-a-nice-lady" smile. The second one produced a puzzled expression on his face. But, at finding the third, he was sure I had hidden something valuable in those Bibles, and proceeded to search each one diligently. He even held one up by its binding and shook it vigorously.

That guard never discovered the treasure I had hidden in those three Bibles. The omniscient Lord Jesus Christ, "in whom are hid all the treasures of wisdom and knowledge" (Col. 2:3), had given it to me. Underlined and marked on those pages was all the direction I had needed for a "chaste and reverent" life-style since I was 18 years old. Line upon line, precept upon precept, God had taught me how to change.

When I have needed direction for my life, has He ever left me groping in the dark, trying to find my way? Oh, no! He has given me His Word as a "lamp unto my feet, and a light unto my path" (Ps. 119:105). And, as I have obeyed His instructions, He has *changed me*, step by step, into the person He wants me to be.

# 3

## *Lord, Change Me for Others Too*

---

THE 14 MONTHS marched silently along with God continuing His rebuking, refining, enlightening, changing. I was aware of each step, but still had not thought of it as anything more than a process for me.

But suddenly the months of searching Scripture "without a word" were over. The "Lord, change me" gestation period which started in June 1968, came to an end and the hidden theme was born. What had been a very private experience in my own life erupted, unplanned, at the 1969 Minnesota Baptist Women's Retreat at Big Trout Lake, Minnesota. Unannounced, it became a principle to be shared with others.

"Did the theme of this retreat change?" asked a committee member.

"To what do you think it changed?" I asked.

"I think it changed to 'Lord, Change Me.'"

"I think it did, too. But I didn't change it. God did."

No, I hadn't changed the theme. I had diligently prepared my messages on the theme those 800 women had chosen for their retreat—but God had other ideas.

Just before I started to speak on the Wednesday night of that retreat, someone slipped a note to me: "Please come to our cabin. We have a problem." I tucked the note in my Bible, promising myself to see about the need after the service.

While I spoke that night, one illustration from a previous women's retreat was to trigger the change of theme. I told these Minnesota women that back in September 1966, right after I had found such exciting answers when I had read only the Bible, I decided to try the *wait* process on the 400 women attending a retreat in the foothills of Mount Rainier in Washington. Having no idea of what God was going to say to them, I sent those women out to read Colossians 3 by themselves. I had instructed them to read only *until* God spoke, and then to stop and pray about what He was saying to them.

In addition to speaking at that Mount Rainier retreat, I told them, I had also served as a counselor. A steady stream of women came to me for advice—talking to me while I brushed my teeth, and even shouting over the shower curtain. I knew I didn't have professional answers for those women, so every time one came to me I listened to her problem and then asked the question: "And where did God stop you in your reading of Colossians 3 today?" I felt I was on safe ground asking that question.

And do you know what happened? *In every instance* the Lord stopped *each one of them* at the answer to her problem. I didn't have to offer a single solution, because the Lord did. In fact, on Saturday night the retreat committee said to me, "God is doing such a great thing, let's not structure the Sunday morning service. Let's just ask the women to share what God has been saying to them out of the Scripture."

171

That Sunday morning for one-and-a-half hours the women kept popping up like popcorn sharing what God had said. I was so overwhelmed that I finally asked them all to jot down on a piece of paper what God showed them when He stopped them in Colossians 3. I went home to Minnesota with a large manila envelope bulging with specific answers—not from me but from God.

I told the Minnesota women that as I was hurriedly throwing things into my suitcase to catch a plane for Minneapolis, a very angry and distraught woman burst into my room. I explained that I really didn't have time to talk with her, but she told me to keep packing while she talked. She trembled with anger as she ranted on about a woman she couldn't stand, a woman who was also attending the retreat. "Why," she exploded, "she actually talks and gossips about our pastor. And I won't go to prayer meeting if she's going to be there because I get so furious when she prays. Would you believe she actually prays against him right in front of him?"

As she raved on, I paused in my packing, turned to her and asked, "And where did God stop you in Colossians 3?"

"In verse 13."

"What does it say?"

"It says, 'Forebearing one another, and forgiving one another, if any man have a quarrel against any; even as Christ forgave you, so also do ye.'"

"Is that where He stopped you?" (Nod.) "How long have you been a Christian?"

"Three months."

"Did Christ forgive anything in you when you became a Christian?"

A look of shock crossed her face. Then she put her head on my shoulder and began to weep. "Oh, it's *my* fault, isn't it? I'm the one who needs to change, not her. I'm the one God needs to change." She had seen that she was to forgive others *as* He had forgiven her—forgiven her of all her past sins when she accepted Him as her Saviour three months before.

I went to the airport with a wet shoulder, but left behind a woman who had learned to forgive as Christ had forgiven her—because God had shown her what was wrong with herself, not with the other woman.

That's the story I told at the 1969 Minnesota retreat before going to the cabin whose members had sent me a note just before the meeting. Though it was a warm September night, when I entered the cabin, I was sure there were icicles hanging from the ceiling. I have never felt a colder atmosphere. All the women were sitting there in sullen silence with their chins slightly jutted and arms crossed.

I soon discovered that they were all from the same small town where their church had recently split. Half of them had stayed in the church and the other half had left. At home they weren't speaking to one another. But the unknowing camp registrar had put them all in the same cabin!

And there they sat—each one blaming the other. My first suggestion was that they read Colossians 3.

"No!" One lady was sitting cross-legged on her bed right beside me, holding her Bible. I asked her several times to read Colossians 3:13 for us, but she stubbornly repeated, "No, I won't."

A couple of hours passed, but I was getting nowhere. They finally agreed on one point: the problem in their town was all the fault of one man—*he* did this, and *he* did that. And if *he* hadn't done that, *we* wouldn't have done that. "Yes," they all agreed, "it is all his fault because our church broke up."

"He sounds like a pretty horrible guy, and I guess it is probably all his fault—or at least most of it is. But," I said,

173

"do you think one percent of the blame might be in this room?"

"No! Uh-uh! There's nothing wrong in *this* room."

But I kept pushing the point. "Could there *possibly* be just one percent?"

Then from the far corner a woman said hesitantly, in a barely audible voice, "I think there's one percent over here."

Then someone else said, "I think maybe there's, ah, ten percent here."

Finally the woman with the Bible, sitting cross-legged on her bed, looked at me and stammered, "I—I think I can read Colossians 3:13 now." And slowly she read: "Forgiving one another, if any man have a quarrel against any; even as Christ forgave you, so also do ye."

At a quarter to one in the morning, we finally ended the encounter with our arms around each other, weeping and praying. And those women prayed only one prayer, "Oh, Lord, don't change that guy back home. *Change me!*"

The next night at our campfire sharing time, the "Lord, Change Me" theme continued. Woman after woman kept saying, "I needed changing—not everybody else." One women's society president said, "Nine of my women had made reservations for this retreat, and I kept saying of each one, 'Isn't that wonderful; does *she* need it!' And then my phone started ringing, and one after another was saying that she couldn't make it. I would hang up the phone and think, 'Isn't it too bad; *she* needed it so badly.' Finally there were just four going from our church. But tonight I realize that it wasn't all the women who couldn't come who needed this retreat; *I* am the one who needed it."

Yes, I knew the theme of the retreat had changed. I had watched it change. But I hadn't changed it—God had. Thus "Lord, Change Me" for groups was launched—to be used with thousands of people, always with the same results, all over the United States and Canada.

## ANOTHER SURPRISE

On the first Monday following that Minnesota retreat, God had another surprise for me in the unfolding of the "Lord, Change Me" theme.

Early in the morning our front doorbell rang and there stood a man my husband had counseled many, many times. He had been married, divorced, and remarried to the same woman. And his life was still a horrible mess. "Could I see the pastor?" he asked.

My mother-hen defense for Chris went up and I said, "It's terribly early and Chris is still asleep. Could you come a bit later?"

"I *have* to tell somebody. Could I tell *you*?"

Monday morning! But I said, "Wait until I turn off the washer and dryer." I returned, pulled my robe tighter around me as I sat down on the davenport and said, "OK. Tell me."

He said, "Do you know what? The most amazing thing happened to me."

And I halfheartedly countered, "Really?"

"Yup. A week ago I was driving my truck down Broadway, and I was blaming everybody for what was going on in my home—my kids, my wife, my employer. But suddenly the Lord said to me, '*You* are the one who needs to be changed, not all the rest of the people. *You* need to be changed.' As I drove I think I even closed my eyes once and prayed, 'Lord, change *me*; Lord, change *me*.'"

I sat there in amazement: *Lord, change me!*

It was all coming into focus. The "Lord, change me" concept had been given to him too. It was spreading. God was spreading it!

"I have had the most marvelous experience," he continued. "I went home, and there was that wife that I had married, divorced, and remarried. We were having such a rough time. And the next morning when I woke up there she was, the same wife. But I loved her with a love I didn't know was possible. I took her in my arms and said, 'Oh, honey, how I love you.' It was just great. I loved her, and I loved the kids.

"Now, I hadn't gotten along with my dad. We hadn't really spoken for many years. I got in the car and went out to see my old dad who had been an invalid for a long time. I went to his bedside, took his hand, and said, 'Dad, I just came here for one reason. I came here to tell you I love you.' And the tears started to trickle down his face as he took my hand and said, 'Sonny, I have waited since you were that high (measuring three feet from the floor with his hand) to hear you say that.'

"Then I went to church on Sunday morning, and there was my wife's lawyer who knew all the dirt about me. I thought I was ready to join the church that morning, but I knew that I had some unfinished business. Instead of going down front to say that I wanted to join the church, I turned around and swung over to my wife's lawyer. The two of us put our arms around each other, and stood there in the sanctuary and wept. The next person I saw was a businessman who had done me dirt—a Christian, a member of our church. I got to thinking, 'I haven't been so honest with him either.' And I walked up to that man, looked him right in the eye, and stuck out my hand. We shook hands.

"Mrs. Chris, I *had* to tell somebody, because all I've been praying is 'Lord, change me.' *And all of these things have happened in my whole relationship with people—just because I prayed 'Lord—change—me!'*"

This is the exciting part of the changing process! Relationships with people do change when we pray, "Lord, change *me.*" And I now realized that God had not given this fabulous thought to me to be kept selfishly to myself—only to see myself change. But He had intended all along that it was to be shared with others whom He also wanted to change.

## "WE WANT A 'LORD, CHANGE ME' RETREAT TOO"

The next morning I went to our weekly prayer meeting with my heart absolutely overflowing. I decided it was time to share "Lord, change me" with my dear women. I told them what God had been doing in my life for 14 months, and then how the process had miraculously erupted, unplanned, at the Minnesota retreat the preceding week. Then I shared the startling story that had been told to me the morning before. When I finished, one wide-eyed member of our prayer group said, "I think we need a 'Lord, change me' retreat too."

So we planned what was to be my first "Lord, change me" retreat. For the next month our president and I struggled, trying to put together an agenda, but to no avail. The day before the scheduled retreat, we communicated five times trying to figure out what to do all day long, but the Lord kept telling both of us, "Just trust Me. Just trust Me."

The next morning I was a little apprehensive as the church parking lot started to fill with cars. The officers of our women's organizations were gathering to form a caravan to a cottage in Wisconsin for our first "Lord, change me" retreat. They were trusting me, as their pastor's wife, just as I was trusting God, and the responsibility was a bit overwhelming. Armed with nothing but our Bibles, we wended our way to our all-day retreat. As we traveled I kept praying silently, "Oh, Lord, just You—just You."

The great part of trusting the Lord is that He never lets you down. I spent the first 20 minutes of that retreat sharing my excitement over what God had done in my own life for 14 months: the Minnesota retreat, the Monday morning visitor, and then the prayer group's request for this retreat. That was all.

From then on that day we let God be in command. I assigned a portion of Scripture, instructing them to "take this portion of Scripture, find any spot you want in this cabin, and read until God speaks to you. Read *only until* He speaks. Don't read any more. If you read on after He speaks, you'll get confused, not knowing what you should pray about. Then, ask God *why* He stopped you at that point, *what needs changing* in your life, and then *what He wants you to do* about it. Be sure to listen as He gently brings answers to your mind. God's speaking to you in the Scripture may be only a little nudge, or you may think some words are popping out in bold print."

Then we prayed a simple prayer. "Lord, remove all our preconceived ideas about this portion of Scripture. We want You to tell us *afresh* what You want changed in us *today.*" I asked for complete silence, explaining that it is impossible for God to speak to us if we are chattering, discussing, and talking to each other. So, a slightly bewildered but willing group sought their private spots with the Lord and began reading.

I sat in the living room wondering what would happen. For almost two years these women had been experimenting with what happened when they prayed, learning to pray first and plan afterward, and then to bear one another's burdens in prayer. Did God have another step for *them* too?

At 11 o'clock we came back together and formed a large circle of prayer on our knees in the living room. Then the miracle began. We had agreed not to talk to each other, but we prayed aloud to God about where He had stopped us in the Scripture portion. I can't find any word to describe what happened next but "revival." Those women wept and prayed on their faces before God, confessing what He had told them was wrong in their lives.

"Lord, I'm sorry. Forgive me. Lord, change me," they all prayed. He had put His finger on specific needs in their lives—all of them out of the same portion of Scripture. Tears were abundant, including those in my own eyes as I

178

listened in amazement at the way God had been faithful to His "just trust Me" promise the day before.

Through the years I have never ceased to be astounded at this process as I've led thousands to read *until* God speaks. He who knows the thoughts and intents of every heart digs deeply into the hidden recesses to search out sins and shortcomings we are often not aware of. And He does it in response to our sincere prayer to be shown what *He* wants to change in us.

During lunch we continued our silence so that we could keep listening to God. As the leader, I thanked our hostess in advance for the noodle casserole, and once again felt a slight anxiety in my heart about the unaccustomed silence. But I was put at ease at our very next session when one woman reported, "It was embarrassing when I first sat down. I sat there eating my hot dish, and I didn't know what to do. And then all at once God started to talk to me about the thing in my life He had convicted me of that morning. He penetrated deeper and deeper. I wasn't aware that there was anyone else at the table because I was alone with God, and He was speaking to me." Most of the women agreed that this was their experience during that time of silence.

In the afternoon of our first "Lord, change me" retreat, we concentrated on what God wanted to change in our circles and women's church meetings. Assigning another portion of Scripture, we prayed asking God to show us specific things He knew needed changing in our organizations. After listening to God speak to us from Romans 12, we prayed together as officers of our individual circles about what God had shown us. Then, just before our day apart was over, we gathered and asked our secretary to take notes as we shared all the things God had said needed to be changed in our circles. Those ladies bombarded our secretary with the ideas God gave them:

Circle officers should meet before each meeting to ask God's guidance.

Pray about purpose of our circles.

Do what *God* says to do.

Make inactive members feel wanted.

We must meet the needs of *all* ages in our circles.

Have a "Lord, change me" night in our circles next month.

Show compassion and love by doing kind deeds, invite, offer to pick up.

Postcards to tell them they were missed.

Help and teach, don't push.

Everyone has a talent; use it to make all feel needed.

I was so astounded at God's advice that when I got home I reread that portion wondering how He ever found some of those things in that passage to tell those ladies.

But the climax came when our shocked president looked in amazement at the women and then at a list she had dug out of her notebook. "Ladies, I have here a whole list of things I thought needed changing in your circles, and gripes from people who have wanted to see this or that changed; but I don't have to read it to you. God has told one or the other of you every single problem I have listed here and what should be done about it. I don't have to say a word!"

Yes, God had another exciting experiment for the "what-happens-when-women-pray" ladies of our church. And He had indelibly written on my heart how He can speak to specific personal and organizational needs without the president or pastor's wife saying a word. "If any of you lack wisdom, let him ask of God, who giveth to all men liberally" (James 1:5).

## A REALITY: 2 TIMOTHY 3:16

"All Scripture is given by inspiration of God, and is profitable for doctrine, for reproof, for correction, for instruction in righteousness" (2 Tim. 3:16).

Sometimes God stops us on something He wants changed in our beliefs only—in our doctrine. But most of the time He deals with the three other facets in this verse—what He wants changed *in our actions.*

God frequently uses this method of reading until He speaks for *reproof*—the process of exposing and convicting of things He is dissatisfied with in our lives. One woman kept coming to me at a retreat asking me what to do about her husband who was not assuming his role as spiritual head of the house. I used every scriptural approach I knew, but nothing seemed to provide the answer.

When I arrived home, I received a letter from her. She wrote, "Dear Evelyn: Please forgive me. I wasn't honest with you, so you couldn't possibly have known my real problem and given me the right answer. But when I was reading our assigned chapter, God stopped me on my real problem—a little three-letter word 'own.' I am the secretary for a pastor. He's my ideal. I get all of my spiritual insights and help from him. At the retreat God showed me while reading His Word that I should 'be in subjection to my *own* husband.'"

About six months later I was visiting in her church, and after the service I heard, "Here's Larry, Evelyn. Here's Larry, Evelyn."

"Who's Larry?" I wondered.

I looked up to see this woman with her *own* husband in tow, happily beaming at me. Then I remembered—he was her *own* husband, the now obvious spiritual head of her house.

A young convert had been invited to one of my retreats to be our Sunday School speaker. It was obvious from the beginning that she had come to show us that she had arrived spiritually and we had not. But at our Saturday night testimony meeting around the campfire, she stood up and said, "I would give anything if any one of you would take that Sunday School hour tomorrow morning. I came here

feeling so superior to you. But I took my Bible this afternoon as I was told and read God's Word. And," she said as
her voice choked, "He stopped me on the word 'humble-
ness,' and I know now that I came here because of pride.
God had to show me that He wanted me to be humble and
have humility. All I have is pride in my own self-attain-
ment. Please will one of you take that Sunday School hour
tomorrow morning?"

I was really shocked at a not-so-typical example of God
stopping at specific problems at one retreat. During our
sharing time there was absolute silence as four pastors'
wives stood up at different times and said, "My husband
left the pastorate (each said some time within the last 12
months), and God has told me out of His Word today that
it was all *my* fault." How God reaches down and puts His
finger of reproof right on the word or words we need.

It is interesting to watch God use *restoration to an upright state* from 2 Timothy 3:16 at our retreats. One Friday
night at a weekend retreat the wife of a seminary student
said her roommate was so angry that she was just about
kicking the furniture because her seminary-student husband
had received a call to a place to which she did not want to
go. She asked me if I would see if I could calm her down
and counsel with her.

"Let's wait until we read in God's Word tomorrow, and
see what *He* says to her," I suggested, and she agreed.

At sharing time the next day so many in the group were
stating that God stopped them in Galatians 5 concerning
the leading of the Holy Spirit, that I finally said, "Everybody
whom the Lord stopped on the Holy Spirit's leading and
their following, please stand up." To my surprise, the angry
wife of the night before stood up (with nearly half the whole
audience—another surprise). As she was telling us all about
it, I leaned over the pulpit and asked, "Does that mean to
so-and-so city too?"

"Yes, it does," she beamed back at me.

I didn't have to say a word. God had put His finger on her problem, and she had said in her heart she was willing to be changed into a willing follower of the Holy Spirit's leading.

A thank-you letter after a retreat said it so well, and only God could have known the need in her heart.

"Dear Evelyn: I'm so thankful for the Key '73 retreat. I learned what it means to have real joy! You see, I was raised in a Christian home, and I knew everything a Christian should do and be. I had it all in my head. But I found Him in my heart. God changed me that day, and I am so thankful. What impressed me was when you sent us out, alone, and without speaking, to read until He spoke to us."

Another note recorded the place God stopped one woman: "Galatians 6:2. 'Bear ye one another's burdens'—and the name of a specific person came to me immediately. Praise the Lord for His *living* Word."

*Instruction in righteousness* from God was evident in this note:

"Dear Evelyn: There wasn't time to share publicly, but my husband and I have considered adopting a child and adding to our family since we have the room and the money. . . . I wasn't sure if it was God's will or just our do-gooder thoughts. I now know that God thinks I can and should do this. James 1:27, 'The Christian who is pure and without fault, from God the Father's point of view, is the one who takes care of orphans and widows, and who remains true to the Lord'" (LB).

## 100 PERCENT OF US?

Every fall our church had a kick-off for our Christian Education administrators and paid staff who were to decide on the direction of their ministries for the coming year. In

September, 1970, I was asked to conduct a "Lord, Change Me" retreat for them. All the C.E. board members, departmental superintendents, the general Sunday School superintendents, staff, and pastors were there. I briefly explained the process of reading until God spoke to them and assigned Galatians 5:1–6:10, then sent them off alone to read.

When we came back together we knelt to share in prayer what God had told each of us. Something astounding began to emerge: person after person prayed about God stopping him or her on some thought concerning the importance of the Holy Spirit's leading in the Christian Education activities in our church. It soon became evident that God had stopped every single administrator and staff person on the same principle—let the Holy Spirit lead. My pastor husband and our assistant pastor, Gary Smalley, were kneeling side by side. When the pattern took shape and included where God had stopped them also, they both put their heads in their hands and wept!

Even more amazing than the fact that God speaks to all individually is that He speaks to many collectively about the same thing. Every time I assign this portion in Galatians, never fewer than 50 percent and up to 100 percent of the participants are stopped on the passage dealing with the Holy Spirit's leading. And this always is absolutely without any instruction as to what they are to look for or expect from God. Whenever this happens, I feel a sense of holy awe sweeping over me. God's *instruction in righteousness*—showing us the direction He wants us to go!

## WRITE GOD A LETTER

Frequently at our retreats, after God has spoken to us through His Word, we write Him a letter. We tell Him what we will change in our lives because of what He has pointed out to us. After having each one seal his letter to God in a self-addressed envelope, I collect the letters and keep them for about a month. Then I put them in the mail so the writer can check up on herself to see if she really *did change*—or if she forgot and went on in the same old condition.

I always "read until" with the others at retreats, and here is one letter I wrote:

"Dear God: You told me that I am hung up on not really accepting 'that person' back into the fellowship of the beloved, and that I am to restore that person who was overtaken in a fault—lest I, Evelyn, should be tempted like that—even though I don't think that is one of my weaknesses. I will restore that person in every possible way. Lord, open doors, make me comfortable around that person again."

The very next day God honored my prayer, and arranged a surprise breakfast meeting. I keep that letter as a constant reminder of how *I* had to change in my attitude toward one who had slipped—of how God had told *me* to change and I had obeyed.

The changes come, however, not when God speaks but when we *obey* what He has told us. We are changed only when we *apply* to our lives what He has said.

A pastor and his wife were chatting with me at a conference last summer. She said, "After our 'Lord, change me' retreat, Evelyn, I went home and practiced letting the Lord change me according to what He had told me at your retreat. And it really worked. Now there is someone else I need to pray 'Lord, change me' about."

"There surely is," agreed her smiling husband.

## ALL-CHURCH PRAYER WEEK

Conduct an all-church prayer week with God speaking instead of people? To do this took courage, but the results of our "Lord, Change Me" prayer week in January, 1970, were fantastic. We observed a strict rule of no preparation, no leading. The week before, we trained all those who would be leading the groups. If they had not had an experience of God speaking personally to them from His Word, they were to find others to lead for them. We formed no new prayer meetings, but used only the existing classes, organizations, and boards of our church as groups.

Spreading this "Lord, change me" process to the whole church resulted in great things. One Sunday School superintendent said, "Every member of the C.E. board had been in a different preparation week prayer meeting, so our chairman had each share how God had already spoken and changed his life. Each one gave a specific request from his area; then we all prayed about it. Nobody was pulling for his pet project; all prayed only for what God wanted done through the C.E. board. There's a different feeling in the C.E. board now."

A woman who had been at the center of our church's prayer life for several years said, "As I walked into the church and saw the 'Silence, Please' signs, sensed the reverence and hush, and then saw the sanctuary set up for prayer with circles of chairs even on the platform, I felt as if something new was coming to our church." And it did. We used the "Lord,-change-me"-Bible-reading process and our "six S" prayer method—subject by subject, short prayers, simple prayers, specific prayer requests, silent periods, small groups. And we had almost 100 percent participation in audible prayer, and at least five times as many people attended as had ever come before.

Our children's worker said, "As a church staff, our feet really never touched ground as we led several training sessions a day during preparation week and watched hearts, attitudes, and lives change as God spoke and these leaders were being prepared by Him to lead prayer week meetings in their respective groups. By the time we got to our weekly church staff prayer meeting during prayer week, there was such a sense of God's presence that tears replaced audible praying."

The results of my 14 agonizing months of letting God change me privately can well be summed up in the words of our deacon chairman when he reported about that first all-church "Lord,-change-me" prayer week: "The tremendous problems we faced ceased to be problems because of prayer week. We found a unification of spirit that never had been in our board before. Our meeting ended with all of us standing in a circle, holding hands, and singing 'Blest Be the Tie That Binds'—with tears flowing. God moved in that meeting. It was 'preparation week,' with God preparing hearts, that made the difference. I think every church meeting should be run like this."

# 4

## *Changed—*
## *When I Study*
## *God's Word*

"SHOULD I LET God change me through devotional reading or Bible study?" That is not a fair question, because *both* are essential for a well-rounded, transformed life. Devotional reading is never a substitute for deep, systematic Bible study—but it is a complement to it. And the Lord does change me *when I study His word.*

Paul gave Timothy excellent advice when he said, "Study to show thyself approved unto God" (2 Tim. 2:15). He also counseled him to: "Remember that from early childhood you have been familiar with the sacred writings which have power to make you wise and lead you to salvation through faith in Christ Jesus. Every inspired Scripture has its use for *teaching* the truth and *refuting* error, or for *reformation of manners and discipline in right living,* so that the man who belongs to God may be efficient and equipped for good work of every kind" (2 Tim. 3:15–16, NEB, italics mine).

I'm so grateful that God did not ask me to give up teaching when I prayed, in June 1968, that He would make

188

me the kind of wife He wanted me to be, for this would have deprived me of great joy. Digging into the Bible always produces a joy and an excitement that *changes* me into a different person. My spiritual barometer, 1 John 1:4, applies here, "These things [are written] . . . that your joy [might] be full." Even if I'm willing to be changed by what God is teaching me, the end result is always joy. Deep Bible study also produces spiritual maturity—Christlikeness—in me.

One of the guidelines we gave to each participant of Key '73 neighborhood Bible studies was "The purpose of this study is for us to find our life-style out of God's Word. This will include accurately observing what the Bible really says and applying it to our daily lives."

This chapter is not intended to be an in-depth guide on how to study the Bible. Its purpose is to show how life-changing a thorough study of God's Word can be.

## PRE-STUDY PRAYER

As I study God's Word, approximately one third of the study time is spent in prayer. This prayertime is divided into four categories: before the study, while observing what the Scripture really says, while interpreting what it means, and when applying it to myself or those whom I'm teaching.

Just approaching my study time in prayer *changes me.* First, I pray about my personal preparation. Praying for *cleansing* before starting to study establishes a clear communication with God. Then expressing in prayer the hunger and thirst after righteousness that I feel in my heart assures me of "God's filling" (Matt. 5:6).

Next, it is important for me to pray, "*Lord, remove all preconceived ideas* about this portion of Scripture I am about to study." It is always possible that something I have heard or studied previously has not been correct. Praying for God to remove all preconceived ideas (for the study time) will enable Him to reveal fresh insights to me. I let my spirit soar as I thrill at new thoughts from His Word!

I also pray that God will *take control* of the study time so that all observations, interpretations, and applications will be *truth*. I must acknowledge my dependence upon Him if I want accurate, powerful, life-changing lessons for myself or those I will be teaching.

Then, *I ask God to be my Teacher*, inviting the Holy Spirit to be operative in me as I study. In John 14:26 Jesus said that the Holy Spirit would "teach you all things." Also, Paul prayed for the Christians at Ephesus that God would give them "the Spirit of wisdom and revelation in the knowledge of Him, the eyes of [their] understanding being enlightened" (Eph. 1:17–18). The Bible is more than a textbook of poetry, history, psychology, law, and letters; it is a living, personal message from God's heart to our hearts! And studying it thoroughly, deeply, and systematically produces *changed* people.

A good Bible study always includes three elements: *observation, interpretation*, and *application*. And as I diligently practice each part, God *changes me*.

## I. OBSERVATION

### A. For Teachers

A great change comes over me as a teacher when I admit my fallibility. Having prayed for God to remove all my preconceived ideas, I am thereby made teachable. Then as I read the Scripture portion to be studied, I *observe* carefully what it really says, admitting the possibility of incorrect or incomplete preconceived ideas.

Since my experience in Hebrews 12 when Judy died, I am convinced that God not only allows suffering but that He sends chastenings our way. It is He who is doing the chastening. But because this is an unpopular truth with many Christians, I found myself at one time watering down this concept to "God allowing, not sending" in order to accommodate them. But while studying for my Bible class in 1 Peter, I was greatly relieved to observe the phrase: "Them that suffer according to the will of God" (4:19). This observation changed me into a much more confident teacher—having found confirmation of what God had taught me years before. So many of our ideas are built on what we think the Bible says, rather than on what it actually does say.

As I studied for that Bible class God gave me some additional help in 1 Peter 3:1 for my 14 months of living "without a word" before my daughter in 1968. For the first time I noticed how that verse started: "In the same way" (NASB) which referred me back to something that came before. (This is like "therefore," showing what a statement is "there for.") As I checked the preceding verses, I found that wives are to act in the same manner as Jesus did in His suffering. He, who did no sin and in whose mouth was found no guile, didn't retaliate when He was reviled or threaten when He suffered. No, Jesus just committed Himself to God who judges righteously (2:22–23). I had additional changing to do—to become more Christlike.

Then as I passed this observation on to my class members, two of them, whose husbands were being unfaithful, also saw God's answer for their own needs. When they reacted in a way that pleased God, they too could commit themselves and their problems to Him, the faithful and righteous Judge.

Pronouns are particularly tricky little words; they can tell us a whole story, for example: on Resurrection morning the angel, talking to the women at the tomb, said, "Remember how He [Jesus] spoke unto you when He was yet in Galilee, saying, 'The Son of man must be delivered into the hands of sinful men, and be crucified, and the third day rise again'" (Luke 24:6–7). That "you" tells us a whole story: (1) The women traveled with Jesus and ministered to Him

191

in Galilee. (2) Jesus gave this teaching to the women (the angel doesn't mention the men to whom this most likely was given also). (3) Jesus taught the women directly while they traveled with Him to Jerusalem. (4) Jesus entrusted the women with some very important teaching. This little pronoun refuted several of my preconceived ideas about the place of women in the ministry of Jesus and changed my thinking considerably.

Plural pronouns can be enlightening. By observing the "us" in 2 Corinthians 2:11 I saw that Paul was talking about *himself* and the Christians at Corinth. "Lest Satan should get an advantage of us." I then realized that if Paul wasn't safe from the toehold of Satan in his relationship with the Corinthian Christians, I had better be a little more alert. Changed by a plural pronoun!

A teacher can get an accurate understanding of a situation by observing verbs. In Matthew 14:22 we read that "Jesus constrained His disciples to get into a ship and to go before Him unto the other side." Since Jesus deliberately sent His disciples into the storm, I reassessed my attitude toward the storms in my life. Does Jesus deliberately send me into storms so that I, too, can see the miracle of His walking on the water and the storm stilled?

Then again the little verb "drove" encompassed a whole theological truth. In Mark 1:12 we observe that "the Spirit immediately drove Him [Jesus] out into the wilderness" (RSV). And He was there 40 days, tested by Satan. Again my preconceived idea had to be changed by one little verb. The Spirit didn't *hinder* Him from going, didn't *allow* Jesus to go; no, the Spirit *drove* Jesus to His temptation by Satan.

Another important rule for teachers to follow is: "Read the Scripture portion *before* reading any lesson helps. Carefully observing all God's Word has to say in the study enables teachers to evaluate lesson helps and commentaries in the light of the Scriptures."

Unless we actually observe first what the Scripture says,

we are apt to accept gullibly all the teachings in other books—right or wrong, and be changed by them—right or wrong.

Accurately observing everything God says in an assigned portion of Scripture is the opposite of teaching by the piece-meal method, where a teacher skips through the Bible, taking a verse or part of a verse to prove a point. (This may be an acceptable method if each section has been carefully studied in context and if the premise to be proved is scrip-turally accurate.) Isolated phrases and sentences put together at a teacher's whim can be made to prove almost anything.

My neighbor was evaluating some Bible class study samples I had given her, and said to me, "We chose this one because it takes a portion of Scripture and teaches what it says. We don't like to jump around. If I took a bunch of letters from someone, cut out sentences here and there, and put them together the way I wanted, I could prove anything I cared to!"

While teaching this process to some senior highers, I evidently got a little carried away with my proving, for after Sunday School I received a phone call from an upset father. "What do you mean teaching our son that all the demons will be saved?" I hurried to explain that I was teaching the young people how *not* to prove something about demons. I had put three "pieces" of Scripture together—all true in their proper setting—and thereby "proved" that all demons will be saved.

1. "I know Thee who Thou art, the Holy One of God" (unclean spirit's words in Mark 1:24).

2. "The demons also believe, and tremble" (James 2:19).

3. "Believe on the Lord Jesus, and thou shalt be saved" (Acts 16:31).

Even the Scriptures themselves can be used to change us in a way that is contrary to God's truth and His will if we don't observe accurately what they say, all they say, and in context. We can be changed—incorrectly.

## B. For Those I Teach

Lorna and Signe, my two prayer partners at that time, and I prayed for two years that I might teach a neighborhood Bible study class. But I had some changing to do before God would allow me to teach. I had to learn that the pupils, too, had the right to observe what God was saying to them and not to rely solely on what their teacher said. If I had used my lecture method, I would have given them what God had taught me through His Word instead of allowing them to discover for themselves what the Bible teaches. When I learned at last that the purpose of a Bible study is to let God be the Teacher, He gave me a wonderful class to teach every week.

When we came together in Ruth's living room, we first of all prayed that God would remove our preconceived ideas so that He could speak to our specific needs.

Then we read individually—silently—the Scripture we were to study that day, so that the teacher or whoever else might be reading aloud would not emphasize the words *they* wanted stressed. I offered no hints as to what God might say to them.

And this wasn't just a casual reading. It was the process described in James 1:25 of "looking into the perfect law of liberty" which meant seeking, desiring, longing for, as when Mary "looked" into the empty tomb that first Easter morning.

We had women from all denominations and walks of life in that Bible study, but none of them was a skilled Bible student. When they finished reading after our second lesson I asked, "Did God say anything to you that you didn't know before?" And 100 per cent of them said "yes" with gusto.

Later, after the reading, I introduced the teaching with, "What did God tell you?" They exploded with excitement. One lady tried to count on her fingers all the things God had said, but she didn't have enough fingers. I almost lost control of the group as they all talked at once. *They* had been taught by God!

Early in the study I learned how to make those who had never studied the Bible before feel that they were a part of the discussion. I would ask them the "observation" question and, just from reading carefully, they would be able to answer intelligently on what the Scripture had really said.

We had one very quiet member who sat through our first few lessons too shy to say a word. But all at once God spoke to her through the simple three-letter word "saw." The fact that Jesus "saw" people burst upon her—how *He saw* Peter and Andrew and James and John. Then she commented that she was at the Bible study because so-and-so "saw" her and asked her to attend, but moved away before the study started. But another person "saw" her and picked her up and brought her here to study the Bible. After almost twenty minutes she stopped abruptly and apologized for monopolizing so much time. She had gained insight into Scripture—just by observing a little verb!

A teacher is humbled when God speaks dramatically to the class before she even gives her introductory remarks. That happened to me as I asked my usual, "Did God say anything to you?" question, and one member said, "Yes, He did."

"What did He say?"

"He said that I didn't know the Scriptures. Well, that's why I'm here—because my church doesn't teach the Bible and I want to learn the Scriptures. But God also said, 'You don't know the power of God either!'" (cf. Mark 12:24)

"Would you like to know the power of God?"

"Yes, I would."

"Right now?" (After all, we hadn't even *started* the lesson yet, and it certainly wasn't time for application.)

"Yes, right now." And before I even started to teach she bowed her head and accepted Jesus as her Saviour. *Changed*— just by observing the Word. Yes, God had some *changing* to do in me with this method of Bible study as well as in the pupils I was teaching.

Another important fact to *observe* while studying God's Word is "to whom a portion of Scripture is written." It makes a lot of difference who needs to be changed and also who is eligible to apply the Scripture to his life. At a Bible study in St. Paul, a woman observed "the eyes of your understanding being enlightened" from Ephesians 1:18.

"My family is not getting along well. How can the eyes of my understanding be enlightened so I will know how to run it better?"

"To whom did we learn this book was written?"

"To the saints which are at Ephesus and to the faithful in Christ Jesus" (Eph. 1:1).

"Are you a saint—one who knows Jesus as personal Saviour? Are you *in* Christ Jesus?"

"No."

"Then you are not eligible for what Paul was praying for."

And at that she decided to accept Christ—right there!

A well-known Christian author and speaker said to me, as we were discussing the way God speaks so specifically out of His Word, "Do you mean to tell me that somebody can find Christ just by reading the Bible?"

"Yes, sir, it really works."

## II. INTERPRETATION

If I'm going to understand and interpret the Bible accurately, I must spend time studying its meaning in addition to observing what the text says. I must rely on Bible scholars for word meanings from original manuscripts and for information on how the cultural setting influenced what was written.

Also, God has spoken to Christians down through the ages, and my failure to study what He has revealed to them makes me poor indeed. I am immeasurably richer when

196

I learn from them, and am inspired by the insights they have gleaned. The Early Church learned these things immediately, for we find in Acts 2:42 that the new Christians "continued steadfastly in the *apostles' doctrine* and fellowship, and in breaking of bread, and in prayers."

And years later Paul admonished young Timothy to "give attendance to reading, to exhortation, to doctrine" (1 Tim. 4:13). In the interpretation we study in depth the meaning of a passage. Minimum study aids include a good commentary, a Bible dictionary, a Bible atlas, and a scholarly dictionary for word study.

God changes me into a *disciplined* person when I obey the command of 2 Timothy 2:15: "Study to show thyself approved unto God, a workman that needeth not to be ashamed, rightly dividing the Word of truth." To study takes discipline. Research is hard work, and time-consuming. It demands a reassessment of priorities—the giving up of some shopping trips, coffee parties, entertainment and recreation—some "good" but not "best" things.

Prayer at this point is essential. In order to be changed by my study the way God wants me to change, I pray, asking God to guard my mind as I read. Just because something is in print doesn't make it true. Then I pray for God to help me be selective. "Lord, lead me to just the books You want me to study." Indiscriminate reading of every book on a subject may not be good stewardship of my time, so I ask Him to show me what will be relevant to me and to those I will be teaching. Then I pray for His wisdom in interpreting and understanding the correct meaning. My greatest insight frequently comes not from reading but from praying.

But there must be a *proper balance* between inspiration and perspiration. I used to bring home all the reference books from my pastor husband's library for the study of next Sunday's lesson, stack them on the dining room table (the pile usually was at least two feet high), and systematically

197

wade through them all that week. Then, after up to 25 hours of study, by Saturday I was ready to put the gleaned wisdom into outline form, dash it off to the church secretary to be mimeographed for the class members, and then go home to pray, "Dear God, please bless my notes."

I asked God to change that procedure, and He did. He taught me there was a proper balance between what other people had to say and what He had to say. A seminary senior, in tears, confided to me, "I've dissected the Scriptures so long that they don't say anything to me any more." My college botany professor gave us some profound advice: "Remember, after you do enough dissecting, you no longer have a flower."

But there is also the danger of all observation with little or no perspiration. By striking a happy medium and not neglecting either, God produced a good balance for me. To maintain this balance, I developed a *work sheet* on which I systematically recorded the various aspects of my lesson preparation. In three vertical columns I recorded: (1) my observations, (2) the meaning to those to whom the passage was written and the meaning to us, today, and (3) application for me and those I teach. This assured me of change through all aspects of study.

Interpretation of the Scripture portion is divided into two categories: (A) What it meant to those it was written to, and (B) What it means today.

## A. What It Meant to Those to Whom It Was Written

God changes my attitude toward Bible teachings when I understand their actual meanings. The meanings of words change through the years, and only by relying on scholars who have studied original meanings can I be assured of accurate understanding. Comparing several of the good translations is helpful also. To insure accurate instruction I must remember that paraphrases are good, understandable Bible helps, but not literal translations. I also keep in mind to whom the portion was written. Does 1 John 1:8 apply to non-Christians, or was it written only to Christians? And when the psalmist prayed, "Take not Thy Holy Spirit from me" (51:11), he was writing before Pentecost, so that it is not a way I ask God to change me today. Then, too, I must not assume that I can be changed by the study of only one portion of Scripture on a certain theme. I must study all His Word teaches on that subject, and not insist on being changed only by my "pet" Scripture.

## B. What It Means to Us Today

Only in the light of what the Scripture meant to those to whom it was written can I know accurately what it should mean to me today. We tend to interpret God's commands and instructions in the light of culture trends in the church and in our world. When I started teaching my first neighborhood Bible study I had to deal almost immediately with the cultures of different churches.

When someone asked the question, "What is sin?" the answers started flowing. "My church believes you can have one cocktail at a wedding reception." . . . "My church allows alcoholic beverages for all adults." . . . "My church only allows beer and wine." . . . "We don't believe in any alcohol!" After agreeing to the rule that we would take as authoritative only what the Bible said and not what churches believed, the problem disappeared.

Then we are prone to put the emphasis on "today," thinking that the moral climate of the age somehow influences what God demands of us. I remember hearing sermons condemning television sets when they first came out, and my husband recalls as a little child his grandfather storming into his home after his father had bought the first radio in the neighborhood, saying, "Well, I never thought I'd see my son on the way to hell." But attitudes change. Most of those who once violently condemned movies now sit glued to their TV sets as old reruns flash right into their living rooms.

God gave our Nancy a good answer to this problem when she was a teenager.

"Mother, is what was sin when you were a girl still sin?"

"Where are you reading in God's Word these days?" I asked.

"Ephesians."

"Let's take that Book and see what God says."

So, as we had done many times before, we both read silently until He stopped one of us. Suddenly Nancy said, "Stop. God gave me the answer in verse 4."

"What did He say?"

"'That we should be holy and without blame before Him.' It doesn't make any difference whether we lived at the time Christ was on earth or a 100 years ago, or whether we live today, we are to be blameless and acceptable in His sight."

God's standard does not change; His yardstick of perfection is not shortened by years or culture; His purpose to conform me to the image of Christ is the same yesterday, today and forever. When I know what God's instructions really meant to those to whom they were written, I can apply the same truths to my life today.

## III. APPLICATION

The real change in me comes when I take the truths I have observed and studied and *apply* them to my life. Only when I apply the Scripture does God do the actual changing in my thinking and my actions.

There are reasons for reading the Bible historically, for an overview of a book or the whole Bible; but the real life-changing comes when we apply, one by one, the precepts that He tells us. "Precept upon precept; line upon line" (Isa. 28:10).

I had been teaching the same Sunday School class of sharp young adults for about 12 years when an unsettling thought

200

started gnawing away at me: "Are those people any different because of all my hours of perspiring in lesson preparation?" Oh, they were a great group, and I would come away from the class with a heady sense of exhilaration from the lively give-and-take discussion on deep biblical subjects. In fact, that class was one of the joys of my life.

But the gnawing persisted—was actually growing—were they really different because of all my efforts?

Then the officers and I met to plan the year's program and curriculum. And I dropped the bomb. "I'm not going to teach this class any more unless I see more evidence that the Scriptures are actually changing lives."

The only audible response was the swallowing of the others in the room. The stunned silence didn't deter me. I launched our paragraph study of the Book of Mark with a new determination. Either they would let God *change* them by what we were studying from His Word, or I was finished as their teacher!

After a couple of months, one Sunday morning I announced to the class that, instead of studying that day's lesson, I wanted them to share with all of us exactly how God had changed them by specific lessons we had studied. It didn't take long to see that God had been at work. One after another stood to share what God had changed in them because of specific Scriptures we had studied. My apprehension and fears were over. They *had* let God change them. Then Bill, our class president, looked at me and said rather meekly, "Did we tell you enough so you'll keep teaching, Ev?"

I remember the advice on counseling that Dr. Henry Brandt gave to the international leaders at Expo '72: "Only listen till the people coming for counseling mention a scriptural precept they're violating. Stop their conversation and give them the scriptural answer. Then send them off, telling them not to come back for more advice until they have *lived and applied* that answer."

During one of my neighborhood Bible studies, the women all were suffering some deep personal or family trial. But as we studied the book of First Peter, we found an amazing thing happening. God gave answers *to live by* week after week to those who seemed to need help the most. I watched as they observed that those early Christians were suffering for a season but were to rejoice as the testing of their faith was preparing them for Jesus' return (1 Peter 1:6–7). The women's attitude toward their problems changed as they applied this truth. They actually learned to smile again.

Most of the women were enduring undeserved suffering (2:20), which was being caused by another family member. And I watched them change from being resentful, defensive and wanting to retaliate to TAKING IT PATIENTLY because it was acceptable to God, and because Christ was their Example of suffering although innocent of wrongdoing. They applied what they studied.

But they were also watching for changes in me, their teacher, for I too was going through a deep family trial. One day while studying the lesson, 1 Peter 4:19, "Wherefore let them that suffer according to the will of God *commit* the keeping of their souls to Him," I discovered that the word translated "commit" was the same word as was translated "commend" in Luke 23:46. Jesus, agonizing as He gave up His spirit on the cross, cried with a loud voice and said, "Father, into Thy hands I commend My spirit." How God lifted my burden as I applied that truth to my own life! Although my suffering was so small compared to that of my Christ on the cross, I, with Him, committed the keeping of my soul to God. And He changed me.

I cannot expect those I teach to be changed by applying God's Word if I have not been changed by it first. But that is exactly what happens when I study His Word. The observations are thrilling, the studying is exhilarating, but the *change* comes when I personally apply what the Scripture means to my everyday life. The "Lord, change me" comes when I let His Words abide, take up their residence, in me (John 15:7). The change comes when I am a doer of the Word and not a hearer only (James 1:22–25). For when I look into the Bible and do not apply it, I am like a person beholding my face in a mirror and immediately forgetting the mess I see. But when I look into God's Word and do what it says, then I am changed into a blessed person. Changed—when I study His Word.

# 5
## Changed—
## When the
## Holy Spirit Reminds

---

MANY TIMES GOD wants to change me now when I'm reading or studying His Word, or when I'm with a group "reading until He speaks." But when I find myself in a situation where I need help immediately, then the Holy Spirit brings to my mind the Scripture that meets my need at that moment. One of the primary reasons for reading and studying the Bible is to provide Him with the Word to bring to our remembrance—*when we need it.*

Jesus said: "These things have I spoken unto you, being yet present with you. But the Comforter, who is the Holy Spirit, whom the Father will send in My name, He shall teach you all things, and bring all things to your remembrance, whatsoever I have said unto you" (John 14:25–26).

Now, some of the disciples would be recording the words of Jesus in some of the books of the New Testament. What a word of assurance this must have been for them. But was this promise of the Spirit's prompting given only to Peter, John, Matthew, and the other disciples who were with Jesus

204

at that time? I think not. Prisoners of war and others who have had Bibles taken from them tell fantastic stories of the Holy Spirit recalling for them the Scriptures they had learned previously. This is one of the most powerful ways God has used the Scriptures down through the ages.

One of the surprises that came out of my analysis and the underlined and dated verses in my three Bibles was that frequently the verse didn't have any immediate specific meaning to me. But when there was a need sometime in the future, the Holy Spirit pulled from my memory exactly the portion of Scripture that fitted the need.

We stay in the Bible, studying and reading devotionally, being taught by God so that the Holy Spirit can bring to our remembrance what He has told us. We tell our children that they can't expect God to help them recall answers on a test if they have never studied the material in the first place. Neither can we expect God to bring to our remembrance answers to our needs if we have not stored His truth in our hearts.

A couple of years ago I was fretting because I was remembering less and less as I grew older. But in a moment the Holy Spirit kindly reminded me of this verse on His bringing all things to our remembrance—His way of dealing with old age! Then I thought back on the chat I had with 82-year-old Corrie ten Boom the month before. "Evelyn," she said, "I never forget spiritual things."

## THAT I MIGHT NOT SIN

I view with awe my neighbor across our cul-de-sac who is working on the world's largest computer. My mind is boggled as he tells of the one million words it can work on at a time and the billions of facts its memory banks can store. But we as human beings possess the world's most sophisticated and complex memory banks—our minds—and they store up all the information acquired by us from infancy.

The psalmist says: "Thy Word have I hid in mine heart, that I might not sin against Thee" (Ps. 119:11). This is the process of tucking the Word of God deep down in our hearts by study and memorization. As we read the Bible, study it, and listen to sermons from it, we are not to dismiss what God says to us, but are to *hide* those spiritual truths in the deepest recesses of our hearts.

But those of us who know the pain of trying to recall some of the information we stored there as a child (even the *old* math), the college material that produced an "A" grade, or even a recipe that seemed so simple 20 years ago, realize the inadequacy of our human memory systems. As human operators we are frequently unable to bring forth even a tiny bit of stored information. But when we need to recall a particular spiritual truth, we have a supernatural computer operator—the Holy Spirit!

When I recognize there is something wrong in my life and I know God wants to change me, I feed the problem into the computer of my mind. Then, when I ask God to give me a solution, the Holy Spirit often *reminds* me of a portion of Scripture—a verse or a single word—that shows me the specific sin that is causing my problem. Many times He flashes back: "pride" (Rom. 12:3) or "worry" (Phil. 4:6).

Occasionally, before I'm even aware that something is wrong, or before I know there is a problem to feed into my computer, my Supernatural Operator is already spelling out an answer to me. He knows the need or the problem before I ask, before I consciously formulate it into words. Jesus said in Matthew 6:8 that our heavenly Father knows what things we have need of *before* we ask Him, and the solution is recalled from my memory bank before I spell out my need. That's even less time than the 1.2 microseconds this largest computer in the world takes to summon answers! Yes, before I even realize my sin, the Holy Spirit is reminding, prodding, reproving with His gentle nudge or stating in no uncertain voice, "That's SIN!"

Our Supernatural Operator, the Holy Spirit, never makes a mistake. In one of our Kurt's junior high classes where the computer forms had the classifications "male," "female," and "other," some shocked students were classified as "other" by the not-too-friendly computer. And how I recall the agony of all the "Christensons" getting mixed up on the computer of our city's largest department store, just before our Jan's wedding. With all the shopping we had to do, we were suddenly lost from the face of the earth. And how embarrassed our senior high daughter felt when her school's computer assigned her to a boys' gym class! But the Holy Spirit never makes an error. Even when we feed in the wrong problem, He comes up with exactly the right answer for our specific need.

Reminding me of a scriptural answer when I ask for it, or even before I ask, is one of the methods the Holy Spirit uses to "reprove of sin," as Jesus mentioned in John 16:8. The psalmist in Psalm 119:11 gives the "why" for hiding God's Word in our hearts: "Thy Word have I hid in mine heart, *that I might not sin against Thee.*" How else could God's Word, hidden, unseen, perhaps even forgotten, keep me from sin except that the Holy Spirit *recalls* it? This is the supernatural process of the Holy Spirit, more accurate than any computer that will ever be invented by man, reaching down and *recalling* for me exactly the answer I need from God's Word at the very time I need it.

My Spiritual Operator, the Holy Spirit, has a favorite one He spells out for me: "B-E Y-E H-O-L-Y; F-O-R I A-M H-O-L-Y" (1 Peter 1:16).

I hid this verse in my heart many years ago, and I'm surprised it isn't worn out from God's flashing it at me so often. But it gets to me every time. I immediately see my God high and lifted up, *holy*—perfect attitudes, actions, and reactions.

And what I've stored in my memory bank from His Word comes clicking back to me. And I know how holy God is— and how holy I'm expected to be! Recalled—to keep me from sinning.

I remember one day while on vacation at our cottage I had a sudden eye-contact with a man. I flushed slightly, enjoying his obvious approval of me. The next morning I asked God to enlighten my understanding of the sin of this type of encounter. Slowly, as if on a screen in my mind, the words "Be ye holy; for I am holy" came forward until they were in focus. I asked God for complete cleansing, and immediately I was *changed*. Communing with God as He gave me several pieces of wisdom for my next book, I was suddenly engulfed with adoration of Him. Welling up from the depths of my being, flowing into every inch of my body was the prayer, "Oh, God, how good is vacation! Time to drink deeply of Your Word, to read good Christian books. Time to adore You rather than working under the tyranny of the urgent." Changed when the Holy Spirit recalled His "old faithful" verse.

## TO COMFORT ME

The Holy Spirit causes me to remember not only to keep me from sinning but also to supply needs in my life. When I find myself in adverse situations, He provides the Scripture I need to comfort me.

The night before I was to speak four times at a retreat high up in the Rocky Mountains, I was reading my Bible and these words spoke to me, "For He shall give His angels charge over thee, to keep thee in all thy ways" (Ps. 91:11). Angels? Why did I need angels when I was securely tucked into a warm bed in a nice private trailer?

But the next morning I woke cold and miserable. The electricity, and thus my electric heater, had gone off in the night; and, although it was only September, the first snow of the season had just fallen. Adding to my misery was a hard case of intestinal flu with its accompanying chills. Shivering violently, I piled all the blankets and coats in sight on me, trying to get warm. Then the Holy Spirit suddenly recalled for me the verse I had read the night before. "Angels? Wow, do I ever need them right now!" And just the thought of God sending His angels to hover and watch over me in that room changed me—warmed my spirit and made those difficult circumstances easier to take. His miracle of making me well enough to speak all that day was to come later, but right then I needed the assurance and comfort of the Scripture the Holy Spirit recalled.

While we were traveling overseas a few years ago, I came down with a severe infection in Jerusalem. As I was lying all alone in my hotel bed, looking out on the Mount of Olives, the Holy Spirit reminded me of Romans 8:28, and I knew that even missing the tour that day was being worked out by God for my good. Then He brought to my remembrance some of the lessons from God's Word that I had tucked down in my heart years before. Again, Romans 8:28—He brought good from the loss of those three pregnancies right after we were married. Then from Hebrews 12—the chapter that was so real to me at the time of Judy's death—He had taught me that even her death was for *my profit*. Lying there, I let God speak afresh about those lessons from His Word of yesteryears.

Surprisingly, instead of lying there rebelling at missing the tour to Bethlehem that day, I found my spirit soaring to the heavenlies with God—*changed*! He enveloped me with a tremendous sense of His presence—caring for, and speaking to me, personally. I spent hours listening to "Jerusalem sounds"—a cock crowing in the morning, a donkey braying in the distance—and had the unspeakable thrill of seeing the rising sun burst over the Mount of Olives, just as it must have done that first Easter morning! And God proved that the Scriptures He was recalling would work again.

Later in the week I was given a tour of Bethlehem by private car, and when I returned to Jerusalem I had the wonderful privilege of spending an hour alone in the Garden of Gethsemane, communing with my Lord.

## FOR TEACHING OTHERS

The Holy Spirit frequently brings to my remembrance Scripture I have hidden in my heart so that I can teach others the truths God has taught me.

Back in 1957 I was scheduled to speak at a women's meeting but could not get a message I felt God wanted me to bring them; every idea I had seemed inadequate. In desperation I arose early on the morning of the day I was to bring the message and sought out my old green "prayer" chair. Prayer and searching of God's Word produced nothing. Finally, in exasperation, I laid aside my Bible and picked up the newspaper. The headlines stunned me. Russia had sent Sputnik I into outer space! The frenzied race to *conquer* outer space was on. (How foolish that word "conquer" sounds now.) President Eisenhower, astonished that the Russians had projectors and propellants which could cast that 184-pound object into outer space, gave a message of comfort and encouragement to the American people on the front page.

But almost immediately the Holy Spirit recalled a portion of Scripture that I had hidden deep in my heart when I had taught that book to my Sunday School class: "For by Him [Jesus] were all things created, that are in heaven, and that are in earth, visible and invisible, whether they be thrones, or dominions, or principalities, or powers; all things were created by Him, and for Him; and He is before all things, and by Him all things consist" (Col. 1:16–17).

I had my message! Jesus *made* outer space! He put the stars and planets, the sun and the moon in place! Jesus *holds* them all together! He makes them run on course according to His will! We are not to fear some nation that can make a little piece of hardware circling our planet. But we are to put our trust in the One who created all that outer space, the One by whom it all consists—Jesus!

Just by recalling a portion of Scripture, that whole shocking news item came into focus. It lost its horror. I could go to that meeting and tell those frightened women that our enemy had invaded outer space before us, but Jesus had been out there creating it and controlling it from eternity past! *Changed*—when the Holy Spirit brought just two verses to my remembrance.

The Holy Spirit recalled a precious portion when I was asked to speak to a women's Sunday School class in Ambo, Ethiopia. None of them understood English, and I wondered what we had in common that I could talk about. As I looked out the window of their church, I saw a mountain in the distance. And immediately the Holy Spirit brought to mind *my* mountain verses from Psalm 121. They understood mountains!

Slowly, with the help of an interpreter, I related the story of how God spoke to me on my mountain. I told them that after having a slight heart problem I had gone to a doctor to find out whether it was advisable for me to travel through the Rocky Mountains in Canada on my way to Vancouver, British Columbia. A group of us were traveling in a caravan of cars, and everything went fine until we reached our first mountain. Suddenly I had trouble breathing and my heart started to beat wildly. We stopped at a motel and, while the others went to a restaurant, I spent the time in bed, gazing out at huge Cascade Mountain, which seemed to go straight up from my bedroom window. "Oh, God," I prayed, "please give me just the Scripture You want me to read. I don't want to be sick and unable to go on to Vancouver. I don't want to break up this caravan. Please give me something from Your Word." Then God flashed Psalm 121:1–2 in my mind. I reached for my Bible and read: "I will lift up mine eyes unto the hills. From whence cometh my help? My help cometh from the Lord, who made heaven and earth" (sco).

Then I told those Ethiopian ladies, "I was looking up to the hills, but they hadn't helped me. In fact, they had caused my heart to act strangely. But there's a question mark after verse one; my answer was in the next verse. My help comes from the Lord who *made* those high mountains. Then I decided to trust God for all the strength I would need to get across those mountains, and right away my heart was OK." Changed!

I told those Ethiopian women that when it was time for devotions the next morning I had the caravan stop on another one of those big mountains, and we all sat down while I read my "mountain verses" to them, telling them of my trust in the God who made all the mountains and who made—and keeps—me. Yes, the Holy Spirit had recalled just the Scripture I needed to teach that Sunday School in Africa that morning.

I was happy that I had tucked some verse down in my heart when I was doing follow-up counseling after a city-wide youth evangelism week. On the last night the leader announced, "Mrs. Christenson will take all those who have finished their written follow-up books and teach them." My mind raced. How could I fill up a whole evening with teaching when all the subjects had been completed by these high schoolers? When a newspaper editor asked to interview a few of my young people, I silently thanked God for the few minutes I had to ask Him what I should tell them.

Then the Holy Spirit recalled several scriptural truths I could share. Changed, I confidently told them that their completed follow-up program didn't mean that the battle was over for them as new Christians (Eph. 6). I reminded them that although temptation would come their way, there is always victory in Jesus (Phil. 4:13), and from 1 John I showed them that when we *do* sin God will forgive us if

212

we confess it to Him (1 John 1:8–9). Then I shared how God would take all of these things, both good and bad, and work them all out for our good (Rom. 8:28).

When the evening was over, one of the other counselors came to me and said, "Whew! I'm glad he didn't give *me* that job. I don't even *know* those verses!"

How important it is to hide God's Word in our hearts so the Holy Spirit can recall it when we need to teach others. It is so great to keep sensitive to the Holy Spirit while teaching and speaking so that He can recall just the Scripture somebody in the audience needs.

### JUST FOR ME

Sometimes the Holy Spirit recalls Scripture that is just for me. I'm not going to teach or share it with anyone—it's just for me.

As we drove down to Bethlehem that day I was given a private tour, I prayed, "Lord, bring to my mind just the Scripture You want me to hear as I view the birthplace of my Saviour."

Looking at the shepherds' fields I expected to hear, "And suddenly there was with the angel a multitude of the heavenly host praising God" (Luke 2:13). But no Scripture came to my mind. And as we approached the town of Bethlehem, I waited for Him to recall Micah 5:2, "But thou, Bethlehem Ephratah." But there was nothing. I strained to hear God say something as we approached the Church of the Nativity—nothing. Then on the marble steps descending to the actual stable level—nothing. Breathlessly expectant, I stepped into the room where tradition states Jesus was born. Even as I pulled back the velvet wall hangings and touched the wall—there was still nothing. Regretfully, I walked up the stairs. Not one portion of Scripture recalled especially for me, from God in that precious spot. But as I stepped out into the sunlight of the courtyard once more—it hit! God

213

recalled a total surprise: "And the Word was made flesh, and dwelt among *us*, (and we beheld His glory, the glory as of the only begotten of the Father,) full of grace and truth" (John 1:14).

The emphasis the Holy Spirit conveyed was on the word "us." I recoiled as my mind went to "me" with my filled teeth, eyeglasses, infection, and recent surgery. Then I looked around at the hunger and pain so prevalent in the Holy Land. Among us? As I almost felt the dirt around me, I wondered at that "Holy Thing" announced by the angel to Mary, being born into this. Yes, a part of it through the birth process. He *dwelt* among *us*?

Then God took my mind back to the preceding verses in that first chapter of John. Jesus Christ, who was God, and who had been with God from the beginning—in heaven's perfect environment where there was no pain, sickness, or death—had come down to earth right at that spot and dwelt *among us*. What a new picture God had given me of my Jesus—not the traditional Babe in the manger—but the holy Son of God who loved me enough to come down here and dwell among us. I was completely *changed*—with a new and deep appreciation of my Saviour's sacrifice—for me!

I've heard of some awful things that are supposed to happen to parents when the last child leaves the nest. The divorce rate for parents in this category goes up, and many mothers fall into an "I'm-not-needed-any-more" depression. Just before leaving for college, our Kurt said to me, "I think this is harder on you than it is on me, Mother."

Two days after he left, Chris and I were driving along holding hands as we returned from a shopping trip that had carried us through what had been our family dinner hour with our children for 26 years. I squeezed his hand and smiled as I said, "Ye have not, because ye ask not" (James 4:2). The Holy Spirit had given us that verse for that weekend. And there had been some desperate "asking" as we saw Kurt's empty bed, the vacant spaces where his clock radio, stereo tuner, and desk lamp had stood, and as we "listened" to the silent bathroom that had resounded so vigorously every morning with splashing shower and buzzing electric comb.

On the last night of prayer together with Kurt, as we thanked God for the almost 18 years of joy, and then gave our son to God in a new and special way to make his own life outside our nest, I turned to a new kind of "asking": "Dear God, fill the void with Yourself," I prayed over and over. Then my prayer progressed, adding another dimension: "Dear Father, fill the void with *You and Chris.*"

The results were incredible. God filled my life to overflowing with Himself and His love through other people. And after reading about Joseph taking such good care of the infant Jesus and His mother Mary, I prayed, "Thank You, Lord, for the way Chris protects me and the security I have in him."

Later that week Chris and I traveled together as far as Denver where I was to speak. Before he took off for the rest of his journey to California, he sat on the edge of the bed and said to me, "I don't know or understand all that is happening to us, but I sure like it."

"Ye have not because ye ask not," said the Holy Spirit. And how right He was! I was a completely changed mother and wife—just because I obeyed the Scripture the Holy Spirit recalled.

## NUMBER ONE

But Romans 8:28 is by far the number one verse the Holy Spirit recalls for me. In fact, He has reminded me of it so often that I have finally adopted it as my philosophy of life: "And we know that all things work together for good to them that love God, to them who are the called according to His purpose." God gave that verse to me at the time I lost my third pregnancy during our college days. He must have known then how my whole life would revolve around that verse—though I certainly didn't know it at the time.

I used to have to struggle to find the "good" in the seeming calamities of my life, but sooner or later I was able to see what God was doing and why He was doing it. And more and more through the years I am able to see the "why" of circumstances as soon as the Holy Spirit says, "Romans 8:28." What used to take time to figure out, now seems to come almost immediately and automatically.

And it works 100 percent of the time. When something especially bad happens, when the roof caves in or the floor falls out from under me, the Holy Spirit still persists, "*All* things." I cannot accept it just 90 percent of the time or even 98 percent of the time. I must accept it *all* of the time. It was hard at first, but as the years have come and gone, it has become easier. I guess it's a matter of faith. As faith is exercised, it grows stronger and stronger. And the faith, of course, isn't in a verse or even a verse turned into a philosophy of life. The faith is in the God of that verse—the One who is working out all things for my good. And the Holy Spirit is really recalling not a verse, but all that God has worked out for me for 30 years.

One of the greatest ways God changes me is by bringing Scripture to mind I have hidden deep in my heart. And He always picks the right Scripture at the right time. What a reason for staying in His Word daily—reading, studying, devouring it. And then what a challenge to stay so sensitive to the Holy Spirit's speaking that He can reach down and recall just exactly what I need at the very minute I need it!

# 6

## *Exchange—*
## *When I Ask God*

ONE OF THE most direct ways God changes me is by answering my prayers for myself. When I ask Him to change some specific trait in me, He frequently lifts that thing out and replaces it with a quality that He desires me to have. As God removes an attitude, a personality trait, or some characteristic of my old nature, and puts in its place His own attribute, the process is a dramatic one. He does not add a little of His strength to my weakness, or a little of His forgiveness to cover my sin. No, there is an actual *exchange* that takes place within me.

And this exchange takes place when I ask Him in prayer. Of course, the key to this process is my *wanting* Him to change me. Now, God's methods aren't always painless, but the end result is an exchange within me, which leaves me with an unexplainable sense of well-being. It is a life-changing process that fills me with His peace, joy, and power—when I ask.

## STRENGTH FOR WEAKNESS

Often we ask God to change us, but then don't *wait* for Him to answer our prayer. A secret I learned many years ago is that God gives me some things only *when I wait*.

Recently in a series of hectic days I had an unusually strenuous one. I drove to Wisconsin for an all-day prayer seminar, lectured for six hours, and then drove back home to Minnesota. I had just one-half hour to cook my dinner, eat, and get back on the road for another two-and-a-half hour lecture. At bedtime, Chris, knowing my rigorous schedule, called me from his travels in Florida. "Just wanted to know how you made it through the day, Honey. How was it?"

"Oh, Chris, all I can say is that it was another miracle. By the time I had driven home from Wisconsin I was so exhausted that I could hardly raise my arms, my stomach was hurting, and it was hard to think straight. But—when I started to speak at Bethel College tonight, I suddenly felt as fresh as if I had had eight hours of sound sleep!"

What had happened? Before the evening seminar I took a few minutes to lie down and pray these words: "O God, *exchange* my exhaustion for Your strength." And it worked. God miraculously reached down, lifted my exhaustion, and then replaced it with His strength.

The same thing happened to me a few months ago at the Greater Los Angeles Sunday School Convention. The night before I left I had taught all evening, driven 50 miles, arrived home at midnight, and then had packed for the trip to Los Angeles. Early the next morning I flew out to California and dashed into the convention center just minutes before I was to speak. That evening I was scheduled to give my final lecture of that day at 8:30 P.M. California time. But that was 10:30 P.M. according to the time on which I was operating! Start again at 10:30? And continue lecturing until *my* 11:45?

During a short break between sessions, I dashed to my motel room, and suddenly realized that my staggering schedule had caught up with my body—my head felt fuzzy, and I was shaking all over. So I went to prayer—not just asking but desperately hanging on to God for help. Here again I practiced that threefold formula which never fails: 1. *Stop.* 2. *Ask.* 3. *Wait.* The results were fantastic. I bounced over to that final meeting and never felt a speck of fatigue all through the session!

Dr. Stephen Olford in his booklet, *The Secret of Strength,* explains that the word "renew" in Isaiah 40:31 ("They that wait upon the Lord shall *renew* their strength") actually means "the process by which the molting eagle *exchanges* its old feathers for new ones." We think of the renewing process as an addition of a little strength, but to God it is an actual replacement.

When we are fatigued, our tendency is to keep pushing and pushing, slower and slower, until we get the job done. But God's formula is so simple. And it takes such a short time to stop, ask, and wait. However, there is a key to this formula: Ask, and then wait expectantly. This requires *faith*— not in the few minutes I might have in which to rest, but in the *One* who is to provide the strength. Hebrews 11:6 explains it so clearly: "But without faith it is impossible to please Him; for he that cometh to God must believe that He is, and that He is a Rewarder of them that diligently seek Him." It is God who *exchanges* my fatigue for His strength. And He does it when I stop, ask in faith, and wait expectantly.

## THE MIND OF CHRIST FOR MY FALLIBILITY

Another exchange takes place in me when I acknowledge my inadequate ideas, my shortcomings or sinful attitudes, and ask God for the *mind of Christ.*

The first step in this process is to recognize that there is something more or something better than I am now experiencing. My needs can be difficult to detect, for my inadequate thoughts frequently disguise a deeper problem, my shortcomings often excuse inactivity, and sometimes my sins actually feel good. When I finally acknowledge that something is wrong, then I can *ask* for the mind of Christ.

The day before I started a prayer seminar in the largest Lutheran church in the world, my son-in-law phoned and said, "Do you want to hear a funny story?"

"Sure," I replied.

"Well, Jan and I were being entertained in a couple's home, and our hostess mentioned Pastor Lyndon Karo. 'How do you know him?' Jan asked in surprise. 'Oh I read about him in a book on prayer.' 'My mother wrote that book,' said Jan. 'Oh,' said our hostess as she glanced nervously around her house, 'if I had known, I would have cleaned my house better.'"

After Skip and I stopped laughing, he continued. "Then our hostess became quiet and preoccupied with her own thoughts. She blurted out, *'I feel as if I'm entertaining God.'"* And at that Skip and I roared with laughter. That surely was a funny story.

But when I hung up the phone, God said to Evelyn—pride! I dropped to my knees and pled with God to *give me the mind of Christ.* "O God, please forgive me for that terrible attitude. I'm sorry. Please give me the mind of Christ." Immediately God brought Philippians 2 to my mind. I knew what that portion said, but scurried for my Bible so I wouldn't miss a single word: "Let this mind be in you, which was also in Christ Jesus; who, being in the form of God, thought it not robbery to be equal with God; but made Himself of no reputation, and took upon Him the form of a servant" (vv. 5–7).

I was overwhelmed. Jesus *was God* (John 1:1). Jan wasn't God. I wasn't God—but Jesus, who actually was God, came to earth *as a servant.* My mind flashed to Mark 10:45 where Christ said of Himself that He "came not to be ministered unto, but to minister." This was the "mind of Christ" I was admonished to have in me—the mind Jesus had when He came to earth from heaven.

"O Lord," I cried, "change me. Make me *only a servant.* Please give me the mind of Christ." Immediately God answered. It seemed that He reached down and scooped out of me the attitude that must have been a stench in His nostrils. And flooding over me was an overwhelming sense of only being a servant. The next morning when I started my seminar in that large church and looked out over all those people, I had the most beautiful sense of being completely *their servant*—nothing more.

Pride over a funny story could have ruined the whole seminar, but God took that story and gave me what He really wanted me (and every Christian) to have—the mind of Christ. The mind of a Servant!

There are also other references in Scripture relating to the mind of Christ and the Christian. While I was teaching my neighborhood Bible study on 1 Peter, we as a class discovered much about suffering. In chapter 4, verse 19, we found that there are those who suffer according to the will of God. And in 3:17 we discovered that "it is better, if the will of God be so, that ye suffer for well-doing, than for evil-doing." And we were told in 1 Peter 2:20–21 that when we suffer for doing well and "take it patiently, this is acceptable with God." We are called to this because "Christ also suffered for us, leaving us an example, that ye should follow His steps." And I wrote in the margin of my Bible next to 1 Peter 4:1, "Lord, change *me*": "Forasmuch then as Christ hath suffered for us in the flesh, arm yourselves likewise with the same mind." As the teacher of the class, I also wrote by that verse, "key verse?" Is this the key to understanding the whole Book of 1 Peter? Yes, we are to arm ourselves with the mind of Christ so that we can see our suffering *as* He saw His.

Also, I found it interesting, and often disconcerting, to

discover the mind of Christ in the four Gospels. Most of the time His reactions were so different from what mine would have been, His attitudes so much more lofty than mine, His thoughts so far above my thoughts. But what a privilege actually to be *admonished* in Philippians 2 to have His mind *in* us.

Whenever I'm in doubt as to how God wants me to change, I am always safe in praying for the mind of Christ. So often I'm aware that my attitude, reaction, or thoughts are not Christlike, but am not sure exactly what God wants to substitute for them. But I never ask amiss, when I pray for *the mind of Christ.*

## PREPARED FOR MEETINGS

When I'm preparing to speak at a seminar, retreat, or a single meeting, I sometimes have trouble feeling a burden for the people to whom I'm to minister. Struggling to put myself in the right frame of mind usually proves useless, but I have learned what does work: asking God to exchange my attitude for His.

When one meeting follows hard on the heels of another and another and another, I occasionally find a lethargy setting in. Then, as I drive my car, or sit in an airplane winging my way toward a meeting, I pray, "Lord, give me a burden for these people. Please, God, take away this lethargy. Help me to feel Your burden." And God always answers that prayer. He *exchanges* my lethargy for His burden. I can feel it descend on me, almost like a weight, surrounding me and pressing from all sides. And I arrive at my destination completely prepared spiritually for the task He has given me.

I pray that same kind of prayer when I'm consumed by "the tyranny of the urgent." I find myself having to leave for a meeting in the middle of an important priority in my life. But it is time to switch gears, to let another priority have all of me. This is often difficult, but, again, I pray for God to *exchange* the urgency of one priority for what He wants me to feel for this new task. And it always works.

I could hardly face a new evening seminar series which was to start on January 3, 1977. In addition to being completely engrossed writing this book, I had spent the day in holiday cleanup and washing our son's clothes for his return to college. I finally took the hour before dinner to get alone with God in my bedroom, seeking a spiritual lift for the new series. Then as I left the house for the seminar a sense of my utter inadequacy swept over me, and I asked Chris to pray for me. Driving down the freeway just a few minutes later I prayed in desperation, "Lord, change me; take away this frustration. Give me joy. Make me what You want me to be at this seminar."

Almost immediately there flashed a tingle of excitement. It flooded into my whole body. I could feel it physically. Then a smile of joyous anticipation spread over my face. I pressed a little harder on the accelerator—all at once anxious to get there! God had lifted all those undesirable feelings from me and exchanged them for His attitude toward the meeting. And I faced that audience absolutely thrilled—and felt their excitement and anticipation in return.

Sometimes God answers a prayer for exchange in unexpected ways. I worked for a month preparing for a "God's Living Word" retreat (mentioned in chapter 2). Without any emotion I was typing into the message outlines the material I had culled from the three Bibles I had used devotionally since I was 18. Then I realized what I was doing—I was recording just dates and facts, not God's personal, dynamic speaking to me through the years. I dropped my head onto the kitchen table and fervently prayed, "Oh, Lord, give me the emotion I need so that this message won't be just statistics and facts. Give me the feelings You want me to have."

Before I finished praying, the phone rang. It was my former prayer partner. "My daughter's baby died last night. She has just awakened, and a flood of grief and an overwhelming sense of being unable to face life has swept over her. She wants me to talk to you. Could you say something to her?"

I wept as I recalled our Judy. And I wept as I cared about her little baby. Then I told her about one of those underlined verses I had just listed for the retreat—from Hebrews 12. I told her that God never makes a mistake, and that He must have something great in store for her and her husband to allow them such suffering. I told that grieving young mother that God was doing this "for their profit," even though they could not understand it now.

And God had *exchanged* my humdrum listing of verses and routine typing with a deep, Christlike caring. I went to that retreat burning with the desire to impart to those women that God's Word is alive; it does have answers for right now.

God changed me in an almost violent way one night as I prepared for a retreat the next day. I had everything all in order on the pages of notes, but somehow I lacked a sense of urgency. It seemed to be just a run-of-the-mill preparation for an ordinary retreat. I realized that my heart wasn't as well prepared as my notes. So I prayed the simple but earnest prayer, "Lord, prepare *me* for tomorrow's retreat. Teach me what You want me to know and feel. Take away this feeling of nothingness."

Just then a deafening crackle resounded through our house, accompanied by a brilliant orange flash. As I sat stunned, the phone rang. My husband, calling long distance, said, "Just thought I'd let you know the tornado that was predicted for our area has moved past. You're safe now."

"Thanks a lot," I said weakly, "but our house has just been hit by lightning." I slowly hung up the phone, and sat in the total darkness. Then I bowed my head and thanked

God for protecting me. After the firemen had examined the house and told us to keep alert for possible outbreak of fire, the children and I knelt by Nancy's bed. Eleven-year-old Kurt was the first to pray, telling God we were just going to trust Him that night and go to sleep.

As I awakened the next morning safe and sound, I had a new sense of God's protection. Driving to the retreat, I found myself following a car with a bumper sticker that read "Protected by Batman." I smiled as I thought, "*I'm* protected by God!" I arrived at that retreat changed. God, through a bolt of lightning, had *exchanged* my run-of-the-mill attitude for a vital, living sense of His protection and leading in my life.

Whenever I'm feeling inadequate for a job to be done and overwhelmed by an "I-can't-do-it" feeling, I quietly commune with God. I ask Him to give me His power, His enabling in place of my inadequacy. I ask this specifically for the task that I am facing, then claim Philippians 2:13, "For it is *God who worketh in you* both to will and to do of His good pleasure." And my attitude changes. I rise to do the task, completely able to do it. God lifts my inadequacy and fills me with *Himself!*

## EXCHANGE: GOD FOR MONEY

Twenty-five years ago, in the apron-hankie-corsage era of payment for women speakers, Chris and I made a promise to God that we would never ask a fee for my speaking. We told Him we would pay for baby-sitters, hairdos, and transportation out of his pastor's salary—a promise we have never withdrawn, although he is no longer a pastor. Even in the early days of my prayer seminars when love offerings rarely covered expenses and prayer-letter mailings, we simply trusted God. Somehow I had always felt He would withdraw His blessings if I started serving Him for the money I might receive.

After my first book came out and my cassette tape sales increased, I was still completely detached from the income. Then people started ordering the tapes by mail. And gradually I became more and more eager to see how many orders the mailman brought. When Chris would ask what was in the mail, I would reply by telling him the number of orders I received.

Then one day as I was returning from a seminar, pushing harder and harder on the gas pedal to get home as fast as possible to see how many orders had come, God said clearly to me, "Evelyn, that attitude toward money is sin!" I was horrified. I slowed the car down and cried, "Please remove all of these thoughts and this attitude right now, Lord. O God, forgive me. O Lord, change me! Please, please You remove this from me." And it was gone—not little by little as it had so subtly crept in; but in one sweep of His mighty cleansing hand—it was gone!

That night God had something to say to me out of His Word. As I was reading my Bible, tucking a thought in my mind to go to sleep on, a phrase in Matthew 6:24 almost jumped off the page at me: "You cannot serve both God and money" (NIV). For three nights I found myself peculiarly drawn to that same verse, from one translation to another. It was as if I wanted God to press it deeper and deeper into my very being. "I cannot serve both God and money!" Why not? God gave me that answer in the same chapter when Jesus was warning us against laying up for ourselves treasures upon earth and telling us to lay them up in heaven. Then Jesus gave the "why": "For where your treasure is, there will your heart be also" (Matt. 6:21).

God didn't say that I never could be paid for my ministry. In fact, He has some explicit instructions about the workman being worthy of his hire; but the problem lay in *where my heart was.* And He *exchanged* my wrong attitude about money for His perfect one.

## MEEKNESS FOR SELF-ASSERTION

Sometimes it's a little risky to ask God to change me. I remember a pastor at a World Day of Prayer speaking on the topic, "Be careful what you pray for—God may answer your prayer." And I learned the truth of this back in 1967 when I asked God to give me a meek and quiet spirit.

While preparing a banquet message on Godlike characteristics in women, I was pricked by 1 Peter 3:4, where it says that we should be adorned, not with outward hairdos, ornaments and clothes, but with "a meek and quiet spirit." Recognizing something to be desired in my steamroller personality, I prayed for five consecutive days, "Dear God, please give me a meek and quiet spirit." This was the prayer on my lips and in my heart.

I must have thought God was going to "sugarcoat" me by some supernatural process, for I was completely unprepared for the method He used. Our sixth-grade daughter had a divorced male teacher who liked to take his female pupils to a wooded retreat for outdoor education. When I refused to let our daughter go to the woods with him alone, he was furious, and came to tell me so. When I answered my doorbell, I saw him standing there with his face ashen in anger. And for the next half hour he raved and ranted at me for ruining his reputation in the community by not allowing my daughter to be alone with him in the woods, etc., etc., etc.! When he finally walked out the door, I had what I had prayed for—a meek and quiet spirit!

Yes, God had *exchanged* my personality trait for the one of His choice when I had asked Him to. But, oh, the process!

## FORGIVENESS FOR GUILT

The most important *exchange* of all takes place when God takes our guilt and replaces it with His forgiveness, His cleansing.

While visiting in California in 1969, I heard a Sunday School teacher talk excitedly about an interesting concept in Psalm 103:12. Those were the days when we all were standing in awe of our space achievements, and she had found the concept of the Hebrew word *nasa* in that psalm. "As far as the east is from the west, so far hath He removed our transgressions from us." The word "removed" conveyed the Old Testament idea of sin being separated from the sinner. And the Hebrew word *nasa* translated "forgive" meant literally to "lift away." What a picture of the dramatic blast-offs of Houston's NASA space ships. The psalmist used the largest measurement which the earth can measure—"as far as the east is from the west," but NASA is now in the business of lifting off from Planet Earth completely!

But the comparison ends there. NASA tracks our satellites with unbelievably precise instruments and brings them back to earth again. But not God. Once He lifts them off, our sins are gone—forever. He doesn't even remember them any more! God is in the business of replacing our sins with His forgiveness.

Of course, the ultimate of this exchange of guilt for forgiveness comes when we ask God to forgive all our sins and invite Jesus to become our Lord and Saviour. The greatest transformation of my life took place when I was just nine years old. At that time 2 Corinthians 5:17 became true in me: "Therefore if any man be in Christ, he is a new creation; old things are passed away; behold, all things are become new." Why is this transformation necessary? Jesus tells us clearly in John 3:18: "He that believeth on Him [God's Son] is not condemned; but he that believeth not is condemned already, because he hath not believed in the name of the only begotten Son of God."

As recorded in the Book of Mark, Jesus began His ministry in Galilee preaching *repent* and *believe*. Somehow today the emphasis is only on believing, and we tend to omit the first half of what Jesus preached (Mark 1:14–15).

228

Then the night before He was crucified, Jesus told His disciples that He would send the Comforter who would "reprove the world of sin . . . because they believe not on Me" (John 16:8–9). Paul puts it so clearly in Romans 3:23: "For all have sinned, and come short of the glory of God."

But when God exchanges His forgiveness for this condemnation, the contrast is fantastic. Paul tells us that "there is therefore now no condemnation to them who are in Christ" (Rom. 8:1). Then in Colossians 1:13–14 he tells us that God has "delivered us from the power of darkness, and hath translated us into the kingdom of His dear Son; in whom we have redemption through His blood, even the forgiveness of sins." We exchange citizenship. And in Ephesians 2:1 we have the greatest exchange of all—life for death: "And you hath He [made alive], who were dead in trespasses and sins."

This exchange transforms our life-style according to the preceding verses. Theories and theologies are of little value if they do not produce *evidence* of their being true, if lives aren't changed.

Several years ago the churches of our city cooperated in a Teen Evangelism Crusade with Dave Wilkerson. About a thousand young people found Christ as their Saviour, and the local newspaper headlines said: "Teens Say Wilkerson Visit Resulted in Changed Lives." Then they quoted some of these young people.

"It has made me a completely new person," said a 16-year-old boy. "It has changed my life. I used to be a Latin Count. I used to feel like I wanted to beat up somebody all the time. I wanted to smash things."

A 15-year-old high school sophomore said, "I don't hate anybody any more. I feel clean inside. I get along with my mom now."

"I am no longer self-centered. Christ is the center of my life," reported a sophomore girl. "Man! If I feel low, I pray to Him—and just like that! My emptiness is gone. I love everybody."

While we were chatting with Eldridge Cleaver the other night, he looked at me and said the same thing, "There isn't anybody I don't love now." What had so dramatically changed the life-style of this former Black Panther fugitive? We had just come from a meeting where he told of his years of running from U.S. justice, and then of the change—beginning with his dramatic experience on the shores of the Mediterranean in southern France to the time when he asked God to forgive all his sins and Christ to be his Saviour. Changed! Yes, he had *exchanged* a life of violent revolt for one of loving everybody—because God had *exchanged* in him his old nature for God's new one. It's almost as if God were in the heart transplant business. He lifts out the old heart and implants a new one.

But even after becoming a Christian there is the necessity for this exchange. John, who lived closer to Jesus on earth than any other person, included himself when he wrote in 1 John 1:8, "If we say that we have no sin, we deceive ourselves, and the truth is not in us."

Someone once said to me that we didn't have any record of the Apostle John ever sinning. "No," I replied, "except that he admitted it himself." His book of 1 John was written only to Christians, with clear directions on how "we" (John and other believers) can confess our sins so that God can forgive them (v. 9).

We spend so much time rationalizing and counseling in relation to what we did wrong, why we did it, what in our childhood made us do it, and on and on, that we lose sight of the fact that God says—confess it *as* sin, and I will remove your guilt. So many of our problems have an ultrasimple solution—confess what we have done or are doing as sin so that God can lift the load of guilt. Dr. Karl Menninger, well-known psychiatrist of the Menninger Clinic in Topeka, Kansas, treats this subject of guilt powerfully in his book *Whatever Became of Sin?* (New York: Hawthorn, 1973).

An interesting thing happens in my prayer seminars and retreats when I read a list of verses about sin from the Bible in preparation for confessing our sins to God in prayer. I watch faces change from a haughty "I-don't-have-any-sins-to-confess" expression, to a blinking in surprise, to horror, which says, "Stop, don't read any more. I can't take it."

I find it is good for me to pray through the lists of sins in God's Word. One of my favorite passages is the first eight verses of 2 Timothy 3. I stop to pray over each specific sin mentioned, asking God to reveal to me where and if that sin is in my life. I'm frequently surprised at what He tells me. But the process always works. I confess it as sin and God lifts the guilt from me. Exchanged!

This is a constant process in my life. God exchanging His presence for my loneliness—His power for my weakness—His healing for my illness—His hope for my despair—His peace for my anxiety—His love for my resentment—His grace for my suffering—His comfort for my sorrow. *Exchanged*—when I ask God.

# 7
## *When I
Ask Others
To Pray for Me—
I Change*

WHEN OTHERS PRAY for me, I change. So when I sense
a need in my life I ask other people to pray. They in turn
ask God to take over and do the changing, with amazing
results. For the past nine years we have kept a record of all
the requests that have gone through my prayer chains and
groups for me, personally. Nothing has so overwhelmed me
as the reviewing of these thousands of requests and answers.
Whenever I read through them, I'm reminded anew that
God really does change me when people pray!

## BEAR YE ONE ANOTHER'S BURDENS

"Bear ye one another's burdens, and so fulfill the law of
Christ" (Gal. 6:2).

Does this law of Christ concerning our responsibility to
one another include *only* physical needs—food, clothing,
shelter? I think not. Many of *my* needs, yes, most of my
needs are not temporal. Could Christ have had in mind
spiritual, emotional, and mental as well as physical needs

and burdens? How I used to appreciate the casseroles that were brought in for my family when I had had surgery, or a new baby, or when I was ill! But was that the *only* kind of support I needed? Was there more?

In 1968 while experimenting in prayer on the theme "What Happens When Women Pray," we felt it was an indication of spiritual maturity when the women started to pray for things that could not be seen with their eyes or felt with their hands. God gave us a new dimension in our praying when we learned that there are other needs and burdens that don't have a fever, stitches, or a cast.

There are burdens that can be borne *only* in prayer.

The deepest need I ever had while in our pastorate was not physical. Nothing temporal was lacking, but there was a desperate need in my life. At the time, the grief was so deep that I did not think I could stand before the audience to speak at an annual Christmas luncheon in one of our churches. I had shared this burden with the women of my neighborhood Bible study, and they, sensing how difficult it was going to be for me, bought tickets for the luncheon. Then they came early enough to take a place closest to the speaker's table, and sat there upholding me in prayer every minute I was speaking.

The results were dramatic. I no longer felt alone and unable to cope, because I was completely undergirded and surrounded by their love and concern. I changed because the God to whom they were praying reached down and gave me the strength, courage, and even the joy and enthusiasm I needed to share with that luncheon audience. Yes, I *changed* when they prayed for me.

At a Sunday School convention luncheon last fall I had the same experience. Three of my advisory board members, sensing my special personal need that day, bought tickets and came to the luncheon. As I passed by them walking up to the speaker's table, I recognized immediately their "we're-here-praying-for-you" smiles. What a difference it made to be able to look down into their beaming faces—knowing they cared enough to spend money and time to come and help bear my burden. But the greatest part was what God did for me when they prayed. He came to that room and *changed* me with His power and strength.

Just sensing that other people are caring and praying for me is great. But the marvel is that God takes over and does what they never could do for me. He only has the power to meet my spiritual, emotional, and mental needs. He really *changes* me when others pray.

## ADMITTING OUR BURDENS

Some of our needs are obvious, especially physical ones; but many of our heaviest burdens are completely hidden to those who would pray for us—unless we share them. How can we fulfill the law of Christ in all its potential if we refuse to admit our burdens to one another?

In order to benefit to the fullest from the prayers of others, we must *admit* our needs to them. In our prayer closets it is often difficult to confess our needs to God, but we find it almost impossible to admit a weakness or need to fellow Christians. However, this is a must if we expect to experience all the prayer support they are willing to give us.

When we first started our experimental praying in 1968, we all had a lesson to learn about praying for one another. One of our committee members had been taught to keep to herself her own needs and the needs or problems in her family, an attitude she found almost impossible to change. She was a terrific pray-er, but it stopped there. She could not admit that *she* had a need.

One day she had to leave our national committee meeting early because of a severe migraine headache. She knew that medication and rest would take several days to alleviate the problem. And she was having a baby shower at her house that night! As the time for the shower drew near, she found herself completely incapacitated. In desperation she finally decided to do what she never had done in her life: "Oh, God," she prayed, "if You want somebody to pray for me, just have them call on the phone. I won't call anyone, but if this is what You want, tell them to call me."

Almost immediately three women called her, one after another. "Hi. Just wondering if there is anything I could do for you tonight," each one said. Stunned, she broke the inhibitions that had been binding her and not once but three times said: "Please pray for me. I don't feel well. I need you to pray for me."

Admitting she had a need was hard, but God honored her honesty and humility. By the time the guests arrived, there wasn't a sign of her migraine headache or nausea. Changed!

Leaders sometimes find it especially hard to admit a need or a burden to other people. Often presidents, pastors (even pastors' wives), chairmen, and teachers feel they are to bear the burdens of other people they lead, but they find it difficult to ask those people to pray for them. Are they afraid of admitting weakness to those they lead? Are they fearful the people will think less of them as their leader if they admit a need? I think just the opposite is true. The greatest leaders surround themselves with the strongest staffs, admitting their need to be supported by them. No man is an island unto himself. Some leaders bear so many burdens unnecessarily—just because they can't admit they have a need.

Yesterday morning my phone rang as I was getting ready to speak to 1,300 people at an all-day prayer seminar. It was the president of the national organization which had invited me. She was responsible for the day's activities and was to lead all the sessions. "Evelyn, I didn't sleep well all night. And this morning I have a terrible migraine headache. I can't even eat breakfast. Would you pray for me?"

As I went to prayer I wondered what would happen to all those people and all those hours of teaching without her leadership. I prayed fervently that God would undertake and have His perfect will in her body.

When I arrived in the convention room, I inquired, "How are you feeling? How's the headache?"

"Oh," she answered a little wide-eyed, "it lifted. It's all gone!" Changed! It was because she admitted she had a need that I knew I should pray for her. And it was because she admitted her need that God was able to answer my prayer.

Just last week it was only because I let a few tears fall and admitted I had a need that my secretary put her arms around me and prayed for me. And then I had the privilege of feeling God lift the burden that seemed so heavy— because she prayed. "O what needless pain we bear!" No human being can carry the burdens of others without having someone else bear his.

As president of our United Prayer Ministries, it is important that I admit my needs to my advisory board so that they can pray for me. Our prayer chairman calls every day for requests for my personal needs, problems, and burdens, then passes them through our prayer chains. In 1975 and 1976 the women on those prayer chains prayed for 1,119 requests—over half of them for me. I could never carry on the heavy schedule I have without all that prayer. When they pray for me I *change*—change into their guided, encouraged, empowered, healed leader—because they pray! I know—because we have all the answers to their prayers dated and recorded.

One of the thrilling things about our over one-thousand-member Metro Prayer Chain in the Twin Cities area is that many Christian leaders request prayer. Admitting that they or their organization has a need activates over a thousand pray-ers—and activates God!

Even Paul, most likely the greatest Christian who ever lived, asked for prayer. In Ephesians 6:18–19 Paul asks the Christians to pray for him that utterance might be given to him, that he would be able to open his mouth boldly "to make known the mystery of the Gospel." And again in Colossians 4:3 he writes, "Praying also for us, that God would open unto us a door of utterance, to speak the mystery of Christ." In the conclusion to his first letter to the Thessalonians, his abrupt request is, "Brethren, pray for us" (5:25). And he begs the Christians in Rome to strive together with him in prayer for his deliverance from the unbelievers in Judea, that his service might be accepted by the saints in Jerusalem, that he might come to them with joy by the will of God and might with them be refreshed (Rom. 15:31–32). Paul was not ashamed to *admit* his numerous needs or to ask the Christians to pray *for* him.

Did Paul really expect to find himself and circumstances around him *changed* because people prayed for him? Why else would he have asked them to pray?

## DEPENDENCE

Perhaps one of the reasons we find admitting our needs to other people so difficult is that by doing so we are admitting we are dependent—dependent upon God and upon other people. We are a generation of "I-can-do-it-myself-God" Christians.

Whether we want to admit it or not, we are dependent on other pray-ers. In Matthew 9:38 Jesus said, "Pray ye, therefore, the Lord of the harvest, that He will send forth laborers into His harvest." Am I a laborer because someone, some time, some place, obeyed Jesus' command and prayed that God would send forth a laborer to the field in which I'm working? This is a humbling thought, and removes all the ego and pride about *my* ministry, *my* calling. Because somebody prayed, did I CHANGE into God's laborer?

If Paul was dependent on his friends to pray for utterance to be given to him, how much of *my* having utterance in my ministry is because somebody, or many people prayed for me? How dependent am I on other people's prayers for enabling me to teach my prayer seminars? In Ephesians 6:18-19 Paul asked prayer for utterance for himself and all saints—me! How much did I CHANGE because of them?

Frequently we don't know we have been depending on the prayers of others until we see the results. When Peter was in prison (Acts 12:5-19), he may not have been aware that "prayer was made without ceasing of the church unto God for him" (v. 5). Perhaps not until the chains fell off his hands, and he walked out of prison as the iron gate opened did he realize that God must be answering prayer. Or was it when the believers finally opened the door of the house and he saw them "praying without ceasing," that he realized why he was freed?

Scripture tells us in 1 Timothy 2:2 that we are to pray "for kings and for all that are in authority." So, whether or not they know it, leaders are dependent upon the prayers of those who obey this command. When God reaches down and *changes* kings and those in authority and the circumstances surrounding them even without their knowledge, they are dependent upon the prayers.

Or when we experience relief from some physical problem before it runs its natural course, it may well be that our fellow Christians are obeying the admonition in James to "pray one for another that ye may be healed" (5:16). When we are miraculously *changed* physically, how dependent were we on God's faithful pray-ers?

How much do I change because other people pray for me? Only eternity will tell. Only God knows who activates the process of change that takes place in me.

## SPIRITUAL WARFARE

Since the Father and the Son are one, I'm constantly amazed that God had need of Jesus' prayers on behalf of others. Jesus must have known that this is the process God uses, yes, expects, when others have needs, for in His high-priestly prayer He prayed for His followers and for us.

And in that prayer Jesus prayed that the Father would keep them and us "from the evil one" (John 17:15). He didn't pray that God would remove us from the evil one's domain, Planet Earth; just that God would deliver us from him. Because Christ is our Example in all things, we too should pray this prayer for other believers.

Jesus also practiced this kind of prayer specifically when Satan wanted to sift Peter. He said, "But I have prayed for thee, that thy faith fail not" (Luke 22:32). But in spite of Jesus' prayer for him, cocky Peter—cocksure he wouldn't fall into the enemy's trap before the cock would crow—denied his Lord. Jesus knew the importance of praying for those who are tempted by Satan.

When Dr. Kurt Koch was in our Twin Cities a while ago to lead seminars in opposition to the occult explosion in America, he begged us to pray for him. He had just cancelled a series of seminars in New York and had to be flown back to Germany because of a severe physical problem that he attributed to the lack of prayer on the part of Christians in America as he spoke on this perilous subject. "Americans don't know how to pray in this battle," he told us. He pled with us to follow faithfully, fervently, Christ's example in His high-priestly prayer. Dr. Koch had changed—for the worse—because of lack of prayer.

In Ephesians 6:18–19 Paul's exhortation to pray always for all saints and for himself is part of the armor that Christians are to use in the battle against spiritual wickedness—the realm of Satan. In 1972 I bravely tackled a Bible study subject of "Ephesians in the Light of the Spirit World" (fools rush in where angels fear to tread), and experienced unusual resistance from the enemy. But in the margin of my Bible next to Ephesians 6:18 I wrote: "2/29/72. Great power first Bible study. Host of people praying. I could *feel* power. Never felt more when speaking." I had *changed* from an intimidated and harassed woman trying to prepare a Bible study that was a threat to Satan—*changed* into an empowered teacher. Because they prayed!

## TELL ME YOUR SECRET

Many times after teaching my whole seminar on prayer in one day (five and one-half to six hours of lecturing), a pastor or priest will come to me and say, "Tell me your secret. How can you 'speak to convince' so many hours in a row? When I finish speaking for one or two hours on a Sunday morning, I'm exhausted. I'm completely overcome with fatigue. What's your secret?"

"I do have a secret," I tell them honestly. "It's my prayer support. It is all the women who so faithfully pray for me."

Yes, I do have a secret. On January 4 of this year after writing every spare minute during the holidays and then teaching a large first-of-the-year prayer seminar the night before, I awoke too exhausted to get out of bed. This was a rare occurrence in my life for I'm an early riser; but, as Chris put a towel over my eyes, I thanked God silently that he was going to a breakfast meeting that morning. Then, suddenly, surging through my body was strength, eagerness to get going on the day the Lord had given me. I was *changed*—there was a complete transformation. What had happened? The prayer chain members one by one were arising and having their quiet times with the Lord—and praying for me!

Not long ago I became aware that at exactly six o'clock every morning I felt a surge of God's power. Questioning the recurrence at the same time every morning, I casually mentioned it to one of the women who had been sending through the prayer requests for one of my prayer chains. I could almost see her blushing in modest humility over the phone as she stammered, "That's the time I pray for you every morning." I could feel the change come over me—as she prayed!

240

One day last fall this prayer request went through the chain for me: "Evelyn in desperate need of strength." Then the record of the answer made a couple of days later read, "Over 3,000 people attended her workshops. Ev stood and talked 14 hours one evening and next day. Experienced Isaiah 40:31."

Last November 23 I asked the prayer chains to pray because I was already tired and facing an all-day prayer seminar. I just reread the astounding answer recorded in our files, "Ev gained momentum as the day progressed." *Changed?* Yes!

When others pray for me, God, the omnipotent God of heaven and earth, reaches down and changes me—because they pray. Because they are willing to fulfill the law of Christ by bearing my burdens.

## FOR ONE ANOTHER

But the greatest joy in prayer is not just being prayed for, but bearing *one another's* burdens. Sprinkled all through our advisory board and other prayer chains are the personal and family needs of our members. What a privilege to pray for one daughter in distress, and then a year later to be praying for her as she leads a Bible study at Urbana—changed! And after praying for a member's arthritis surgery, to be told of the dramatic, almost painless success of the operation, or to pray for a Christian college professor's son from another state who was on alcohol and marijuana, and then to receive a thrilling letter that there is victory—changed! There was the mother with a stroke, the woman with the migraine headaches, the opening of a new Christian bookstore, and the responsibilities of the "Here's Life" city-wide prayer chairman—circumstances and people—all changed according to God's will for them because we prayed!

Yes, it's hard to admit we need to be changed and it's very hard to admit to other Christians that we need them to pray so that God will change us. Yes, it is a humbling process, but it's so rewarding. When others pray for me—I change!

before she was born (as we have all our children), this situation was different. It meant literal releasing—Jan was of legal age. I almost felt like Hannah as she gave her weaned child, Samuel, to the Lord. It was similar to what I experienced when the doctors told us that our Judy could not live. As I prayed for her that night, it wasn't until I *released* her to God for *His* will to be done that the battle was over. Not the grief—but the battle was over. I changed that night. I had released her to God!

Even the releasing of our children to God's care every day as they left for kindergarten and continued on through high school taught me so much about this process. Releasing them to God's protection and guidance when I couldn't accompany them to school, when my empty hand ached to hold theirs in this big, frightening world, was preparing me for the actual releasing that would take place in the future.

Releasing Jan to God intensified my prayers for her. So often what I do for a child is too little, too late. But God always does everything in the right way, at the right time. What I want for a child may be dictated by selfish motives—the best-paying job, the place of greatest honor, the highest grade, the biggest house—things the world equates with success. But not God. He always wants for them what will teach them the most, and that which will make them the finest gold.

I'll never forget what a mother of several teenagers once said to me. "I'm not sending my kids to a Christian college only to have them go to a foreign mission field, as my brother did, and leave *me* all alone in my old age."

I see this process of releasing take place in our prayer seminars so frequently. The most life-changing session we have is the one where we learn to pray in God's will. At the close we think of the most important thing in the whole world to us, and then give it to God in prayer. This is the point at which we release to God our right to that person or thing which is more important than anything else to us at the time.

While conducting a prayer seminar in a friend's church in California, I watched an astounding change take place in her pastor. His wife is a beautiful, talented, and charming hostess—but she is gravely ill with cancer. Throughout their pastorate, she has been his supportive co-worker. When I arrived for that seminar, I was introduced to the most heartbroken pastor I ever have seen. But a miracle happened while we were praying in our small groups after studying how to pray in God's will. That pastor released his wife to God for *His* will for her—not his own. As he came to the pulpit to close the session in prayer, I couldn't believe my eyes. "Is that man radiating?" I whispered to my friend. His face seemed literally to glow as he smiled at his congregation and told them what had happened. "He's radiating!" she whispered back. The wife hadn't changed—but the one who released her had!

Talking with a woman at a seminar yesterday, I listened as she told me that her husband who had had surgery several times had been told by his doctors that he could not get well. It was only a matter of time. She told me of her days and weeks of struggle and rebellion against God and of her refusal to give him up. "But," she said, "the miracle came when I released him to God. *I* was the one who changed. The battle was over." Then she added, "Oh, by the way, he's the gentleman you were just talking to over there. He's completely cured." But his recovery wasn't the only miracle. The miracle that happened when she released him to God was just as life-changing.

Perhaps the most difficult time to release our "human possessions" to God is when He is disciplining them. How we love to protect our children, our spouses, and our loved ones from God's discipline. At a recent retreat I was counseling a woman whose pastor husband had been having an affair with another woman. Having been discovered, he was in deep depression. She told me that she was asking God not to deal with him any more because she was afraid he wouldn't be able to take it. She was trying to protect him from God! I told her that the only hope for her husband was for her to *release* him to God, the only One who could convict him of the *sin* of his actions. Then her husband could assume his responsibility before God and confess his sin. "Stop trying to play God," I told her.

The first time Jan faced final exams at college after I released her to God in 1968, I remember how different were my prayers for her: "God, don't necessarily give her all A's, but teach her everything she needs to know this first year of college." I remember Jan jokingly (but deep down inside, seriously) telling her friend not to have her mother pray for her. "She'll pray you right out of all A's." Well, I really wasn't the one who caused the one "B" that first semester, but in a way I felt responsible, for I *had* prayed that God would teach her *everything* He knew she needed to know. And He obviously knew (as I was to learn later) that there are more important things than all A's earned immediately upon entering college. Of course, all A's were as exciting to us as to her, but I had submitted to His will. I had released her for Him—not me—to teach her.

A missionary used half a box of Kleenex as she tearfully told me her story at a retreat. God had called her and her husband back to the United States and had given them a pastorate. She told me between her sobs that both she and her husband were absolutely positive that it was God's will that they were here. "But," she sobbed, "people won't release us. 'Once a missionary, always a missionary,' they say. It's the people *who pray for us* who won't give us to God for *His* will in our lives. They want to tell God where we should be serving Him."

How we love to play God in other people's lives—especially in those for whom we are diligently praying. But God wants *us* to change—to release them to Him for His will.

Jesus taught us to pray for them that way in the Lord's Prayer in Matthew 6:9–10 when He said, "After this manner . . . pray ye . . . *Thy* will be done in earth, as it is in heaven."

When I was president of our faculty wives' association, we planned a "Lord, change me" retreat. While announcing it, I explained to the college and seminary faculty and staff husbands that we were going to draw apart at a retreat center and let God tell us from His Word what He wanted changed in us. "I don't want my wife changed. I like her the way she is," quipped one professor.

I held my silence, but how I wanted to say to him, "But does *God* like her the way she is?" There's a difference!

I praise and thank God for a husband who has released me to God for *His* will in my life. How beautiful our marriage relationship is, since Chris is interested not in what *he* wants for me, selfishly and personally, but in what *God* wants for me. Yes, it involves sacrifice to release a loved one to God, but the beauty of that submissive, changed life is great to behold.

## RELEASING OUR SPIRITUAL CHILDREN

We often have a tendency, too, to be over possessive of our "spiritual children." I had been telling my telephone prayer chain chairman about talking long distance to a woman who had led many people to the Lord and was now physically and emotionally exhausted from trying to keep them all afloat. As she was discipling, mothering, and coaching, she found herself collapsing under the strain.

"Release them to God," I had advised her, "and let Him give them back to you one at a time for only those things He wants you to do for them."

The next day my prayer chairman called and said, "I took personally the advice you gave the other person over the phone. I suddenly realized that I was spoon-feeding my

246

neighbors, feeling totally responsible for all of them all of the time. And I, too, am under a doctor's care, not able to take the strain any longer, so I just *released* these neighbors to God. I won't stop being concerned. I won't stop discipling and nurturing them; I'll only stop playing God."

Babies never learn to walk if adults refuse to let go of their hands. New Christians never learn to walk if we insist on carrying them. Although discipling is a necessary part of helping those whom we have introduced to Christ, there comes a time when we must *release* them to fly by themselves with God.

When we release our right to our own will for our "human possessions," we change—becoming submissive to God's will rather than demanding our will for them. But there is an added bonus in this process I had not counted on, and certainly had not sought. While God was changing me, He was also teaching me the effectiveness of *His* changing others for whom I was only praying, not "preaching at."

I saw myself in a new role—changed! On intercessor's knees, I found it much more effective to talk to God about things in their lives of which I didn't approve and letting *Him* handle them. Gradually I learned that there is more power in praying for people than in preaching at people, especially when I have released them for God to answer my prayers in any way He desires.

## CHANGED—WHILE I PRAYED

One of the greatest privileges for mortals on this planet is to be able to come boldly to the throne of grace (Heb. 4:16). When I exercise this privilege, I change. I see the worth God has placed upon me when He allows, yes, invites me to come into His presence in prayer. I, a mere mortal, have the overwhelming joy of bringing those for whom I'm concerned right to the throne of the God of the universe. I have the attention of the omniscient, omnipotent, omnipresent God—and this changes me!

The reason we are continuing our 24-hour "Here's Life" prayer chains in our churches now that our "I Found It" saturation is over is that many pray-ers have told us they don't want to give up the privilege of intercession. The joy they experienced on their 24-hour-prayer-chains, even when their hour to pray was scheduled in the middle of the night, was tremendous, they told us. The privilege of having access to God in that very special way is something many are not willing to give up.

Also, while I am praying for others, I am fulfilling the admonition of Colossians 3:1–2, "If ye, then, be risen with Christ, seek those things which are above, where Christ sitteth on the right hand of God. Set your affection on things above, not on things on the earth." Keeping my mind in the heavenlies, being transported mentally into the presence of God the Father and Christ His Son, changes me. When Jesus took Peter, James, and John up into a mountain to pray, we read that "as He [Jesus] prayed, the appearance of His countenance was altered" (Luke 9:28, RSV). It was *while He prayed* that Jesus' appearance changed. Matthew tells us that His face "did shine as the sun" (Matt. 17:2). And as I pray, God changes me. While I am directly associating with my holy God, high and lifted up, I become more Christlike, more conformed to His image.

We read in the Book of Acts that two of these same men were brought prisoners before the rulers, elders, scribes, and all the kindred of the high priest. And when they saw Peter and John, "they took note of them that these men had been with Jesus" (Acts 4:13, NIV). We teach our children they will be like the people with whom they associate. Is there really something different about us when we have been with Jesus? Yes, we really are changed—so much so that even *our* enemies also can tell the difference.

## SOMEBODY NEEDS ME

Inherent in each human being is the need to be needed. It gives us a sense of self-worth, a zest for life, and a reason for living.

In our prayer seminars we discover the worth of ourselves as we practice intercessory prayer. As the urgent and often heartbreaking prayer requests are handed in, pray-ers find—many for the first time—that *someone* really does need them, and their prayers.

Corrie ten Boom told me that when she was five years old and had just received Christ as her Saviour, her mother said to her, "Corrie, now you are an intercessor." And she found that the people living around her home needed her prayers. What a great way for a little child to find her self-worth.

Trying to motivate and instill a sense of self-worth in teenagers at a prayer seminar proved to be a difficult experience. These were 200 members of a confirmation class who, along with a church full of adults, were learning to pray. But their presence was not voluntary, and the paper wads, bubble gum and paper airplanes displayed on the first night showed me what they thought of themselves as pray-ers.

At the second session one of them came to me and said she had a prayer request. "My ten-year-old sister cannot hear," she said. Fearing I'd never be able to motivate them if God chose to answer some way other than healing her sister, I decided on a plan. I challenged those 200 teenagers by giving *them* the request. I told them it was *their* responsibility, *theirs* to do whatever they chose with it. I held my breath all that next week waiting for the outcome. At the next session my fears proved to be in vain. I found myself surrounded by a whole gang of the girl's teenage friends as she excitedly announced, "Guess what happened to my sister?" I waited with bated breath. "She can now hear without her hearing aid!" Those 200 teenagers had found the worth of themselves to someone in need.

After the last session of that prayer seminar, the pastor's wife came to me with tears in her eyes. "Do you remember the boy who was shooting paper airplanes and paper wads that first night? (How could I forget him?) Do you know what he just prayed in our little group? He prayed, 'Dear God, please teach my dad what You've just taught me!'" Oh, yes, we change when we discover we are needed.

## GOD NEEDS ME

Some of the greatest untapped potentials in our churches are our infirm members. Many of them were great spiritual giants while their bodies were still strong, but now that disease or old age has forced them to become inactive for God as they are confined to their rocking chairs, wheel chairs, or beds, their spirits often become as shriveled as their bodies. But I've discovered something exciting in our prayer seminars. Relatives and friends frequently bring these people to a seminar, and occasionally they even come by bus from nursing homes. I challenge these infirm Christians that God *still* needs them, and I tell them that they can once again exercise as much and perhaps more spiritual power than they did before. I love to watch these bypassed citizens of God's kingdom unfold like a rose as they rediscover that God needs them.

While experimenting in prayer back in 1968–1969, we assigned these people as prayer support for our neighborhood Bible studies. What a release of God's power and what changed results we saw in the Bible studies as the teachers and hostesses kept their "pray-er" up to date on all the needs and problems of the class!

One of our outstanding primary department teachers became physically unable to teach her class. Home-baked cookies and deep personal concern for every pupil had made her a teacher who was deeply loved. But after having to relinquish her class, she launched a new project from her hospital bed and home confinement—she spent the Sunday School hour praying by name for each pupil in her department and for the teachers and the superintendent. Almost immediately the other teachers began to report that amazing changes were taking place in that department. Discipline problems went almost to zero. Did God *need* her more in that capacity than teaching her class of primary boys and girls? Evidently. Yes, God had allowed her to be changed from an active to an inactive person, but instead of folding up in her confinement, she was changed into a powerful intercessor.

While I was conducting a prayer seminar in a large southern city, a psychiatrist told me, "You know, my profession isn't known for its cures, but I am discovering something interesting. I've been a Christian for only two years, but I've started to pray for my patients—deep, fervent prayer. And," she continued excitedly, "I'm finding that those for whom I pray," she took a deep breath before finishing, "actually get well." And *she* was a changed psychiatrist, overawed that God was actually doing something for her patients when she prayed for them.

When we first started experimenting in prayer in January 1968, the thing that changed the Original "eight gripers" into motivated and faithful pray-ers was the discovery that God actually needed them. And I have found this to be true through the years as I have taught thousands to pray. Watching people change from skeptical doubters to exuberant pray-ers, when they discover God is using *them*, is a constant thrill to me. A pastor's wife told me this morning that sometimes she prays for a need that only she knows about and for which no one else is praying, then *knows* it is *her* prayer that God is answering. The startling discovery that God is using *us* does change our sense of self-worth.

We are changed—needed—people. And that makes us joyful people!

## SWEET AND BITTER WATER

When I become an intercessor, praying *for* other people, I find the truth of James 3:11–12 becoming evident in my life. I find it is impossible for two attitudes to be in me at the same time. "Doth a fountain send forth at the same place sweet water and bitter? Can the fig tree, my brethren, bear olive berries? either a vine, figs? So can no fountain yield both salt water and fresh."

When I pray for others, it takes my mind off my trivial or perhaps very real complaints. There is always someone worse off than I, and when I go into deep intercessory prayer for that person I change from a self-centered complainer into a person with genuine concern and love for that one for whom I pray. Somehow I can't concentrate on myself and pray out of love for others at the same time.

I find, too, that it is impossible to pray for and gossip about a person at the same time. One of the great results of a telephone prayer chain is that the pray-ers stop gossiping about other people's troubles when they start praying about them. Also, "roast pastor" is no longer a Sunday dinner main dish when we really start praying for him.

And I can't thank God for all the good things about a person and be filled with accusations at the same time. Somehow those two diametrically opposed attitudes can't be expressed simultaneously. This is one of the subtle results of thanking God for all our acquaintances—especially our enemies. During the process, *we* change.

I also find it impossible to pray for and be angry with a person at the same time. Could Christ have had something more in mind than the persons for whom He commanded us to pray, when He said in Matthew 5:44, "Pray for them which despitefully use you"? Could one of the results of praying for those who despitefully use us be that we, the pray-ers, are changed *as* we pray for them? But in order to effect this change, our prayers must be genuine. We cannot utter a few sweet words in prayer while the bitterness remains deep down inside. No, real prayer is the overflow of the heart.

The first step to take to insure the sweetness within is to forgive the person who has despitefully used us. It is at this point that we change on the inside. We are changed *when* we forgive others.

A retired missionary came to me yesterday and told me that the women in her church were studying *What Happens When Women Pray*. Tears came into her eyes as she said, "The crisis chapter of that book is the one about forgiving others. One thing after another is cleared up between people when they forgive each other. It is making such a difference in our church."

A woman attending a seminar in a Minneapolis suburb wanted me to play "Ann Landers" and advise her on how to tell her mother-in-law off. I asked her to wait until the next week when we would study how to handle such situations. The following session included the formula for forgiving others—and she prayed through! The next week she came bouncing into the seminar a completely changed person. A sweet spirit had replaced her acute agitation; a smile had replaced her troubled countenance. I never met the mother-in-law. Whether she continued to be her evidently rather miserable self or was changed as her daughter-in-law's attitude toward her changed, I will most likely never know. But this I do know—a radical change took place in the one who forgave her.

Two college girls burst into the dean of women's office after I finished teaching their prayer-week session on forgiving others. "I'm free. I'm free!" cried one. "I forgave her, and now I feel free!" Although I didn't have the foggiest idea who had been involved or what the problem was, the dean of women nodded and smiled an understanding smile. Something had been solved on that Christian campus. And the one doing the forgiving had the privilege of being changed. Free!

A very agitated woman from Germany came to Hansi ("the girl who loved the swastika"), telling her she could not stand her mother. They got along all right as long as the Atlantic Ocean was between them, but she had just received word that her mother was coming to America!

"Why don't you come to the prayer seminar at my church tomorrow night?" Hansi suggested. She came—and we just happened to be having the lesson on forgiving others. As the rows of people turned to pray together, Hansi found herself facing this angry woman. After having chosen her mother as the one person to forgive during prayer time, she looked up at Hansi and said, "Oh, now my mother can come from Germany!" Who changed? The mother? No, *when* she forgave her mother, *she* changed!

God wisely gave that little formula in 2 Corinthians 2:5–11 to those who have been grieved. We somehow feel that the person who grieved us is the one who needs to change, but God wisely places the responsibility on us when we have been despitefully used. There isn't anything in that formula that tells the person who has caused the grief what to do, but only what we, the grieved ones, must do. God knew all along that when we forgive someone and pray for him out of real love, we change.

Yes, when I pray for others, I change! *My* priorities, *my* rights, *my* attitudes, all change as I pray for other people.

*Section III*

# MAKE SURE
# IT IS GOD
# DOING THE CHANGING

# 9

## Source No. 1,
## My Sensual Self

NOW THAT WE'VE looked into the methods God uses
to change us, the haunting question arises: How can I be
absolutely sure it is God who is changing me? How can I
know that my life-style, the sum total of all my wisdom
put into action, is really from Him?

God showed me the fact that the Book of James mentions
four sources of wisdom from which I can obtain knowledge
that will change me. And these four are constantly vying
for my life-style; and I discovered that only one of them is
God. Only one of the four is a trustworthy source of direction for the changes in my life. The other three are mentioned in James 3:15: "This wisdom descendeth not from
above, but is *earthly* [from other people], *sensual* [from
within our sensual selves], *demoniacal* [from demons]" (SCO).

Is there any way, then, that I can test the source of wisdom that is producing my life-style? James says the proof
is in *what it produces:* "The wisdom that is from above
[from the Lord] is first pure, then peaceable, gentle and easy

to be entreated, full of mercy and good fruits, without partiality, and without hypocrisy" (3:17). This is in contrast to what the other three sources produce: "But if ye have bitter envying and strife in your hearts, glory not, and lie not against the truth. This wisdom descendeth not from above, but is earthly, sensual, demoniacal. For where envying and strife are, there is confusion and every evil work" (3:14–16, sco).

Sometimes it is difficult to discern which source of wisdom has produced a change in me, because it is possible for the sources other than God to produce temporary satisfaction with the good life, but the end result in me will always be the opposite of what God wants to produce in me. Superficial happiness may be produced from one of the other sources of wisdom, but there will be an absence of real joy and peace down deep within me.

I discovered this frightening fact while reading devotionally in James 3 one Sunday morning several years ago. Anger over something a relative had said nine years before suddenly welled up within me. I had forgiven and been forgiven at that time, so why this recurrence of these feelings? As I read this portion of Scripture I knew God's answer: that attitude was not from Him! Horrified, I noted the other three sources of wisdom, and then realized that wisdom from God would not produce the anger I was experiencing. It had to be from one of the other sources.

In these final chapters I will discuss these four possible sources of wisdom which can produce changes that collectively result in my life-style.

## SOURCE NUMBER 1:
### MY SENSUAL SELF

One of the sources from which I can receive wisdom is my own sensual self—the part of me that is controlled by my senses. It is the natural man that Paul struggled with

258

in Romans 7. "For I know that in me (that is, in my flesh) dwelleth no good thing" (v. 18). "So then with the mind I myself serve the law of God; but with the flesh the law of sin" (v. 25b).

Christ, on one occasion when "He had called all the people to Him," painted a word picture of the human heart that was far from complimentary: "For from within, out of the heart of men, proceed evil thoughts, adulteries, fornications, murders, thefts, covetousness, wickedness, deceit, lasciviousness, an evil eye, blasphemy, pride, foolishness: All these evil things come from within, and defile the man" (Mark 7:21–23). James wrote about a source of sin that was within us: "But every man is tempted, when he is drawn away of his own lust, and enticed" (1:14). And Jeremiah lamented, "The heart is deceitful above all things, and desperately wicked: who can know it?" (17:9)

**Deceiving Myself**

After reading what the Bible says about my sensual self, I'm appalled that I can deceive myself into thinking I know what direction my changing should take. A profound proverb says, "The way of a fool is right in his own eyes" (Prov. 12:15). And in Romans, Paul describes those who "when they knew God . . . became vain in their imaginations, and their foolish heart was darkened. Professing themselves to be wise, they became fools" (1:21–22). Then, because "they did not like to retain God in their knowledge, God gave them over to a reprobate mind, to do those things which are not convenient; Being filled with all unrighteousness, fornication, wickedness, covetousness, maliciousness; full of envy, murder, debate, deceit, malignity; whisperers, backbiters, haters of God, despiteful, proud, boasters, inventors of evil things, disobedient to parents, without understanding, covenant-breakers, without natural affection, implacable, unmerciful" (1:28–31). Are all these things really the end results of rationalizing and following my own feelings and senses? The possibility of any of these consequences being a part of my life sends me scurrying to God's Word for His direction on how to change.

What can I do about this sensuous self? God has some good advice for me. In Ephesians I read that henceforth (from now on, since I am in Christ Jesus), I am not to walk as other Gentiles walk, *in the vanity of their mind*. . . . But I am to "put off concerning the former [manner of life] the old man, which is corrupt according to the deceitful lusts; and be *renewed in the spirit of* [my] *mind*" (4:17ff). God wants to change me, wants to give me wisdom from Him that will produce the opposite of these sins of the flesh.

So in prayer I cry to God with the psalmist, "Search me, O God, and know my heart; try me, and know my thoughts; and see if there be any wicked way in me, and lead me in the way everlasting" (Ps. 139:23–24). "Don't let me be changed by what *I* think or feel. Give me the wisdom for changing that is from You."

## I Think

What I think really isn't very impressive according to God's Word. There is only one Truth, and that is God Himself. And the only absolute truth on which we can depend for the right kind of changes in our lives is found only in God's Word (John 17:17).

We have a rule about this at our house. Last summer I overheard two of our children discussing it: "Mother always said truth is truth. It doesn't matter if you believe it or not. And not believing it has nothing to do with the fact that it is truth, and it will not change from being truth just because we choose not to believe it."

Yes, whether or not I agree with something has nothing to do with whether or not it is true. My "I think" about a subject neither negates it nor insures its being true.

But we are so prone to believe our "I thinks" are very important. Many times what is billed as a Bible study turns out to be an exchange of our "I thinks." We read the Scripture portion and, using it as a springboard, dive immediately into the inner pool of our "I thinks" and begin a discussion of whatever comes to our minds. When we are finished telling what we think about the subject, other class members usually retain what they think, and I keep what I think. It may have been a great discussion, but no one acquired any new truth.

A rule for Bible study that assures us of getting wisdom from the only worthy Source, God Himself, is that we don't discuss anything that is not answered in the portion of Scripture being studied on a given day. The teacher, and hopefully the pupils, will have studied the actual meaning of the text, and the answers no longer will be the participants' "I think" but God's Word. Then we know that the changes we make in our lives based on that lesson are not from the "I thinks" of people but from God Himself.

I was conducting a retreat in an eastern state, and on the Saturday morning we were to practice reading God's Word individually until He pointed out something in our lives that needed changing. The hearts of those women had really been prepared during their cabin devotions the night before. Someone had listed some excellent questions on "How do you react when . . . ?" The object was to discover if one's reactions were Christlike or not. But something went wrong. I sat in the corner quietly listening to their discussions. They became more and more heated as the women exchanged their "I thinks"—disagreeing, ignoring, and vying for the floor. The next morning I asked how many could honestly say they learned something during the devotions the night before, and not one single hand was raised. But in another way they had learned a tremendous lesson, and were eager to listen to God that morning.

A professor at one of our large seminaries told me that the school was changing its teaching policy because the students had requested less group-interaction sessions and more teaching sessions. These students felt that there was far too much to learn to warrant so much time being spent in sharing their "I thinks."

However, this does not mean that we cannot learn from each other. Sharing can be a profitable source of wisdom— if the wisdom shared is from a worthy source. If the source has been what God taught that person, then the sharing will be profitable indeed. If the teacher says, "I think," the pupil well may respond, "So what?" And the same holds true when the teacher verbalizes his or her own feelings. They are not grounds for expecting or demanding change in the pupil. But when the teacher's source of wisdom has come from God or those who also learned from God, then the "I think" becomes positive wisdom.

This, too, is why we do not approach Bible reading or study with our minds full of our own preconceived ideas.

Asking God to remove preconceived ideas *before* writing would have helped the author of a widespread women's study to interpret and teach Genesis 1:26 and 28 correctly. Approaching the Scriptures with the preconceived idea that God gave the male the roles of dominion and procreation had blinded the author's eyes to the pronouns being plural, not singular ("them," and not "him"). The accurate reading gives male and female equal dominion and procreation roles and thus negates the basis of the thesis of the study. And looking up the meaning of the words "Adam" and "man" in this portion in a good Bible word study would have revealed that both words are plural—also disproving the preconceived thesis.

Sometimes our "I thinks" are produced by inadequate Bible study. A young male student assailed me after I had led a prayer seminar in his college prayer week. After teaching them, I had asked the student body to stand and make small groups for prayer. "You know very well," he exploded at me, "that nowhere in the Bible does it tell women to tell men to do anything."

"Oh," I said in surprise, "except Jesus and the angels on Resurrection morning both told the women to go and tell the men—not only that Jesus was not dead—but to go to Galilee where He said they would see Him too."

His preconceived "I think" had robbed him of seeing the truth about how the most important fact in the history of mankind—He is risen!—was revealed and then relayed to Christ's male followers.

A lawyer in a class I was teaching in the Book of Mark came to me after class and objected, "Why are you teaching all this about Satan and demons? You know very well there's no such thing."

In our verse-by-verse study, I was not choosing topics but simply teaching whatever subject was covered in the text, and the first few lessons had all included some encounter with these beings.

I replied, "You are a very intelligent man. I want you to do something for me. Take at least the Book of Mark, and all four Gospels if you have time, and write down as if you were preparing a legal case every time Satan or demons are mentioned, who said what, how each reacted, who was victorious, etc. When you have finished, tell me your decision about the reality of these things and I promise to abide by your decision as to whether or not I will teach about them."

By the next Friday a note had arrived in my mail box: "Dear Mrs. Chris: Please forgive me. I only thought I knew what the Bible said about that subject. I hadn't really read it."

Sometimes we take a perfectly good word from the Bible (such as "chastisement," "suffering," "submission," "healing," "God's justice"), dive immediately into our pool of "I thinks" and weave them subtly and securely around that word, leaving the impression that all of our "I thinks" about the word actually were included in the scriptural meaning of the word.

Also it is important to base a theological premise on *all* the Scriptures dealing with the subject and not from our ideas from just one Scripture portion. It is easy to believe that prayer should be made only in a closet, only holding up holy hands, only kneeling down or only lying in bed when we take what that particular Scripture has to say about prayer. But, in order to get a true, complete picture of scriptural prayer, all Scripture on that subject must be viewed collectively.

So also it is easy to get a lopsided view of women staying home and being keepers at home, whereas many of Paul's co-workers were women. Priscilla traveled with Paul (Acts 18:18), taught Apollos, and the four Gospels abound with women traveling with Jesus. And these same women made up a large part of the 120 waiting and praying together with the men after the ascension of Christ back to heaven (Acts 1:14). Then we next see them still with the apostles and other men at Pentecost with the Holy Spirit falling on *all* who were in that prayer group, and *all* of them speaking to the visitors in Jerusalem from many different countries—in their native tongues. Peter explained this phenomenon not as *being* drunkenness, as was supposed, but as the fulfilling of Joel's prophecy: "But this is that which was spoken by the prophet, Joel; 'And it shall come to pass in the last days,' saith God, 'I will pour out of My Spirit upon all flesh: and your sons and your *daughters* shall prophesy, and your young men shall see visions, and your old men shall dream dreams: And on My servants and on My *handmaidens* I will pour out in those days of My Spirit; and they shall prophesy'" (Acts 2:16–18).

Many of these verses, you may have noticed, have to do with the role of women within the Church. Lest someone suspect that I as a woman am anxious to advance my own "I think," I will assure you that the issues growing out of these passages are the ones that have been coming up week after week in the prayer seminars around the country.

Many women have shared with me how they have allowed someone's "I think" to thwart their usefulness and to render them almost subhuman. Bookstores are filled with women's books, some advocating total submission to men, others suggesting ways a wife may manipulate her husband to "keep him happy and save the marriage"; still others suggest that Christians abandon male-female roles altogether.

Few topics of late have been so popular—or so polarizing. Because so many men and women are being hurt because of a misunderstanding of male-female roles in the home and church, it is especially important for all of us to put aside our "I thinks" and allow God's Word to speak.

Ideas are only as good as their sources. It is possible that the interpretation we are familiar with has been only some speaker's or teacher's "I think." But when we let God speak, having had our minds cleared of our own preconceived ideas, we receive from Him exactly what He wants to teach us—the method He wants to use to change us.

Sometimes we even back up our "I thinks" with Scripture that we feel supports our own ideas. "The heaven, even the heavens, are the Lord's; but the earth hath He given to the children of men" (Ps. 115:16), was used by many to prove that man was confined to this planet in the solar system and that he would never be able to land on the moon or any other planet. But this "I think" idea was shattered on July 20, 1969, at 10:56 Eastern Daylight Time, when Neil Armstrong uttered the now almost immortal words, "That's one small step for a man; one giant leap for mankind" as he put the first, but not the last, human foot down on the moon. This process of disproving one's "I thinks" and proving the Bible has been going on for centuries.

Galileo, the 17th-century scientist, believed the now-accepted fact that the earth is not the center of the universe.

But in 1633 the Church forced him to kneel down and, with his hand upon the Gospel, renounce his belief because of what "they thought."

Sometimes we superimpose a change on others because of what we think the Scripture means. I remember being told of a minister, who ran a home for displaced children and young people, having sexual relations with the teenage girls in his care. He firmly believed he was doing the right thing because he thought they needed to experience love (a good scriptural concept). These girls were changed because of his "I think," but certainly not according to the kind of love God would have used to change them. This type of "I think" is spelled S-I-N in God's Word.

### How Smart Are You?

While I was being entertained as the guest of honor at a dinner party in a large southern city, a young man trained in handwriting analysis suddenly asked me, "What's your I.Q.?"

All conversation ceased as those around me listened for my answer. "Sorry, no way am I going to talk about that," I replied, embarrassed at the silence.

"Oh, come on, I've already analyzed your handwriting, and I know how smart you are."

I suddenly realized he meant business and was ready to tell me all he knew. "OK. I'll tell you how smart I am." He smiled a little "I won" grin as all eyes focused on me. Slowly and very deliberately I said, "I'm smart enough to know that I don't know" (I could almost feel the shocked silence). "But," pointing upward, toward God in heaven, I added, "I'm also smart enough to know who does know." Proverbs 3:5-6 says: "Trust in the Lord with all thine heart; and lean not unto thine own understanding. In all thy ways acknowledge Him, and He shall direct thy paths." Yes, I know I don't know how to direct my own life. When I lean on my own understanding, I become more and more stubbornly entrenched in my own ambitions, rights, and ideas.

How, then, can I avoid getting my life-style from wisdom that is within myself—a source that produces bitter envyings, strife, confusion, and every evil work? (James 3:16) God has promised if I *don't* lean on my own understanding, He will take over and direct my paths. Then He will teach me through Bible study, guide me through devotional reading, and recall Scripture when I need it. And He will give me wisdom when I admit I need it and ask Him for it—wisdom that changes me according to His perfect will.

# 10

## *Source No. 2,*
## *Earthly*

ANOTHER SOURCE OF wisdom by which I am changed
that James mentions is *earthly*. This is not that which
attacks me with fiery darts from Satan's emissaries, nor my
own "I thinks" welling up from deep within my sensual self,
but it is the wisdom that bombards from the world around
me. This is the constant barrage of communicated suggestions which pellet me from every angle: people, books,
newspapers, radio, and television. The parade is endless and
unrelenting. Bit by bit they push, press, chisel, and invade
until I am changed—unsuspectingly—into a composite of
their messages.

The advertising media have learned the power contained
in suggestions that flash so rapidly on my TV screen. I am
not even aware of them, but I am motivated to get up out
of my chair and go to the kitchen for something to eat or
to go out and buy their product. These hidden persuaders
are not only on TV; they are subtly at work on me all day
long from a myriad of sources.

In Romans 12:2 Paul refers to the results of this process as *conforming* to the world. He writes, "And be not conformed to this world." To conform is to become similar to, to bring into harmony or agreement with, to act in accordance with. CHANGED! Changed to conform to what? The *world*. The age in which we live. The principles and practices of this present order of things. The world becomes our source of wisdom which in turn changes us into conformity to it. Paul warns us against this. James says that this wisdom "descendeth not from above [from God], but is earthly" (3:15).

Peter puts it this way: "Wherefore gird up the loins of your mind . . . as obedient children, not fashioning yourselves according to the former lusts in your ignorance" (1 Peter 1:13–14). What are these former lusts? Paul defines them in Ephesians 2:1–3: "And you [Christians] hath He quickened, who were dead in trespasses and sins; Wherein in time past ye walked according to the course of this world, according to the prince of the power of the air, the spirit that now worketh in the children of disobedience; Among whom also we all had our conversation [way of life] in times past in the lusts of our flesh, fulfilling the desires of the flesh and of the mind; and were by nature the children of wrath, even as others."

## BOMBARDED BY A RELENTLESS PARADE

What becomes commonplace changes me. I can remember the times when I hurt inside if anyone took God's name in vain, when I winced at some of the four-letter words so commonly used on TV today—words I never allowed to enter my home by any other way. I never tolerated a child's playmate or a crude adult friend using those words, but now I am frequently unaware of the vile language so casually used on the TV in my family room.

And God's standard for marriage is steadily eroding as the

ever-present marriage triangle on TV now involves not just the bad guy but our heroes, the "nice guys." Sleeping overnight with someone else's wife or husband doesn't carry a hint that it might be wrong. Soap operas constantly feature the third person in the marriage relationship, and on one of the current top ten programs a divorced mother and her two daughters talked freely about not "doing it" until "Mr. Right" comes along. And little by little we are a bit less shocked as we grow accustomed to that kind of life-style.

In today's popular music there has crept in a gradual changing of moral values. We find ourselves actually sympathizing with the lovers who have to keep their "beautiful" love a secret till they both are free from the selfish culprits to whom they are married. And the young woman alone in her room at night convincingly laments that there is some man out there missing what she has to give.

I recall the startled expression on the face of a member of my Sunday School class when we read Jesus' words in Matthew 5:28 that "whosoever looketh on a woman to lust after her hath committed adultery with her already in his heart." Horrified, he exploded, "Does it really say that?" Yes, God's "flee fornication" still stands, no matter how much the world tries to change our thinking.

I wonder how many Christian young people are getting their moral standards from this relentless parade, and how many adults unwittingly lower their ideals because of this invasion by the world. And when does turning our heads and ignoring it change into condoning? *Changed*—first in our thinking and then in our actions.


## GULLIBLE—IF IT'S IN PRINT

A returned missionary shared with me that he felt God was calling him to translate good literature to send to the nationals he had just left. "They believe anything that is in print," he lamented. But it happens here in America, too.

270

A national denominational women's executive said to me one day, "What can we do about the gullibility of our women? Now that women are 'thinking for themselves' they are reading and studying everything they can get their hands on. And they are believing anything, as long as it's in print, swallowing everything printed under the name of 'Christian.'"

We should test every book we read by the Bible's standards, but the tendency today is to make the Bible's teachings fit into those of a book—secular or religious. In a Sunday School class a teacher was using a popular secular book, attempting to conform biblical concepts to the ideas expressed in the book. After a few sessions of this study, a doctor's wife became extremely agitated and said, "I personally studied this material in a seminar conducted by the author, and by nine A.M. he was 'bombed.' And we Christians are evaluating the Bible by what this alcoholic's book says!" Many of us act as if the Bible is on trial, whereas we should judge every book by what the Bible says. And this includes Christian books. An internationally known Christian psychologist startled me one day when he said that he didn't know a single Christian book that did not have in it something he considered to be contrary to the Scripture.

And we must evaluate *all* the teachings in a book. A national Christian radio personality told me last week that she had been reprimanded for reviewing a certain book on the air. In her hurried perusal of that book, she had missed the one antiscriptural teaching in it. But she learned that it was necessary to check out all the teachings of any book before she reviewed it. I've heard people say in defense of an author, "But that book has so much good in it." Great. Take what is good and true, and accept it. But we must reject anything, even from our favorite author, that is not consistent with biblical truth. A lot of truth in a book doesn't automatically make everything in the book true.

## A SOURCE OF WISDOM WHEN WE TEACH

Discerning an author's source of wisdom is also wise. When an author has been taught by God, what he has written can be a valuable source of wisdom for my changing. But I must be alert to things in print which are a result of the author's having received wisdom from Satan's realm or from his own "I thinks." If the teachings in a book are contrary to the Scriptures, the source of the author's wisdom could not have been from God, but from one of the other three sources—sensual self, demonic, or earthly.

Many times our preconceived ideas, our "I thinks" about what we want the Scriptures to say, color our interpretation. I was appalled as I read a Christian couple's paraphrase of Proverbs 31 in a Christian magazine. It obviously was their idea of the perfect wife, but it had little to do with the actual description of the virtuous woman recorded in the Bible portion. They wrote, "Your own clothing will be modest, but chosen in colors to please your husband," while the Bible actually said she made herself coverings of tapestry and her clothing was silk and purple (v. 22). And they said, "There may be many beautiful and intelligent women in the world, but I wouldn't trade you for any of them," whereas the Bible says the virtuous woman opens her mouth with wisdom (v. 26). Again they wrote of her buying fresh fruits and vegetables and, in consultation with her family, organizing the day's responsibilities. But the Bible said she considers a field and buys it—an independent businesswoman (v. 16). And the purpose of her making fine linen and girdles was to sell them to the merchants—not only for her family. This virtuous woman must have been an intelligent and clever businesswoman, for even the civic leaders in the gates praised her for her work.

A pastor's wife recently said to me, "I get that doctrine all straightened out until I go back and read so-and-so again." How easy it is to accept gullibly some author's "I think" about the Bible and be changed by it, not stopping to test it by what the Scripture actually says. But wisdom is only as good as the author's source, and is only worthy as a source of change for us if God has been his teacher.

Several years ago a teacher at a parent-teacher night said that our first-grade child had picked a book from the school library which she, a Christian teacher, questioned. Knowing we were a preacher's family, she said, "Oh, honey, you don't want to read *that* book, do you?" "Well," was the reply, "we don't have to *believe* everything we read." Did that little first grader know something many adults have not yet learned? Do we accept without question and are we changed by anybody's printed wisdom regardless of its source?

Those of us who write and teach have a grave responsibility to make sure of our source of wisdom. To admit we are wrong and change our teaching is admirable; but in doing so we must admit that our former source of wisdom could not have been from God for it expressed an opposing view.

This puts an awesome responsibility on my shoulders to make sure that *before* I teach others my source of wisdom has not been my "I thinks"—the results of being squeezed into the world's mold or the contemporary Christian culture, or by what is acceptable thinking and behavior in my specific Christian community. Or that my teaching has not been colored by the sensual welling up from within me. The really frightening responsibility is to make sure my source is not from demons. Satan can appear as an angel of light (2 Cor. 11:14), and some of his subtle persuaders look so right and feel so good that I sometimes have trouble catching those deceptions. But if I pass those on as I teach, they become heresy. I'm sure most antiscriptural teaching is done in complete innocence, the teacher having been convinced that his or her source of wisdom was God. But Paul warns us in 2 Corinthians 2:11 that we are not to be ignorant of Satan's scheming ways.

Then the question comes, *how can we retract and correct teaching that we have received from the three sources of wisdom other than God?* I may be able to reach a few, but the seeds I have sown multiply and in turn are scattered by those I have taught. How imperative it becomes for me to pray *before* I teach, asking God to remove all my preconceived ideas which may have been from the other three sources, and then to ask Him to guard and guide my mind as I study and teach.

There are some excellent books for husbands and wives these days that are God-inspired and tremendously beneficial. There are others that have not been inspired by Him. Here again, the author's source of wisdom makes the difference—God's holy Word or Hollywood. Is it advice that will change me into what God wants me to be? One husband complained to me, "My wife is acting like God is the Hugh Hefner of the sky." Also, where the author is in his or her personal life at a given point in time may not be the direction God wants us to take. We may be changed—but not according to God's will! Someone may be "teaching for doctrines the commandments of men" (Mark 7:7).

## TEST BY WHAT IT PRODUCES

Inadequate Bible study and basing our teaching on an inaccurate premise of what we think the Bible says produces the wrong kind of changes in our lives. Many women have come to me angry, depressed, or in tears because they studied material that was not accurate according to the Scripture, and they had tried to change into the persons God did not intend them to be.

An extremely frustrated and guilt-ridden author and teacher came to me one day because what she taught a woman had produced a husband who, instead of becoming the head of the house, had taken a gun and blown his brains out. Silently, I questioned the source of wisdom resulting in such tragedy. Reading through just the first six pages of her study course, I found a long list of things that I did not believe were scriptural, including the basic premise of the whole study. I went to prayer asking God to reveal the mind of Christ to her—not what Evelyn thinks for I can be right *or wrong,* and what God is saying to me for my life might not be what He is saying to her.

If our new life-style produces rebellion in our mates, it is good to check the source of wisdom that is affecting our changing. One husband whose wife had been following step-by-step a course of study finally exploded, "Honey, I married you because you were a bubbly, outgoing, beautiful hostess. I loved you the way you were. Will you please stop this idiotic behavior? I can't stand you this way." The changes in her life had infuriated him. And many husbands have been insulted and embarrassed that men in their social circles or neighborhood have all been receiving the same planned treatment each week. Discovering that their friends' wives and their own were changing their behavior toward their husbands in exactly the same way has caused deep hurts.

If what we teach produces bitterness, confusion, guilt, embarrassment, rebellion, insult or even divisions among Christians, we need to check the source of wisdom from which we are deriving our teaching. James 3:17 and 18 tell us: "But the wisdom that is from above is first pure, then peaceable, gentle, and easy to be entreated, full of mercy and good fruits, without partiality, and without hypocrisy. And the fruit of righteousness is sown in peace by them that make peace."

## NOT TO MANIPULATE

My motive for changing is not to manipulate other people. When I pray, "Lord, change me" I am only concerned with my changing into what He wants me to be.

Peter said my changed actions and attitudes will *affect* the people around me. Others will change as they see and observe my "chaste and reverent behavior" (1 Peter 3:1–2), but God takes care of changing them. I am responsible for me.

Some of the books and studies for women these days are designed to manipulate the husband into a certain response when the wife follows a certain pattern of behavior. One course of study teaches the wife how to manipulate her husband so that she with him will qualify for a higher place in heaven. And another study switches from God's plan to that of movie stars for manipulating men, husband or not.

One man said to me recently, "I am insulted that my wife is trying to manipulate my behavior in this way."

God's Word abounds with instructions for both husband and wife which are sufficient to produce all the joys, privileges and beauty of the marriage relationship. Letting God change us into warm, loving, responsive mates physically, emotionally, and spiritually is His will for us—not the manipulation of one another, but for each to be changed into what He wants us to be. Paul says in Colossians 2:8, "Beware lest any man spoil you through philosophy and vain deceit, after the tradition of men, after the rudiments of the world, and not after Christ."

## SQUEEZED INTO THEIR MOLD

One of the ways we conform to this world is described in J. B. Phillips' version of Romans 12:2 "Don't let the world around you squeeze you into its own mold."

We are exposed these days to courses of study that would squeeze us into the mold of the world. Many of these courses, in the areas of mind expansion, philosophy, and social behavior, are strictly from a worldly perspective with no consideration as to God's teachings. In them a clever, persuasive teacher can present the material in such a way that it produces dramatic changes in thinking and actions—frequently opposite from God's way of changing.

We tend to believe a teacher if he or she draws a large crowd. And we instinctively feel all those people can't be wrong. But as I read through the text of Mr. Sun Myung Moon's speech given to the standing-room-only crowd at Madison Square Garden recently, I realized the error of this thinking. He cleverly twisted and misinterpreted Scripture to "prove" that Jesus did not come to earth to die, the cross was not God's will for Christ, the crucifixion was a mistake, and Jesus thus could not save us totally. Then he went on to "prove" that Jesus was not coming back in the clouds but would be born again as the third Adam in the flesh.

A distraught leader of a large denominational district rally told me her daughter had left home to live at Mr. Moon's headquarters in our city. After I spoke to the gathering on this subject, the denomination's leader stood up and said, "I hope you paid attention to Mrs. Christenson, for right now, this week these Moon representatives will most likely knock on your door. It is our community they are saturating this week with their philosophy." Moon's followers are missionaries to Christians—trying to squeeze us into their mold. Trying to change us—but not as God would have us change. God's Word says, "Let no man deceive you with vain words" (Eph. 5:6).

## ADVICE FROM OTHER PEOPLE

As a young pastor's wife in our first city pastorate, I was eager to please everybody, and slacks were still questionable attire for women. But on our first Christmas in that pastorate my mother-in-law gave me a pair of lovely maroon wool slacks. I immediately put them on to go to the train station to meet an arriving relative. Just as I stepped out of our front door, an elderly member of our church passed by, stuck her nose in the air and said, "Harumph. Women in pants!" Then strode defiantly on past our house in the howling wind. Should I rush back and change into a skirt and be late for the train—or chance it?

As I stood on the train platform with the winter storm raging about and the plaid of my new slacks getting louder by the minute, I suddenly shrank back into the shadows. Another female member of our church! But I was too late. She bounded over to me and sighed, "Well, at last we have a pastor's wife with enough sense to dress for the weather!" Which one was right? Which one's reaction should I heed? It couldn't be both. In my confused state I dug out my Bible and once again found the answer from God—Acts 5:29: "We ought to obey God rather than men [people]."

This past Christmas my husband and I sat looking at the family picture on the Christmas card from our former assistant pastor and commenting on what a lovely family they were. He is now the assistant to a successful national leader of thousands of people. "Oh to think I advised him not to go with that man," recalled Chris. (At the time Chris gave that advice that new boss was a relatively unheard-of youth leader.) "That's why we obey God rather than men," I commented.

I went home and cried after receiving some advice from another person at a retreat. In a little exercise of giving something to each other she said to me, "I give you a spirit of adventure."

I was crushed. "Lord," I prayed, "have I missed it that much that people think I need a spirit of adventure?" Reviewing that very month, I realized how wrong that advice had been. I had turned fifty—which in itself took a lot of courage. And I enrolled in my first seminary class, started speaking on a then very misunderstood subject in churches and schools—"The Dangers of the Occult," organized my first St. Paul telephone prayer chain, conceived and planned the first of the annual Founder's Week luncheons for women at our college and seminary—and on the list went.

I'm sure I needed advice, but a spirit of adventure was not it. I could have used "Learn to say no," "One thing at a time," or, "Try eight hours of sleep some night." But a spirit of adventure—hardly. I'm sure the advice was well-intended, but missed my real need completely. Psalm 118:8 says, "It is better to trust in the Lord than to put confidence in man." Advice from other people can chisel away at us until we are reduced to a fraction of all that God intended us to be. God's wisdom enlarges, matures, and fulfills us.

However, the worth of people's advice is determined by their source of wisdom. There is much Christian counsel that is worthwhile and beneficial. But all advice must be evaluated in the light of the advice God gives in His Word. If the counseling is contrary to the Bible's instructions or from the person's "I thinks" it can never change us into the persons God intends us to be. "And my speech and my preaching was not with enticing words of man's wisdom, but in demonstration of the Spirit and of power; that your faith should not stand in the wisdom of men, but in the power of God" (1 Cor. 2:4–5).

How precious is the counsel of the godly to us, and how good to be changed by it; but even Job (Job 38:1–2), Christ (Matt. 16:21–23), and Peter and John (Acts 4:18–20) had to firmly reject being changed by the advice from people so that they could follow God's instructions and leading in their lives.

Changed? Yes! But by the only infallible, consistently reliable Source—the Lord.

# 11

## *Source No. 3,*
## *From Demons*

As I DISCOVERED, in James 3 that Sunday morning, the four sources of wisdom by which I could be changed, the most horrifying one to me was the wisdom from demons. Although I was well aware of this subject doctrinally, the sudden realization that it was possible for me to receive and be changed by wisdom from demons completely unnerved me.

Then I began to wonder. How much of the "confusion, strife, bitterness, and evil work" in my life have been caused by an input from Satan's kingdom? The possibility of demons literally shaping my life-style by the wisdom they were giving me suddenly loomed as a dark, threatening menace. I thought of the anger over a remark made years before that had seemed to come from nowhere as I read my Bible that morning. God had forgiven, and when He forgives, He forgets. So who dug up something settled nine years ago? Not God! I looked at the other three sources. Not the earthly source from other people—I was alone in my living room. My own "I think"? I couldn't make any sense out of that one since the incident hadn't been a part of my thinking, at least not that I was aware of, for nine years. I was left with just one source of wisdom that was producing that un-Christlike attitude in me—from demons!

## SPIRIT OF DISCERNMENT

One evening we had taken Corrie ten Boom to dinner at the top of our new IDS tower in Minneapolis. Ignoring the breathtaking view across our city, she suddenly asked, "What is the gift of the Holy Spirit least sought after these days by Christians?" Several shook their heads, wondering what Corrie was going to say. "I think I may know, Corrie," I said. "Is it a spirit of discernment?" (1 Cor. 12:10) Her eyes lit up. "Yes!" And she was off on one of her wonderful little sermonettes on a subject about which she was feeling deeply.

God had shown me this three years before in 1 Corinthians 12:8 and 10, "For to one is given by the Spirit . . . discerning of spirits." At that time I had prayed that He would give me that gift, the ability to identify the source— which spirit it was that was producing my life-style and that of others.

Then Corrie said, "It's a poor soldier, indeed, who doesn't even recognize the enemy."

Peter recognized and discerned the source of wisdom which caused Ananias to lie: "Why hath Satan filled thine heart to lie to the Holy Spirit?" (Acts 5:3)

Perhaps Peter recognized this source so easily because Jesus had identified it in him when Peter in his rebellion declared that Jesus could not go to Jerusalem to die—doing His Father's will (Matt. 16:22–23). Just saying, "I don't believe that can happen to a Christian" doesn't change the truth of our enemy's tactics one bit. We do receive wisdom from demons.

## BY WHAT IT PRODUCES

I learned from the Book of James that I can identify and discern the source of wisdom by what it produces. Bitter envyings, strife, confusion, and every evil work are always the input of Satan's kingdom. How frequently I have to claim God's "sound mind" of 2 Timothy 1:7, when I find this state of confusion in me, and let God change me!

I also discovered that fear is another product of this demonic source of wisdom. Several years ago, while reading our Bibles until God spoke, another woman and I were puzzled as to why God stopped us both at 2 Timothy 1:7. I tucked this truth down in my heart, but didn't need it until the following September. While conducting a retreat near Banff in the foothills of the Canadian Rockies, I was to speak on a Sunday morning on the subject of victory over Satan. On the night before, our campfire sharingtime near the horse corral was broken up by a pack of wolves. Around midnight when I returned to my bedroom in the far corner of the lodge a sense of uncanny fear came over me. I felt I was not alone, though a thorough search in closets and under the beds revealed no one. Turning out all the lights except the one over my bed, I took my Bible, zipped up my sleeping bag, and began quoting 2 Timothy 1:7: "For God hath not given us the spirit of fear, but of power, and of love, and of a sound mind." Then, telling Satan to get out of the room (James 4:7) and claiming 1 John 4:4, I went to sleep— a beautiful, restful sleep—and awoke the next morning changed, with actual tears of joy in my eyes. Completely changed by recognizing the source of that fear—and claiming the Scripture God had given to me six months earlier.

I saw this fear displayed in a college student from the University of Montana who was sitting next to me on a plane flying to California. He was telling me how deeply he was into meditation.

"Tell me, do you ever hear anything?" I asked.

With a fear in his eyes that I cannot describe, he said, "Lady, if I'd tell you everything I've heard, they'd come with a straitjacket and take me away. I hear bells, voices . . ." and with that his voice trailed off. It wasn't hard for me to discern the source of that fearful life-style, but he wasn't interested in changing it.

As I teach young people on this subject, I can usually tell which ones are getting their wisdom from some supernatural source other than God by the peculiar fear they exhibit. As many share their problem quite readily with me, I show them from the Bible that this way of life is not from God. What a joy to watch them change as they pray, asking God to forgive them. And I know the change is complete when the big smiles spread over their faces, demonstrating their happiness and relief.

Yes, the gift of the Holy Spirit least sought but so needed these days is the gift of discerning the spirits—the gift which enables us to discover the sources of wisdom that will change us, and to avoid those which will certainly not change us for the better.

## TEST THE SPIRITS

Now for the question: "How can we tell which kind of spirit is changing us?"

The Apostle John gave us a good test of the spirits: "Dear friends, do not believe every spirit, but test the spirits to see whether they are from God, because many false prophets have gone out into the world. This is how you can recognize the Spirit of God: Every spirit that acknowledges that Jesus Christ has come in the flesh is from God; but every spirit that does not acknowledge Jesus is not from God" (1 John 4:1–3, NIV).

John warned us not to believe every spirit; not to accept wisdom from those that are not of God, not to be changed by what they teach, say, or suggest to us.

And we are to test them according to whether or not they confess that Jesus Christ came in the flesh, that is, He took on a body with flesh and blood for the purpose of shedding that blood on the cross to defeat Satan (1 John 3:8). Every spirit that does not confess that Jesus is come in the flesh is not of God.

God said in His Word that "without shedding of blood there is no forgiveness" (Heb. 9:22, NASB). But because Jesus did come in the flesh, He redeemed us from sin by shedding His blood on the cross. "Forasmuch as ye know that ye were not redeemed with corruptible things . . . but with the precious blood of Christ" (1 Peter 1:18–19). (See also Matt. 26:28; Col. 1:14; Eph. 1:7.)

Sometimes it's difficult to discern what people who receive wisdom from demons really think of Jesus. A woman in our area, a popular speaker at local occult conventions, supposedly receives messages from dead loved ones by automatic writing. Our local newspaper quoted her as saying that God was great, the great Creator, etc., but farther down in the long article she was quoted as saying, "But the confusion comes when we try to put a *body* on 'it.' God can be an 'it' force in the universe, but don't put a body on 'it.'" This reveals what she thinks of Jesus having come in the flesh!

I was hoping someone dressed in a colonial costume would approach me at the Philadelphia airport when I was there on July 6, just two days after our 1976 Bicentennial birthday, and I was not disappointed. A lovely young girl in a bonnet and a long dress started telling me about our country's spiritual heritage. I beamed back and said, "Yes, I love God, and love and serve His Son, Jesus." At that she gave me a long speech about how great a teacher Jesus was and how wonderful He was. As I nodded in agreement, she continued, "And He was one of the ways to God." I blinked and started to listen more closely. "Oh, yes, He was *one of the ways to God.* There are many ways to God. Let me tell you about mine. I'm a Hare Krishna girl . . ."

"Hold it, honey," I interrupted. "I think you are doing a very diabolical thing here in Philadelphia at this, our nation's birthday celebration. Our country was founded on belief in God through Jesus, and you are saying how great He was and at the same time that He is just one of the ways to God. But Jesus said of Himself, 'I am the Way, the Truth, and the Life: no man cometh unto the Father, but by Me' (John 14:6). Now, He is either a barefaced liar, or He is who He said He is—the *only* way to God." What the Hare Krishna followers think of Jesus!

Krishna, whom she follows, says in chapter ten of the *Bhagavad Gita,* "I am the prince of demons." Test the source of that kind of wisdom before believing and being changed by it. Jesus said in John 8:44 that Satan was a liar and the father of lies.

Sometimes it is difficult to test the spirits. Three people supposedly dressed in costumes such as Abraham and Sarah might have worn came to one of my prayer seminars. They would not let me touch them as I tried to shake their hands in welcome because, they said, they were from Am.

"Where's Am?" I asked.

Surprised at my ignorance, they replied, "Oh, that's heaven. God sent us to earth, and He has been saying 'Evelyn' to us. When we saw the sign for your prayer seminar in front of this church, we knew you were the Evelyn."

I immediately started to pray for protection and discernment. (Several others in the audience sensed the need and prayed also.) After the seminar the female of the trio threw her arms around me to give me "a double portion of God's power" because, she said, I had taught everything that night that God had sent them to earth to tell. Perhaps I'll never know the source of those three, but I immediately knew and sensed the protection of Jesus Christ.

## DOCTRINE OF DEMONS

False teaching seems to be taking on a new dimension these days. The investigation of inner space and outer space (not authentic exploration) is producing a new kind of wisdom. It's possible to listen to lectures by "beings" from outer space, browse through endless shelves of do-it-yourself inner exploration, attend teaching sessions on the power of the mantra, reincarnation, dreams and the inner world, and astrology as cosmic patterning. Or we can bask in the Caribbean sun on a yoga vacation with Swami Vishnude Vananda or retreat to a Buddhist monastery in the Catskills. The September 6, 1976 issue of *Newsweek* put it this way: "There are more than 8,000 ways to awaken North America."

A University of Chicago anthropologist claims twenty million Americans belong to "fringe religious cults" such as the Hare Krishna movement, spiritualism, and Scientology. The market is flooded these days with cheap or expensive ways of changing with "wisdom" from every source mentioned in James 3 except the true God in heaven.

Paul warns us against the *doctrine of demons*, in 1 Timothy 4:1: "the Spirit explicitly says that, in later times some will fall away from the faith, paying attention to deceitful spirits and doctrines of demons (NASB)." This is not the doctrine *about* demons, but the doctrine *of* demons.

After a recent prayer seminar a woman in her 20s said to me, "I was deeply into TM, but recently while meditating I heard a voice say, 'That is of the devil.' Now, I'm from a church where we never talk about the devil, so that word could not have come from within me. It had to be God." God warning about being changed by the wrong source?

A faculty member of a southern Christian college asked for prayer at a prayer seminar. She had just returned from doing research for a postgraduate dissertation in Iowa near where the Maharishi Mahesh Yogi has established his university. Anxious for any mind-expanding help she could get, she took the

TM course and practiced it, but God spoke to her, telling her that this was of Satan and was not for Christians. She immediately renounced the practice. But what she asked us to pray about was that her secret mantra (that Hindu worship word) kept bonging and ringing in her head. No matter what she did or how hard she tried, she could not get rid of it. She had been changed in a way she didn't want to be changed.

According to *Time* magazine (March 1, 1976), students enrolled in TM classes at their high school in Maplewood, New Jersey, brought fruit and flowers to be placed on the altar before the picture of the late Guru Dev. Then, kneeling at this ceremony performed at the TM center in Union, New Jersey, they were given a mantra, the secret word that must be repeated to aid meditation.

These students were being changed, not by their own "I think" but by other people whose source of wisdom was not the God above. They were being changed by worshiping a pagan god.

Jesus said this method of meditation is used by pagans when they pray. But He told His disciples, "But when ye pray, use not vain repetitions as the pagans do" (Matt. 6:7, sco). Repeating one word over and over is not a method Jesus would use to change us.

However, there are biblical methods of meditating on our God who is in heaven. The Scriptures abound with examples. Dr. Herbert Benson, cardiologist and assistant professor of medicine at the Harvard Medical School discovered that, although meditating with a Hindu mantra did beneficially lower blood pressure, meditating in ordinary ways without a secret religious word also produced the same beneficial results. Christians call it prayer. The danger comes not from meditating, but from the spiritual powers to which we open our minds.

A professor in one of our large theological seminaries said, "If you want to find demons today, go to the pulpits of our churches on Sunday morning." I questioned the possibility of such a thing until I heard a sermon based on the best seller, *Jonathan Livingston Seagull.* Although the author himself speaks freely of occult healing power (having actually stopped the flow of blood with supernatural power when he cut himself) and of a "voice" telling him what to write in the book, his philosophy was used as a basis for many sermons. And one local pastor leads a group in "healing from the cosmos" every Tuesday evening. At eleven P.M. they meditate and get vibrations from their California headquarters, giving them power and the ability to see auras around people. Are preachers immune to this source of wisdom, or are they unusually vulnerable because their wisdom influences so many other people?

The book, *UFO Missionaries Extraordinary,* compiled by Hayden Hewes and Brad Steiger, could cause much deception about Jesus' second coming. In an interview with Bo and Peep in chapters 7 and 8, in which two "people" claim to have existed before and to have been sent to a woman's womb from the heavenly kingdom by a spacecraft that came close enough to earth to make contact, there are profuse references to Jesus and the Bible. They say they are part of a preparation for Christ's coming. Their teachings sound so plausible and are so near what Christ taught. When Jesus really comes back and Christians are taken up to be with Him, will people turn back to this book and believe those Christians went to the next level in a space ship?

A fine Christian woman with an important job for God in our area called me and said, "I've just read the *Reader's Digest* condensation of the book *Life After Life* by Dr. Raymond A. Moody, Jr. It's about people who died, left their bodies and then were brought back to life. They all (unless they committed suicide), whether Christian or nonChristian, had such a beautiful experience. There was nothing unpleasant, no judgment, and a warm being of light was seen by most of them. We Christians may have to reevaluate our position on what happens after death in the light of all that evidence!"

288

Taken aback, I recovered enough to say to her, "You are in a very important position for God in our city right now. You are especially vulnerable. Let me pray about this and I'll get back to you."

A few days before reading that book condensation, I had asked God to guard my mind and give me wisdom as to its truth. After the phone call, I prayed asking God to give me His answer to that book. Immediately it came to mind, "It is appointed unto men once to die, but after this the judgment" (Heb. 9:27). I suddenly realized what God was saying, "If those people are back here to tell the story, they did not really die." The death process was not complete. It is after we *really* die that there will be judgment—and eternal damnation for those who do not know Christ. The whole biblical teaching, of the wages of sin being death, must be discarded if there is only pleasantness, warmth, and light after death. Jesus said in John 3:16, 18: "For God so loved the world, that He gave His only begotten Son, that whosoever believeth in Him should not perish, but have everlasting life. . . . But he that believeth not is condemned already."

The "doctrine of demons" may not be popular with some Christians today, but in December 1971, a completely new thought illumined me as I was reading 1 Timothy 4:6: "If thou put the brethren in remembrance of these things, thou shalt be a good minister of Jesus Christ." Looking back to see what "these things" were, I realized Paul was talking about the *"doctrine of demons."* I don't like that subject either, but if I put other Christians "in remembrance of these things," I will change into a better minister of Jesus Christ.

## HOW WE OPEN OURSELVES
## TO WISDOM FROM DEMONS

"Where did we go wrong?" lamented a mother of a college girl who had left her Christian college to enroll in and later become a teacher in a local school for witches. I'm sure this is the question being asked by many agonizing and anxious parents. There are many ways Christians can open themselves to wisdom from demons, sometimes without being aware of what is happening.

There is much actual teaching of occult practices in our public schools and universities these days. During a question-and-answer period at a workshop conducted by an HEW member in Washington, D. C. last spring, I heard a schoolteacher from a large Florida city ask what could be done about the occult practices that were being taught in public grade schools by immigrants who brought their voodoo and witchcraft practices with them to Florida.

And a public school administrator in another large city told me she was terrified that we would get prayer legalized again in the schools. She told me that she knows personally Satan worshipers and witches who are teaching in their schools and added that in a democracy if Christians get the right to lead their pupils in prayer, so will the Satan worshipers and witches. And, she said, if our children are exposed to that kind of praying year after year, I'm not sure we'd ever recover them.

A rather new source of wisdom coming to our area is called "The Way." A distraught mother told our prayer chain chairman that the people of this movement were teaching her daughter that she should follow them if she wanted to be like Jesus, because He disobeyed His parents when He was twelve. That wisdom didn't come from God. They were seeking to change that little girl to be just the opposite of what the Bible says about obeying parents.

How many people discerned that the "I Got It" bumper sticker was the slogan of Werner Erhard's "est" and not at all related to the Here's Life "I Found It" slogan? Instead of accepting the fact of new life in Jesus Christ as deliverance from past sin, Werner Erhard believes that there isn't anything but spirituality, which is just another name for God.

He denies the past and thinks we should ignore the future consequences of our actions. Having removed moral and ethical considerations Erhard decided he was "God in my own universe."

"Why did God stop all eighteen of us individually on the word 'sorcery' in our cabin as we were reading Galatians 5 until He spoke?" asked a retreat chairman. "You had better tell *me* why," I answered. Then came a startling discussion of how they were using occult practices, such as Ouija boards for advice, in their farming procedures. Wisdom from God? In prayer those women confessed this as sin. God changed them by stopping them all on the same, very frightening word—sorcery.

Sometimes we deliberately ask for wisdom from demonic sources. Perhaps the most common way these days is by reading horoscopes. Millions of Americans get their daily life-style from the newspaper columns. God forbade this ancient practice, along with many other occult practices which are prevalent today, in instructions to Moses as the Children of Israel were entering the Promised Land. God said that those who do such things are an abomination to Him (Deut. 18:9–12).

At a retreat we were attending, a pastor's wife became concerned because there weren't any newspapers available. "I won't know how to run my life today," she moaned. "I won't be able to read my horoscope." Being susceptible to the power of suggestion from a source God calls an abomination to Him is dangerous indeed. And it certainly can't lead us in the direction God would have us go.

Believing and following predictions of psychics is another way of getting wisdom from a source other than God. We are warned, in Deuteronomy 18:21–22, that unless everything which is prophesied comes to pass, that prophet is not of God. Check the percentage of accuracy! The *National Enquirer*'s article of July 6, 1976, revealing the predictions of ten leading psychics for the second half of 1976, included the information that Castro would be ousted; Frank Sinatra was to emerge as a national hero after foiling an assassination attempt; the Six Million Dollar Man, the Johnny Carson Show, and Kojak would no longer be on TV; Billy Graham would suffer a heart attack forcing him to end his career; a gigantic earthquake in California would tear apart entire mountain ranges revealing the biggest gold deposits ever discovered—all before the end of 1976! And we gullibly swallow and mold our life-patterns—are changed—by that source of wisdom!

A frightening number of our children and young people are opening themselves up to wisdom from demons through occult practices these days. Students in a Christian school were disrupting their school playing Mary Worth—calling forth this witch's image on mirrors in darkened restrooms. At their parents' request, I explained to them that the people who practice this (and get wisdom from Ouija boards, tarot cards, séances, and all the other methods they told me they were using) are an abomination to God. How they changed that day as they asked God, one by one in audible prayer, to forgive and deliver them from this.

A mother told me that her daughter had solved a slumber party occult practice. She discovered that the other girls had no power when she prayed. And when they found out that she was the cause of their "games" not working, then they wouldn't allow her in the room when they were practicing them.

Another mother told me her daughter worried for years over a palm reader's prediction that she would die by the time she was sixteen.

Satan engineers our behavior without violating our free will. Weeping, an 18-year-old girl told me she had given her body for Satan worship with all its obscene acts because she was dating a boy who was involved in it. At the time, a pain had come in the pit of her stomach, and she had not been able to get through to God in prayer or understand anything in the Bible. After breaking up with the boy and renouncing Satan worship, she tried desperately to free herself from Satan's clutches and these symptoms, but could not. I prayed for her, using the same simple words Jesus prayed in His high priestly prayer in John 17, "Dear Father, deliver this dear one from the evil one." Then, according to James 4:7, I just said, "Satan, in the name of Jesus of Nazareth, get out of this dear girl."

The change was instantaneous and dramatic. She grabbed her throat as if choking, became a little light-headed, and then jumped up and threw her arms around me. "It's gone. The pain's gone. I'm free!" Changed by Jesus Christ!

A graduate of a Christian college, someone I know, was watching a TV program on Satan worship from San Francisco. He foolishly said, "If you're real, Satan, prove it." And Satan did. For over a year, though he struggled against it, power and direction for his life came from voices speaking to him in the shower and through inner compulsions. It is possible to voluntarily open ourselves to direction from Satan's kingdom.

Books on occult practices abound even in our best bookstores. Anyone desiring to be changed in this way has only to buy a book describing in detail the method he has chosen. But this is not new. Acts 19:19 tells us, "Many of those also who used [magical] arts brought their books together, and burned them before all men; and they counted the price of them, and found it fifty thousand pieces of silver." A huge sum compared to the worth of our Christ to Judas—sold for *thirty* pieces of silver.

Yes, we do receive wisdom from demons in so many different ways, sometimes by deception, sometimes by unknowingly opening ourselves, and at other times, deliberately. But the results are the same—change into a life-style opposite of what God would choose for us.

## KEEP YOUR MIND ON JESUS

An unusual demonic influence was described to me by a distraught woman in a Western city who had 14 immediate ancestors who were witches. They had practiced voodoo and palm reading on her from the time she was two years old, and a pastor had recently cast out the demons, but she was left with what she described as a hole in the pit of her stomach. I had no idea what she was talking about, but promised to meet her the following Saturday. On Thursday morning I awoke early and begged God to give me an answer for her. And He started recalling Scripture—Colossians 3:1–3, "Seek those things which are above, where Christ sitteth on the right hand of God"; Philippians 2:9–11, "That at the name of Jesus every knee should bow"; Ephesians 1:3, "In heavenly places in Christ"; Ephesians 1:19–22, "When He raised Him [Christ] from the dead and set Him at His own right hand in the heavenly places." I jotted the references down in my notebook, and when I met her I said, "The Lord gave me some answers for you out of His Word."

"Great," she said. "He gave me some too."

"Mine are in my notebook. I'll turn it face down on the desk while you tell me what Scriptures He gave you."

"God told me I was to get my mind off those demons and get it on Christ. He gave me Colossians 3:1–3; Philippians 2:9–11; Ephesians 1:3, 19–22." Exactly the same verses God had given me!

"And the hole in my stomach disappeared, too. All week long you have been teaching us how to pray and study the Bible. All you've talked about is Jesus. And the void in the pit of my stomach has been filled with Jesus."

What a change. She started that week confused, bitter, and frightened, but finished it radiating her newfound peace and excitement in Jesus.

In August of 1972 I prayed for the first time, "Lord, keep my mind from the evil one." Jesus prayed this prayer for us in His high priestly prayer, "Father, I pray . . . that Thou shouldest keep them from the evil [one]" (John 17:15).

God also provides us with the armor to withstand in our battle against these "principalities, powers, rulers of darkness of the world and spiritual wickedness in high places" in the battlefield of our minds (Eph. 6:12–18).

When I keep my mind in His Word, the sword of the Spirit, I have the weapon for the battle. One of my favorite verses is 1 John 4:4, "Greater is He that is in you [Christ], than he that is in the world [Satan]." When I am experiencing an onslaught of fiery darts, I quote it, and I immediately change into a victorious—not vanquished soldier for Jesus. One day, just reading that "Jesus . . . went about . . . healing all that were oppressed of the devil" (Acts 10:38), lifted the oppression I had been experiencing.

Kathy Barrow, the beautiful singer sponsored by World Vision, said to me the other day as we were talking about this battle, "I know how it comes out." And pointing to her Bible said, "I have read the end of the Book!" (See Rev. 20:10.) Yes, even Satan knows Jesus came to earth to destroy his works (1 John 3:8), and that Jesus said, in Matthew 25:41, "Depart from me, ye cursed, into everlasting fire, prepared for the devil and his angels." And even the demons recognized Jesus as He started His public ministry, crying, "Art Thou come to destroy us? I know Thee, who Thou art, the Holy One of God" (Mark 1:24). Victory in Jesus!

Sometimes I feel my shield of faith needs to be as powerful as the heat shield of a space capsule to quench the fiery darts of Satan. But it never fails because my faith is in a Person, the risen, glorified, Lord Jesus Christ.

All this armor listed in Ephesians 6 is to protect my thought life—to withstand the wisdom of Satan and his emissaries, the demons. But there is no mention of falling, only standing and withstanding when I wear God's armor! James did show us that frightening source of wisdom—from demons. But he also gave us a promise: "Resist the devil, and he will flee from you" (James 4:7).

It is imperative to admit the reality of this source of wisdom and be alert to discern it, but it is equally important to keep it in its proper perspective. It's good to remember the advice the mama spook gave to the baby spook, "Don't spook unless spooken to." Even though "the whole world lies in the power of the evil one" (1 John 5:19, NASB), it is also true that the earth is only God's footstool. This little speck of dust in the universe we call Planet Earth is temporarily Satan's domain, but the heaven of the heavens cannot contain my God (1 Kings 8:27). And He lives in me!

Yes, it is possible for me to be changed when I receive and respond to wisdom from demons. But this is not a necessary process in my life. I have been given all the resources and power I will ever need to resist this source of wisdom and be changed only as God wants me changed—with wisdom from Him.

# 12

## Source No. 4,
## The Lord

"AND BE NOT conformed to this world; but be ye transformed by the renewing of your mind, that ye may prove what is that good, and acceptable, and perfect, will of God" (Rom. 12:2).

Transformed! The opposite of being conformed to this world!

"Lord, is this what You had in mind when You led me to pray, 'Lord, change me' so many years ago? God, do You mean I can actually be transfigured just as Christ was on the Mount of Transfiguration? (Matt. 17:2) It's the same Greek word, Lord. Really changed like that?

"I guess You meant it, Lord, because You said, 'Be ye transformed.'

"You wouldn't have said that if You didn't mean it, Lord. Is this what You've been doing all these years? Transforming me?

"Lord, I know You are the only Source of wisdom worthy to be used to produce my life-style, and You've taught me all these ways to obtain Your wisdom; but *how* have You been accomplishing this transformation in me? It's been a huge task, Lord! How have You done it?"

## THE SOURCE IS ALSO THE MEANS

We have an oil painting of my husband's favorite verse on one of our walls, and every time I walk by it I am reminded of how the Lord accomplishes this changing, this transforming in me: "For it is *God* who worketh in you both to will and to do of His good pleasure" (Phil. 2:13). The Source of wisdom to change me is also the Means. It is God Himself who is working in me, producing the change. When I try to pick myself up by my own bootstraps I can fall so flat on my face. Even when I know how to change, doing it myself is practically impossible.

But there is a Person involved. A divine Means. Back in November 1971, I wrote "Lord, change me" in the margin of my Bible by Hebrews 11:6. Then I added, "I believe You will do it." "Without faith it is impossible to please [God]," but the faith is not in the seeking or the changing process; faith is in a Person. God will reward me and work in me when I diligently seek Him. God is the divine Means for my changing.

"How, then, Lord, do You bring about this changing?"

## BY THE RENEWING OF YOUR MIND

How does God accomplish this transformation in our lives? When we accept Christ we become a new creation (2 Cor. 5:17). The Book of Romans was written to those who had become new creations (1:7); and, according to Romans 12:2, there is a process that should be going on in the lives of these people, for the phrase "be ye transformed" is in the present continuous tense. And these new creations have within them the potential of this ongoing process of being transformed.

These new creations are to be transformed *by the renewing of their minds*—not "in the vanity of their own mind, but by a change in their pattern of thinking" (Eph. 4:17–23). It is in the realm of our thinking that we are bombarded by the three wrong sources of wisdom listed in James 3:15, but it is also in this realm that God does His changing.

Proverbs 23:7 tells us, "For as he thinketh in his heart, so is he." To realize that I am actually the sum total of all that I think is frightening. But it is also exciting, for God is in the continuous process of changing what I think—and thus changing me. He is providing both the wisdom and the means to change my thinking. And the result is a transformed me!

## I'M UNIQUE

How I thank God that He created me a unique individual. Nobody else is just like me. And God's finished product, "Me," is different from any other He has planned.

But I must realize that every other Christian is unique, too, and God is changing them according to His divine blueprint. I have a tendency to feel that if some changing is right for me, then God must want everybody else to change in the same way. But that is not true. The way the Lord changes me does not automatically become a pattern for every other person. Only the omniscient God of heaven has clearly in mind the finished product for each of His children, and I must let Him, not Evelyn, be every individual's Source of wisdom. I must direct others to the Designer of their individual blueprint—the Lord of glory.

And having God's unique blueprint in my spiritual genes also makes me responsible; accountable for all the potential He put in me; answerable to God for how I let Him change me into what He ultimately wants me to be. "So then every one of us shall give account of himself to God" (Rom. 14:12).

This places the ultimate responsibility on each individual before God. In the final judgment each person will answer for himself. God has only children, no grandchildren. I will be accountable *only* for me—only for what I have allowed God to do in and through me. "Oh, Lord, change ME!"

## CHANGED—SO THAT . . .

Change for the sake of change doesn't make much sense. In the natural realm, the new isn't always better than the old. Romans 12:2, however, gives us the reason for our being transformed. And this is not only better but best. "Be ye transformed by the renewing of your mind, *that ye may prove what is that good, and acceptable, and perfect, will of God*" (italics mine). This is that will of God which is in itself pleasing to Him and which results in actions on the part of His children that are pleasing and acceptable to Him. Changed so that all the words of my mouth and the meditations of my heart are *acceptable* in the sight of my Lord (Ps. 19:14). Changed, so that I will be and do what He wants.

Changed, also, that others may observe my behavior— which has been changed because my thinking is acceptable to God (1 Peter 3:1–2). So often our lives reflect "do as I say, not as I do," but the Book of 1 Peter says my husband (and other people) are changed and won when they see my changed life.

A psychiatrist who attended one of my prayer seminars wouldn't accept anything I said until she saw me in action with other people. Not knowing she could read lips, I questioned her intense gaze from the other side of the room as I interacted with and counseled several different people at a dinner party following the seminar. My speech at the seminar was of little value to her until she saw me prove myself in action. James says a person who is really wise *shows* it out of a good life (3:13).

The first spring we lived in our house in St. Paul, I came down to the dining room one morning to see it alive with brilliant color. The whole room was aglow with little rainbows all over the walls, ceiling and furniture. The rising sun had come far enough north to be directly in line with my small kitchen window, the dining room door and then our crystal chandelier. And the piercing white light of that morning sun was producing hundreds of rainbows by diffusing through all the crystals every color of the spectrum. I swung the chandelier ever so slightly, and the colors danced and flashed around the room. I stood spellbound at the spectacular sight.

How similar that is to God's penetration of my life. Webster's *New World Dictionary* defines white as "the color of radiated, transmitted, or reflected light containing all of the visible rays of the spectrum." And God, too, is the sum total of all that exists. He is infinite. One of His attributes is infinity—that quality of being limitless, to which nothing can be added. And He enters me as pure white piercing light. God in me, my Source of change, wanting to *radiate* through me all the visible rays of the sum total of all that He is. God's acceptable will for me is that I will let Him change me until I sparkle and glow and radiate Him into my whole environment.

## THERMOMETER OR THERMOSTAT?

Changed—so that we become a thermostat, not a thermometer.

So much of the time we are like thermometers, registering the temperature of the atmosphere around us. We respond to a cold shoulder, a chilly remark, a cool reception with a plunge of our own thermometers. Or a hot accusation influences us to flash back with a hotter retaliation.

We find it difficult to keep cool heads with heated arguments going on around us, and a warm, suggestive look frequently fans into a burning temptation. But when we let God change us into what He wants us to be, we become thermostats—changing the climate around us, not just registering it.

And when it is God who sets the dial, our environment always changes for the better. When the suggested change comes from our sensuous self, Satan's Kingdom, or from other people, the temperature extreme may get worse instead of better. But when God changes us, a cold piercing glance turns into a tender look, a sharp tongue utters a soft answer, an aloof stance melts into a loving caress, a clenched fist into a squeezing hand.

But we must have complete confidence in the divine Changer. He always knows when the temperature needs changing to better the environment, and He always knows just how many degrees to turn the dial.

## MY SPIRITUAL BAROMETER

For over 20 years my spiritual barometer has been 1 John 1:4, "These things write we unto you, that your *joy* may be full." The amount of time I spend in God's Word, letting Him change me, seems to register on my spiritual personality indicator. The more time I spend seeking after God's wisdom, the more joy He produces in me.

As I grow older I find that fewer things cause a "tingle" in the pit of my stomach. The first snow of winter, bare feet on the first spring grass, the first squeeze of my teenage boyfriend's hand all produced an exhilarating sensation. But these impressions seem to diminish with age. However, there is one thrilling sensation that becomes stronger every year and seems to come more frequently with passing years—the thrill of having God speak to me out of His Word!

God changes me *as* I turn to Him for advice on how to change. Proverbs 2:10–11 is underlined in my Bible: "When wisdom entereth into thine heart, and knowledge is pleasant unto thy soul, discretion shall preserve thee, understanding shall keep thee." In the margin I wrote, "*Pleasant*—not rebelling against or negative to but my spirit soaring in JOY." Yes, God's wisdom is written down for me so that I might be changed—that my joy might be full.

## THE NEXT PLATEAU

God always changes me to lift me to a higher level. Sometimes God's changing takes me through hot fires, deep valleys, grief or suffering; but after a while the "God of all grace" makes me perfect, established, strengthened and settled (1 Peter 5:10). These unpleasant experiences have prepared me for the next and higher plateaus of my life.

After an extremely deep valley in our family, I recorded in my Bible my cry to God, "O Lord, when is after a while?" But it was exactly a year later that I added the note, "*Now* is God's after a while! Great joy again!" It had taken a year for God to do His changing in me and turn that difficult circumstance back to normalcy.

When the violent learning season is over, God settles me down—but not where I was before. As I'm changed, according to His will, He places me on the next plateau that He has prepared. There's always an open door and always power to go through it when I am changed into what He wants me to be.

In June 1968, when I prayed, "Lord, make me the kind of wife *You* want me to be," instead of removing my speaking engagements, God did just the opposite. He opened a whole new life of ministry. He had an exciting succession of open doors ready for me (and many since then). And through those 14 months of searching, letting Him *change me,* God was preparing me for those doors He was waiting to swing wide open for me.

But even going through His open doors sometimes requires sacrifice. A woman in my group on a World Day of Prayer, commenting on "If any of you lack wisdom, let him ask of God" (James 1:5), said, "Sometimes I don't want wisdom. It's easier to sit in a corner and do nothing than to know what to do and then have to do it." ·

As my advisory board and I pray through each new door God seems to be swinging open for us, I realize more and more that obedience requires sacrifice. And it involves sacrifice on my husband's part, also. But God always gives more than I give Him. He has rewarded my obedience with more joy, acceptance, and respect for each other than Chris and I have ever known before. And God is changing me bit by bit into becoming more like that virtuous woman in Proverbs 31 of whom it says, "The heart of her husband doth safely trust in her" (v. 11).

## FOR MY GOOD

When God gave me my life verse, Romans 8:28, in 1946, I had no idea how good the things He was working out for me would be. As I look back, I can see so clearly the way He has picked up the shattered glass of my life and carefully fashioned the stained glass window He is now making of me. Lost babies, surgery, heartaches, grief—all have been used by God to change me. And always for the better.

How I thank Him for the privilege of growing older so I can reflect on what He was really doing. And I'm sure I won't begin to understand all of this until it is explained to me in heaven. God, the Source and the Means of my changing, working out all these things that change me—all for my good.

## THEREFORE

This morning I was very tired and felt I could not get out of bed to start the day. As I lay there communing with my God, He brought Isaiah 40 to my mind. Reaching for my Bible I was sure it was verses 28 to 31 about our strength being renewed that He wanted me to read. But I started reading at the beginning of that chapter and found something completely different.

My heart soared as I read about my God—*who He is!* Nobody taught Him. "All nations before Him are as nothing. . . . [He] sitteth upon the circle of the earth, and the inhabitants thereof are as grasshoppers . . . [He] stretcheth out the heavens as a curtain. . . . Lift up your eyes on high, and behold who hath created these things . . . the everlasting God, the Lord, the Creator of the ends of the earth, fainteth not, neither is weary. There is no searching of His understanding" (Isa. 40:17–28). I clutched my Bible to my heart as tears came to my eyes. Who He is!

Then I noticed I had written in the margin of my Bible by Isaiah 40, "12/23/71, see Romans 11:36 to 12:2" with the "2" underlined several times. Turning to Romans, I discovered that I had written on that same day "12:1, therefore." God had connected these two passages for me in 1971.

Now whenever we see the word "therefore" we look back to see what it is "there for." In Romans 12:1–2 Paul is "therefore" beseeching us to give God our bodies, not to be conformed to this world, and to be transformed by the renewing of our minds. So what is this transforming process "there for"?

Looking back to the four preceding verses I found what it is "there for"—because of *who God is.* And the words are quoted from Isaiah 40! I am to be transformed by the renewing of my mind because of *who* God is.

"O the depth of the riches both of the wisdom and knowledge of God! How unsearchable are His judgments, and His ways past finding out! For who hath known the mind of the Lord? Or who hath been His counselor? Or who hath first given to Him, and it shall be recompensed unto him again? For of Him, and through Him, and to Him, are all things: to whom be glory forever. Amen" (Rom. 11:33–36).

## A PROCESS

I wish I could say that I have arrived, but I can't since this word "transformed" in Romans 12:2 isn't a once-for-all happening. It is a *process*. And whenever I feel that I have arrived, or that I am just about what God had in mind for me to be, He starts changing me again. And this process has been going on all my life.

When I was a little girl I longed for God to change me—into an angel. My sister, brother, and I each had a special Christmas tree ornament that was our very own. We could hang it any place we wanted on the tree. Mine was a beautiful pink angel. And I would hang it on a low branch, way inside, near the tree trunk where it could not be seen except from my favorite, private spot—under the tree. Lying on my back, I spent hours gazing at that lovely, fragile, glass angel and dreaming my favorite dream: "If only I could be an angel!" How I wished I had been made an angel instead of a little girl.

But the words in a song, "Holy, holy, is what the angels sing," that became popular when I was a young teenager, brought it all into focus for me:

"But when I sing redemption's story,
They will fold their wings;
For angels never knew the joys
That our salvation brings."

No, created in all their beauty, power and intelligence, no angels will ever have the privilege I have of being

306

changed by God, step-by-step, into conformity to the image of His dear Son, Jesus (Rom. 8:29). The angels probably aren't going through the often hard, deep and fiery changing process, but neither are they *becoming conformed to Jesus' image!* Nor have they been promised some day *to be like Him.* Yes, they see Him now and have seen Him for eternal ages past, but they are still not like Him. But I, a mere mortal, *when I see Him will be like Him.* "When He shall appear, we shall be like Him" (1 John 3:2). Whether I leave this world through death or am changed "in the twinkling of an eye" when my Jesus returns, the process will be complete.

"Behold, I show you a mystery; we shall not all sleep, but *we shall all be changed.* In a moment, in the twinkling of an eye, at the last trump; for the trumpet shall sound and the dead shall be raised incorruptible, and *we shall be changed"* (1 Cor. 15:51–52).

I shall be perfect as He is perfect! My long "Lord,-change-me" struggle will be over. I will be like Jesus!

"Dear Father, I have so far to go. I fall so short of what You want me to be. Please keep changing me on this earth until there won't be so much left to change when I see my Jesus. LORD, CHANGE ME!"

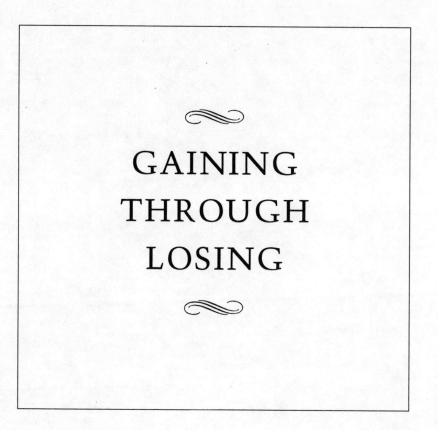

GAINING
THROUGH
LOSING

# Contents

To my dear ones who prayed fervently and unceasingly for fourteen months while I was writing this book, praying God's will for each thought and every word:

My prayer chains who not only communicated my every physical, emotional, mental, and spiritual need, but fervently and faithfully prayed—

Mother and Rollie who prayed daily whether or not they knew my specific needs—

Mother Chris who spent so many of her hours in her rocking chair praying for me—

Chris who understood and undergirded me in prayer when the hours were too long and the task too great—

All those other dear family members and friends who sensed needs and prayed so often—

To them—my indescribable thanks.

To God—all the glory.

# Discovery

I HAVE DISCOVERED through the years a most astounding principle at work in my life: gains actually come through the seeming-losses.

When I was just 23 years of age, I took as my philosophy of life the promise in Romans 8:28—that God was working out all things for my good because I love Him. But *how* He was doing it has slowly unraveled before my eyes year after year. God has not removed every loss, hurt, or difficulty. But He has worked *through* them—turning each of them into a gain.

Every one of my *gaining-through-losing* experiences is backed by a biblical precept. And God has put the two together—my experiences and His teaching—until my losses due to circumstances and this world's natural course of events have produced a life of gains. I have sometimes failed to do my part, but even so God has *always* worked out every loss for my gain—when I let Him.

313

But I have two regrets in writing this book. The first is that there was not enough space to include the myriad of other gains through losses—some small and others large—which came into focus as I reviewed and analyzed my life in the writing of this manuscript.

The second regret is that some of the most profound gains have come through losses which cannot be recorded in a book. There are those heartbreaking experiences which I've worked through with family and friends that are much too private to share. Those times when together we've discovered God's amazing gains as He counseled, comforted, and healed us.

Then there are those deep times of my life that forever will be only between my God and myself. Wounds and losses that are not for human eyes nor human understanding. Those times when God has walked so closely by my side, sometimes explaining the whys and other times just silently assuring me of His presence.

And then there must be an eternity full of surprises. Those millions of gains-through-losses which I never even knew happened here on earth. Waiting to be unveiled to my astounded mind—in heaven.

But here *is* a whole book full of fabulous gains I've already discovered and which I *can* share. Share in the hope that they will help you discover in your everyday hurts or calamitous tragedies that God is also standing by—ready and anxious to turn your losses into gains.

# Section I
# GOD'S
# "SO THAT" PLAN

# 1

## *Gaining Through God's "So Thats"*

DO YOU ALWAYS win? Or do you sometimes lose? If you do, God is in the business of turning your losses into gains.

It was back in 1965, as I lay fretting in my hospital bed recovering from gallbladder surgery, that God began to teach me the gaining through losing principle. Here I was struggling against having to be in that bed because I was missing all the exciting things He was doing in our church those days. As I reached for my pillow radio receiver, I searched the local stations until I heard a familiar voice. It was that of a pastor friend chatting to us "shut-ins" between musical numbers and poetry reading. Suddenly I heard him say, "The title of this poem is 'Gaining Through Losing.'"

And I was about to discover one of the greatest of all discoveries about God—as he read:

*I asked God for strength, that I might achieve,*
*I was made weak, that I might learn humbly to obey,*
*I asked for health, that I might do greater things,*
*I was given infirmity, that I might do better things.*

*I asked for riches, that I might be happy,*
*I was given poverty, that I might be wise.*
*I asked for power, that I might have the praise*
*of men,*
*I was given weakness, that I might feel the need*
*of God.*
*I asked for all things, that I might enjoy life,*
*I was given life, that I might enjoy all things.*
*I got nothing that I asked for—but everything I*
*had hoped for.*
*Almost despite myself, my unspoken prayers were*
*answered.*
*I am, among all men, most richly blessed.*

Suddenly I came alive. I had discovered God's "so that" principle!

As I've studied the Bible, I have discovered that every facet in God's dealing with His people—with you and me—seems to include a "so that." In effect God says to us, "I am permitting this unpleasant experience *so that* you may *gain* . . . *so that* you may *gain* a new insight, *so that* you will be *richer* in your experiences and thereby help someone going through a similar problem." Nothing with God is haphazard, coincidental, or happenstance. Problems in our lives do not mean that God has lost control or that He is no longer on His throne, but they give us the glorious opportunity to prove God's "so thats"—*so that* we might gain through our losses.

That anonymous poem, believed to have been found on the body of a Civil War soldier, had jolted me—yes, shaken me out of my self-pity. Could it be true? Could God take what seems to be a loss and through it give me something better? Could He turn bitter losses into fabulous gains?

From that day to this, I have been discovering God's "so thats" throughout the Bible and His applications of them in my personal life. Through the years God has unfolded some of the magnitude of this principle to me. When we let Him, He takes our losses and shows us His great "so thats"—so that we can have or be more than before. He works our losses all out for our gains. That day, I thought the poem applied to the giving of my body to the Lord, but that was only the immediate result. Today, I can fill this whole book with God's "so thats"—how He takes our *losses* and turns them into *gains*.

What do those two little words *so that* really mean? *The Random House Dictionary of the English Language* (p. 1350) gives these definitions for *so that:* "in order that," "with the effect or result." It involves the reasons, the whys of life. Even the little word *that* is defined as "expressing cause or reason, purpose or aim, result or consequence" (p. 1470).

The Bible is full of God's "so thats." Paul tells us that the things which happened to him had "fallen out rather unto the furtherance of the gospel; *so that* my bonds in Christ are manifest in all the palace and in all other places" (Phil. 1:12–13). He also explains a "so that" to the members of the church of the Thessalonians: "You became followers of us, and of the Lord, having received the word in much affliction, with joy of the Holy Ghost; *so that* you were examples to all that believe" (1 Thes. 1:6–7). Then Jesus, before restoring sight to the man blind from birth, must have startled His disciples with His answer to their question, "Who did sin, this man, or his parents?" He replied, "Neither has this man sinned, nor his parents; but *that* the works of God should be made manifest in him" (John 9:3).

## JESUS' "SO THAT" PRINCIPLE

Jesus both taught and lived this "so that" principle. He repeatedly explained it in the seeming paradox of "gaining through losing." He summed it up in His words, "Whosoever will lose his life for My sake shall find it" (Matt. 16:26). Lose life *so that you* can gain it? Yes, Jesus said you must lose your life so that you can find it. It will be *through* your

319

loss that you can actually gain. Then Jesus used the most valuable possession we have to teach this lesson—our lives.

For whosoever will save his life shall lose it: and whosoever will lose his life for My sake shall find it (Matt. 16:25).

How unpopular that philosophy must have been in His day! And how unpopular it is today. Somehow people can't handle losing. We don't think of losing as something that can be positive. We are a success-oriented society. Losing is unpleasant. Losing is failure, and failure is doom. We are taught how to win, but we have little or no teaching on how to lose.

Can losing life actually produce gain and the finding of life? From our rat-race perspective, it seems that Jesus had things a little mixed-up. Was He not facing the reality of the hard, cold facts? Didn't He understand the sting, pain, and sorrow of losing—especially losing what we call *life?* "Whosoever *loses* his life for My sake shall *find* it"?

## WHAT IS LIFE?

But what is life—that elusive something we humans are chasing, seeking, and so frantically pursuing? Is it utopia, a never-never land of euphoric happiness? Is it what we Christians are seeking to have "more abundantly"? Intangible, indescribable, yet we believe we will recognize it when we find it.

We seek *life* in health spas for the body beautiful, in doctors' offices for vigorous health, in a regimented lifestyle for longevity. We look for it in ever-changing sports fads, in shorter workweeks, in hobbies to take the boredom out of our leisure time. We hoard money in banks to ensure a life of comfort. We invest in stocks and insurance for security at retirement, or in property to achieve equity. We search for life through education, equal rights, mind-expanding

320

programs, and through the passive search for tranquility. We strive for it by moving up to the right neighborhood, being involved socially, getting to the top professionally, by being needed. We know we will reach it when we are free from an addiction or a habit or a confinement. And we will clinch it all by marrying the love of our life and moving into our dream house. Then there will be life—lived "happily ever after"!

But somehow, no matter how many of these we find, there is always the haunting feeling that there must be more to life than this. One of the highest incidences of suicide today is among the affluent, popular so-called "beautiful people"—those who have attained most of these.

Well, then, perhaps life after all is just the seeking of it —that life is found in the process of seeking it. Is it true that the pursuit of it, to which we are all constitutionally entitled, brings happiness? Or can we really find it?

Then, if we can find life, will we really find it through Jesus' mind-jarring paradox of "gaining it through losing it"? I decided to find out.

A word of caution here: This principle has nothing to do with a martyr complex or suicidal tendencies. Jesus never leads us to commit suicide. Nor does this principle have to do with the masochistic tendency to seek gratification from pain, deprivation, or self-denial. It does not apply to those who enjoy losing, but to those plain, ordinary, everyday followers of Christ who are *willing* to lose their lives—for His sake.

One evening, while looking up the biblical definition of that word *lose* for this book, I was shocked at the synonyms: "kill, annihilate, put an end to." Turning to my husband I said, "Chris, I can't write something I can't live. How do I really lose, put an end to, my life for Christ's sake?"

"Well, I think you have already accomplished 99 percent of it," he reassured me.

"Then this must be a huge 1 percent with which I'm struggling," I sighed.

The next Sunday was Easter. Before dawn I spent three hours in deep prayer, begging God to show me what it meant to lose my life. Agonizing prayer—punctuated with hot tears. Then gradually, the answer seemed to come from God: "Empty yourself of all of you, Evelyn."

I thought I had done this many times before. I had certainly tried to through years of serving Him. But God showed me there was still more of self to be relinquished. Looking back, I see that there always had been more. After I would pray, "Nothing of me Lord," sooner or later He would show me another area of my life to lose. And so that Easter morning, I struggled hard to discover the "all of me." I was confident that God had just given the answer, but somehow the whole sense of "losing" was not there yet. I still strained to find it.

The next morning my secretary came to work with a puzzled look on her face. Then she said, "I was really struggling in prayer early yesterday morning. But it wasn't for me. I kept saying, 'But this is Easter, Lord. I should be rejoicing, but I'm not!' Ev, it was somebody else I was praying for, but I don't know who." Then I told her how I too was struggling during those very same hours. She looked up at me in amazement and exclaimed, "Oh, it was *you!*"

Then I decided to try an experiment. I can handle things in little slots of time better than attempting something forever and ever. So the next Friday I said, "Lord, this weekend I want to lose my whole life completely for Jesus' sake as I go to Canada to bring this prayer seminar." Then, at the Holiday Inn in Ottawa before starting to teach on Saturday morning, I spent more than an hour in sincere, expectant prayer. "Father, today is the day. Empty me of all of me."

I had prayed that prayer a thousand times before, but this time it was different—deeper, more desperate. "Take *all* of me. Every deep, hidden, unspoken, unrecognized desire for acclaim. Please, no *desire* to have anybody talk about how my books are selling; no *desire* for praise or statistics; no *desire* for people's gratitude for the ministry; no *desire* for Evelyn even to be seen or her voice heard. Take it all out, Lord—*all*."

As my prayertime drew to a close, there was an unexpected shift in the direction of my prayers. Something was *coming* instead of *leaving*. It was a surprise because I really wasn't expecting the answer to be something I could feel. I'd only had vague thoughts about somehow nothing of me in the seminar that day. But suddenly I felt pouring into my very being a sensation I had not known before. A brand-new emotion I'd never experienced in 48 years of walking with God. Something warm and radiant, soft yet bright, swelling inside me until it engulfed me. I stayed motionless on my knees, hardly daring to breathe lest I disturb that new something. What was it? Life? The kind of life Jesus promised when we lose ours for His sake?

A couple of hours later, I sought to explain my new exuberant attitude in the opening remarks at the seminar, but words failed. I tried *joy*. No. I've had joy from God before, lots of joy. *Fulfillment?* No. After a great expression of family love or a deep moving of God in a seminar, I've often said, 'If I get any more fulfilled, I'll explode." But there it was. The *life* Jesus gives—that came when I wanted to lose mine for His sake. When I wanted to give all of me for Him. Abounding, exuberant, unspeakable life!

A week later I received in the mail a poem entitled "Treasures," by Martha Snell Nicholson. How well it expresses what God had taught me.

> One by one He took them from me.
> All the things I valued most
> Until I was empty-handed;
> Every glittering toy was lost.

323

And I walked earth's highways,
  grieving,
In my rags of poverty.
Till I heard His voice inviting
  "Lift your *empty* hands to Me!"
  (italics mine)

So I held my hands toward heaven,
  And He filled them with a store
Of His own transcendent riches
  Till my hands could hold no more.

And at last I comprehended
  With my stupid mind and dull
That God could not pour His riches
  Into hands already full.
  (*Her Best for the Master*, comp.
    F. J. Wiens, Moody Press)

We frantically scurry around looking for life in all the things we have and do, when all along the secret is in the *losing.* We can't be filled with two things at one time; so it is a matter of being emptied—emptied *so that* Christ can fill us—with His life.

I'm sure there will always be more. More of Him when there is less of me. But for now I'm also sure I have discovered the secret, the formula for finding and gaining life— radiant, abundant life. *Losing* it for Jesus' sake.

Losing my life *so that* I can find it.

## JESUS' "SO THAT" FORMULA

Let's look at Jesus' "so that" formula for finding life in its scriptural setting. (See Matt. 16:13–27.) His teaching, "Whosoever will lose his life for My sake shall find it," was given to His disciples right after His command: "Follow Me." Follow Him? Where? How?

In the preceding incident, Jesus had just told them that His own "so that" would be *losing* His life through suffering and dying *so that* the *gaining* could come in resurrection on the third day. From Peter's reaction in rebuking Christ, it seems that he heard only the losing. He apparently missed Christ's intended *so that*—His absolute, once-for-all victory over sin and death on that cross. Peter missed Christ's triumphant rising which gave assurance to all future Christians (see 1 Cor. 15). He missed the fact that the cross was not the end, but just the "so that" of unleashing the redeeming power that was to surge throughout all of Planet Earth.

In fact, Peter decided to nip the whole process in the bud. He probably was feeling a little puffed up. Hadn't Jesus told Peter that his declaration that He was "the Christ, the Son of the living God" had come to him from the Father in heaven? So Peter, thinking he knew God's ways even better than Christ, rebuked Him with an "I won't let this happen to You" attitude (Matt. 16:22).

How often I have played Peter and looked at others, deciding that their seeming-losses could not possibly be God's will for them! It has taken years for me to begin to recognize God's perfect "so that" plan for those I love or counsel. I too prefer to protect them from God's frequent way of giving gains through losses.

It is frightening to see that Jesus' answer involved calling Peter "Satan." His words must have stung: "Get thee behind Me, Satan. Thou art an offense unto Me; for thou savourest not the things that are of God, but those that be of men," (v. 23). How could Peter have come so far from knowing God's way since God had just revealed such great divine information to him?

Satan, that supernatural being, the Adversary who *always* opposes God's will, was, of course, especially against the event that would bring his own ultimate and utter defeat— the Cross. It was frightening too since two members of the Godhead, the Father and the Son, definitely were ascribing to this "gaining through losing" process. I wonder how many of Satan's seeming-gains he substitutes for God's process of gaining through losing. Temporary gains, which he knows all along will be our ultimate loss. Satan's plan is always for our eventual and then eternal loss.

I wonder too how many times Jesus ascribes my misunderstanding of God's way for myself and others to Satan's desire for me to miss God's will. How much *life* have I kept others from experiencing because I could not see God's "gaining through losing" process, His "so that"? How does Jesus view my thoughts when I think God could not possibly want me to lose something for Jesus' sake? How many of His "so thats" have I missed?

But that "Follow Me" was the last of Jesus' three-part formula for finding life.

Then said Jesus unto His disciples, "If any man will come after Me, let him deny himself, and take up his cross, and follow Me" (Matt. 16:24).

If anybody will come after Me, triumph with Me, experience the victory I am going to experience—here is the formula:

First, *deny yourself.* That was what I was trying to learn to do Easter week. But what is myself? Is it my personal ambitions, my aspirations, my self-seekings, my self-assertions—doing what I like to do? Must I voluntarily abandon all these? Must I always say *No* to me?

After I had struggled in prayer on that Easter morning, I sat alone reading through John's account of Christ's resurrection and the events which followed. I stopped abruptly when I came to "Peter . . . lovest thou Me more than these?" (John 21:15) Peter, with the other disciples, had gone back to his former occupation—fishing. When he recognized Jesus on the shore preparing breakfast, Peter, having denied not himself but Jesus on the way to the cross, jumped into

326

the water in his eagerness to reach Christ. When breakfast was finished, Jesus turned to Peter and asked that piercing question, "Lovest thou Me more than these?"

I pondered the "more than these" for a long time. *More than what? All the things Peter had gone back to even after knowing Jesus was no longer dead? Back to fishing, the challenge of the sea, the wind in his face, the familiar roll of the boat? An occupation, a miraculous catch of fish?* I wondered too what *my* "more than these" might be. The boat spray in *my* face, *my* house, *my* loved ones?

That afternoon at our family Easter dinner, I was still thinking about my "more than these." I looked at my children whom I love so deeply. My heart was aching as I silently prayed, "How could I stop loving *them*, Lord? Lose them for Your sake? My own flesh and blood?" Then suddenly, as if He were seated at the table with us, He clearly said, *"More*—don't love them more than you love Me." And then I knew that for me "these things" were anything I put ahead of Him—my priorities.

In our prayer seminars when we are giving the most important thing in our lives (material possessions, a human relationship, or a circumstance) to God for His will, many are hesitant to pray that prayer, fearing that God will automatically take away all they give Him. But that is not usually the case. God only wants us to be willing to give up all for Him, to love Him more than we love all these other things.

I have found that when I really learn to do this, the process of gaining through losing starts in my life. Then, and only then, do I begin to find *life* as Jesus intended it to be for me. Then I begin to understand the marvel of His "so that."

The second part of Jesus' formula for finding life is not getting rid of something, but *taking up* something—my cross. The disciples knew well what taking up a cross meant. Many times they had seen the condemned ones compelled to carry the instruments on which they would be killed. Did Jesus mean that we were to take up the life for which the cross stood—a life of sacrifice? Did He mean that even when our cross would be bearing a trial that points to even a worse one to come? Are we still to pick it up willingly?

God explained to me a little of His secret of gaining life through the losing process of the cross at Arrowhead Springs. In the fall of 1970 in the wee hours of the night, I was praying about living the victorious Christian life. Suddenly, the chiming of bells filled the still night air with "Jesus, lover of my soul, let me to Thy bosom fly." I arose and stood on the porch in silence, spellbound as the full moon glistened on the softly rustling palm fronds. But my eyes looked heavenward, pleading with God. "I can't live this life," I prayed. "I can't do it."

"No," came the answer, "but Christ can live it in you." Then, as I waited for more, God brought Galatians 2:20 to my mind. The mystery of that verse began to unravel before me.

I am *crucified* with Christ. Nevertheless I *live*. Yet not I, but *Christ lives in me*. (Here and in all succeeding biblical references, the italics are mine.)

Not just *into* a cross experience, but *through* a cross experience—into life. Jesus living His life in me—resurrected, victorious *life!*

Yes, point three of Jesus' formula is "Follow Me." Did Jesus look at Peter when He said that? Was He telling Peter and all the rest of us to get behind Him and follow Him, not try to lead Him? "You do the following, I'll do the leading." I almost can hear Jesus saying, "Follow Me—even though it is going to involve denial, sacrifice, and losing yourself. Whosoever will save his life shall lose it, and whosoever will lose his life for My sake shall find it."

So the losses of life don't need to stop at being losses. In God's hands they can be *so that* we can gain life—real life—not only for eternity, but also for right here, today.

## GAINING THROUGH LOSING

*Losing* my self-seeking *so that* I can *gain* Christ's fulfilling, joyous, abundant life? That's quite a bargain!

"O God, help me *lose* my life *so that* I can *gain* Christ's in me."

# 2
## *Paul's Gaining Through Losing*

---

PAUL'S WRITINGS SEEM to exude, almost overflow, with this gaining-through-losing philosophy of Jesus. Was his victorious, abundant life the result of having actually lived Jesus' teaching that we find life through losing it? Yes, Paul himself sums up his attitude toward life in his letter to the Philippians:

But what things were *gain* to me, those I counted *loss* for Christ (Phil. 3:7).

God has used one of Paul's "gaining through losing" experiences in my life through the years. It is recorded in 2 Corinthians 12:7–10:

And lest I should be exalted above measure through the abundance of the revelations, there was given to me a thorn in the flesh, the messenger of Satan to buffet me, lest I should be exalted above measure. For this thing I besought the Lord thrice, that it might depart from me. And He said unto me, "My grace is sufficient for thee; for My strength is made perfect in weakness." Most gladly therefore will I rather glory in my infirmities, that the power of Christ may rest upon me. Therefore I take pleasure in infirmities, in reproaches in necessities, in persecutions, in distresses for Christ's sake; for when I am weak, then am I strong.

Since I was 18, I have underlined, dated, and made notes beside these verses in all the Bibles I have owned. They are Paul's account of what he *gained* at the time he *lost*, received a "no" answer from the Lord. He reveals what he gained *through* a seeming-loss when he prayed three times for his thorn in the flesh to be removed.

I too have prayed about a disfiguring, annoying, hindering thorn in my flesh. For more than 10 years, one or both of my eyes occasionally swell almost shut. Although God has spoken to me through this portion of Scripture many times, He brought it into focus in May of 1965 when I prayed, as Paul did, that He would remove my thorn.

## POWER OF CHRIST

I was scheduled to bring a prayer seminar to Agape Atlanta, the pilot project of the international Here's Life undertaking. Six hundred Christians were to gather the next day to learn the power of prayer for this endeavor. Since it was one of my early attempts to teach all the precepts of my book, *What Happens When Women Pray* in one day, I had planned carefully. I had timed and recorded the points which could be included on each subject, sifted to find material which best illustrated these points, and then separated each subject into individual file folders to keep the five-to-six hours of lecturing and prayer exercises organized.

Just before going to sleep on the night before the seminar, I was reading 2 Corinthians 12. When I came to the end of verse 9, "that the power of Christ may rest upon me," I closed my Bible, held it close, and prayed a simple prayer: "Lord, tomorrow I want the power of Christ, only the power of Christ." Then I went to sleep with that prayer on my lips and on my heart.

The next morning I awoke aghast. My eyes were swelling! I knew that if the swelling continued, I would not be able to read any of my so carefully prepared notes! Envisioning the potential confusion, I panicked and started praying desperately that God would take care of the problem. Then He gently asked me a question: "What did you pray last night?"

"Oh," I said almost aloud as I remembered—"I want the power of Christ tomorrow." Then a new kind of prayer emerged: "Lord, if You are going to show me the power of Christ by my inability to refer to my notes all day, OK. I'm willing to speak to 600 people and trust You to tell me what to say." The swelling stopped at the point of my barely being able to see. I relaxed, and went to that seminar without the ability to glance at my notes—but with a tremendous sense of the power of Christ resting in me.

Studying that word *rest* as used by Paul in 2 Corinthians 12:9, I found it meant "pitching a tent over me, taking up dwelling in me." In the margin of my Bible near that word, I had written, with the Atlanta date, "I could *feel* it!" For the first time I too had experienced what it was like to have the power of Christ resting on me. Not that I hadn't experienced His power before, but this was so tangible. Speaking for five hours with more strength at the end than when I started!

I also found this process which I discovered that day was not a once-for-all experience. I am frequently astounded at the way I gain momentum as I teach and share at seminars hour after hour without a break. My normal human power during a long day unwinds like a clock running slower and slower until it stops. But not Christ's power. His limitless, divine omnipotence actually takes up residence in me. What a gain for a seeming-loss!

Apparently Paul was not asking for a "so that," but it was what the Lord gave him. I certainly wasn't praying for a "so that" either. Paul most likely prayed fervently, expectantly, for a "yes" answer, but the Lord taught him that there are times when He answers "NO"—*so that* He can give something better than what was prayed for. Gaining through losing!

## GOD'S "NO" ANSWER

As far as we know, the Lord's "no" answer to Paul stood for the rest of his life. God did not remove his thorn in the flesh. In verse 10 Paul identifies his thorn as an *infirmity* (sometimes translated "weakness"). Vine's *Expository Dictionary of New Testament Words* (Revell, p. 204) defines this word as "want of strength, inability to produce results." This word in the Greek always means a physical weakness.

This same word *infirmity* was used by Luke the physician to describe a woman Jesus saw. For 18 years, she was "bowed together" (indicating a curvature) with a "spirit of infirmity," and could not straighten up. Even the source of her problem, Satan, was the same as Paul's. But when Jesus laid His hands on her, "immediately she was made straight and glorified God" (See Luke 13:11–17).

It is interesting that Paul had addressed these three prayers, not to the Father, but to the Lord—to Jesus. I questioned in my heart why this same Jesus took opposite action with those two whose problems were identified by the same Greek word. Also did one of them glorify God more than the other? Evidently not, according to the Scripture. The woman glorified God in her healing. Paul glorified Him in his continuing infirmity.

That opposite dealing by Jesus with similar results took place in a recent prayer seminar in California. Just before the prayertime when we give every facet of our lives, including our bodies, to God for His will, I was preparing

333

the participants for His possible answers. I told of times when God had gloriously healed. Then I told about Elmy, my friend, for whom we had prayed much. God did not make her well. But He used her continuing infirmity, which kept her at home, to enable her to be the chairman of our Rockford telephone prayer chains and to become one of the most powerful intercessors I know.

We broke for lunch after audibly and individually, in our groups of four, giving all of ourselves to God for His will. As the session closed, two women with similar "infirmities" came to the platform to talk with me. The first, a former missionary, came bounding up the several steps, exclaiming, "Look at me, look at me. I walked up those stairs!" Noting my puzzled expression, she beamed triumphantly and went on: "Because of a knee problem and surgery, I haven't walked up steps for four years. I also have a heart condition, and I get severe headaches because of the osteoarthritis in my neck." Later she wrote a letter assuring me that the pain and inability to walk, which disappeared the moment she gave them to God, still had not recurred.

Then the other woman, her neck in a thick brace, laboriously made her way up the steps. "I prayed the same prayer too." And she beamed just as triumphantly. "But God did not choose to heal me just now." She told me of her former deep involvement in serving God, but then she was struck with a disability which stopped it all. Lowering her head and her voice, she added with a smile, "I am one of your Elmys. I have been called to pray. I sleep in traction every night and spend hours praying, and I now have time to pray during the day. God has shown me the magnitude of the job to which He has called me." Which one had the better answer from Jesus? The greater gain?

Sometimes we can experience *losing* through *gaining* when there is a "yes" answer. The psalmist tells us that "He gave them their requests, but sent leanness into their soul" (Ps. 106:15).

In her magazine, *The Hiding Place*, Corrie ten Boom says it like this:

I see certain things that I asked for which were not granted. In recalling each individual circumstance, I am grateful now that God did not give me what I asked for. This shows that we should always pray with an attitude of reverent submission to the overruling wisdom and love of our heavenly Father.

Had God responded "Yes" to my desperate prayer to keep my eyes from swelling, what leanness of soul might I have had? I would have missed the great experience of sensing the identifiable, overwhelming feeling of the power of Christ on me all through that strenuous day! What a loss would have been mine! And how about Paul? How could God give him *gain* through a "No" answer to his petition for the removal of his infirmity?

## LESSONS FROM THE "NO" ANSWER

Paul explained that the Lord told him how this would be turned into gain. He was teaching Paul two of life's greatest lessons. Lessons that apply in turn to all those who can call Jesus "Lord," those who have a living personal relationship with Him.

The first lesson Jesus taught Paul was, *"My grace is sufficient for you"* (see 2 Cor. 12:9). As long as he had this infirmity (evidently up to the time of his death), there would be grace enough to cover all the difficulties brought on by it. How Paul would need that lesson, not only in his infirmity, but also in the trials, tribulations, imprisonments, shipwrecks, and eventual martyrdom that were to come!

Then in His answer, the Lord taught Paul another powerful lesson. *"My strength is made perfect in weakness"*

(v. 9). (Paul repeated this thought in verse 10 by concluding with, "for when I am weak, then am I strong.") It is not physical strength that counts, but the power of Christ which takes up its abode, and pitches its tent over our bodies when we are weak. What was Paul's (or my) maximum strength compared with Christ's omnipotence? In comparison to Christ's infinite, limitless power, all the strength we could ever muster, rolled into one gigantic push, would pale like a firefly competing with a nuclear explosion. What did Paul gain when the Lord said "No" to his being at his best physically? What do I gain? The *strength of* the omnipotent Christ!

Listening to my husband preach over the years, I have become acutely aware of the unusual, powerful strength of his messages when his body has not been at its best. Somehow when there has been no way Chris could deliver a sermon in his own strength, that was the time the Lord stepped in and poured out His power through Chris. No "bootstrap Christianity" this.

If you are losing what you think is best for you by getting an apparent "no" answer from the Lord, take heart. It was *because* Paul's thorn in the flesh remained that the Lord could show him His mysterious dealings with His own— how He equips us through our seeming-losses. How much more powerful, effective, and fruitful Paul was because of that "no" answer! Enough grace and enough power!

## LEST PRIDE

The dates and notes in the margins of my Bibles marched on. There was a progression of events in my learning through my swollen eyes. Atlanta was only the beginning of my being taught from 2 Corinthians 12. That same May held more lessons.

The swelling of my eyes is not particularly painful, but

it is definitely disfiguring. The last Sunday of that month I was to teach a large Sunday School class and, for personal reasons, I felt I had to be at my best. Again I woke with my eyes swelling. But this time the answer came first. God simply said to me, "Exalted above measure" (v. 7).

Again I prayed—this time not that God would keep them from swelling—but only that He would *cleanse the sin of pride.* Then I asked Him to bring other sins of pride to my mind, one at a time. And He did. The events of the previous week marched before me in an ugly parade. On Monday the religion editor of our largest local newspaper had featured the leading Christian influences in our area, my ministry being among them. I found myself basking in comments from all directions. Tuesday I was puffed up from congratulations given at a faculty appreciation dinner. Saturday noon found me smugly acknowledging recognition at a college alumni luncheon. That same night a speck of haughtiness welled up within as I brought greetings from faculty members of a great seminary with whom I had been teaching an extension course.

Horrified at what He paraded before my mind, I begged God to forgive all those awful attitudes. Then I prayed that He would cleanse me of them all.

I had recorded in my notes: "Suddenly I felt one of those rare experiences—could *feel* the power (of Christ) come into my body. Very real!" I had learned a little four-lettered reason for my thorn in the flesh—*lest* pride.

Paul obviously struggled with pride too, for he used this word *lest* to introduce the reason for his thorn in the flesh:

Lest any man should think of me above that which he sees me to be, or that he heareth of me. And lest I should be exalted above measure . . . there was given to me a thorn in the flesh (2 Cor. 12:6–7).

*Random House Dictionary* (p. 822) defines *lest* as: "The *so that* used negatively to introduce . . . an occurrence requiring caution." "For fear that"—God's yellow caution flag. Watch out!

Paul said *so that* I won't be exalted above measure by others or myself, God allowed a deterrent—lest.

The other day another author and I were discussing how pride makes me a loser. "When Satan can't get at me in defeat," I told her, "he gets me in my successes—with pride."

Then she asked, "How do you handle standing ovations, announcements of booksellers' ratings, and so forth?"

"I constantly keep in mind that God spells pride just one way, *s-i-n*," I explained. "And when there is sin in my life, I know from years of experience that God does not come in power in my ministry. That knowledge becomes the greatest deterrent to sinning that there is in my life. I don't *dare* give pride a place."

Some authorities have suggested that Paul's "infirmity" most likely was disfiguring. We don't really know. But whatever it was, it kept him from being proud. It was used by God as a deterrent in his life too.

Who of us has not had some physically disfiguring thorn? Not many of us feel that there is no need for improvement. Too fat/skinny, too short/tall, noses too big/ small. Then, how many of us have something that is *really* disfiguring? Are we as willing to learn as much from our thorns as Paul was willing to learn from his? Can we really say we have *gained* as much as Paul gained by a "no" answer, a *loss*?

An infirmity is not only a deterrent to the sin of pride. How much nicer Paul must have been to know, to be close to, when there was a *loss* in his life. We too tend to be slightly arrogant, unreachable, overly self-confident when everything is a *gain* for us.

It took me a long time to face the fact that perhaps the *why* of my swelling eyes was a deterrent—to the sin of pride. Had it been an answer to my mother's daily prayer, "God, don't let Evelyn get proud?" Could God's "way of escape" (1 Cor. 10:13) from the temptation of pride possibly be a disfigurement?

## MORE LESSONS?

But there was more instruction for me from 2 Corinthians 12. The following September I flew to British Columbia after finishing speaking at a three-day retreat on Mount Rainier the afternoon before.

I awoke exhausted, shattered, and unnerved the next morning—facing an all-day seminar, a dinner meeting, and then a rally that night. I didn't know how I could get through that day. And there it was again—a badly swollen eye. The notes I jotted down that morning are interesting now: "None of the other lessons from this Scripture fit." So I prayed, "God, teach me the lesson You have for me." "Suddenly," continued my notes, "I could *thank* Him for this eye, asking, pleading for Him to be *glorified* through it."

Then Philippians 4:13 flashed into my mind: "I can do all things through Christ who strengthens me." "'*All things*'— even this schedule," I wrote. As I turned to read it in my Bible, I was struck by the preceding verse, ". . . I am *instructed* both to be full and to be hungry, both to abound and to suffer need" (v. 12). I turned over on my back, looked up to God, and started to pray Ephesians 3:20: "Now unto Him that is able to do exceeding abundantly above all that we ask or think . . ." Tears popped into my eyes—HIM! CHRIST! The power of Christ of 2 Corinthians 12! Jesus!

I concluded my notes with, "A few minutes later the eye is draining already. Usually day or two later. Instructed *enough?* That's what I'm feeling."

The lessons are progressing. Just before a large seminar in California this spring, my eyes started to swell. But my only reaction was to smile up at God and relax in Him. I'm learning His will!

## "THANKS, GOD, I NEEDED THAT!"

As I write this chapter, I'm at a booksellers' national convention. Have I learned the last lesson? Evidently not.

My assignment yesterday was to speak about the power of books—my books. In the middle of the night I agonized in prayer over what I said. Was there too much of me? Was I too cocky? I asked God to please make me only what He wanted me to be, to give me the attitude He wanted me to have the next day.

Yes, when I woke up one eye was swelling. Immediately, I shot a prayer to God: "Thank You, Lord. I needed that. Thank You for *Your* way of answering my prayer." The thanks I felt had not just been a mouthed thanks, but one that welled up from deep within me. Is this what God has been so carefully instructing me to do? Does God know that I am beginning to understand His *gain* when a thank-you automatically wells up within me at the time there is a seeming-*loss*?

### PAUL'S PROGRESSION

But Paul's progress was different from mine. Paul's was within the confines of one lesson. He started with one thorn in the flesh. Then when he received a "no" answer, he included more than one physical problem, saying he would glory in his infirmities—plural (2 Cor. 12:10). Next he came far enough along in the lesson to say he would take pleasure in an expanded list of seeming-losses—reproaches, necessities, persecutions, and distresses. He must have been a better pupil, a more rapid learner than I am. It has taken me years.

In addition to seeing that the Lord would give grace and strength for all his problems and not just his thorn in the flesh, Paul saw two "therefores." They are *because* words.

If Paul's "glorying in his infirmities" stood alone without the "therefore," he would be classed today as a person enjoying his infirmities. *Therefore* points to the reason why

340

Paul said it—because the Lord had answered "No," and had given grace and strength in its place. There is a danger in this kind of glorying, for it tempts people to bring on themselves difficulties in which they can glory. Not Paul. He had prayed repeatedly, expectantly, and fervently for his thorn to be removed *until* his "no" answer, and then he adjusted to it.

"Therefore will I rather glory . . . [so] *that* the power of Christ may rest upon me" (2 Cor. 12:9). What a *gaining*! Paul learned it almost 2,000 years before I learned it, but there it is. One of life's biggest gains for a seeming-loss. The Lord's "no" answer was actually a great positive which empowered the rest of Paul's ministry. *Gaining through losing.*

The second "therefore" mentioned is in verse 10. "Therefore I *take pleasure* in infirmities, in reproaches, in necessities, in persecutions, in distresses . . ." There is no indication from the scriptural account that Paul *wanted* to lose *so that* he could gain. He not only prayed expectantly, but prayed persistently, repeating three times his prayer that his infirmity would be removed. He didn't invite his losses so that he could receive gains. (However, if we have willfully brought losses upon ourselves, when we ask God to forgive us and let Him take over, He will still bring us gains through them.) But Paul was definitely not getting satisfaction from those difficulties. There is a great gulf between *wanting* losses and *accepting* them, and then receiving the gains which God will give through them.

Paul did not say that he took pleasure in them for themselves, but because he had learned and accepted the *gaining through losing* principle. It was not for his sake. As stated in chapter 1, losing here was also for Christ's sake (v. 10). Taking pleasure—not for his own sake, but for Christ's sake!

California pastor Dr. Tim LaHaye, founder of Family Life Seminars, asked me what the title of my new book was. When I replied, *"Gaining Through Losing,"* a dark scowl crossed his face. Thinking I meant we should *try* to lose so that we can get gains from God, he wisely disagreed with that premise.

"Oh, no, it would be 'sick' to think that way," I agreed. "I do not mean that we deliberately bring losses upon ourselves; but that when they do come—and they come to all of us— then God goes to work in us turning those losses into gains."

## REMOVED HINDRANCES

I'm fascinated by street sweepers—those massive lumbering machines which loosen and vacuum up debris on the roads. Knowing the magnitude of the task to which the Lord called Paul on the Damascus Road, doesn't it seem logical that He would have sent His supernatural "street cleaner" to dislodge and remove all the hindrances in Paul's pathway? He could have swept the path clean before sending Paul onto it, or at least vacuumed the obstacles as they confronted Paul. But the New Testament tells us that God did neither. We see rather that they were left there—deliberately. The whole list which Paul adds to the "infirmities" was left in his path intentionally *so that* he could learn and grow from them. Left *so that* the power would be Christ's omnipotence and not Paul's puny human strength. From man's point of view they were *losses*, but in God's hands they were turned into gigantic *gains*.

I guess the "narrow way" on which Jesus sends me on my journey to heaven hasn't been swept clean either. Even when the source of the annoyance is Satan, as was Job's before the cross and Paul's after the cross, God can and does use that *loss* for *gain* in me too.

Which one of us at some time in life has not wished for, even longed for, a life like Paul's? Full of adventure, fruit, rewards! Changing the world in which he lived! Then influencing people all over Planet Earth! Could the secret be that Paul learned and accepted God's *gaining through losing* principle? God's *so thats*?

342

What did Paul *lose*? Being delivered from infirmities, re-proaches, necessities, persecutions, distresses. What did he *gain*? Christ's grace and power and strength—resting on Him!

Have you discovered God's divine "so that"?

## Section II

# WHAT
# CAN YOU BEAR?

# 3
## What
## You Can Bear—
## Your Capacity

IN THE MIDST of a deep loss in your life, have you ever cried, "This is more than I can bear"? When a severe financial crisis crashed about you, when shattering news about your health bent you low, or when a calamity in the family sent bitter waves of grief over you, have you felt pressed down till you knew you could not *bear* another minute of it? Years ago I found myself crying out in sorrow after sorrow, "I can't bear it!" Then I decided to find out what the Bible had to say about those crushing times.

As I read the conversation between God and Satan in the Book of Job, it appeared to me that God asked Himself how much Job could *bear*. Then, completely confident of what Job could endure, He gave Satan permission to test him. After Satan left the presence of the Lord the calamities began to fall. Raiding parties and lightning killed or carried off all of Job's animals and his servants, and a desert wind swept down demolishing the house and killing all of his children. Then boils from the soles of his feet to the top of his head left Job mourning in the ashes. The possessions that made Job the greatest man in the East, all of his children, and even his health were *lost*.

As we, like Job, experience testings and trials of varying degrees from time to time, we too feel we cannot bear another minute of the suffering. We ask ourselves what possible *gain* could come out of these horrible *losses*. Seeing the immediate or eventual gain is not only difficult, but often impossible. However, as with Job, there are astounding *gains* for the believer because of his trials and testings.

## JOB'S CAPACITY

The first comforting *gain* in the midst of Job's difficult losses was his receiving the unconditional confidence of the God of the universe! The Creator knew the stuff of which Job was made. He affirmed Job's *capacity to bear*. God also knew how Job had lived out the qualities in his life thus far, and said to Satan:

Have you considered My servant Job, that there is none like him on the earth, a blameless and upright man, who fears God and turns away from evil? (Job 1:8, RSV)

God also had absolute confidence in Job's future reactions. He trusted Job not only under the ideal conditions of being the greatest man in the East, but also when everything except his life would be taken away from him.

This truth is wonderfully expressed in a New Testament "capacity" promise for those who believe in Christ today when they, as Job, suffer losses in their lives.

God is faithful, who will not suffer [*allow*] you to be tempted *above that you are able*; but will with the temptation also make a way to escape, that you may be able to *bear* it (1 Cor. 10:13).

This is a loving God allowing only what we too can bear—endure.

348

What a comforting thought for our day that God knows the capacity of the believer, just as He knew Job's! And He will not allow us to be tested above what we can bear. How well He knows the capacity of a Corrie ten Boom and a Joni Eareckson. And He also knows *our* capacity to bear!

What a *privilege* to have God say of us, "There is one of My servants who can stand any testing or trial you can give, Satan!"

## SUFFERING A COMPLIMENT?

So we can see that testings and trials are actually a compliment from God. There is not a hint of God questioning Job's ability to withstand and bear. Thus, God could say to Satan, "Everything he has is in your hands, but on the man himself do not lay a finger" (Job 1:12, NIV). God gave Satan permission to do anything except take Job's life. What a confidence in His servant, Job! What a compliment from God!

Last year an extremely fine Christian mother who had just lost her 10-year-old daughter stood weeping in the back hall of a church where I was conducting a seminar. Pressing both her hands in mine, I gently explained that God knew her inmost capacity and what she was strong enough to bear. "So," I told her, "this is actually a compliment from God to you." I watched her expression change—from grief, to surprise, to a hint of a smile. God's compliment, His trust in her began to fill the void of her loss.

One of my greatest joys as a pastor's wife was explaining to those suffering deep trials the surprising fact that God knew their capacity to bear—then watching the healing begin as they accepted His compliment. Gaining through losing!

## GOD ALLOWING

God seems to use His knowledge of our capacity to bear to regulate His allowing. I like to think of a complete, unbroken circle representing the permissive will of God—what

He allows. Then a dot in the center of the circle represents the believer. Nothing can penetrate the circle of God's permissive will unless God allows it.

In Job's case God could have said "No" to Satan, but He did not. Why did God permit Satan to attack Job? Here again is God's *allowing* role. I like to think of how much simpler and nicer life would be without it! God could have avoided all the trouble Satan brings to this earth.

There is still another "allowing" question that has stumped the experts for generations. When my pastor-husband was to begin a Sunday night series of sermons about Job, he challenged the congregation to read the first chapter and then participate in a "stump the pastor" night with our questions. To generate interest he promised a dollar reward to anyone whose question he could not answer.

On Sunday afternoon our seven-year-old Kurt laboriously plodded his way through the first chapter. Then, that night as my husband was confidently fielding all the questions, Kurt raised his hand. The audience smiled as this little one stood and asked, "Dad, since one of the reasons the Father forsook and could not look on His Son, Jesus, while He was bearing our sins on the cross was because the Father could not look on sin—how come God would let Satan into heaven to talk to Him?"

The congregation exploded with laughter as Chris slowly reached into his billfold, took out a dollar bill and handed it to the grinning little boy. Another one of those "allowing" conundrums in the Bible!

Do you too have some questions you want to ask God about His allowing? I keep telling myself that if *I* were God, *I* would not have allowed those things. But that's why I'm not God! When God finally spoke to Job after his friends stopped talking, God asked, "Who is this that darkens counsel by *words without knowledge*?" (Job 38:2) That word *counsel* here means that God had been dealing with Job, not irresponsibly or haphazardly, but according to His consis-

350

tent, intelligent design. A loving God allowed according to His absolute infallibility.

The amazing fact about God's allowing is that Job had done nothing to deserve the suffering God allowed to come on him. Sometimes we do suffer because we have broken a natural law or God's law. But not so with Job. Job's friends tried to elicit a confession of sin from him, trying to prove that Job's problems were retribution for his sins. But both Job (who could have been wrong) and God (who could not have been wrong) stubbornly clung to Job's innocence.

It was God who brought up the subject to Satan by saying, "Have you considered My servant Job? There is no one on earth like him; *he is blameless and upright,* a man who fears God and shuns evil" (Job 1:8, NIV, italics added). Then, after the first onslaught of disasters, God repeated these words to Satan, adding, "And he still maintains his integrity, though you incited Me against him to ruin him *without any reason.*" Finally, at the very end of the book, God still confirmed Job's innocence (see Job 42:7).

Yes, this is God *allowing* Satan to pierce through the protective circle of His permissive will to get at one of the choice believers of all history! God allowing suffering! What possible *gain* could there be in that?

## WHY ALLOW?

So then I must ask *why* God allowed catastrophe, suffering, and loss in Job's Life. (My husband just said, "Honey, you are tackling one of the greatest theological mysteries of the ages.") Perhaps, but this is the question we all are asking, "Why?"

Could it be *so that* He could *set the stage* for a gain? God in His omniscience knew from the beginning the outcome and the gains He would bring through losses. But whether or not Job's gains could *only* have come through these catastrophes, only God knows—the Bible doesn't tell us.

351

Was God getting Job's attention *so that* He could reveal Himself to him in a new way? Did it take the loss of Job's human and material possessions and the scraping of his overspreading sores with a piece of pottery on an ash heap—all of this to get his attention? Or was it just God using what He had allowed to bring Job face to face with Himself?

There is a New Testament account in which Jesus seemed to be *setting the stage* for a tremendous gain through a loss. After Mary and Martha, the sisters of Lazarus, had sent for Jesus to heal their brother, Jesus strangely enough waited till Lazarus died. (Even the crowd at Lazarus' tomb questioned if Jesus, who had opened the eyes of the blind, could not have kept *this* man from dying.) Because Jesus was about to reveal a profound truth about Himself, did He deliberately *create the climate* for this revelation by tarrying and thus allowing all the suffering and grief of death? Was He allowing the death *so that* it would set the stage for a revolutionary verbal and visual revelation?

Or was it just that, *since* He had tarried, and thus allowed the natural course of events to proceed, Jesus would *take advantage of the situation*? My husband, now employed by Bethel College, says one of the things he misses most about the pastorate is funerals, because the bereaved are often so tender and open, so willing to listen to God speak to them during grief.

Or perhaps Jesus allowed the agony to *get Martha's attention*. Had Jesus longed to reveal great things to her, but because life was going on as usual had she refused to listen? Martha did not automatically choose the "better part." She was a doer, substituting shopping, cooking, and entertaining the Master for the better—being taught by Him. (The Bible doesn't tell us what profound things Jesus taught Martha's sister, Mary, as she sat at His feet completely absorbed in learning from Him. We only know that she, according to Jesus, anointed Him with oil just before His death because she *alone* understood His death.) Did Jesus have to *allow* Martha to go through something that He could have avoided in order to get her attention?

I too have plenty of opportunities to listen to God. Does God sometimes have to get my attention through hard things in my life also? Am I, like Martha, too encumbered with the tyranny of the urgent to spend time letting God speak to me through His Word and in quiet prayer—until there is a grief that sends me fleeing to Him? Could it be with me too that the greatest revelations come when the sorrow is the deepest?

Sometimes I wonder if God allowed the Watergate scandal in the United States to get our attention—even after millions of Christians had just fasted and prayed all day that April 30 in 1974. We suddenly became the Ugly Americans overseas, lost our national self-respect, and saw ourselves as we really were. But God had our attention! It was for many the beginning of the turning to Him for direction and the coming out into the open on the part of millions of silent Christians. God *allowing* to get our attention?

Whatever the reason for the allowing in the death of Lazarus, the fact remains that Jesus deliberately allowed death and grief which He could have averted. Although we may not understand, Jesus knew His "why"—the gains He would bring through the loss.

During her loss, Jesus gave Martha—a common, ordinary, domestically inclined woman friend—one of the greatest announcements that Planet Earth has ever received:

"I AM THE RESURRECTION AND THE LIFE!"

That proclamation from Jesus must have sent her grieving heart reeling and her throbbing head spinning. Then He proved the credibility of this startling message by calling forth the deceased one before the eyes of the stunned crowd. I remember standing in awe at the small ground-level opening to Lazarus' tomb just outside Jerusalem, wondering what kind of power had propelled that body, bound from head to foot, out of that cramped cavity in that hillside.

But the world-changing impact was not made by Jesus' tremendous display of power in raising Lazarus from the dead. Although he was resuscitated, Lazarus would eventually die again. Also, Jesus had already raised another without this kind of impact. But the power of that moment was that Jesus was declaring and proving that He Himself really *is* the Resurrection and the Life. No other religion on earth offers this! And, in living and walking on earth among them after He also had died, Jesus proved that I too shall live again (see 1 Cor. 15).

He hadn't tarried too long! Jesus knew His "why" for allowing Martha's sorrow all along! What a fantastic *gain* for Martha. What a privilege—in her *loss*—to be the one used by the Master to reveal the greatest news ever to reach Planet Earth!

## JOB'S GAINS FROM HIS LOSSES

So now we turn again to Job's gains through his losses. In addition to God's confidence in what he could bear, Job's gains were many.

The most obvious gain was in *what God restored* to Job. Twice as much as he had before! Fourteen thousand in place of seven thousand sheep and goats; six thousand camels replacing three thousand lost ones; one thousand yoke of oxen in the place of five hundred; a thousand female donkeys to replace five hundred. His lost children were replaced with seven more sons and three more daughters—these fairer than all the women in the whole land. Then Job was given another 140 years to live and see his children's children to the fourth generation. *Gaining through losing.*

But in our concentrating on what God restored to Job, we fail to see all the *gains* throughout the suffering of the *losses*. Did God allow Job's suffering simply to show him that He could restore twofold? I think not.

The key to the Book of Job is seen by many to be Job's statement in chapter 23, verse 10: "When He has tried me, I shall come forth as gold." There are several possible gains which could be inferred in this declaration by Job. The first is the *purifying power of affliction*—God allowing suffering to strengthen Job and purify him as precious refined gold. God producing the patience through trials for which Job is so well known (James 5:11). Suffering producing purer gold! How I have clung to this outcome of God's dealings in my own life since my early 20s. How I have seen myself, and then my husband and my children, grow and stretch during times of affliction.

But there is another possible meaning in this great verse. Another gain—*the vindicating power of affliction.* Was Job vindicating his innocence, clearing his name? Was he saying to his accusing friends, "You'll see. When God is done trying me, you will know that I really hadn't been sinning against Him. It will be proved that I have been good all along."

Then the gain spoken of in Job 23:10 might also be the *proving of his faith through suffering.* Though Job's complaint came through in his speeches during his suffering, he never lost his unequivocal and unshakable faith in God. In reply to his friends' accusations, he stubbornly defended his relationship with and faith in the God who was allowing all his suffering. In the midst of their accusations Job cried out, *"Though He slay me, yet will I hope in Him"* (Job 13:15, NIV). "The God who is allowing all this testing is still my God!"

What a lesson has come to us down through the ages. Job declared to himself, his friends, and to all future generations that no matter what happened, his faith in his God was unshakable!

As I have been reading the Book of Job while at work on this manuscript, God keeps bringing to my mind a gain

tucked down in the last chapter—the *when of restoration.*
It was *after* Job prayed for the friends who had given him
wrong advice and accused him in his sorrow that God restored Job's possessions. God finally told Job's friends that
He was angry with them for not telling the truth about
Him; and that, after their burnt offering was made, "My
servant Job will pray for you, and I will accept his prayer
and not deal with you according to your folly" (Job 42:8,
NIV).

God, the great Psychiatrist! How much change of attitude
it must have taken Job to be willing to pray *for* his friends.
Did God give a *principle* here that we are just now discovering in modern psychiatry and Christianity? I have seen
it happen so many times in my own life that when I get
my mind off *my* troubles and concentrate on *praying for
others*—that much is restored to me—emotionally, physically, and spiritually. Gaining through losing!

Another tremendous gain for Job came in his learning to
*discern the voices.* First he learned not to accept all the
advice of his well-meaning friends. Job firmly resisted their
assumed omniscience. Perhaps the kindest thing Job's
friends did for him during his sorrow was just to sit with
him for seven days—in silence. For when they did speak,
God summed up their long speeches with, "You have not
spoken of Me what is right" (Job 42:7, NIV).

Often I find myself desperately grasping at advice from
others when I am deeply hurting. How easy it is for me to
listen to their "reasoning." But how important for me too
to sort out the truth from their sometimes misguided help.

Then at times the voice I hear in my sorrow is not that
of another, but, like Job, it is my own. My voice of self-pity.
Or self-justification—when I am trying to convince *myself*
of my innocence. Or sometimes it is my own voice of self-
defensiveness against what others are saying. But I cannot
see myself clearly while in the depth of my sorrows, for my

tear-filled vision distorts my perspective and thus the advice I give myself. My interpretation of the Bible becomes distorted. I find a focus that soothes and smoothes me—but fails to help me see clearly the truth about myself.

However, the greatest *gain* of all came when Job stopped listening to his own voice and *put his hand over his mouth.* When God finally answered, Job cried, "Behold, I am insignificant; what can I reply to Thee? I *lay my hand on my mouth*" (Job 40:4, NASB). It was when Job finally learned to keep still that his greatest gain came—he heard God!

Yes, Job heard the God of the universe in a fresh and new revelation of His grandeur and power never before heard on Planet Earth! There were no books or other resources to enlighten Job at that early date in history. But God showed Job the animate and inanimate wonders of the universe. Then when Job finally heard the True One speaking, he saw himself from an accurate perspective for the first time. God gently yet firmly chided him as a parent questioning his offspring, "Where were you when I laid the foundation of the earth?" (38:4, NASB) The defensive, argumentative Job had no answer. Having seen himself in contrast to God, he lowered his accusing voice to whisper, "I am of no account."

Yes, it was when the human strife of words was over that Job's greatest gain came—He had heard God! And Job put his hand over his mouth.

Surprisingly, after all of Job's trials, when God did speak, He spoke out of a whirlwind and out of a storm. Hadn't Job had enough problems without God speaking out of a storm? But somehow I too find that God doesn't usually speak out of the soft, gentle breezes to me. It is in the storms that He speaks in very special ways to me as He did to Job in his distress and to Martha in her severe storm.

This does not mean that God never speaks in the calm. As a young woman and I sat in my mother's porch swing this past summer, she asked, "Is there something wrong with me that I'm not suffering? I've never really suffered." (Yet some people might say she was, for she had been serving Christ in evangelism for two years without pay!)

I assured her, "No, you are in the circumstances God wants you in now. Suffering may come. Just prepare yourself in your relationship with Him in prayer and Bible study so that if the suffering does come you will be ready. Job knew God to the best of his ability *before* his suffering. Just be sure you know God well enough to *hear* and *recognize* His voice if and when the storm comes."

But I believe one of the most beautiful gains for Job came in the *fulfilling of a wish*—wishing that his words would be preserved for posterity, not on parchment which would decay, but on stone with iron—forever. At the low point in his life, when things looked the blackest, Job cried: "Oh, that my words were recorded, that they were written on a scroll, that they were inscribed with an iron tool on lead, or engraved in rock forever" (19:23–24, NIV).

Then came his spontaneous burst of unshakable faith:

I know that my Redeemer lives, and that in the end He will stand upon the earth. And after my skin has been destroyed, yet in my flesh I will see God" (vv. 25–26, NIV).

Centuries before Jesus revealed to Martha the secrets of resurrection, which we read in the Bible today, Job tenaciously and unwaveringly clung to the certainty of living after death. Preserved through all the ages, for all generations of suffering saints—in the world's all-time number one best-seller—the Bible. Job's wish was granted!

We have an unannounced contest in our family—who gets Christmas going earliest—the first gift purchased—the first decoration displayed. At our recent October family birthday dinner, Skip, one of my sons-in-law, announced, "Ev won. She has already listened to *The Messiah!*"

But I don't just *listen* to Handel's *Messiah*. I *feel* it! That day I had turned the volume up so that the whole house reverberated with, "I *know* that my Redeemer liveth!" Thousands of years after Job! Then the exploding crescendos that have brought concert goers to their feet since the 19th century: "Hallelujah, Hallelujah . . . and He shall reign for ever and ever!"

What would Christmas be without Handel's *Messiah*? But what would his *Messiah* be without Job? And what would Job be without suffering?

Although Job didn't know I would even be born, his words have been preserved just for me. A decade ago a deep tragedy happened to one of our children which I still cannot share. That crushing event which came into my life as a parent should have left me bleeding and broken. But just today as I was leafing through the Bible I had used during that calamity, I discovered I had written the name of the child to whom it happened in the margin of that Bible by Job 19:25, not with Job's questioning, or with his complaining—but with his outburst of undefeatable faith. "I *know* that my Redeemer liveth!" In *my* storm I had echoed Job's unshakable faith!

But Job's experience was not recorded just for my big, earth-shattering disasters. Last night I came to the end of a particularly frustrating day. Each succeeding phone call ended with a "wait until something else gets straightened out." As the evening bore down on me with frustration, tenseness, and inner sputtering, I absentmindedly flicked on the record player as I walked by. Suddenly the whole house was alive again with "I *know* that my Redeemer liveth!"

The transformation was instantaneous. My negative attitudes melted. My whole being was soaring, praising, and worshiping—God! Job's wish was fulfilled again.

What fantastic *gains because of* Job's horrible *losses*. Gains Job could not have even dreamed possible. Were Job's *gains* worth his *losses*? Who would even dare ask God that question?

## "WHO" NOT "WHY"

Have you ever asked "Why" during your trials? Neither Martha's nor Job's "why" questions were ever completely answered, and the mystery of the drama of heaven between God and Satan was never revealed to Job.

But whatever the reason for God's allowing of the grief really doesn't matter—for it was in their sorrows that God chose to reveal Himself in new and magnanimous ways. As I settled down to once again read of the way God revealed Himself to Job in the 38th and 39th chapters, God kept getting bigger and bigger and bigger. How Job must have felt himself shrinking and shrinking as his knowledge of God kept expanding and expanding—*who He is.*

It was when God finished giving Job the new revelation of who He really was that Job could cry, "My ears had heard *of* You, but now my eyes have seen You" (Job 42:5, NIV). Then Job suddenly knew all was well with him and with the whole universe! God was, and always has been, in control. The combatant turned into the worshiper. And all of Job's "whys" turned to "Who."

I had lunch recently with Arvella Schuller, wife of Dr. Robert Schuller of the "Hour of Power" telecast from Garden Grove, Calif. I was amazed and thrilled as she radiantly smiled and kept reaffirming the gains that had come through her recent losses—the motorcycle accident in which her beautiful, vivacious daughter Carol's life was hanging by a thread before the leg amputation; endless, exhausting daily therapy; and in the midst of it all, the verdict of her own cancer, and the surgery which followed. She summed it all up by saying that when people say that it certainly must have been a rough year, she replies, "Oh no. It has been a blessed year filled with the presence of God and surrounded by the loving arms of many people." Then she added, "Evelyn, I saw a different side of God's face, and it was tremendous!"

During the first years of my marriage, I found myself almost drowning in a sea of "why" questions as trials flooded over me—and I just knew I could not bear them. But gradually I detected an emerging pattern. It was in those times of engulfment in a sea of sorrows that God would speak to me in a new way. Little by little I saw it. God was choosing to reveal Himself to me at those times, in each instance showing me a deeper, more profound side of Himself—one I'd never seen before.

One of my author-friends who is in my personal prayer group, after I had asked for prayer for God's will in overseas ministries invitations, commented, "You really do live a 'Cinderella' existence, don't you?"

Taken aback, I replied, "If I do live a life like 'Cinder Ella,' now, it's because I've spent so many years on the *ash* heap with Job!"

It has been many, many years since I have asked God "why" in my trials. With a shocking report from a doctor, a calamity in a child's life, or some shattering news in the family, I find myself searching for that "more of my God—my Who. I, with Job, have heard much *of* God, but it has always been in those difficult times of my life that I have seen Him—ready and eager to reveal more of Himself to me. What a fabulous *gain* through my *losses!*

Have your "whys" turned to "Who"?

# 4

## *What You Can Bear— Your Potential*

---

THERE IS ANOTHER meaning of the word *bear* in the Bible. This time not only what we are *able* to bear—our CAPACITY, but how much we *can* bear—our POTENTIAL. God knew how much Job could stand, but Jesus explained another use of this word—how much we can produce.

As we rode to a seminar in California last winter, my hostess and I passed field after field of ugly, bleeding stumps with wires strung above them. Finally I asked her, "What on earth are those?"

"Oh," she said with obvious pride, "they're our grapevines!"

As I gazed on them in silence, my heart cried out to God, "Father, am I that ugly when You are pruning me?"

### GOD OF THE GRAPES

Jesus' words from John 15 kept whirling around in my mind. "I am the true Vine, and My Father is the Vinedresser. . . .

362

Every branch that beareth fruit, He purgeth it . . ." (John 15:1–2, sco). It is the Father, said Jesus, who holds the pruning knife in His hand and prunes those who are His own. How I cringed at this vivid example in those vineyards of that seldom-mentioned concept of God—bending over us, cutting away—The Vinedresser.

I found a little consolation in Jesus' assuring words that it is only the branches who are vitally, organically connected to Him (not just those who go to church or follow His ethics and teachings) whom the Father prunes.

But as Jesus' words kept marching through my mind like the rows of vines flashing past our car, a surprising thought emerged: it is those of us who are already bearing fruit whom God prunes! So why the pruning process? *So that* we can bear—not just *some* fruit—but *more* fruit!

It was winter in California when I was glimpsing those ugly stumps from the car window. Suddenly God showed me there are winters in my life too. In fact, He said, as with grapes, all the seasons are represented in our lives also. But not necessarily one following the other in predictable solar-induced regularity. Usually they tumble unscheduled according to the needs we have as human branches.

But I don't like some seasons. I hate dormant periods when the "sap" has retreated, and sadly there doesn't seem to be much happening through me. Then there is the growing season, that time when I'm being fed and nourished by the Vine when the fruit is ripening and I spoil it by impatiently straining to pluck it. I certainly don't care for the pruning season when the wielding of that sharp knife mercilessly prunes away the abundant leaves and long stems of my just-past time of productivity. No, I definitely prefer the glorious, rewarding fruit-bearing season.

Then I wondered about God. Does His heart bleed with the branch when He knows the only way to produce more fruit is to get out His pruning knife? Does it hurt Him more than it hurts me? Does He like the fruit-bearing season best too?

363

Mentally I dug into my past losses—sorrow, suffering, lost babies, surgery, family difficulties—and wondered if some, or many of them, had occurred because God had put his pruning tools to work. I had definitely been left feeling like a bare, bleeding stump after those experiences. Yes, I had been pruned by the hand of the divine Vinedresser!

## TOUCHED BY GOD

I have been touched by the hand of God in so many different ways. I've felt His strong supporting hand beneath me when I've crumpled in grief. Have been securely held in the hollow of His hand when life engulfed me. When there was no power of my own, I've felt the omnipotence of His hand. I've known His firm hand steering the course of my life. Experienced the restraining of His hand when I would run ahead. Felt the tenderness of the divine Gardener's hand pressing mine. I've been made well by the touch of the hand of the Great Physician. And I've felt His cooling hand on my hot feverish brow. But I have also felt the sting of the pruning knife in the omniscient Vinedresser's hand.

Somehow in our imaginations we have invented a God whose hand gives only love pats. But this is not what the Bible tells us. Job, at the low ebb in his suffering, cried, "The hand of God hath touched me" (Job 19:21). Paul, after being touched by God on the Damascus Road, was blinded for a season. Jacob, before he crossed the Jabbok River to be reunited with his estranged brother, Esau, wrestled and felt the touch of God on his thigh, and he was permanently crippled—by God. As the sinew shrank, Jacob said, "I have seen *God* face to face" (Gen. 32:30).

The place where I felt God's presence the most while touring the Holy Land was at the Jabbok River where Jacob had wrestled all night. I slipped away down the bank and sat alone, motionless, absorbing every bit of that Presence.

The surrounding hills formed a natural amphitheater; and reverberating, echoing across the valley from hill to hill—God!

I pondered in that place: *Was losing the full use of a part of his physical body and limping for the rest of his life worth what Jacob gained?* The answer was overwhelmingly "Yes." Personally blessed by God! Blessed beyond his fondest dreams. Then given a new name. Not Supplanter now, but Israel. "A nation and a company of nations shall be of thee, and kings shall come out of thy loins" (35:11). And he was given power with God—and power with men.

## WRESTLING

I too have wrestled spiritually with the Lord and felt the surprising result of having a leg touched by God. Because of frequent questions by Christians who had sometimes seen God heal physically and sometimes not, I fervently and persistently prayed during the summer of 1977 that God would give me His answers. Then in September I prayed, "God, teach me everything about healing that I need to know." Once again He used my own body to teach me what I had prayed for. In October the process started.

I had come home from a speaking engagement in the Bahamas with a severe virus which had attacked the nerve roots of my spine. Ten days later, as I left for the East Coast for three upcoming seminars, I wondered if I could handle the pain. One morning after struggling with the almost unbearable task of getting my nylons over my toes, I stood up, stopped attempting to get ready for the seminar—and wrestled with God. "Lord," I prayed, "either take this pain away—or give me the grace to stand it."

To my astonishment, the excruciating pain began to lessen, and in a few minutes had all but vanished. But, even more surprising, my left leg went limp. I dragged myself up the stairs to breakfast and stood on my "good" leg for the five hours of speaking on that day, and for many seminars after that one. Touched by God!

Much of our wrestling is *against* God. There is a difference when we wrestle *with* Him. Jacob wrestled *with* God until He blessed him. Davy, in *A Severe Mercy*, wrestled all night with God, giving Him herself for His will in her life (Sheldon Vanauken, Harper and Row, p. 146). So I too was wrestling *with* God until He had His will in me.

As I look back at two years of wrestling with this leg problem, I realize that not once did I wrestle *against* God. The whole experience has been without rebellion of any kind. I couldn't always say that about previous physical problems. I was in complete rebellion against being on the shelf during that hospitalization for gallbladder surgery—until the sweet joy of surrender to His will came after hearing the poem "Gaining Through Losing" over the air.

Contending with the swollen eyes has been a series of gradual learning of God's *so thats*. But not with this leg. These months have been so different—not always understanding why, but always knowing God knew why and what He was doing. So the wrestling has been with Him—to gain all He has for me. Wrestling as Jacob wrestled, over and over again *until He blesses me*—and gives me what He wanted to give me all along.

How did wrestling and being touched by the divine Vinedresser produce blessings in me? The only time I shed tears while still in the hospital was when I had to face the cancellation of a large seminar in another state. But God had more fruit in mind all along. I had no choice but to send another person in my place—Loree, a close prayer associate whom God had been marvelously preparing for years for that very task. And the great results of her seminar proved that God was doubling my prayer ministry here in the United States.

Then I saw another "why." With Loree's teaching, God released me from the total ministry here to permit me to begin an overseas ministry to which He had called me for two years. More fruit—when pruned!

## THE EXPERT PRUNER

Recently my friend Jane brought me a small purple passion plant which she had started from her own. While I was anxiously waiting for it to grow in its new environment, it suddenly shot straight up, resembling a purple and green bean pole. Common sense told me to pinch off the top, but I could not muster the courage. For several weeks I approached it, fingers poised, only to lose my nerve and retreat. I could not bear to hurt my little plant. Finally I steeled myself, gritted my teeth, and pinched. To my surprise, in just one week many new shoots appeared on the stalk, filling out the ugly leafless spots. But later when I returned from a speaking tour, to my horror, a long sprout had shot out from the top at a very awkward angle, and the main stem had compensated by bending in the opposite direction to keep from falling over. Again I resolutely gathered all my courage—and pinched. Then I came to one conclusion—I am not an expert pruner. I just don't know how to do it.

I learned at my last California seminar that it takes an expert to prune effectively. The wife of a grape grower said to me, "Do you want to know something about pruning? Very few people can prune. We go to great trouble to hire the very best expert available."

God is the Expert Pruner. The supernatural divine Professional. He never pinches or cuts too soon lest He damage my tender branch. He never lets me get too far out of control before he draws His knife. He knows just how far to let me sprawl. He understands which part of me and just exactly how much of that part He must prune. How precious to know that the care of me as Jesus' branch will never have to be entrusted to a human vinedresser. My Vinedresser is an Expert. He is God.

## HE'S SOVEREIGN

Since *pruning* means "purging by removal," "cleansing by separation from," and "cutting away living parts," we must ask, does God just *allow* or does He actually *do something* that hurts His own? Here we have one of the theological battles of the ages.

During my son Kurt's first summer, before he learned to walk, I would put him out in our sunny backyard to play. The first thing we had done after moving into our parsonage on a main street was to fence in the backyard and secure the gates with locks to protect our children from that busy traffic. One day I answered a ring at the front door and a stranger stood holding our Kurt in her arms. "Is this your baby? I found him crawling into State Street." I numbly reached out and took him from her arms, too shocked to do more than mumble a weak "thank-you" as she turned and disappeared.

I've thought of that stranger often. What if she *hadn't* rescued that little one from the relentless stream of traffic? Would she have *caused* his death? Who would have been responsible for it? An older neighbor-child who had un-locked the gate? The mother for trusting the fence and locks? Or the woman who could have snatched him from the wheels of the cars? We would say—the one who deliberately allowed the child to be hit. The one who was fully aware of the danger and had the power to avert the tragedy.

Is it so with God? Since He has the power and ability to stop any difficulty in our lives, what is His part? Most people can agree that God allows suffering but feel that His sending unpleasant or difficult things into our lives is inconsistent with His being a God of love.

The writer of the Book of Hebrews states that God *was able* to save His Son, Jesus, from the death of the cross (Heb. 5:7). Jesus even cried with strong tears to His Father who *was able to save Him.* But God did not. It was God the Father's will that His Son should suffer and die. (We know that technically Satan caused Christ's death when he brought sin into the world and made the redemption on the cross necessary.) But God could have chosen a less severe method of redemption. God could also have prevented Job's suffering by saying "No" to Satan and not allowing the suffering, but He did not. Jesus could have prevented Lazarus' death and thus avoided Martha's suffering. But He did not. So did He cause Job's and Martha's grief?

To be sure, I sometimes bring suffering upon myself. When I break God's moral or physical laws carelessly or deliberately, I must reap the consequences. Sometimes sorrow is the result of a natural course of events here on this fallen planet. But sometimes it is of God. God defended Job when his friends declared that Job's suffering was the consequence of sin. The Old Testament abounds with instances of God sending affliction (see Num. 14:28, 33; Pss. 66:10–11; 119:71, 75: Isa. 9:1). Our preconceived ideas about God may not be consistent with what His Word says about Him.

At Bethel College's 1980 Founder's Week, I witnessed two vivid examples of God choosing not to prevent suffering. One of our speakers, Cliff Barrows, pulled an object from his pocket and showed us one of his most precious possessions—a glass eye. It was given to him by his close friend and associate, blind singer Kim Wickes, who had gotten a new one.

Then I watched the U.S. Army chief of chaplains place the Order of Aaron and Hur medallion (the highest honor bestowed by the chaplain's corps) around the neck of one of my husband's dearest friends, retired commandant of the U.S. Army chaplain school, Chester Lindsey. This great Christian was in the final stage of cancer. And my heart cried out to God, "You can—why don't You—give Kim *real* eyes and Chet that healthy, vibrant body we used to know?"

But such questions aren't for Christians to ask. We must not only look past the losses to the gains, but we *must see the real God at work.*

At a convention this past summer, I asked Joni Eareckson if she would give me a quote for this book. She cheerily responded, "Sure. Come to my room when I'm through speaking tonight." Still in braces from her shoulders to her hands and feet, she lay on her bed talking to me about questioning God and praying to be healed from the paralysis which resulted from her diving accident. Then she wistfully recounted her gradual climb up through those reactions to her present beautiful relationship with God. As we discussed whether God just allowed these things or actually had a part in sending them, she suddenly broke forth in a beaming smile and exclaimed, "Oh, that isn't even a good question, is it? *He's sovereign!* He's in control of everything!"

Joni—the one I had seen the year before receiving an award at the national Christian Bookseller's Convention for being the Number One author reaching today's Christian teenagers. Why? *Because* of her tragic accident!

Sovereign! The expert, supernatural Vinedresser who gives the perfect season, the perfect nourishment, the perfect protection, and the perfect pruning—to His precious branches.

### FRUIT

By now are you saying you don't want any part of a God like that? Are you thinking, *With a friend like that, who needs enemies?* James explained in his epistle that when we

can look back and see what the Lord has brought about
through suffering, we will realize that He really was good
all along.

Brothers, as an example of patience in the face of suffering, take the prophets who spoke in the name of the
Lord. As you know, we consider blessed those who
have persevered. You have heard of Job's perseverance
and have seen what the Lord finally brought about. The
Lord is full of compassion and mercy (James 5:10–11,
NIV).

Jesus explained that God's reason for pruning is never to
hurt us but to produce more fruit. That glorious season we
love so much. *Fruit-bearing!* Accomplished by God's all-
loving, all-wise process!

Fruit? What is fruit in our lives? In the New Testament, fruit
occasionally means the winning of souls. But usually it means
what is produced in our personality—*our potential.* Those
visibly expressed character traits which the Holy Spirit produces in us—"love, joy, peace, long-suffering, gentleness, goodness, faith, meekness, self-control" (Gal. 5:22–23).

I recall how I busily jotted notes at Urbana '70 as Dr. John
Stott explained that *fruitfulness* almost always means
"Christlikeness." I wrote this quotation from him: "Prun-
ing—pain, sorrow, suffering, frustrated ambition, grief.
Much of our suffering is the chastening of Hebrews 12:10,
*'That we may share in His holiness'"* (NIV).

It is amazing to study Scripture and see *how* these personality gains are produced. James wrote, "My brethren,
count it all joy when you fall into various trials, knowing
this, that the testing of your faith worketh patience. But let
patience have her perfect work that you may be perfect and
entire, lacking nothing" (James 1:2–4, SCO). Our potential
is fulfilled through trials. Paul wrote, "But we glory in tribulations also; knowing that tribulation worketh patience; and
patience, experience; and experience, hope" (Rom. 5:3–4).

Penned beside Romans 8:28 ("All things work together for good. . . .") in my old Bible is the simple, now fading word, "Judy," the child we lost in infancy, with an arrow pointing to the pruning verse John 15:2. Pruned! For my good. To produce fruit—more Christlikeness—in me.

In California I was told that if grapes are not pruned, a fuzzy, ugly, hairlike growth appears on the branches of the vine. I may think everything being produced in my life is the luscious fruit of the Spirit. But God, seeing the real me, gets out His pruning knife and cuts away at the branches.

There are many extensive and expensive courses being taught these days to help people discover their full potential. But God's 2,000-year-old formula has been available to us all along. And through it—*gained*—*the rare privilege of actually realizing our full potential!*

## SPIRITUAL FRUIT OF THE WOMB

But as mentioned previously, there are some examples in the Bible of the other kind of fruit being produced in our lives. There is the fruit of the womb—spiritual offspring. This comes as a result of "bearing" a witness (see John 15:27). Jesus told His disciples, "Lift up your eyes, and look on the fields; for they are white already to harvest, and he that reapeth . . . gathereth *fruit* unto life eternal" (John 4:35-36). With this same idea, Paul expressed his desire to visit the Romans that he might have some *fruit* among them (see Rom. 1:13).

It was because of Mary and Martha's grief that Jesus had the opportunity to demonstrate His power at the grave of Lazarus which produced the fruit of souls. "Many of the Jews who came to Mary [and Martha], and had seen the things which Jesus did, believed on Him" (John 11:45; see also 12:11).

Recently a woman wrote, "Dear Evelyn, I am really going to watch for your next book, *Gaining Through Losing*. I

372

gained through losing my husband. . . . He was fatally injured by his chain saw. . . . My five children ranged in age from 21 months to 15 years. . . . It's a long story how the Lord used Ron's death to bring us all back to California, and how, *one by one, each of us came to Him.*" Eternal fruit!

At an annual convention of the auxiliary of the Home World Bible League in one of Chicago's large motels, the previous manager had overbooked. As a result 2,000 women waited for hours in tedious lines for rooms, some being shuttled to less desirable hotels and arriving back late for meetings. Torrential rain had flooded the below-ground-level convention room. Just two hours before the first session began, maintenance people had siphoned two inches of water from the floor. The 94-degree temperature and an inadequate air-conditioning system for a crowd that size had turned the room into a literal steam bath. Disaster reigned.

Just before I closed the last session, the new manager asked for time on our program. After explaining that his predecessor had lost his job because of the frightful overbooking, he thanked those ladies profusely for their beautiful spirit all that weekend. "If I had had this many traveling salesmen, they would have been fistfighting in the halls over the rooms. But not one of you complained once." Then—to thunderous applause—he said, "In fact, ladies, you have made a believer out of me!"

*Gained*—the privilege of being one of the branches God chooses to prune—*so that* I can realize my full potential of what I can be—*so that* I can bear eternal fruit!

## GOD IS GOOD?

Back in 1943 my mother-in-law, 42 years old with two young children and a grown son away at war, answered the phone early one morning. It was the family doctor bearing the message that her husband, recovering from minor surgery, had just been found dead in his hospital bed. Being in

*Section III*
# BORN LOSING.
# REBORN GAINING

# 5
## Aloneness

ALONENESS—THE RESULT of one of the greatest losses we can experience—that sometimes sudden and ever-deepening realization that we have been deprived of human companionship. The loss may come through death, separation, divorce, rebellion, or distance.

Aloneness is serious, frequently producing mild to severe physical, emotional, or mental stress. Numerous studies cite a definite correlation between loneliness and frequency of illness, length of hospitalization, admission to mental institutions, and a higher death rate. Writing on this subject, Dr. James J. Lynch, psychologist at the University of Maryland School of Medicine in Baltimore, states:

Individuals who live alone—widows and widowers, divorced and single people—may be particularly vulnerable to stress and anxiety because they continuously lack the tranquilizing effect of human companionship (*The Broken Heart: The Medical Consequences of Loneliness*, Basic Books).

Since the loss of human companionship at some time in life is inescapable, must the inevitable result always be complete loss for us? Must we endure these shattering losses alone? Is there no one to take up the role of companionship, to produce a tranquility in us?

Yes, there is. Jesus. He is the One who promised those who love Him, "Lo, I am with you always, even unto the end of the world" (Matt. 28:20). Always and forever! Companionship with Him is always available to us. He will never forsake His own, never rupture the relationship, never sever the bonds of love.

But there is still another dimension in aloneness for the Christian. There is the hope of actually *gaining* through the *losing* of human companionship.

## GOD COMES IN PROPORTION TO OUR NEEDS

Theologians tell us that God is omnipresent, that is, He has the ability to be everywhere at once. But does this mean He is in all places at all times in the same proportion? It does not appear so.

An amazing characteristic of God's nature that I have observed is: *He always comes in proportion to our needs.* The deeper the sorrow, the more comfort He gives; the larger the void, the more God fills it; the greater the need, the more we have of Him. "The Lord is *nigh* unto them that are of a broken heart"(Ps. 34:18).

I have found in my own life that God always comes in proportion to my need. It is more than just, "Lo, I am with you always." That is God's "when"—always! But there are differences in my "whens." Difficult circumstances require an added measure of this strength and grace. At those times I can be sure He will be with me in that same proportion.

There is a quality and a seeming quantity of His presence that changes with life's needs. It is like the "as" of Moses' beautiful promise to Asher during his final benediction to the 12 tribes which has been a comfort to every succeeding generation of believers: "As thy days, so shall thy strength be" (Deut. 33:25). More strength is given when more strength is needed!

Sharing some ideas for this book with Joni Eareckson last summer, I told her about God always coming in proportion to our needs. Lying on a bed in her braces, she became quiet, pondered my statement, and then said, "Oh, that really ministers to me, Evelyn."

A woman in her 30s came to me in a large Midwestern church with a horrifying story: "My husband seemingly went out of his mind temporarily and beat me with a hammer, trying to kill me. The excruciating pain was almost more than I could bear. Nobody was around to help me in that awful moment. But in that terrifying aloneness, something astounding happened. I saw Jesus standing right by me. I was not alone!"

As I listened, there welled up within me a sudden longing to actually see Jesus like that. I had never seen Him in that way. But then I realized—I've never needed Him to that extent either. However, the premise still is true. He has always come to the degree that I have needed Him—in proportion to my need!

This knowledge has given me a wonderful assurance for the future, since through all these years He has never failed to come in the exact proportion to my need. I can face whatever life may bring, little problems or huge tragedies, and know absolutely that Jesus will be there in the exact ratio to my need.

When we *lose* the security and help of human companionship, the *gain* we experience is that fantastic proportion in which God gives of Himself to us. It was in a hospital that I first learned this concept. Hospitalization produces a particular kind of aloneness—the loss of the security of all familiar human companionship. Absent too are all the familiar sounds, smells, and sights of our usual surroundings.

The night before surgery brings a very special kind of aloneness. I was just 34 when I entered a hospital for my first surgery. A lump in each breast foreshadowed an almost certain verdict of cancer. I had an overwhelming need—and God knew it.

After my husband and all the hospital personnel had left me, an amazing thing happened. It was not just that I was opening myself up to Him more, but I could suddenly sense God actually filling that stark, white room with Himself. As I lay on that bed, I was acutely aware of His presence permeating the room right up to the corners of the ceiling. He was there—all that I needed of Him. More of Him than I could ever remember experiencing before. *God understood the magnitude of my need, and came accordingly.*

When the chaplain came for his usual cheer-up-tomorrow's-surgery-rites, I didn't need him. Perhaps he didn't appreciate God usurping his rights, but God had already come!

What a *gain* in that *losing* situation! *Gained*—that unique privilege of having my room filled with the overwhelming presence of the God of the universe! The God even the heaven of the heavens cannot contain! And *gained*—the lifelong realization that no matter how great my need, God will infuse it to the extent that it needs filling. God coming in proportion to my need! Although the next day's surgery proved the tumors to be benign, I had learned one of life's most important lessons.

Through my years as a pastor's wife I have assured apprehensive, frightened, hospitalized friends that it was a privilege—yes, a privilege—for them to be in that hospital with a very deep need—because they too could experience His coming in proportion to that need. What do we *gain* when we *lose* all familiar human support? More of God!

But my third surgery—gallbladder—produced a surprise for me. At 4 A.M., just 12 hours before check-in time at the hospital, I was facing a frustrating schedule of last-minute loads of washing, the final mopping of the kitchen floor, the preparation of food to be stored in the refrigerator—wondering how I could ever get it all done before 4 P.M. As I lay beside my husband in the silence of the predawn darkness, I cried out to God in my special need: "God, I'm leaving my little ones, my home . . . so much undone . . . surgery!" Then I felt God coming in a powerful, but different way than He had come before the previous surgery. He was so real that I almost felt myself lifted and mingled with Him. I spent a long time just lingering in this precious presence—finding strength, comfort, encouragement. All the things I needed so badly for that day.

Then I shook Chris and woke him exclaiming, "Oh, Honey, God came early this time!"

Chris smiled and held me close. "He must have known you needed Him early this time." Of course, He did. He had come in proportion to my need—again!

So once again I learned the lesson. Now as I reflect on the gentle progression of God teaching me through hospital experiences, I realize that this principle had been in operation without my recognizing it all of my Christian life—God coming in proportion to my need.

## DEATH: WHEN GOD SEVERS
## A HUMAN RELATIONSHIP

The greatest aloneness we ever experience is in the violent rending of loved ones by death. The loss is gargantuan. Almost unimaginable. *Can God, does* He come in *that* great a proportion?

My first years of marriage seemed to be full of losses. Death was everywhere. Losing at three months the unplanned baby conceived on our honeymoon produced a psychological and, surprisingly, physical void entailing an adjustment that for me was deeper than any postpartum blues I later experienced—a body shocked at premature loss. Aloneness!

The loss of our second baby occurred at a period of great loss for the whole world—World War II, a time when we parted with people and things most dear to us—husbands, sons, doctors, sugar, tires, gasoline, shoes. For me it was a time of losing my husband to fight in a war just weeks after becoming pregnant.

This time the child was stillborn—a daughter. After all the tests said "dead," my mother would sit by me long hours, head cocked like a mother robin—watching, longing, hoping against hope for a flutter of life. Then came two days of unimaginably hard labor assisted only by student nurses—our regulars lost to the war. The coming of our family doctor to deliver that death, then his pacing outside my hospital room, wringing his hands in bewilderment. Why was his other new mother cursing and refusing her newborn while I, so eager to have mine, was wiping away tears—alone?

We had counted so heavily on that baby to fill the void, the aloneness, left when Chris' dad died so unexpectedly in his sleep following minor surgery just five weeks before. The new little grave dug next to his still fresh one turned Chris' second emergency leave into blackness and despair.

How God came in proportion to my need was amazing! Looking back, I realize there had been a deep, underlying assurance during those losses. Although at that young age I wasn't given to analyzing feelings and experiences, I remember the awful blackness being filled with an unusual presence. I recall vividly a special something, a quality in those bitter days of death that had not been there before. Nor after! It was just for that time. It was then that I had underlined Psalm 34:18 in my Bible: "The Lord is nigh unto them that are of a broken heart." I know now it was not a quality but a Person—God, coming in proportion to my need.

But God in His infinite wisdom knew that I had other needs in addition to being comforted with this enlarged

382

proportion of Himself. He came in other, sometimes surprising and almost shocking ways during my aloneness through death. The number of different methods God used to produce gain for me is fascinating to explore.

## CALLING ME TO SERVE OTHERS

With my first pregnancy loss, that miscarriage, God filled my aloneness in a way I certainly had not expected. How startled I was when our very wise pastor visited me, assured me of his understanding, and then promptly asked me to be the superintendent of our upcoming Daily Vacation Bible School. I blinked in disbelief. How could he even *think* of anything else when I had just lost part of my very life? (Six pregnancies later, I smiled at how I had just known there would never be another baby.)

But life really hadn't come to an end. God showed me another way He comes and fills voids—*by calling me to serve others.* While I poured my whole being into those 300 eager pupils for two exhausting weeks, I almost completely forgot my own loss. And I certainly was no longer alone. Yes, God had come in proportion to my need, when I didn't even know what my need was—filling the void by calling me to serve others.

## EQUIPPING ME TO TEACH OTHERS

Another gain I discovered years later was that God had actually come in my need by preparing me for the privilege of teaching others—through these and subsequent baby-losses. Opportunities came in surprising and unexpected ways.

Back in the '60s when the problem of earth's exploding population was just beginning to surface, I was asked to speak at a Zero Population rally at our local Rockford College. After arm-waving speakers startled the students and members of the community, I found myself speaking on my assigned topic, "The Worth of a Human Soul." Wide-eyed, the audience hung onto every word as I explained the physical shock to my body at the involuntary aborting of a fetus and the psychological trauma of losing desperately wanted baby after baby. I had been invited to bring a "balance" to the rally, and I saw it happen. The crowd quietly dispersed, sorting out their thinking perhaps for the first, but certainly not for the last time. Another *gain* through my *loss*—the privilege of bringing another side of a controversial issue to those future leaders of our state.

## PREPARING ME TO COUNSEL

How God came in proportion to my need and produced a most important *gain* because of the *loss* of my stillborn baby wasn't to be realized till years later. He knew my future need, and was preparing me for my role of listening to the heart cries of many young wives as a seminar leader.

In one of my prayer seminars, a young wife of a seminary student stubbornly refused to pray for God's will in her life. In her bitter anger toward God, she belligerently explained to me, "We prayed and prayed for a baby, and finally God answered and I became pregnant. He even gave us a name for our baby. Then three months later, right at Christmas, I lost it. I will never pray 'God's will' in my life again."

After much listening and comforting, I finally said, "Did you ever stop to think that the purpose of that baby's life was perfectly fulfilled? God's purpose—to bring you as a future pastor's wife to a place of complete and total surrender to His will—the absolutely essential ingredient for an effective ministry."

Wide-eyed, she pondered . . . understood . . . and literally crumpled before God. Then she prayed, "Only *Your* will in

384

my whole life. Take all of me—for Your holy will." What a privilege I had *gained* because of my similar and equally shattering losses!

But I experienced another type of loss when one of our children died in infancy. A new kind of loss—aching, empty arms. But in this too, God came in proportion to my need. In addition to filling the awful void with His presence and undergirding arms of love, He came in the future tense—equipping me to meet the needs of others He knew I would be counseling.

After a "Lord, Change Me!" seminar in Canada this spring, a young mother in the autograph line, instead of handing me a book, said, "I want to talk to you. My little girl has just died." While she waited, I watched her struggle to keep the facial contortions of grief under control. After the last person left the line, she threw her arms around me and sobbed uncontrollably.

As I held her tightly and let her sorrow flow out in tears on my shoulder, I gently asked, "When did she die?"

"Last Sunday." Six days ago!

As our Judy's death at seven months flashed into my mind, I felt I should ask an all-important question. "Was your baby well?"

"No, she had brain damage."

Instead of giving her the standard Christian answer, "God was good to take her home," I took a completely different approach. For a moment I vividly recalled the sting when the wonderful doctor who delivered Judy said that to me at the time of her death. I had remained silent then, but my grieving heart was screaming, "A lot *he* knows about it! Sure, she was paralyzed from the waist down and couldn't ever walk. But he can't possibly understand that she's been the sunshine of our home, smiling and laughing with her eyes following every movement as I cheerily chatted at her." Of course the doctor was right, but in my grief, my

385

brain hadn't been ready to sort out *that* fact yet. I knew that the one sobbing in my arms wasn't ready yet either.

So I said to her, "You know, I just have a feeling that God is going to use you to help other people who have children like your little girl."

Earlier that day she had participated in the seminar's exercise of reading the Bible *until* God speaks and then stopping and praying about what He said. (See *"Lord, Change Me!"* chapters 2 and 3 for complete coverage of this exercise.) The assignment had been Galatians 5:1 through 6:10, and I asked this young mother, "Where did God stop you in the Bible reading today?"

"Oh, He didn't say much," she mumbled and blew her nose. "Just Galatians 6:2."

"Hey," I beamed at her, "that's what He said, *'Bear ye one another's burdens.'"* Startled, she seemed almost shocked back into reality and the fact that there still was a tomorrow. "Now," I continued, "you just let God comfort you and heal you. Don't miss anything He wants to do for you *right now.* Then when someone comes to you who has just lost a child that wasn't normal, you can comfort her with all the comfort God has given to you—when He came in proportion to your need."

A feeble, relieved smile spread across her tear-stained face, and she hugged me again. This time not sagging in my arms in despair, but with the hope—and even a little flicker of confidence. I sent her on her way with 2 Corinthians 1:3–4 to cling to in the difficult days ahead:

> Blessed be God . . . the God of all comfort; who comforteth us in all our tribulation, that we may be able to comfort them which are in any trouble, by the comfort wherewith we ourselves are comforted of God.

Gaining? Oh, yes. In her grieving *aloneness* experience God was equipping her too to fulfill the law of Christ. Now she would be able to understand and help bear other people's burdens in the future. In the same way, He had equipped me through those dark, stumbling days of death in the early years of my marriage—to meet the needs of others.

## GOD EXPLAINING WHY

But all the ways God came in proportion to my need were not only for the future. Finally, during my third pregnancy-loss, God actually explained to me *right then* what my gain was through losing those three babies. At that time I had stayed in bed for 14 days with my feet elevated more than a foot, trying desperately not to lose again. But I did.

That wasn't to be the last death-loss for us, but it marked the time I began to see *how* God fills the void with Himself. God was starting to show me the gains He had planned for me. Things finally began to come into focus, a focus that was to continue throughout my life.

It was in my utter hopelessness that I cried out to God for His "why." And He answered—coming in a gigantic way in proportion to my gigantic need. He flashed before me "Romans 8:28," who He was—the God who was working out all those losses for my good. To those who love Him— to those who are called according to His purpose. (See *What Happens When Women Pray*, chapter 6, for complete story.) His *purpose*. But my *good*? Yes, it was God showing me that had those three babies lived, we could never have gone back to the college and seminary campus for seven years to be equipped for the life to which He had called us. Chris' dad was dead, leaving two children who were minors; and my own dad was an invalid. *His* purpose. And *my* good!

## JOY

Understanding the "why" from God produced another gain—unbelievable joy. After those 14 days of living "upside down" in bed, the final verdict from the doctor came—dead.

But this time God came in proportion to my need in a more personal way—just for me. He replaced the loss with *joy*.

I smiled inside at the eager young intern who, at seeing my joy, concluded he had uncovered a then illegal abortion right there in his hospital. His sleuthing intensified as he saw my doctor's name—the obstetrics teacher in that hospital! It was futile to try to explain during the intern's countless cross-examinations that God had turned my loss into joy. He didn't know, couldn't know, how God had come in proportion to my need.

After this "why" explanation from God, complete trust in Him started to come. It was then that His purposes for my whole life began to come into focus. I was gaining through my losses. Although I would not yet articulate that in those exact words until finding them in that poem several years later, it was then that *gaining through losing* took shape in me. Through the *loss* of an unborn baby's death.

Oh, how rich I am because God always took my death-losses and turned them into gains—for me and then for others!

*Gaining through losing*. It all came into focus the other day. The wife of the "little boy next door" from Rockford met me in front of the seminary where he is now an administrator. She had lost their expected baby in a miscarriage a few days before. I fought back the tears as she said to me, "God brought you into my life for such a day as this."

Has God come in proportion to your need?

# 6

## *To Die*
## *Is Gain?*

---

To DIE IS gain? The person is gone—forever. Everything that belonged to the deceased—money, property, family, life itself—all lost to him. But isn't it from our earthly perspective that we measure the losses of our loved ones? In our grief it is difficult for us to see that death is all gain for one who has died in the Lord. Paul wrote:

For to me to live is Christ, and to die is gain (Phil. 1:21).

This is our assurance, and we can cry with Paul, "O death, where is thy sting? O grave, where is thy victory?" (1 Cor. 15:55). My sister expressed it this way in a thank-you note for flowers sent for her saintly father-in-law's funeral: "Grandpa would have been 89 today. He can celebrate on a far higher plane than he could have with cake and candles!" If our loved ones have known Christ as Saviour and Lord, then we can have absolute assurance that for them all is gain. It is *our* sense of loss that makes us want them to stay here with us—not theirs.

But death *is* loss—crushing, numbing loss.

As we stepped into the mortuary right after my brother's death, Mother momentarily froze in her steps just inside the entry door. Gone! Then, bracing ourselves, we walked stoically into the room marked, "Mr. Luhman." As we stood by his casket, I took my frail little mother in my arms and, pressing my cheek against her white hair, whispered, "Mother, this is the ultimate Romans 8:28!" That had been our secret—ours through the years when life had crumbled and collapsed around us. When by earthly standards life wasn't worth living, we could always with a squeeze of the hand or an understanding glance whisper, "Romans 8:28." God working everything together for *our good*.

But that day this concept took on a new dimension—God working all things for *Bud's* good. Yet, somehow it was more than good. It was triumph! What was our *loss* was Bud's *gain*. Yes, we were gazing down at "to die is *gain*."

But my loss at my brother's death still jumps up at me in unexpected places—a plane stopover in Detroit, for instance. While Bud was living, every time a flight I was on made a stop in Detroit, I would get off, dash into the terminal and call him on the phone just inside the gates. The first time I came into that airport after he died, my feet dragged into the waiting room. A great void swept over my whole being. My stomach did a peculiar flip-flop as I shuddered inside. But it was my loss—not his!

Just last month while I was being driven to the Detroit airport following seminars, a vaguely familiar sight flashed past the car window. It was the fire department which housed the emergency squad Mother had summoned to try to resuscitate Bud. And there it was again. The loss welling up, unheralded, inside me. My loss—but not his!

## OUR GAIN THROUGH THEIR GAIN

Our gain comes through knowing that it *is* gain for our loved one, not utter loss in an eternity without Christ. To have the assurance that our loved one has truly found with Paul that "to die is gain" makes such a dramatic difference in our grief. It changes our despair to hope.

God gave this assurance in an unusual way to a young woman grieving over the sudden death of her mother. Knowing that her mother had attended a "Lord, Change Me!" retreat (where we individually read His Word and write God a letter about what He has said to us), the daughter wrote in a letter to me:

I found your *"Lord, Change Me!"* book in my mother's room when I was sorting out things after her sudden death in January. . . . And I found a letter she had written God at one of your retreats. I knew from reading it that she had accepted Christ as her Saviour.

Her feeling of hopelessness had turned into confident assurance.

## THEIR GAIN—PARADISE WITH JESUS

During the loss of a loved one, we can start the process of turning it into our gain by lifting our eyes, as our loved ones have, to their gain—Jesus. Frequently, we hear of the glorious experience of a Christian glimpsing heaven during the dying process. It happened to Stephen. He saw Jesus— not only ready to receive him when he drew his last breath, but also lifting him out of the misery of the lethal stones that were snuffing out his earthly life.

But he, being full of the Holy Ghost, looked up stead-fastly into heaven, and saw the glory of God, and Jesus standing on the right hand of God. And said, "Behold, I see the heavens opened, and the Son of man standing on the right hand of God" (Acts 7:55–56).

Transcending the stoning, Stephen transfixed his eyes on his Lord—Jesus—in heaven. Then there is recorded for us one of the most remarkable conversations ever heard on earth. Stephen, as he was being stoned, asked Jesus to receive his spirit. His last words were addressed, not to those humans around him, but to the Lord. Stephen knelt and cried with a loud voice, "Lord, lay not this sin to their charge" (7:60). Jesus was so real at the time of death that Stephen actually talked to Him.

To have communication with Jesus seems to be the privilege of many of God's children while they are dying. My stepfather told me that one morning his first wife, who was dying of breast cancer, told him that she would die that night—and she did. Her doctors and nurses had said, "She is not that close to death yet." But she knew that she was. Then he smiled as he reminisced: "Her face absolutely glowed that morning as she told me. And it glowed all that day." She had heard from her beckoning Lord, her Jesus!

How sad that some feel the dying one must be given drugs to provide a false euphoria or a dulling of the senses right out of reality. Depriving them of the right to die with dignity. Denying them the privilege, with the saints through the ages, of the experience of valiantly clinging to the greatest of all Comforters, the Lord Himself—"The Lord is my Shepherd; I shall not want. . . . Yea, though I walk through the valley of the shadow of death, I will fear no evil; for Thou art with me" (Ps. 23:1, 4). Pain relievers—yes. But the right to deprive the dying person of the privilege of being lifted, alert, into the arms of Jesus? Hardly.

And even our little Judy—just seven months old—seemed to sense Jesus' presence just before death. My husband was sitting by her hospital crib while she lay, unconscious, with her little fists tightly clenched. Suddenly, she opened her right hand, raised it upward as if reaching for something, held it there for a moment, dropped it—and died. Reaching for what—for whom? Jesus?

My heart thrilled again as my mother recently recounted how my dad, after being in a coma for several days, sat up in bed, raised his arms toward heaven, looked up and, smiling triumphantly, exclaimed, "Jesus!" Then he slumped back on his pillow in death.

## PREPARED

I had watched the price my mother paid for the privilege of knowing that my father was prepared to spend eternity with Jesus. For 25 years she had lived her Jesus before him, always in love and sacrificial giving of herself, never compromising—then came that moment when his doctor told him he was dying. After calling his denomination's pastor (whom he had never even met) to administer final communion, he said, "There's more to it than this, isn't there, Mother?"

"Do you really think so?" She once again repeated to him, "Just ask God to forgive all your sins, Daddy; and ask Jesus to come in as your Saviour." He did. Her Jesus became his Jesus!

Through the years my mother has paid the price for gaining the privilege of rejoicing in the certainty of the eternal destiny of many of her close relatives. Actively pursuing, loving, sacrificing, sharing Bible promises with them—until they too were ready. Her *loss*—their *gain*. With *their* Jesus!

As I was typing the manuscript for this chapter, the phone rang. It was someone calling long distance with a prayer request. "My boss' mother is dying of cancer. The doctors have given her two months to live. I just arrived to take care of her. She is angry with everybody—her children, the doctors, and me. Everybody. All I can feel is hate in her. Last night I even dreamed she was trying to poison me."

"She is reacting that way because she is afraid," I explained to her. "Afraid, because she knows she is going to die and is not ready. What she needs is your love and your Jesus. Share Jesus and His promises about heaven with her.

Read John, chapter 14 ('In My Father's house are many mansions . . .') to her."

"Oh," she exclaimed, "before I left home, her daughter said God had given her a Scripture portion for me to take to her mother. That's the Scripture—John 14!"

A completely changed lady called me a week later, "I did as you said—just shared my Jesus and loved her. And she just melted. She then wanted what I had. She accepted Jesus. Now she is a totally changed person—relaxed, joyful, not afraid to die." Prepared!

Many parents agonize for years over their children's readiness to meet God at death. For 30 years Mother had prayed every day for God to bring her boy back to Himself. The rest of us had prayed fervently too, though sometimes spasmodically. We interceded through all those years of his rebellion against God, and when he finally had said, "There is no God. I know there is no God!"

For two years Mother had prayed, "God, do anything You have to do to bring Bud back to Yourself." Then the accident. The car was traveling 50 mph and my brother, a pedestrian, was hit. Tubes, pumps, and intensive care were all that lay between him and eternity when our family arrived at the hospital. And Mother, almost collapsing, shuddered and sobbed, "Is it *my* fault—for praying that way to God?"

The next morning two of us could see him for ten minutes every two hours. Mother and I were first. I bent over his seemingly lifeless body and said slowly, deliberately, "Bud, . . . God . . . loves . . . you." The God he declared didn't exist! But at that moment there came the first flicker of life. Bud stirred. The minutes ticked by. I waited, fearing that any sudden shock would push him, unprepared, into eternity. But in desperation I knew I had to say something more.

"Bud . . . can . . . you . . . trust . . . Jesus . . . today?" I intoned. Suddenly he was awake, and through the tubes and hardware, he grinned at me and mouthed a strong, affirmative, "Uh, huh!"

God gave him over two more years to live, and it was again Mother who took care of him when the doctors could do no more. In the last couple hours of his life here on earth, he reviewed for her his whole spiritual journey with God since he was a little boy—loving Him, leaving Him, denying Him, and then returning to Him. "I'll see you in heaven, Mother." With that he went to sleep. Just two hours later, with a violent lunge, he found himself in that heaven. Loss for her—but indescribable gain for him!

"Today shalt thou be with Me in paradise," promised Jesus (see Luke 23:43)—to the dying thief on that other cross—and to my brother. What a *gain* suddenly to be transported into heaven to be with Jesus, the very Son of God!

## GAINED—A PLACE

After the long years of questioning our brother's eternal destiny while he was alive, my sister still had a gnawing fear that perhaps Bud really hadn't known Christ as his Saviour when he died. When we met for the first time after his funeral, she asked, "If I could only *know for sure* where he is. Do you know for sure Evelyn? Has God told you?"

"Yes, I believe He has. It happened the first day I was home after Bud's funeral." And I told her exactly what I had scrawled in my notebook that morning.

Just before 5:30 A.M. woke with a start from a deep sleep. Looked out window. Cloudless sunrise! Shakily crawled out of bed and groped my way down to the dining room. It was alive with color. The sun radiating through the crystal chandelier at its peak.

As I stood in a mixture of trembly exhaustion and awe, I asked God to *recall* a Scripture. Searching my mind had produced nothing in that early morning stupor. *"In My*

*Father's house are many mansions. If it were not so I would have told you!"*

My notes continued:
He knew my need. *Hope.* Not to look back to funeral, casket and cemetery, but *forward,* upward! *Bud.*

Then a sight I never had seen before. The sun kept striking the crystals and shooting blinding rays back into my eyes. Brilliant, all colors. Just a few, four or five at a time from the different crystals. Had I never stood exactly at that angle before? I don't know why, but *this morning was by far the greatest display of brilliant beauty ever.*

Then came, "You believe in God, believe also in Me!" *God!* The One who woke me out of a deep sleep at *exactly* the right minute. The One who recalled *exactly* what I needed to start living life normally again—*hope.*

Next my notes revealed my answer from God:
How could I *not believe* in the God who would do that? Happenstance? It would take a lot more "faith in happenstance" than I can muster this morning.

"I go to prepare a place for *you.* And if I go . . . I will come again and receive *you* unto Myself; that where *I* am, there *you* may be also!" Bud *was* prepared. He *is* preparing mine (my place) now.

Suddenly, praying was fantastic, *thrilling*—"I love You, Jesus." *Praise. Feeling* Him so real, tingly. Feeling God when I'm *alone.*

I can't wait to see all the gorgeous colors of the place God has prepared for us. Every foundation stone a different precious jewel with the glory of God lighting it and the Son of God the Light—intrinsic light, radiating through those jewels. A note in the margin of my Bible dated 4/16/74 (another time when the rising sun was in the right position to shine through my kitchen window and radiate through the

396

crystals of the dining room chandelier) says, "Kurt, Dad, and I looking at spectrums on dining room ceiling. Read Revelation 21:18–23. What will heaven be like with, not the sun, but the glory of God shining through the precious foundation stones?"

Then I wondered how many more colors there are in addition to the visible rays of the spectrum we were viewing. New technology has already allowed us to see infrared and ultraviolet. How wide is God's heavenly color spectrum? After Bud's funeral I could see only the rays of the spectrum visible to the human eye. But what is Bud seeing?

## WHERE ALL LOSSES TURN TO GAINS

How important it is for us to lift up our eyes to that place where all of the losses of earth turn to gains for the one entering eternity!

*Angel Choir.* My husband had a unique glimpse of this after he returned to his cadet training in the U.S. Air Force following his father's death. As Chris and his flight team were flying out over the Gulf of Mexico, someone had switched the dial from the radio range station to a regular broadcasting station to practice navigating by radio compass. Chris had hung his radio headphones up in the cockpit and leaned back, deep in thought about his father's recent death. Suddenly from those headphones, ethereal strains of music filled the cockpit:

There's a land beyond the river,
That we call the sweet forever,
And we only reach that shore by faith's decree.
One by one we'll gain the portals,
There to dwell with the immortals,
When they ring the golden bells for you and me.

In his mind Chris was standing in the midst of that great celestial angel choir in the presence of both his earthly and

397

his heavenly Father. His emotions accelerated from awe, to joy, and then to hope!

Helen, a woman with whom I have prayed for eight years, recounted a similar experience. Her father, Dr. Henry Wingblade, to whom I was a secretary for four years when he was president of Bethel College and Seminary, was one of earth's spiritual giants. During his final illness, he was being cared for by Helen in her home. One day, while kneeling by his pain-wracked body singing hymns to him, she suddenly became aware of singing *with* an angel choir. And he was gone—to join that angelic host.

*Whole.* Chris and I were just reminiscing about our reactions to our Judy's death after she had lived seven months. From birth she had been paralyzed from the waist down. "The most important thing to me," he said, misty-eyed, "was that with a perfectly whole body she was running and jumping in heaven. No more handicap. Her life after only seven months here was perfectly complete with Jesus. She had accomplished on earth everything that God had purposed for her in that little deformed body. Judy standing— complete in Jesus."

"The fact that she was physically whole was the most important to me too, Chris," I recalled. In the days right after her death, I found myself imagining, almost fantasizing, that she was coming back down from heaven—healed. Sometimes coming into our home or sometimes with a dramatic descent into our church congregation as they gathered for worship—but always whole. However, gradually David's words after the death of his son by Bathsheba became a reality to me: "I shall go to him, but he shall not return to me" (2 Sam. 12:23). Heaven became so real to me I almost felt it was an addition we had built on our parsonage.

*Reunion.* Our children too have gained a special view of heaven as a real place because they have a sister there. Although only our oldest child Jan knew Judy, the two younger children, when they were small, always counted four children—including sister Judy. They knew there was a *place* and part of our family was waiting for us there.

The other day as I was sorting out a hoard of our son Kurt's favorite keepsakes for storage, I read for the first time what he, as a seven-year-old, had recorded on the "deaths" page of his Bible. He had not only included Judy, but had added an "Unknown Christenson" for our stillborn—who went to heaven 15 years before he was born. Another gain from a loss—a seven-year-old's thinking on death already in proper perspective.

As Chris watched our Judy die, his thoughts went to his dad and mine who would be meeting her for the first time. He saw our *enlarged family* forming in heaven. And when my brother died, I had an overwhelming sense of Daddy and Bud greeting each other. For years they had worked together in state highway construction. Then Bud was alone—so many years without his dad—until then. Gained—a family reunion!

## RELEASED—TO BE WITH JESUS

Death is God's way of taking His own from this place of sin and sorrow and pain into His place of joy and peace and wholeness. So, since it is such tremendous gain for those who go to be with God, why is it so difficult for us to release them to Him? I think it's because the loss is ours. Because of the deep, devastating void it leaves in our lives. A grieving pastor whose wife had just died, wrung his hands in agony as he said to me, "Evelyn, we prayed and prayed and prayed, but she died anyway. She's gone."

Why are we horrified when we think we may have hastened the process by submitting to God's will, releasing them for His will? Doing so does not *cause* death. No, it just prepares *us* for the loss we will experience.

At a recent prayer seminar, we had prayed in the session just before lunch, giving God the most precious possession

THE POWER OF PRAYER

we owned—for His Will. The wife of the pastor of one of the largest and greatest churches of that area had prayed, "Lord, I've been holding back. I give you my whole family." It was a touching scene.

As we dismissed for lunch, a police car pulled up with the news that her husband had just had a severe heart attack. All I could do was mouth, "We'll pray," through the closed window of her car as it swept past me. Then, as we reconvened for the afternoon, the shock waves reverberated in the auditorium as we heard the announcement, "She didn't make it in time to see him before he died."

Had her releasing him to God *caused* his death? No. It was just God's way of preparing *her* for her loss in those next devastating hours.

A similar thing occurred when I revisited a federal penitentiary. The inmates shared with me what had happened to them through prayer since I had taught them to pray on my first visit. A female prisoner told us that at that time, she had released her most valuable human possession, her father, to God. Two weeks later she was informed by the prison administration that they had lost the official paper that should have informed her of her father's death and funeral. She decided to check through to see exactly when he had died. Horrified, she found it was two hours after she had released him to God. She burst into tears as she told us how the guilt of perhaps causing his death had haunted her all these months. "Did I kill him?" she cried.

"Was he a Christian?" I asked, trying to ascertain if death had been a gain for him.

"Yes, a fine one," she sobbed. Then I assured her that giving him to God had nothing to do with his dying. Her releasing him to God had prepared her for the shocking news of his death. Gain? In what way? By being prepared for the loss that was God's will—and her father's gain.

Why do we so tenaciously cling to the feeling that somehow it *has* to be better to stay here on earth? Paul struggled with the conflict of his willingness to stay here for the benefit of those he loved and his desire to be with Christ—which is far better. (See Phil. 1:22–23; 2 Cor. 5:8.)

A nurse in one of my Bible studies told me that her doctor-husband had obtained the best medical team available to operate on his elderly widowed mother whose leg needed to be amputated because of a circulation problem. After the surgery, the doctors huddled outside her room listening as she prayed and prayed—in Swedish. Frustrated at not being able to understand her, they asked, "What is she saying?"

"She's asking Jesus to take her home."

"She won't die," they all chimed at once. "The operation was a complete success. There's not a medical reason in the world for her to die." But she did. God had taken this saintly mother to be with Him—in that place of perfection and wholeness—and reunion with her husband. "For me . . . to die is *gain*."

We have a tradition at our house. The person celebrating a birthday or a special day is served breakfast in bed. The first Mother's Day after my brother's funeral, our son Kurt, getting up to cook my breakfast, found me at the phone downstairs in the family room.

"What do I have to do to keep you in bed so I can serve you your breakfast there?" he asked, feigning sternness.

But I had a reason for arising so early. "I'm calling Grandma, Honey. Uncle Bud died just one month ago, and this is her first Mother's Day without one of her children. There is a time change between here and there, and I wanted to get her early." I had visions of her being in deep despair and grief.

But I was amazed when she answered the phone. She cheerily said, "Hello," and seemed so on top of it all.

Apprehensively I asked, "How are you, Mother?"

Then she answered with, "What greater privilege could there be for a mother than to have one of her children in

401

heaven on Mother's Day?" Yes, there continues to be that hurting void in her life. Yet it is always transcended by—where he is.

But I would not have you to be ignorant, brethren, concerning them which are asleep, that you sorrow not, even as others who have no hope (1 Thes. 4:13).

How good it is to watch the beautiful thing which is happening at many Christian funerals these days—turning an almost pagan ritual of despair to a victory celebration for the one who has experienced final, glorious gain—heaven. With Jesus, who, by His own death, secured once and for all the fact that dying *can be gain*.

We were not created by God to die—to have our bodies separated from our souls. This was the result of the fall in the Garden of Eden. But God took away death's terror by making death itself the doorway to heaven.

"O, death, where is thy sting? O grave, where is thy victory? . . . But thanks be to God who giveth us the victory through our Lord Jesus Christ." For many years I have asked my family to have the "Hallelujah Chorus" from Handel's Messiah sung at my funeral. Turning their *loss* into *gain* by lifting their eyes and hearts to the glorious place of total and eternal joy—reigning with Jesus!

Culmination? No! Coronation!

Will your losses all turn to gains—when you die?

# 7
## Forsaken

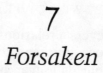

IS SEPARATION BY death the only cause of aloneness? Is there a *loss* of human association that can be even more difficult to bear than death?

In death there is generally the factor of God's sovereignty. We can find solace in the fact that the ultimate controlling force in death is God. Whether we accept it or blame Him, we still hide behind the knowledge that, after all, death is really beyond our control.

But not so when a loved one deliberately chooses to sever or replace a relationship. Forsaken! This can sometimes be a far more devastating loss than death.

Soon after my husband's father died, my mother-in-law and I shared a deep hurt with a mutual friend who had just learned that her husband had been unfaithful to her for several years. My heart ached as we watched her smile valiantly in public but writhe in agony at home as she struggled to swallow that bitter medicine.

403

When a loved one severs a relationship—especially when it leads to that final loss, divorce—the wound can be even deeper than death. It bleeds longer and festers. Whereas in death the departed one (if in Christ) gains, in divorce both lose. They lose the security, the oneness given them by God in marriage. Even in the mutual agreement to "part as friends," they both lose a stockpile of shared experiences, hopes, dreams, and possessions. And the innocent party (years of counseling heartbroken spouses have led me to believe there *are* some of those) not only suffers the same losses as the one who leaves, but frequently loses self-esteem, and goes on living in guilt and remorse. Guilt because of a sense of failure; remorse because things might have been done differently. Perhaps, just perhaps, the final break could have been avoided.

## GAINING THROUGH LOSING?

What can possibly be *gained* in this kind of a ruptured relationship? This kind of *loss*? Except for those horrible cases in which anything would be better than suffering the physical or emotional battering and brutality at the hand of a spouse, is there any hope of coming through this kind of *losing* and actually *gaining*?

I have listened, astounded, as the forsaken ones have told me how God has met them at the point of their devastatingly deep needs. How He has taken over and filled the void with Himself. How they have been able not only to cope, but actually to find something given to them by God to replace the lost relationship.

This does not suggest that it is God's will that a marriage be broken. "What therefore God hath joined together let not man put asunder" (Mark 10:9). But God can pick up the pieces of the shattered life and put them together, so bound with His love, that the scar tissue is stronger than the natural flesh.

A beautiful, radiant, victorious woman came to me at a large Sunday School convention. After I'd taught the prayer lesson on the necessity of forgiving others, she told me an amazing story. She shared with me her struggles at trying to be a better wife in every way she could think of while her husband had been seeing a girlfriend for the past several years of their marriage. The other woman was even brazen enough to call and ask for her husband when she, the wife, answered the phone. Not wanting to give up the home-cooked meals, the laundry service, and the additional earnings his wife provided, he wanted to "have his cake and eat it too."

She told me of the three-stage progression through the years: first the bitterness, anger, and hurt; then the turning to God for advice and support; and finally experiencing *His* love replacing the human love she had lost. She said God had given her such a fantastic relationship with Himself that it was even better than the love she had *ever* known in marriage. Of course, God's *first* choice for her was not this loss of human love. But when, because of her spouse's rebellion against God's marriage plan, she was forsaken by her husband, God was there in proportion to her need. She said to me, "I've found Jesus absolutely sufficient. I still love my husband, but I have turned to Jesus and find all I need in Him. I can never begin to explain how much I love Jesus and how He fills and fulfills me."

I gave her a squeeze, then stepped back and gazed into that beaming face. "All I can see is Jesus radiating out of your beautiful face." It was true—that was all I could see.

## NOT FORSAKEN

How did this *gain* come about through her *loss*?

The answer is in this beautiful promise: "For He hath said, '*I will never leave thee, nor forsake thee*'" (Heb. 13:5). This promise follows a rather startling series of brief statements of practical advice which includes: "Marriage is honorable . . . the bed undefiled . . . whoremongers and adulterers God will judge . . . be free from the love of money, being content with what you have." Then, "*For* He hath said, '*I* will never leave thee, nor forsake thee.'" Interesting context for that promise.

This promise is a restatement of several pledges made in the Old Testament, one of which was the time-tested assurance Moses gave to Israel. How horrified, how alone the Israelites must have felt when Moses announced that after leading them from Egyptian bondage and through 40 difficult years of desert-wandering, he would not be going into the Promised Land with them. Forsaken by their leader!

But then Moses gave them the promise that proved to be true in that day, in New Testament times, and still today:

"Be strong and of a good courage, fear not, nor be afraid of them; for the Lord thy God, He it is that doth go with thee; *He will not fail thee, nor forsake thee*" (Deut. 31:6).

After the similar promise is quoted in Hebrews 13:5, there follows one of the Bible's great "so thats"—"*so that* we may boldly say, 'The Lord is my Helper, I will not fear what man [people] shall do unto me'" (31:6). We can confidently know the source of our sustenance—the Lord. We don't have to be afraid of the possibility or reality of being forsaken by human beings. What worked for the Israelites works for us. Because of their example we can say with absolute confidence: "The Lord will never leave me nor forsake me."

## MISPLACED EXPECTATIONS

Perhaps the reason so many are seeking alternative human companionship is because they have never found an adequate source to fulfill their needs. They may be expecting more than God intended from a human being. Should we expect anyone to be able to meet all of our needs at all times?

The daughter of a friend of mine recently had a discussion with a peer, at a Christian college in the South, who feels her husband is not meeting her needs. Summing up that conversation, her daughter said, "Mother, it is unrealistic that one person could meet another's needs for a whole lifetime."

"Yes, it is unrealistic. You are absolutely right," answered the mother. "No human being could do this. Only God can meet *all* our needs. *That is why we have God.* As we grow and change, our needs change in the same proportion, and we expect our mates to change and grow ahead of us and be able to meet our needs. But this is not possible.

"God does not *expect* any human to be able to do that and meet *all* of our needs *all* of the time. That is God's business. Today in marriage we are expecting a mate to do what *only* God is equipped to do. We are to live each day in the fullness of enjoying our mate, but never expecting him or her to be God."

Another wife said to me, "When my husband and I were first married, I had just found Christ and didn't fully understand what a Christian really was. I was dependent on my husband for all my needs, and he was just like God to me. Then I would criticize him because he didn't measure up to what I thought a Christian should be. My husband is head of our house, but he is not infallible. How much better it is to discover that we can't expect our husbands to be what only God can be."

Then she went on. "God is sufficient for every need that *I* want Him to be sufficient for. Sometimes we just *want* to feel sorry for ourselves, to nurse along the feeling that my mate 'doesn't understand my needs,' thus justifying the turning to forbidden ones. But God *is* sufficient for every need."

I too have found that not being understood, not having my needs fulfilled, involves a very difficult kind of loneliness, a sense of being forsaken. But in this *loss* I have found an overwhelming *gain.*

407

When a parent, a friend, a roommate, or a spouse cannot or will not meet my needs, it is really an advantage. For this has always driven me to the One who not only understands but cares. To the One who is always there to meet my needs. I have learned that a fantastic relationship with the Lord only develops in this kind of loneliness. What a privilege! The *loss* produces a *gain* that no human companionship could ever match. Fellowship with the Lord—who always understands. And bids us come to Him!

## THE BIDDING ONE OR FORBIDDEN ONE?

Many people who are alone have told me about their beautiful, spiritual "love affair" with Jesus—being fulfilled in the pure and holy love of their Saviour. But all love affairs are not holy. It is possible in loneliness to turn not to the Bidding One, but to a forbidden one to find human companionship.

An attractive, unmarried 30-year-old Oriental woman confided to me at a seminar, "I'm in love with a man I can never have." Then hesitatingly she asked, "Will God really supply *all* my needs?"

"Yes, He will," I quickly answered, thinking she was referring to Philippians 4:19: "My God shall supply all your needs. . . ."

"No," she explained, "I mean *all* my needs," and suddenly I realized she was talking about her sexual needs.

Then I said, "To find sexual fulfillment from forbidden fruit is *never* God's way of meeting our needs. That is Satan's way. Ask God to forgive you and be done with that relationship."

I become weary of all those who, because they are deprived of a legitimate partner, defend to me their "right" to sexual gratification. I remember back in my college days there were two graduates who hadn't "landed their educated man" and decided that they had the *right* to sexual fulfillment. They pursued this life with two married men acquaintances.

Did the needs God supplies exclude those needs? Or didn't He even know they had a need? Jesus said that the Father knows what we have need of before we ever ask Him (Matt. 6:8). So He knows our needs, and in Philippians 4:19 we are told that the *person* supplying them is God. And how many of them? All!

Of course, there are always those men who feel it is their "duty" to fulfill the needs of the lonely young girl, the wife whose husband is cold, the widow, the single adult, the divorcée. There are also women who feel it is the ultimate in kindness to give of themselves to the lonely young boy, the husband whose wife for a myriad of reasons is not available at the time, the widower, the divorced, or the never-married.

How does God supply *all* these needs? I vividly recall the indescribable loneliness I felt as a young wife, married just 11 months, when my husband was called into the service during World War II. My invalid dad would sit by the radio and keep track of the B-17 bombing raids in Europe announced on the daily news. No matter how recent a letter I had received from my pilot-husband, I always wondered whether I was a wife or a widow. I was never really sure till the day I sank weakly into a chair, clutching the cable that read, "Missions all done. Coming home. Love, Chris."

How I cringed in those war days at so many "alone ones" all around me who were seeking forbidden companionship—in the factories, in the bars, in the churches! Yes, the temptation and the opportunity were all around.

But I found that God would and did supply all *my* needs in that aching loneliness. The secret? He took away those needs and gave me complete satisfaction when I immersed myself in the Bidding One—Jesus. In His Word. In talking to Him. Receiving support, comfort, and guidance from Him. And immersing myself in serving the Bidding One—

five times a week with the junior high schoolers of our church. And He was always there—loving me, occupying my time, controlling my emotions. Supplying *all* my needs.

But there is a forbidden one more terrifying than any human being. It is Satan, who goes about as a "roaring lion . . . seeking whom he may devour" (1 Peter 5:8). A college dean of women called me to counsel one of her freshmen, the daughter of a missionary couple on a continent where demon possession was common. Experiencing the loneliness of cultural and educational shock, this young girl had turned to fantasizing. "I'm having sexual intercourse with the Holy Spirit," she informed me.

"Oh, no, you aren't," I stated firmly. "You know, Satan is the deceiver. He counterfeits many pure and good things God has given us." The forbidden one! But for that lonely, forsaken college freshman, there was available the Bidding One—Jesus. "Come unto Me," He said to her. "I will never leave you nor forsake you. I will supply *all* your needs."

## INNOCENT VICTIMS—FORSAKEN

The greatest tragedy resulting from a broken home is its effect on the children. Forsaken! Whether the loss has been precipitated by deliberate separation on the part of the parents or by God through death, the children seem to suffer most—they experience the greatest loss. They understand least the trauma of separation. Often they experience *guilt*: "It was my fault that Mother and Daddy couldn't stay together. I caused it." Or *remorse*—wishing they had been better children so that a separation might not have occurred.

But children are sometimes faced with another problem when their parents are separated by divorce or death—they lose both parents. In some areas today, schoolteachers are being taught to handle children who have lost one parent as though they had lost both parents—for many times they have. The parent left with the children changes, indeed

410

must change, in order to cope and to assume the added role of the departed mate. That parent becomes a different individual with whom the children must become reacquainted. So the loss may be doubled.

A schoolteacher told me recently how much she appreciates her principal. When she could not seem to do anything with a little third-grade boy who lost his father just before Christmas, she asked her principal to talk with him. The boy came back to the classroom all smiles. Later she asked the principal, "What on earth did you do to him?"

"Well," he said, "I talked and talked and got nowhere. Then I took that little boy on my lap and told him I understood, because I too lost my father when I was a boy. And that little guy put his head on my shoulder and cried for 20 minutes."

I was reminded of Kum Ja, a beautiful little girl with an angelic voice who was a member of the Korean Orphan's Choir when they sang in our church several years ago. I can still see her splashing in our YMCA pool, relaxing, and having fun after a grueling concert tour. Today she is a citizen of the United States and is working on her doctorate degree in music.

Last summer she reminisced and shared with me some of her experiences as an orphan in Korea. With no one to care for her, she ate out of garbage cans and slept in doorways. You can imagine how startled I was when she said to me, "But I am one of the most privileged people in the world. With no human source of support, I had learned by the time I was two years of age, that God would take care of me. I came to know Him in a way few people ever have the chance to know Him. I am indeed a privileged person to have been deprived of all human relationships when just a little child, for I came to know Him in such a wonderful way."

Astounding? Yes. In her indescribable need, God had met that need in a way rarely experienced by most people. Abandoned? Certainly, although not intentionally by her deceased parents. But in her little mind—*forsaken*. Forsaken—until the God of the universe came in that fantastic way that almost defies human comprehension.

Jesus explained to His followers that He would not leave them *comfortless* when He left them (bodily) but would come to them (John 14:18). The meaning of the word *comfortless* in the original Greek surprised me: "forsaken and abandoned ones . . . *orphans*"!

"I will come to them." He promised!

Children have a keen sense of being forsaken and abandoned when they are deprived of one or both parents. Do we lead them to the God who understands, fills the void, and supplies their needs? Have we given them the assurance that there is one Friend who will never, never leave them nor forsake them?

## NOTHING CAN SEPARATE

But there are other reasons for feeling forsaken in addition to death and broken homes. At times, security, acceptance, and fellowship are wrenched from us by our *own* actions or by the actions of *others*. And there are even times when separation is unavoidable. But no matter what the cause, the aloneness and sense of having been forsaken can be just as real and the need just as great as in death and in broken homes.

There is an assurance in the Bible for these times, too:
Who shall separate us from the love of Christ? Shall tribulation, or distress, or persecution, or famine, or nakedness, or peril, or sword? . . . Nay, in all these things we are more than conquerors through Him that loved us. For I am persuaded, that neither death, nor life, nor angels, nor principalities, nor powers, nor things present, nor things to come, nor height, nor depth, nor any other creature, shall be able to *separate us from*

*the love of God*, which is in Christ Jesus, our Lord (Rom. 8:35, 37–39).

To be excluded, separated from one's peers as a high schooler, can be particularly painful. Kari Malcom, a daughter of missionary parents in China, told me of her feelings when she found herself in a Japanese concentration camp while still in high school. She had lost her father and all her material possessions, except what she could carry. "But my hardest loss came," she explained, "in a break with my close girlfriends with whom I had been through thick and thin. We daily met for prayer, asking God to take us out of that concentration camp. But God eventually convicted me of that prayer," she said, "and finally I could go to those meetings no more."

Her girlfriends became angry with her and ostracized her. She was excluded—emotionally and physically—forsaken by her close friends in a hostile, friendless environment—a concentration camp.

But Kari told me that the reason she had stopped asking God to release them from the concentration camp was that she had discovered a different prayer: "God, I will stay in prison the rest of my life *if I may only know You.*" Yes, she had found a relationship deeper than one with a peer group. She had found a Friend closer than any of her earthly friends. Then she beamed at me and declared, "Since praying that prayer, all that matters is my relationship to God." Nothing could separate her from her God!

## JESUS UNDERSTANDS

Jesus too must have known what it is like to be misunderstood and excluded from the close friends with whom He grew up and played as a child. His teenage group.

When He returned to Galilee with His fame spread through all the regions round about, Jesus found it to be quite different in His hometown, Nazareth. He stood up to read and preach in the synagogue, and His friends recognized Him only as a member of a local family, not as the Son of God. They "were filled with wrath, and rose up, and thrust Him out of the city, and led Him unto the brow of the hill whereon their [also His] city was built, that they might cast Him down headlong" (Luke 4:28–29). Jesus was more than emotionally ostracized by His childhood friends. He actually fled for His life as they violently forced Him toward a cliff so that they could push Him over to His death. His teen-age group!

This past summer I heard a prominent Russian pastor speak just two months after being released from a slave labor camp. He said, "I had to wear red stripes because I was considered the most dangerous kind of criminal in the camp. I was not allowed to fellowship with other prisoners. If the guards saw me talking to others, they would put us in separate barracks. Other prisoners were brainwashed against me as I was declared to be worse than a murderer."

But then he told us that no matter how segregated he was, he always had great fellowship with his Lord. His captors could not take that away from him! Separated—but not from God's love and companionship!

Jesus also understands what it is like to be ostracized by those in authority. Throughout His public ministry, there was a running battle between Jesus and the religious leaders of His day. They called Him a liar, attempted to stone Him, took counsel together to put Him to death, delivered Him to the civil authorities unjustly—until they finally cried to Pilate, "Crucify Him, crucify Him" (Matt. 27:22–23). Ostracized by religious leaders—but not separated from His Father's love.

A recent college grad poured out her heart to me for more than an hour. She said, "In college I had almost a 4.0 average and at graduation was given the highest scholastic honor my university bestows. I led the largest Christian organization on our campus for more than three years, my resumé is outstanding, and I'm going to be a high school teacher this fall." I sensed I was listening to a positive, deeply committed Christian.

"But," she went on, "I'm panicking. I'm going out into the world *alone*. I will be living in a little efficiency apartment—*alone*. I will no longer be a part of a group. I don't think I can handle it. All my friends from college are going their own ways or getting married." She had been sure that a certain young man was going to ask her to marry him. But instead at graduation time he said, "You are going to be happily married someday, but not to me!" Then he turned and left her—alone. Graduation—bringing not joy, but a horrifying sense of impending loss.

She told me she then prayed, "Dear Jesus, I'm afraid of being alone."

I asked her if all through her life and on that college campus there had ever been a time when God had not been with her in proportion to her needs. Thinking back for a few moments, she finally answered, "No, there has never been a time."

"Then," I continued, "there is no reason to think He isn't with you now, is there? God is always there to help in proportion to your need. If the need is great, He will be there in that proportion. When you are alone in that little efficiency apartment, look up at the ceiling and into the corners and know that God is filling every inch of that room. He *will be* there."

Tears welled up in her eyes. She threw her arms around me with a great big thank-you and good-bye hug all rolled into one, and stepped confidently out the door—into a waiting world. But not alone!

What had she gained in her frightening losses? She had learned that when feeling forsaken—even when the separations are unavoidable—that the panicking heart can be calmed with the assurance that God is there. Not alone! "Nothing can separate us from the love of God."

## SINGLENESS

Clinging to believing the promise that the Lord never leaves us is not always easy. Feeling forsaken by all those who might have, could have, or wanted to marry us can be difficult—especially when feeling forsaken *for* another—the one they did marry.

Does the Lord understand singleness? Did He feel that kind of loneliness? Did He feel cheated? *Or*, because He was without a mate, did He experience His Father in heaven being with Him in a special way—as He glorified His Father and did His Father's will in all things?

A well-known Christian author and radio personality who has never married told me many years ago that she found singleness to be a blessing. She had discovered in her aloneness that she and God had a very special relationship. When she had said that, inside me a slight sneer raised its ugly head as I piously smiled and strained to agree with her. In my youthful inexperience, I thought she was only trying to justify her singleness.

Then I remarked a little smugly, "I have the best of *both* worlds. I have the privilege of having a husband *and* knowing God that way." But did I? Perhaps those of us who live in the security of mates who comfort, love, and provide necessities for us have never had the privilege of depending as completely on God—knowing Him to that depth. Had she merely become resigned to the state in which she found herself, *or* had she really found a relationship with God that only comes in aloneness? Since God understands our need for companionship—He created us that way—how natural and understandable that He will fill that need with Himself.

Jesus never married, yet at the end of His life He could say, "I am not alone, because the Father is with Me" (John 16:32).

## LIFE'S SEPARATIONS

Life is full of separations for all of us. Times of feeling alone, abandoned, forsaken—unavoidable or deliberate. College . . . a new job . . . marriage . . . moving . . . a working spouse . . . hospital . . . nursing home . . . when we hit the bottom—or the top. These can bring anxiety, apprehension, and tension. They are real losses, and all need a solution.

This morning I witnessed a traditional family ritual out by our curb. Little shoes were shined, hair freshly cut, new jeans still stiff, eyes shining—or were there tears? The last-minute clicking of the cameras ceased. The big yellow bus pulled away. Tears were blinked back. The first day of kindergarten!

As I watched, my mind whirled back over more than two decades of similar performances in our family—a series of separations in the pattern of our lives. The last one to flash on the screen of my mind was Kurt leaving for college. How similar it was to our first child going to kindergarten. I can still feel the depth of Chris' and my prayers that night for the boy whose newly vacated bedroom was next to ours. And our prayers for us. The empty-nest syndrome!

But again God showed me I was not alone. While reading the 15th chapter of John the next day, I wrote in the margin of my Bible, "Already feeling God's love when I'm alone. Kurt gone to Bethel last night." But then the note continued—another dimension—"I will be alone Monday night without Chris. Asked God to give me a great experience with Him." God answered my prayer then, and over and over again since—as He had done for so many years. Time-tested for over 35 years. Great experiences with God when I'm alone!

The year before, when Kurt left for college, I had spent much time alone with God because of my leg problem. My

417

notebook bulged with recorded experiences with God—alone. When I returned home from the hospital after being in traction and was to stay in bed two weeks, my husband had to leave for the West Coast. At first a sense of aloneness swept over me like a flood. Kurt, popping in and out between college activities, worried aloud, "Mother, I should not leave you alone. But I have so much to do."

"Oh, Honey, I'm fine! I had the most wonderful day." And it was true. My notebook records that while praying alone that morning, I had felt an overwhelming love for God. I lay in bed—just reveling in His love, but mostly *my love for Him*. God had taught me years before that one of the definitions of *abiding* is "feeling My love when you are alone." Underlined right then in my Bible in purple ink were the words from John 16:32, "I am not alone—3/9/78." Jill Briscoe said this so well at a 1979 Bethel College Founder's Week service: "When your husband leaves and you are left alone, you can wallow in self-pity and drown *or* use the time positively. The greatest transactions take place when we are alone."

Our prayers when our children leave home are not only for them—but for ourselves. When either Chris or I must leave the other, we too have very special needs. While I was in Texas this summer, I sensed Chris was sad as we talked during our "good-night" phone call. Flashing through my mind was, *Oh, if only I could be there to comfort him*. I was torn between a strong impulse to just fly home to him and a desire to serve God there. But I could not leave, so I prayed to the One who would provide the comfort Chris needed: "Dear Father, only You can comfort him. Please, come in proportion to his need. You love him and comfort him the way I would if I could be there."

I first learned to pray this way for my husband at a time when he and I had flown as far as Colorado together. I stayed there for a seminar. The next day he was to fly on to California. As we knelt by our bed the night before he left, I became aware of a battle going on within Chris over leaving without me. He lingered in prayer, struggling with being separated from me—again. I prayed the prayer aloud for him then, but all through the night I kept praying silently, *O, Lord, You go with him. Surround him with Yourself. Lift him up. Give him joy. All the things that You can do.*

When I feel frustrated and helpless, sometimes a thousand or more miles away from Chris, what a privilege it is to know that not only am I not alone, but that he too is not alone. For my God is his God—who never forsakes him. From whom *nothing* can separate him.

But sometimes I am the one who travels alone. Unfamiliar airports, strange motels, stranger food, new faces. It is very lonely out there. As long as I am surrounded by the security of familiar places and loving people, I am not aware of needing God as much. But it is when I'm alone that my utter dependence on Him comes into focus. It is then that "I will never leave you nor forsake you" takes on real meaning. It is then that He really does come and meets all my needs—spiritual, mental, emotional, and physical.

I, with the Israelites of old, have the promise that has never failed—them or me: "I will never leave thee nor forsake thee."

## JESUS WAS FORSAKEN

Jesus understood being alone—forsaken. Toward the end of His ministry on earth, the huge crowds that wanted to make Him their king turned against Him—and followed Him no more. As He entered Jerusalem for the last time, they sang, "Hosanna in the highest" and instituted the first Palm Sunday by strewing palm branches at His feet. But by Thursday night, the forsaking had begun. His disciples, His closest friends, betrayed, denied, and forsook Him in His hour of great need. There were no familiar, friendly faces, no trusting supporters at His trial—not one!

419

But Jesus knew that He would be forsaken. He had already told them, "[You] shall leave Me alone." But He added, "Yet I am not alone, because the Father is with Me" (John 16:32). That fact is also true for all of us as followers of Jesus—we are never alone for the Father is with us.

But it was while suffering on His cross that Jesus had a sense of being forsaken that will never be experienced by any true follower of His. The Father was always with Him—until that excruciating moment when Jesus cried with a loud voice, "My God, My God, why hast Thou forsaken Me?" (Matt. 27:46). As Jesus hung on that cross, the Father had to turn from His Son in order that the Son could experience and bear our sins in His death.

That forsakenness will never be ours. We who deserve to be forsaken by the holy God will never be—because Jesus, who had never sinned, undeservedly bore that sin for us. We will never be forsaken as Jesus was—for us.

## DON'T WASTE YOUR FORSAKENNESS

Forsakenness comes in degrees—from the shattering of death or divorce to the first day of kindergarten. But don't waste one of them! Practice experiencing all of God's unchanging steadfastness in the little bumps and in the enormous disasters so that, no matter what kind of forsakenness engulfs you, you can experience what Paul did. Join him in his absolute assurance, born experientially out of every conceivable loss, through temporal adversities and spiritual conflicts, summing up with almost ecstatic confidence: "[Nothing] shall be able to separate us from the love of God, which is in Christ Jesus our Lord" (Rom. 8:39).

Confidence *gained* through our *losses!*

One evening this past summer, Chris, his sister Shirley, and I were hiking along the shore of Lake Michigan. We were exhilarated and chatting happily when suddenly my weak leg started to drag, making marks in the sand. There

420

was only one thing for me to do—turn back. I felt a twinge of forsakenness as I turned to walk to the cottage—alone. But as I saw only the lake and the sand stretching out in front of me—no other person in sight—my heart suddenly leaped within me. "I love You, God. Just You, God. What a great feeling. All alone with *You*."

I recalled how I felt just before Chris and I were married, when there were places it was not proper to be alone with Chris. And that insatiable thirst to be alone with him. "This thirst is how I feel about You, God."

I hiked, my heart soaring. Then I sat on the sand, just so the lapping waves missed my feet, and watched the progressing sunset. I hugged my knees. A thrill tingled down my spine. Not forsaken! Not alone! God!

Don't waste your losses!

*Section IV*

# LIFE'S PARADOXES
# OF LOST RIGHTS

# 8

## *Losing*
## *My Right to*
## *Run My Own Life*

NO MATTER HOW important the loved one whom I have lost in separation or death may have been to me, there is one other human possession who always wants to be Number One—the one I cling to most dearly and struggle so hard to keep; that being who is called by my name—myself. It is the "I" in my life, the "I" that I strive the hardest to protect and nourish.

Even in dealing with losses by death, I have clung to this prized possession—protecting, pampering, and preserving this "I." At times it becomes very difficult to give up the "rights" of this prized possession of mine. The rights I feel are legally, rightfully mine.

How like William Ernest Henley we are in forcefully asserting, if not aloud to others, at least in the secret recesses of our hearts the words of his *Invictus*:

It matters not how straight the gate
How charged with punishments the scroll,

I am the master of my fate;
I am the captain of my soul.
(Arthur Quiller-Couch, ed., *The Oxford Book of English Verse*, Oxford University Press.)

We feel we have the right to sovereignty over our own lives. But do we? Is this, or has it ever been, the *right* of the Christian? Is it the difference between knowing Christ only as Saviour or as both Saviour and Lord?

Thomas, on seeing the wounds in the risen Saviour's hands, immediately enjoined the disciples' familiar name for Jesus, "Lord," with the absolute title of deity: "My Lord *and* my God." After that there is no record of that Greek word *kurios* ever being used by believers in addressing any but God and the Lord Jesus. It was a term they used interchangeably with God—and Jesus. (See William E. Vines' *Expository Dictionary of New Testament Words*, Revell, Volume III, p. 17.) Sovereignty—not I but Jesus.

Peter, after the resurrection and ascension of Jesus, told those who had crucified Him that God had made Jesus *both* Lord and Christ (Acts 2:36). It was because of that resurrection, he explained, that the full significance of the title *Lord* could be understood. Lord—having power and authority. Also we as believers have been translated by God "into the *kingdom* of His dear Son" at redemption (see Col. 1:13–14). Jesus spoke of His sovereignty in Matthew 15:24, "If any man will come after Me, let him *deny* himself."

## THE HANDMAID

From my teens on I have consciously worked at allowing God to be sovereign in my life. At every prayer seminar that I teach, I personally re-pray my commitment along with the others as we bring ourselves into total conformity to the will of God.

I always thought I had submitted completely to God's will. But in the fall of 1977 at a retreat in Indiana, God gave me a word that solved the whole problem of sovereignty for me: *handmaid*. While I sat on my bed with two friends at that retreat, studying Peter's explanation of Pentecost in Acts 2:14–18, the word *handmaidens* in verse 18 just seemed to jump off the page at me. The letters momentarily appeared to be eight inches high and half-an-inch thick. God was saying "handmaid" to me.

With that impact I struggled in prayer trying to submit absolutely to God. He was suddenly pointing out the two areas of my life I just *thought* I had surrendered to Him. Then in a flood of tears, I bowed before Him till my head touched the mattress—in complete, total submission. "Lord, I want to be Your handmaiden."

Flashing across my mind came Mary's response to the Angel Gabriel at the Annunciation: "Behold, the *handmaid* of the Lord; be it unto me according to Thy word" (Luke 1:38). Mary responded immediately after he told her she was to be the mother of the coming Saviour. I couldn't wait to get home to my reference books to see if *my* word was the same in the original as the one word Mary had used. Had I said to God what Mary had said? Elated, I discovered—yes, I had! Then I looked up the definition of the word *handmaid* in many reference books. In Mary's day it meant the lowest term in the scale of servanthood—"one who gives up her will to do the will of another." Sovereignty!

Tucking the exciting discovery into my heart, I went to bed, but lay awake, pondering in the night what Mary had been willing to give up, to *lose*, in order to be the handmaid of the Lord. What losses would result from making God, not herself, sovereign?

Mary was a Jewess who knew that according to the law she could *lose her life* by stoning if found to be pregnant out of wedlock. Still she was willing to allow God's will to be accomplished in her body. Willing to live contrary to the expectations of the existing religion of her day. Willing to *lose her reputation*—a most precious human possession. Willing to endure the suspicions and whispers and peering eyes of the neighbors in that little town of about 15,000 persons. Willing to *hurt Joseph*, the love of her life, when he learned she was pregnant by another. Willing even to risk *losing her beloved* and giving up all the plans for her future with him, knowing that legally he could give her a private writ of divorcement or divorce her in a public scandal. Mary—willing for God's will. But probably she was hoping she wouldn't have to change her lifestyle, dreams, and priorities—but willing!

I gulped, "Lord, did I really say *that?*"

Later, when I took inventory to see if I really was willing to apply what God had said to me at that retreat, I found myself struggling. It was easy to pray, "I want to be Your handmaid, Lord," but was I actually willing to *become* the handmaid now that I understood what it really meant? What would be the losses in my life?

The big possibility loomed—the love of my life—Chris. What if God would want him? Could I be willing? Or even willing to hurt him? On the morning of Chris' next birthday I found myself praying for him—and then for me. Struggling with the thought that *if* this was the year of his life that God would call him, was I willing? That wrestling with God took a couple of hours before I could honestly say, "Lord, You are sovereign."

Was I willing to lose *my* reputation? This spring I reported on *that one* to my Advisory Board, citing three almost simultaneous examples. First, phone calls from a large Canadian city had me stumped. The reservations for my upcoming seminar had suddenly stopped cold. They had poured in for a while, then nothing. Checking, we discovered that a Christian leader in that city had spread some rumors with this question: "How does that Evelyn Christenson have the nerve to come up here to teach us to pray when she and her husband are in the middle of a divorce?" Convincing them that Chris and I had never been happier turned the tide (and my hurt pride). The seminar was filled—with several hundred turned away.

Then I told my board that next my publisher was frantically trying to locate me. When he did, he said, "Call Australia immediately. Your speaking tour there is being questioned." After much probing and questioning . . . "Have you ever?" . . . "Did you and your husband . . . ?" the transoceanic call ended in hearty peals of laughter. We decided that the information "from a very reliable source" had really been lies. Halfway around the world. Rumors really do fly!

Lastly, I reported to my board that at a recent retreat, after four of the five days had lapsed, one of the administrators confessed over pizza that she had been assigned to keep an eye on me to see if I really was doing so-and-so, and if I had sort of flipped since last being with them and was now carrying on like a mad woman. Someone had warned them that it had happened to me just two weeks after our last retreat. My question, "And did you *see* me acting like a mad woman?" released gales of laughter and then a great big, affirming hug.

Our treasurer had listened intently as I verbally licked my wounds, then asked a question that was a good reminder for me, "Haven't you been praying to lose your life for Christ's sake, Evelyn? Well, what is more you, your life, than your reputation? That's *you!*" Yes, the human possession I'm most fearful of losing is *me*.

And I too had to admit I wouldn't be overly anxious for my friends to peer out at me and say, "Tut, tut. Look what that Evelyn is up to now." And being misunderstood by *my* status quo church or Christian friends? Being God's handmaid involved more *losses* than I had counted on. The magnitude of what I had prayed overwhelmed me.

## THE HANDMAID'S GAINS

But were there no *gains* through Mary's losses in becoming God's handmaid? Oh, yes, they were legion. What awe must have swept over her when she realized that from among all the Jewish virgins through the centuries, *she* had been chosen to be the mother of the Son of God—bursting forth in her Magnificat that "henceforth all generations should call her blessed" (see Luke 1:46–55).

What a thrill to have the familiar prophecies about the coming Messiah fulfilled in her! What a privilege to actually be the one chosen to experience Isaiah's prophecy concerning "Immanuel," "God with us" (see Isa. 7:14)—inside her own body! What sensations of ecstasy must have welled up, unheralded, in her whole being when she realized the little one kicking in her body was in reality the very Son of God.

While in labor in the town of Bethlehem, how overwhelmed Mary must have been as she recognized God's timing in placing her, because of the taxation, in just the right city. Micah was right. Bethlehem! The rest of that prophecy was being fulfilled—"Ruler in Israel; whose goings forth have been from of old, from everlasting" (Micah 5:2)—being born right then from her very body. A preexistent Deity!

What kind of anticipation must have been Mary's as she gazed down into that newborn's face—knowing that this was the One who would save His people from their sins? What did she ponder in her heart when the arriving shepherds told of hearing the announcement of His birth by a host of angels over their fields near Bethlehem? "A Saviour—who is Christ the Lord!"

What joyous reverence must have swept over her when later the wise men found Him after following a star in the East until it stood over where the young Child was. They fell down and worshiped Him—knowing that He was the

430

King of the Jews. How dazzling for a poor, humble Jewish girl to see all of that wealth—for Him—her offspring!

Perhaps the most mind-boggling gain for Mary was that God used her own body to produce her own Redeemer! He was coming to save His people, of whom she was one, from their sins. Then, some 30 years later, after the agonizing sorrow of watching her son being crucified for all our sins—to be given the unutterable joy of seeing Him after He had risen from the dead. Her Saviour. Having paid the price of sin once and for all.

Then Mary was in the Upper Room with the 120, hearing the apostles, flushed and glowing with excitement, reporting that they had seen her Son ascend to His Father in heaven in the clouds. Gains? Unspeakable! But all because she was willing to *lose* the sovereignty of her self and become God's handmaid.

## THE MISSED PROMISE

Were there to be *gains* for Evelyn too for having prayed that prayer? Using Mary's word *handmaid* just before falling asleep that first night home from Indiana? In the middle of that night, as I sleepily groped my way to our bathroom, six more words from Acts 2:18 flashed into my mind: *"I will pour out . . . My Spirit."* A light burst upon my thinking. I had been concentrating so hard on being the handmaid, *I had missed the promise!* It was Joel's promise that we had been reading in Acts 2, the promise which Peter said was being fulfilled before their very eyes. God's Holy Spirit would be poured out—on His servants and His handmaidens (see Joel 2:29).

Back in bed I saw it all come into focus. Was the Annunciation the only time the Holy Spirit had been poured out on Mary? Oh, no. She was listed among those 120 gathered in the Upper Room for prayer (See Acts 1:14), on whom this part of the prophecy was being fulfilled. She had experienced

431

the other prophecies being fulfilled in her—enough to produce the actual Son of God in her body. But was she expecting to be *one* of *these* handmaidens? This is the last *gain* recorded for Mary in the Scriptures. Her other handmaid-experience had been so singular; in a way, no other person ever had or ever will be a handmaiden in that sense.

I wondered how those 120 were praying between the Ascension and Pentecost. The apostles; the women; Mary, the mother of Jesus; and His half brothers. Were they praying about their desire to be only *His* bondservants and handmaidens—and thus having the prophecy fulfilled in them? Was Mary reviewing her submission to God's will that she had prayed more than 33 years before? Were the brothers of Jesus claiming their elder brother as *their* Lord—expressing their desire to be His bondservants? Were the apostles who had deserted Jesus and even denied Him—and then had seen Him ascend to His Father in glory—were they submitting to be His bondservants? Were the women who traveled with Jesus, who supported Him with their funds, and who were the first to see His resurrected glory, praying this prayer? His bondslaves! His handmaidens!

Lying there in bed I suddenly saw it—for me. On those who completely submit to Him, *He pours out His Spirit.* Understanding this concept explained why at that retreat the very next morning God had poured out His Spirit on those over a thousand women—as they confessed their sins aloud in prayer, wiping away their tears of repentance. "The only thing wrong with this retreat," they complained, "is that you forgot to tell us to bring our boxes of Kleenex."

We had experienced the *Holy Spirit in His rebuking and reproving role!* It explained why a couple hundred of them who followed me to my next prayer seminar just exploded with excitement over God's response to their retreat praying—it had changed them, their husbands, relationships within families and their pastors. Again the *Holy Spirit—healing, reconciling!*

At that seminar the Holy Spirit reproving *the world* of sin (see John 16:8–9) came into focus as two bewildered young women stood before me. As we entered a vacant Sunday School room, they blurted out, "We don't know if we really have Jesus as our Saviour." I questioned if they had ever asked Him to come in as their Saviour.

"I did when I was a little girl, and I feel as if I'm slapping Jesus' face to ask Him in again today," one answered.

"I don't think I ever did," said the other.

Then I explained that if they weren't sure, Jesus would understand and wouldn't be hurt. They could pray that prayer just in case they hadn't meant it before, if they wanted Him now. They both started to cry, and I put one arm around each of them and held them close. As their tears formed wet spots on my shoulders, two young women made sure of their eternal destiny that noon. *The Holy Spirit wooing!*

I see it now, God's promise given through Joel that the Holy Spirit would be poured out—with His convicting, wooing, empowering—on and through those who were totally submitted to God. His *bondservants*, His *handmaidens*. I had struggled so hard with the submission that I'd missed the promise! I had experienced the promise without recognizing it for what it was.

## THE BONDSLAVE

While studying the word *handmaid*, I discovered that it was the feminine equivalent of the masculine word, *bondslave*. Some of those men praying in the Upper Room before Pentecost described themselves as bondslaves in their epistles in the New Testament. Peter, who betrayed His Lord, used it of himself in introducing his second letter. Even Jesus' half brothers, James and Jude, opened their respective books referring to themselves as bondslaves of Jesus Christ. It was a favorite description of Paul for himself. Bondslave—the one (this time a male) who gives up his will to the will of another.

But what about the man in Mary's life? Did God choose a bondslave to be the husband of His handmaid? Although there is no record in Scripture that Joseph called himself a bondslave, I noted as I studied his life that his actions and attitudes proved him to be one of God's greatest. When the angel came to him explaining that Mary was pregnant by the Holy Spirit and would bring forth a Son who would save His people from their sins, Joseph's immediate response was to rise up . . . and take his wife. No questions. No hesitation. Just instant obedience.

Then I questioned—what "rights" did Joseph surrender, lose, in order that God's will be done? Joseph gave up the right to be *included in the Annunciation.* Spontaneous acceptance of God's exclusion of him from the most important announcement on Planet Earth up to that time— the Messiah was coming! I've often wondered how Joseph felt when Mary, not he, found favor with God and when the angel came only to Mary—not to both of them together. There is no indication that he submitted grudgingly or angrily—only that he complied completely with God's wishes for his espoused wife's life.

Joseph also gave up the right to *clear his name* of fathering a baby before marriage, which he could have done by giving Mary a writ of divorcement. That really took a big man! And he gave up the right to his *feelings of embarrassment* at taking a ready-to-deliver *espoused* wife to be taxed with him when legally they had no right as yet to have come together (see Luke 2:5). How my heart ached for him.

Also, Joseph gave up the right to marry a maiden who wasn't pregnant. The right to father the first child of his bride. My opinion of Joseph was growing by leaps and bounds.

But Joseph became the most beautiful example of a bondslave when he gave up the rights of a bridegroom. He put aside all his human needs and wants and lived a life of self-denial. He kept his bride a virgin through their honeymoon and their marriage till her baby was born—so that God's prophecy in Isaiah could be fulfilled.

When Joseph unhesitatingly obeyed the angel's message, he knew that he had given up the Jewish father's right to name the baby (for God had already named Him—see Matt. 1:21). He also gave up the father's right to direct his child into his life's work (God had already planned His life).

My discoveries of what Joseph had given up, his *losses*, continued after the baby Jesus was born. He was God's bondslave to the extent that he gave up the right to go home to his honeymoon cottage in Nazareth after the birth of Jesus. Rather, he was forced to flee from Bethlehem to Egypt in order to save Mary's (and God's) Son from the wrath of King Herod. Then he had to spend the first two years of their marriage in a foreign country among strangers.

Although Joseph may not have known it, he gave up the right to have the lineage recorded in his name as was his prerogative. He received no credit in the Holy Spirit-inspired genealogy in the Gospel of Matthew. The wording changed from the long line of "begats" to the feminine singular, "Mary, of whom . . ." Confirming Mary's virginity—yet excluding Joseph with divine finality.

I concluded we have not given Joseph enough credit. What a specimen of manhood—a newlywed bondslave of God. I saw Joseph as one of the most powerful examples in recorded history of a man who was willing to give up his will—physical fulfillment, reputation, and personal plans— to the will of God. Bondslave!

## THE BONDSLAVE'S GAINS

But was it all *loss* for Joseph? Oh, no. Because he was willing to give up his rights, he won staggering *gains*. I eagerly tallied his rewards.

First, Joseph was chosen by God to be the head of the home into which God was entrusting His only begotten Son. God was giving Joseph the privilege, according to Jewish custom, of *training* one of the preexistent members of the Godhead—the Son—through His formative years on earth. And what overwhelming waves of awe must have swept over him from time to time as he looked at the little boy learning at his feet—knowing He was destined to save His people from their sins.

What a privilege for Joseph to be entrusted by God with the *preservation* of the Saviour of the world—before, during, and after His birth. How carefully Joseph must have protected that unborn fetus; how seriously he must have taken his responsibility of aiding in the birth of the very Son of God. How Joseph must have tingled as God confirmed His confidence in him, telling him in a dream to flee to Egypt to preserve the world's Saviour.

Another gain for Joseph was that he was given the fulfillment of *providing all the human needs* of the very Son of God while he was growing up—food, clothing, shelter, security. That incentive must have lifted the weariness during those long hours in his carpenter's shop.

How Joseph must have reveled in the fact that both he and God had picked the same maiden—he, for his wife; God, for the mother of His Son. The woman God had chosen to be the most blessed among all women! *Gains* inexplicable!

## THE MARRIAGE TRIANGLE

I believe there was one more gain for Joseph and Mary, when together they submitted their wills to the will of Another. God did not break up their love affair, but most likely gave them the best marriage imaginable.

A third human invading the marriage relationship always spells disaster. Hurts, suspicions, lost trust, broken homes, forsaken families, disturbed children—all results of the third party intruding where he has no right to be.

But there is One whose presence creates just the opposite effect when He is asked to be included in a marriage. This One expects submission, obedience, loyalty, and love which, instead of disrupting a marriage, enhance it. Instead of dividing the marriage, becomes its cohesive force.

The only third Person capable of doing that for a marriage is God Himself! Instead of forcing a wedge between the couple, God draws them together. Inviting God's will into a marriage unites them until, side by side, they are so close it is hard to distinguish that there are two people forming the triangle, with God at the apex.

And so it was with Joseph and Mary. The perfect example of God's sovereignty—two separate lives—in unspeakable joy becoming one in Him. A bondslave and a handmaid —married! Both being willing to give up their own rights to obey God's will. What perfect material for the creation of a perfect marriage!

## WHO'S NUMBER ONE?

Without my knowing it, God was preparing me this summer for a showdown decision. At a convention attended by several thousand, I had felt a great moving of God during our prayertime. The next morning as I prayed for that day's meetings, I asked God to send a great revival to that conference—at the grass roots level. Then I asked Him, if it was His will, to allow me to be an instrument in it.

"O God," I corrected, "not an instrument. Organs are great musical instruments, and many times I have heard them praised for what *they* are. Make me only one of the *empty pipes* through which *You* pour Yourself in glorious music—powerfully moving the people."

Returning home I went to a physiatrist for some leg exercises and he routinely took my blood pressure. His stern eyes never left mine as he said, "Your leg is only the oil stick of your whole physical condition. Your blood pressure has skyrocketed. You may have two days to live—maybe two months—maybe two years. In fact, you may not get home from this office in your car. You'll have to stop trying to hold the whole world in your arms. You'll have to change your lifestyle and take time for Evelyn—*every* day. You're going to have to start looking out for Number One."

Numbly I drove home, sorting out the priorities in my life, reviewing my standing commitment to God—wanting only His will, whatever that might be, all my life. Should "I" become Number One in my life? I struggled in prayer, but by the time I went to bed I had settled it—once for all. Reaffirming my lifelong desire, I prayed, "Lord, *You*, not Evelyn are Number One in my life. It doesn't matter for how long. I am Your servant, Your handmaid."

During my following retreat at Mount Hermon, Calif. unbelievable problems were being shared with me. I found myself holding those women one by one in my arms, weeping with them, praying for them till past midnight. After sleeping three hours that Saturday night, I was wide awake pleading with God. "Lord, I want to hold every one of these hurting women in my arms. Every one."

As I lay there in unbroken communion with God, I was offering, not actions, but my whole self to God—to be expendable for Him. Then a burden started to come from Him. I felt that commitment growing and growing inside me till I could see—not Mount Hermon, not the state of California—but the whole world.

"Lord," I cried, "let me hold the *whole hurting world* in my arms!"

What happened the next week was just a sample of the fantastic joys, open doors, and gains that God was planning for me. To minister around the world!

The phone started ringing. "When can you be in Hong

Kong for a seminar?" . . . "Trans World Radio in Guam just finished playing both sets of your tapes—to one fifth of the globe." . . . "Kathy leaving for round the world. Will check on the Japanese translation of your book and your trip to Japan while there." . . . "Transoceanic call firmed up Australia and New Zealand itinerary." . . . "Friends from San Diego want books and tapes. . . . Leaving for Singapore in two weeks to teach prayer." . . . "Publisher's meeting— England and South Africa must be next," they said. I was reeling.

I put my head on my kitchen table and sobbed, "Lord I'm not worthy!" No, I'm not. And neither was Mary—or Joseph. But it is on His handmaids and bondslaves, those who are willing to give up their wills to the will of Another, that God pours out His Spirit!

Perhaps the concept of *gaining* through *losing* my rights to myself is best summed up in a Christmas present from our daughter, Jan, last year. The previous summer she had painstakingly transcribed for me on the typewriter, word for word, the tape recordings of the actual prayer seminar from which I produced the book, *What Happens When Women Pray.*

The letter accompanying the Christmas present said:

Dear Mom,

It's almost hard for me to give this present because it's like giving a piece of myself away. It's letting you peek inside me for just a minute. I wrote this poem for and about you while I was typing your manuscript several summers ago. I want you to have it, not because it's good, but because it's me. And it's you. And it's the mingling of us both. So here I am—like your little blonde-braided girl again, holding out a bunch of dandelions to you—just because I love you. With love brimming out my eyes—Merry Christmas to the most wonderful Mommy in the world. . . .
Your Janny,

439

Her personally hand-painted, beautifully framed Christmas present said:

Let go
Unclench
So you can hold
The wonders of His will
Exchange your finite
for His infinite.

Who's number one in your life?

# 9

## *Losing My Right to Harbor an Unforgiving Spirit*

---

HAVE YOU EVER battled with your right to harbor an unforgiving spirit? When you are hurt by what someone says or does, do you feel you have the "right" to turn that person off, shun him, or even hate him? When things just aren't the way they used to be, do you feel you have the "right" to keep it that way?

I have been teaching the biblical precepts of forgiveness from my book *What Happens When Women Pray* for several years now. I used to wonder how effective this teaching was—if the actual forgiving really worked.

But I don't wonder anymore. One of my greatest joys has been watching these instructions bring visible results in the lives of those doing the forgiving. I have been astounded at the *gains* that have come to those who have been deeply hurt and then, by forgiving, have indicated their willingness to give up, *lose* their "right" to nurse a wounded spirit.

Many have said I should write a sequel to that first book. So here it is—at least in part, telling what happens to those who have forgiven someone as they have prayed. I have used many of these illustrations in subsequent prayer seminars, but now here they are for you who are reading this book. Some of the *gains* I have observed:

## TRANSFORMED LIVES

Watching the changes take place right before my eyes as hundreds of thousands have forgiven someone right in our seminars has been enlightening to me. Each time the participants pray aloud in their little groups of four, I stand amazed as burdens which have been carried for years are lifted, as people are set free from debilitating attitudes. I see them enfold weeping prayer partners in their arms, and I catch the surprised expressions of indescribable joy spreading across faces as they are released from feelings of hatred and bitterness. And then watch the hugs of reconciliation.

So many participants as they stop to say good-bye, beam, squeeze my hand and say, "You'll never guess what happened to me today." And then their story—victory! Or some will press a note in my hand telling me of the depth of the hurt and then the height of the relief as they forgave that day.

I have been inundated with letters from people who have read the chapter on forgiveness in *What Happens When Women Pray,* and have bowed in prayer—applying the scriptural teachings—with such fantastic results. I have met strangers who are just exploding with the life-changing results because they applied those simple principles and took the step of forgiving. The *gains* for the ones doing the forgiving have been astronomical!

Arriving at a large southern prison to teach the principles of prayer, I was stopped by a tall blond male inmate with a fine athletic build. "I just must talk to you—alone. I have to tell you what your book did for me." To find a place to be alone in a prison is difficult, but we were told

442

we could sit in a corner of a heavily trafficked hallway to talk.

"Evelyn, I have been a Christian since I was a little boy, played football at a large Christian university, then earned my first million dollars playing professionally. After I was injured and could no longer play, I squandered my million trying to keep up the lifestyle I'd learned to love. When the money ran out, I panicked and turned to organized crime. I ended up on the FBI's 'Ten Most Wanted List,' was eventually caught, and drew a 240-year-consecutive sentence.

"I have a delicate wife whom I love dearly. I protected her so well when I was on the outside that I never let her even carry a bag of groceries. But since I've been in here, she has had to hold down two jobs to support our four children. It just breaks my heart."

He dropped his head in his hands momentarily before he could continue, then he said, "Two weeks ago I had word from her that she has cancer of the throat. I almost went crazy with grief—especially when I didn't even have enough money to call her long distance. We have to pay for calls in advance. But one of the assistant chaplains of this place saw my distress and said, 'Ralph, you may come to my office and use my phone to call your wife. This is an emergency.'

"While I was in his office making the call, that chaplain suddenly burst in the door, turned on me, and yelled, 'Get out of this office. You know this phone is for legal use only. You have no right to use that phone.'"

Ralph's face whitened as he relived that moment, and then he continued. "I was so angry that I was afraid of what I might do to him physically. So I marched right to the warden's office, banged on his door with my fist, and shouted, 'Warden, put me in maximum security. I demand that you put me in maximum security.'

"But," he added, relaxing his clenched fists, "thank goodness he didn't but instead sent me back to my cell to cool off. When I got there, I picked up the book I was reading—your little paperback *What Happens When Women Pray*. I started to read the next chapter—'Forgiven As We Forgive.' Evelyn, I looked at all the blood on my hands" (trembling, he held them out for me to see what only he could still see), "and I suddenly realized that Jesus said in the Lord's Prayer and then in the next two verses that if I didn't forgive others, God would not forgive me the sins I, as a Christian, had committed either.

> And forgive us our debts, as we forgive our debtors.
> . . . For if ye forgive men their trespasses, your heavenly Father will also forgive you: but if ye forgive not men their trespasses, neither will your Father forgive your trespasses (Matt. 6:12, 14–15).

Horrified, I knelt down and asked God to forgive my attitude toward that assistant chaplain and then asked Him to give me love for that man. He did, and I went back to his office, knocked softly on his door, and said, 'I just want you to know I have forgiven you and love you.' Evelyn, *that was the turning point in my Christian life!*"

Many letters to and from Ralph and his family, and a follow-up visit have confirmed his changed attitudes and behavior. A Christian—radiantly transformed in that prison!

## WHAT ABOUT THEM?

Surprisingly, I seldom hear from those who have been forgiven. Almost all of the reports are from those who have done the forgiving. Frequently, the ones being forgiven don't even know they have wronged someone or that a grudge was being held against them. Surprisingly, the one who has committed the wrong has often not been injured by attitudes nearly as much as the one who needs to forgive them. The reason Ralph was so changed was not because of the *response* of the official he forgave (he didn't even bother to tell me that). It was because of what happened *to him*.

I find so many people counter this command to forgive with, "What about *them*?" "What if they don't want to be forgiven?" "What if they don't *accept* my forgiveness?" "Why should I be the one?"

These are questions that usually pop into my mind too. But they have nothing to do with *our* obligations to obey biblical teachings on forgiveness.

The one who has wronged us has his or her own responsibility to confess that sin before the Lord. But that is not *our* concern. "Avenge not yourselves. . . . 'Vengeance is Mine; *I will repay*,' saith the Lord" (Rom. 12:19).

So frequently I hear, "God is unfair to expect *me* to go to those persons who hurt me. Shouldn't *they*, since they wronged me, come to me?" There are many reasons they don't come to us—an unawareness that they have hurt us, pride, stubbornness, the idea that they have a "right" to harbor wrong attitudes. So we don't wait for them; we take the initiative ourselves.

How we love to play the "I-will-if-you-will" game. But that never produces the *gain* which can be ours if we, by taking the initiative, forgive from the depths of our hearts. Somehow, most of the life-changing results occur in the one doing the forgiving. When we give up, voluntarily *lose* our "right" to harbor an unforgiving spirit, *we* are the recipients of huge *gains*.

## STATISTICS OF EVIL

Are you aware that each of us has an internal "bookkeeping" system? We have one column in the ledger where we record the good things which happen to us, and another where we keep track of the wrongs leveled against us. Year after year these accumulated statistics tip the balance one way or the other. The side outweighing the other has a strong effect on our whole being. If it is the "bad" side, it can affect us adversely.

I heard of a woman who actually has a little book with a page for each acquaintance. She makes an entry each time they say or do something against her. Then when she comes to a predetermined number, she draws a dark diagonal line across that page—slashing off her list of friends! Statistics of evil. ·

But forgiving does a strange thing to the forgiver's column of hurts. It wipes clean the evil statistics which have been hoarded in the internal ledgers. In 1 Corinthians 13:5, that great love chapter, we read, *"Love keeps no score of wrongs"* (1 Cor. 13:5, NEB). In other words, as in the Phillips translation, "It does not keep account of evil."

It is so easy to compile, keep adding up, the score of wrongs committed against us. We poke them deep down inside ourselves, layer upon layer, instead of forgiving and being done with them. Doctors tell us we actually can make ourselves ill when we push hurts and resentments deeper and deeper down inside. These attitudes eat away at us *from the inside out,* causing emotional and sometimes physical ills.

Interesting research is taking place on this subject. Leafing through a Western Airlines flight magazine while flying home one night, I took time to read an article by a medical reporter. The bold-type quote caught my eye:

"To the physiologist, general terms such as frustration, anxiety, pressure, worry, job tension, conflict, and anger translate into quite specific events taking place *inside* the body" *(Western World,* March–April, 1979).

Recently, I listened to a speaker who was blaming the church (perhaps rightly) for not forgiving him for a sin he had committed. But, as I watched his revealing facial expressions, I felt that his bitterness at not being forgiven was eating away at him like an internal ulcerated sore. I kept getting the message that if "they" would only shape up in their attitude toward him, he would be just fine. But my heart kept crying out to him, "Oh, dear man, your load could be lifted just by forgiving them for not forgiving you."

We may feel there is a personal *gain* in the satisfaction we derive from exercising our "right" to refuse to give up our angry, negative, accusing, wounded spirit. But in reality just the opposite is true. We are the *losers.* The emotional and physical *gains* come when we take our spiritual eraser and wipe the ledger clean—by forgiving.

I was sitting with the dean of women of a Christian college in her office after completing the "forgive" lesson in a chapel series. A group of freshmen girls knocked excitedly on her door. Jumping up and down and waving her arms like a cheerleader, one of them grinned and exploded, "I'm free, I'm free! I forgave her!"

Although I had no idea what she was talking about, the dean's knowing expression and affirmative nod let me know that a campus problem had just been solved. And a pretty freshman student had been released from the burden she had been carrying. She had erased it—by forgiving.

In my seminars I have seen thousands who were defeated and bitter, instantaneously released from burdens they had carried—sometimes for many years. Released, almost with a shudder, as if something that had become a part of their very being was torn loose.

Or sometimes it is a fresh hurt. A weeping, young mother came to me the minute I said the last word at a recent seminar. "I just have to talk to you," she pleaded.

I drew her back of the stage curtains where we could be alone. "My two preschool children, a boy and a girl, were molested two weeks ago by our nephew who was babysitting for us." I enfolded her in my arms as she poured out her story and her tears. "But today I've forgiven him!" As she straightened, she said softly, "It's OK now."

Then I prayed a prayer for healing—physical, but most of all, emotional—for the children. And then prayed that God would completely heal the hurt in this dear mother's heart. She stepped back a little and, still clinging to my hands, smiled, "It's all right now. It's more than forgiven—

447

it's OK." Then, as if she had to convince me even further, she said, "It *really is* OK," and disappeared into the crowd. Eyes still moist, but shining with deep, profound victory. A ledger wiped clean!

So who are the *losers* when we keep compiling, adding up those statistics of evil against others? And how do we become winners? The ones who *gain*, who are victorious, free from the crippling canker that eats away at us, are not the ones we forgave. They may not even have known there was a problem. No, the ones who gain are the *ones who do the forgiving!* The "statistics of evil" column of the internal ledger—which can cause so many emotional, mental and physical ills —in our whole being—has been wiped clean!

Sometimes it is easier to "forget" than to "forgive *and* forget." Instead of really wiping it all clean, we feel that just to "forget the whole thing" will take care of it. But it won't. The evil statistic is still inside us—gone only *temporarily* from the conscious mind. Then every time we feel like licking our wounds, accusing that person, or vindicating our hurt again, the ugly statistic comes popping up at our bidding to assist us.

There is one more important erasing that must be done in order to have complete emotional and physical healing. We sometimes forget there is one other person involved—myself. After we have forgiven others and God has forgiven us, we must wipe *us* off the ledger of evil statistics too. Forgive ourselves!

## PREVENTATIVE MEDICINE

An added dimension to a clean internal ledger is: *Don't let evil statistics accumulate in the first place.*

One of the most strikingly beautiful women I have ever seen is a 60-year-old fellow speaker whom I met at a retreat. After we had prayed through our exercise of forgiving someone, she explained to me, "Evelyn, I honestly could not think of anyone to forgive. You see, for years I have practiced forgiving immediately. Never holding anything against anybody."

Frequently, people try to tell me that, but their faces contradict their words. But the radiant glow on her face and the spring in her step attested to the truth of her statement. Here was a beaming, radiant woman in her 60th year who was living proof of what happens to a face that through the years has not compiled statistics of evil. Preventative medicine! Handsome men and beautiful women!

I've heard it said that we are responsible for our own faces after 40. The lines and sags distribute themselves according to the expressions we have exercised through the years. No matter how perfect the features, facial beauty disappears from the countenance harboring the "right" to be touchy, to hold onto grudges or an accusing spirit. The most beautiful features can never compensate for a mouth pursed with resentment, and with corners drooped in touchiness; eyes narrowed with vindictiveness—surfacing from their statistics of evil column. But the plainest features somehow come alive with a radiance and beauty when they exude, not peevishness, anger and resentment, but love—unconditional love. *Gaining* through *losing* the right to harbor an unforgiving spirit.

Modern medicine is stressing not just healing for existing ills, but preventive measures as well. But the formula has existed for 20 centuries in the Bible. In all my Bibles I have used since I was 18 years old, I have underlined Ephesians 4:32, "Be ye kind to one another, tenderhearted, forgiving one another." Here was God giving *me* a prescription for preventive medicine through all those years.

## FAMILIES REUNITED

One of the greatest gains I have observed from simply forgiving is the reuniting of families when one member gives up his or her "right" to harbor an unforgiving spirit against another.

A young married woman confided to me that her pastor-father had severely wronged her mother by being unfaithful. She bit her lip to keep from crying as she confessed, "I'm having a terrible time forgiving him. Pray for me that I will be able to."

Then she handed me her name tag to remind me to pray for her. I did—then and since—that she would be able to forgive—to reunite a bleeding family.

I remember how many years it took me to really forgive my daddy for a wrong I felt he had committed against my mother. I was the *loser* for all those years. I now look back and see how my mother was so much more the *gainer* by her ability to forgive—so much sooner than I.

A daughter-in-law came to me during a local seminar angry, uptight, bitter toward her mother-in-law. "What can I do? She's impossible to get along with," she moaned.

I told her to wait till the next lesson—which just happened to be "Forgive." A couple of weeks later, a completely changed daughter-in-law grinned at me and winked. Peace, tranquility, Christlike maturity communicating to me she had found the answer—forgiving her mother-in-law.

While I was leading a prayer seminar in the church that Hansi (author of *The Girl Who Loved the Swastika*) attends in California, a woman came to her and wailed—in German, "I can't stand my mother. She did so many cruel things to me when I was a child. So I came to America. And we get along just fine as long as there is an ocean between us. But I just got a letter that *she* is coming to America!"

"Why don't you come to our prayer seminar tonight?" Hansi suggested. Again the topic was "Forgive." When the alternate rows of people turned around to form prayer groups of four, Hansi found herself in that woman's group. As they each prayed forgiving someone, the woman forgave her mother for all her childhood hurts. As she opened her eyes, she was looking right into Hansi's. Surprised, she exclaimed, "Oh, *now* my mother can come from Germany!"

At a college, the students shared with each other what had happened after forgiving someone at the seminar the week before. One freshman said, "The courts took me away from my mother four years ago for what she had done to me. After forgiving her, I took the weekend off and went home. Sitting across the kitchen table from her, I said my first words to her in all those years—'Mother, I want you to know I love you.'" Reunited!

In a large southern city, a woman came to me with tears in her eyes and said, "I haven't talked to my mother for 18 years, but last night I forgave her." Then, beaming through her tears, she announced, "And I'm going home for Thanksgiving!"

Then there was the woman in Alaska who knelt, trembling, at my feet as I sat autographing books. Putting her arms around my waist, she lifted her tearstained face and whispered, "I have hated my mother for 24 years. Today I forgave her." Compiled statistics of evil!

"When I was 15 years old, my father committed a crime against my body so severe that he went to prison for it," said a deeply hurt 70-year-old woman. "I became a Christian, but never forgave him and never talked to him so I could share my Jesus with him. Today he is in a Christless eternity, and it's my fault. What can I do to confirm the love I feel for him now that I've forgiven him today?"

"You will never be able to make it right with your dad in a Christless eternity," I explained. "All you can do now is make sure it is all settled between you and God," I explained. How sad to refuse to forgive and to carry a burden like that—for 55 years!

## MARRIAGES TOO

Not only families, but also marriages are frequently mended by the simple act of forgiving. After my plane landed in the East for a seminar, the pastor's wife briefed me on their church's prayer chains and groups. "We've had a miracle take place. If so-and-so tells you her story, listen. It's a miracle!"

At lunch I was sitting next to so-and-so who told me, "My husband was fooling around with his secretary and decided to leave the children and me to live in a motel, so he could spend his nights with her. When I helped him pack his bag, I tucked in a Bible, even though he never reads one." (I stopped her and said, "Hold it, Honey. I've been told this story is a miracle, and it surely is. If my husband ever leaves to spend his nights with his secretary, *he can pack his own suitcase!*" But, of course, I knew that really wasn't the miracle.)

"Every day," she continued, "the children and I prayed for our daddy, and every week the prayer chains and groups at church prayed for him. Then one Saturday morning after he had been gone several months, I read in my morning devotions:

> The Lord hath been witness between thee and the wife of thy youth, against whom thou hast dealt treacherously; yet is she thy companion and the wife of thy covenant. And did not He make one? . . . Therefore, take heed to your spirit, and let none deal treacherously against the wife of his youth (Mal. 2:14–15).

Her eyes narrowed with resolve as she continued: "'Hey,' I said to myself, 'I'm the wife of his youth. He doesn't have a right to treat me like this.' And I began to pray, 'Lord, send him to Malachi 2.' *Oh, what a stupid prayer.* 'Dear Lord, send him to Malachi 2.' *What a dumb prayer. He never reads the Bible.*

"But *that very night* my husband came to his senses. Realizing what he had done to his children and me, he started pacing the floor and was contemplating suicide. Then he flung himself on the bed with his head hanging slightly over his partially unpacked suitcase. And there in

452

plain view, out from the midst of the clothes, was—yes, that Bible." (Now you've probably guessed the miracle.)

"He grabbed it and, in desperation, just opened it at random. Yes—to Malachi 2! He read those words, ran home, and begged us to forgive him, which, of course, we so eagerly did." Another family together again.

But on the way back to the plane, the pastor's wife exclaimed, "That story was only half told. That wife was in my prayer group today. While we were forgiving someone, she just stood there, relaxed. She already had forgiven him. But suddenly she became stiff as a board. Then she blurted out her prayer—forgiving *the secretary!*" Wiping the ledger clean!

As a seminar closed in Canada, a lovely woman said to me, "I was to go to my lawyer next Wednesday for the final step in my divorce. But, after forgiving my husband today, I'm going home and tell him I love him instead. You saved a marriage today." No, not I, but *she* saved a marriage that day—by forgiving. Wiping her ledger—full of a long list of evil statistics—clean!

## FURTHERING GOD'S WORK
## ON EARTH—BY FORGIVING

We have all seen many examples of the way forgiving furthers God's work here on earth. In Genesis 50:20 we read of Joseph, the young man so deeply wronged by his brothers who sold him into Egyptian slavery. But God meant it for good . . . that many people should be kept alive. What a "right" Joseph had to hate them! But, because he was willing to forgive them, God's chosen nation was preserved.

A missionary on furlough shared a particularly moving experience when she was our guest at our United Prayer Ministries Christmas party. During Idi Amin's reign of terror, hundreds of refugees fled for their lives to her compound, which was right across the border from Uganda.

453

She said, "For the most part they were professional people who had lost all their material possessions and many even blood relatives to his plundering, torturing, and brutal murders. I had to go to another mission for 10 days, and was worried about them not having anything to keep their minds off their troubles. So I gave them your *What Happens When Women Pray* to read while I was gone. They were shocked to read what Jesus said about the sins of His followers being forgiven only if they would forgive others.

"When I returned," she continued, "I couldn't believe my eyes. One by one they were kneeling in prayer—*forgiving Idi Amin!*"

After all their losses, who of us wouldn't say they had the "right" to their feelings against Idi Amin? How horrifying were their columns of statistics. But when they were willing to *give up* those rights, their gains were almost unbelievable. Transformed refugees!

Their new lives in Christ couldn't be contained. With a new peace and joy, they went out to witness as others watched the incredible example of what Christ really can do in the lives of those who are obedient to Him. Then our guest beamed and said, "In all my life as a missionary, I have never seen such powerful witnessing."

In our own state, we have had the privilege of observing a forgiving spirit on the part of our Christian governor. Right after the Americans had been taken hostage in Iran, some Iranian students reportedly attempted to kidnap the governor of our state. Shortly afterward, we were enjoying hot cider while talking with one of the governor's close friends. "How did he handle it?" I queried.

"He is the most amazing man. His concern was his love for them. No matter what people do to him, he always reaches out to them—in love—forgiving them!" Exuding Christ's love.

A seldom-mentioned teaching of Christ deals with the matter of forgiveness. When we bring our gifts to the altar, if our brother has anything against us, we should leave our gifts and go *first* and be reconciled to him. When the matter is settled, then we should come and give our gifts. We like to omit the reconciling, thinking that somehow enough of the gift-bearing will replace that obligation. (See Matt. 5:23–24.)

Even in our churches, the cause of Christ is often thwarted by the members' refusing to forgive. At a church where I was to speak, the Sunday bulletin had already been printed with my subject listed. But at 11 o'clock Saturday night, God suddenly directed, "Change your topic. Speak on 'Forgiving.'"

At the close of the church service, I did something I had never done before. I asked anyone who had anything against anybody in the church to come to the front and kneel. To my surprise the pastor was the first one. Then another man came and knelt, putting his arm around the pastor. Many others from the congregation met by twos at the front. As he drove me to his home for Sunday dinner, the pastor demanded, "Who told you?"

"Told me what?"

"To change your message to 'Forgive.'"

"God did—last night at 11 o'clock. Why?"

His words tumbled out. "I am on a national committee that voted for something with which I do not agree theologically. Although I told my people that I had spoken and voted against it, one man didn't believe me. He then started a campaign to oust me as pastor. Today some of the members were circulating a petition for my removal. I thought I had completely forgiven this man, but while you were speaking, God showed me I really hadn't. So I came to kneel and forgive him altogether."

Can you guess who the man was who knelt with the pastor? For several years since, I have watched with interest the way Christ has worked in that church—with the same pastor!

## REVENGE—FORGIVENESS

A stately black woman, a clinical professor of surgery in a large southern hospital, was addressing us in the Bahamas. I listened carefully as she described the racial hatred and sex discrimination through which she had to claw and crawl to become the first black woman surgeon in the South. Then with a beautiful, radiant smile, she said, "But no revenge is so complete as forgiveness."

Revenge—forgiveness? I pondered that puzzling statement for days. What did she mean? Not revenge by her fabulous success story? Not by showing them that she could do it. How had she *won by forgiving*? She had wiped all the resentment and bitterness out of her heart—in the act of forgiving! She was changed. She was released. She was the beautiful, radiant surgeon—transcending and living victoriously above all their hurtful acts. No statistics of evil left in her to eat away at her from within. Her ultimate victory—forgiving!

Jesus demonstrated this kind of victory on the cross. Triumph over His enemies came not only when He was raised from the dead. Oh, no. It also came *during* the physical torture and spiritual anguish. Victory came as Jesus, while suffering excruciating physical and spiritual agony on the cross, practiced His own admonition to us: *"Pray* for them which despitefully use you, and persecute you" (Matt. 5:44). The complete victory was in His prayer, "Father, *forgive them*; for they know not what they do" (Luke 23:34). Why? Because *they were no longer His enemies.* He was Victor!

I wiped tears as Tim Showen reviewed for me and showed me pictures of what he was going to share at Judson College Chapel before I brought a message on forgiving. And many students also wiped away tears as he told his story:

"Our theme for today is going to be on forgiving as we forgive, and I would like to share with you some Scripture from Colossians 3:13:

Bearing with one another, and forgiving each other, whoever has a complaint against anyone; just as the Lord forgave you, so also should you (NASB).

"It's the first time I've really been able to speak in front of people about this, but about nine months ago I was involved in an auto accident that just changed my entire outlook on life. I was then enrolled in Indiana State, and one day I had spent the whole day with my fiancee—making honeymoon reservations, picking out the tuxedos, and everything. We were two months away from being married.

"And a quarter to 4 that afternoon—from nowhere—a drunk driver hit us head-on. I looked over at Rita, and it didn't take much to tell that she was dead. I was filled with rage and I didn't realize that I was hurt myself. I was in shock and I burst out of the car and ran over to the car that hit us. I was pounding on the car with my fists. I was calling the driver a murderer and inside, inside I was really thinking if I could get in that car I was going to kill this man, and I mean that.

"And all through the months of last summer, I went on with the burden of this hatred in my heart, and I knew it was wrong but I really didn't care. I wanted revenge because he had taken away something that was precious to me, and it really hurt. The strength that I had in the Lord kept me going, but still there was something wrong.

"Then I had to go back to Indiana for the trial of this man who had hit us. I had never seen him since the day of the accident. A friend said, 'I'll be praying for you, for *there is something you have to do,* Tim. You have to forgive this man.'

"I looked at him and said, 'What are you talking about? You want me to forgive this man who took away someone who was more precious than anything to me—just took her away from me?'

"Then he quoted to me, 'Father, forgive them, for they know not what they do.'

457

"But I'm not Christ. I don't have the strength to say anything like that. I hate this man.

"In court, after waiting and pacing all day, I sat down in the witness stand and would not look at him. The prosecutor gave me a stack of pictures of both cars. And then there was a short recess.

"In that quiet courtroom I saw the picture of his car and my blood all over it. All of a sudden the Holy Spirit convicted me and shook me and said, 'Tim, look. Look what you've been doing. You wanted to kill this man. And this man was drunk and he had no intention of killing someone.'

"I was really convicted and remembered what Christ went through on the cross—the nails going through His hands and His feet, and the thud as the cross fell down into the ground. And He just said, 'Forgive them. They don't know what they are doing.'

"I glanced over at the man. At the same time, he looked up at me—and I couldn't talk to him. That was not allowed. But in that exchange of glances, I think I was able to communicate: 'I forgive you. Do you forgive me?' And that was really hard to do. But Christ said we have to forgive.

Is there something *you* have to do?

# 10
## *Losing*
## *My Rights to*
## *My Money*

WHEN I WAS a little girl, I divided everybody into two classes: givers and takers. In my mind I didn't see people as short or tall, black or white, fat or thin—only as givers and takers. It was not the giving or receiving of money that was discernible to me at that young age, but much more obvious things. The givers shared what they had while the takers were always trying to get or keep. The takers were the scrooges of the neighborhood, always building their own "empires," reputations, egos. The givers always offered bunches of grapes or carrots from their gardens; but the takers' harsh words or threatening gestures sent little feet scurrying home.

Yet somehow at the end of the summer, the givers never seemed to lack carrots to preserve or grapes for jelly. I sorted out those facts early and filed them away in my little mind for future reference.

Then there was the friendly iceman who always chipped off little extra pieces and conveniently looked away as hot,

THE POWER OF PRAYER

sweating children clamored aboard his wagon. And there was the grouchy iceman who didn't need to bother to yell his cross warnings to us. We knew who was who!

We had all the cooks pegged as givers and takers too. The mothers of the neighborhood baked homemade bread or buns every Saturday, and we knew which ones never "had enough" in the batch and which ones we could count on for a hot treat smeared with melting butter.

I puzzled over the fact that the takers never got richer than the givers. And the givers never seemed to lack more often than the takers—even through the Great Depression.

But my little preschool mind had also figured out a pattern. The givers not only shared their goodies, they shared themselves. It was the givers who would return the "Hi," who freely gave their smiles.

As I grew older, the categories remained. We knew the ones we could count on to buy whatever we were selling; the ones who would always thank us for working so hard to collect for that "very worthy cause."

Then I made a really big discovery. The takers were usually grumpy and sour; but the givers were pleasant to be around. They were the happy people!

Now I know that those principles I saw lived out in my neighborhood are the same ones we have been given in the Bible.

## SEEMING-LOSSES IN SCRIPTURE

The Bible seems to say such harsh things about our possessions. So opposite to our culture today. It does not commend the accumulation of wealth, but instead the giving up and losing of it.

A professor of New Testament at a seminary who just returned from a sabbatical in Sweden talked with me about our current grasping, materialistic lifestyle. He said, "While away I became more and more overwhelmed with what Jesus had to say about material possessions in Luke 14:33:

So therefore, no one of you can be My disciple who does not give up all his own possessions" (NASB).

"Evelyn," he continued, "that *give up, forsake*, in the King James Version, literally means '*bid farewell to*.' It is the same word used by Jesus when He sent the multitude away and went alone to pray on the mountain" (see Mark 6:46).

Jesus said these jarring words on the way to the cross. Many of those following Him thought they had latched on to an earthly ruler who would usher in material utopia. But Jesus set their thinking straight. Unless they bid farewell to their possessions, they could not be a disciple of His. A distant follower, perhaps, but not a disciple.

There are many other seemingly harsh words spoken by Jesus about money and possessions: "You cannot serve both God and money" (Matt. 6:24, NIV); "With what difficulty shall they that have riches enter into the kingdom of God!" (Mark 10:23, SCO); "Woe to you who are rich, for you are receiving your comfort in full" (Luke 6:24, NASB). And on the list goes.

## TESTING

It is not easy to write about the subject of money— especially since God has tested me personally on the theme of every chapter in this book as I've been writing it.

Driving Mrs. Tim LaHaye, author of two best-selling books, from our airport a while ago, I shared this fact. "Is it true with you too, Beverly?" I queried.

Thoughtfully she agreed, "Yes, in everything I write, God tests me also."

While working on this chapter, I have joked with my secretary, Sally, telling her she had better sit on the checkbook as I write. But our slight uneasiness is not without grounds. Sally was there the last time I tried to write about money. She watched as I kept trying to type the story about it

461

in the *"Lord, Change Me!"* manuscript from my penciled notes. I kept ripping the paper out of the typewriter and crumpling it—only to try again—in vain. Although the story was absolutely true, I could not get it typed.

Then the phone started ringing. Three times. The first call was from a woman who had collected all the reservation fees for a large seminar and luncheon at a hotel, while I had signed for the expenses on my American Express card. She said she had some personal debts and had used the seminar money to pay them—assuring me the $1,200 would be forthcoming immediately. (That was three years ago, and to this date I have received a total of $8.) The next call was equally shattering. A seminar chairperson had reversed her agreement with us so that she, not we, would have the profit of the sale of over a thousand books. This profit usually took care of our overhead expenses. The next call was so relatively insignificant I can barely remember the details—except that the losses represented in those three phone calls totaled $2,400—out of my checkbook! More than was there!

Shocked, I got up from the typewriter, put my arms around Sal and let a few tears fall. Then, settling it, I prayed aloud, "O God, it's all Yours. All my money. It's OK!"

The burden lifted instantly. I smiled and said, *"I guess all God wanted was my attitude."* I sat down and immediately typed the illustration. Not that I hadn't given God all I owned before that. No—this was just His testing!

I sat on the edge of the bed last night and said to my husband, "Chris, it really is true that God has tested me on every chapter I've written for this book. I've relived every loss about which I'm writing. Are we *really* ready for me to write about money—or should I take another subject for this chapter?"

He looked up at me and softly replied, "It's okay. We've been without money before." All He wants is our attitude!

## LOSING THROUGH SEEMING-GAINS

Although the current philosophy seems to emphasize striving for and amassing material wealth, Paul has some frightening words about the outcome of that process:

But those who want to get rich fall into temptation and a snare and many foolish and harmful desires which plunge men into ruin and destruction. For the love of money is a root of all sorts of evil, and some by longing for it have wandered away from the faith, and pierced themselves with many a pang. But flee from these things, you man of God (1 Tim. 6:9–11, NASB).

Paul uses three little terms here that clarify the biblical position on the dangers of wealth: WANT. LOVE. LONG FOR. All three result, not from having, but from trying to get money. Our attitude! Sounds like three terms I might have used as a child to describe the takers of my neighborhood.

The things that appear to bring gains to us can have just the opposite effect. Money and material possessions, God's Word says, actually can bring severe and devastating losses into our lives when they become the ruling force of our existence.

Greed has created many sad, lonely people. "I haven't spoken to my brother since our parents died and the inheritance was divided up several years ago," shared a woman at a prayer seminar. "My brother and sisters became very angry with me when the estate was settled. I kept trying to communicate with them with no response until seven years ago when I sent my last Christmas card to my brother. When he didn't answer, I said to myself, 'Phooey to you. If that's the way you want it, OK. I'll never write again.' Then at yesterday's session I forgave him, and last night spent many hours tracing his several moves by long distance telephone calls. When I finally found him living in another state, I told him I had forgiven him and loved him."

"Oh, Sis," was his reply. "Since our family broke up, I have become a Christian, and I have looked and looked for you but couldn't find you. I've wanted to tell you that I loved you too."

Typical? Yes. Broken relationships over money at the death of a relative are the most common result of those three little terms. Years of loneliness and lost love come because of bitterness and greed. How easy to sell the love of family, security, and oneness for a few dollars, some old china or furniture.

But even worse, these three little terms can produce a broken relationship with God. Jesus warned about that possibility. "You cannot serve both God and money" (Matt. 6:24, NIV). He did not say, "You cannot *have* money—but you cannot *serve* God and money."

How easy to "go away sorrowing" like the rich young ruler because of *wanting, loving,* and *longing for* material possessions. When Jesus told him that the one thing he lacked was the willingness to sell all that he had and give to the poor, and thereby gain treasure in heaven, his face fell and he went away grieved (see Luke 18:18–27). What could God have done with that young leader? He had it all—authority, wealth, and the vitality of youth. A whole life to give to God. But lost—the joy that might have been his. And ours?

Then Jesus sadly said to His disciples, "How hard it is for those who are wealthy to enter the kingdom of God!" (v. 24, NASB) When Peter reminded Jesus that the disciples had left it all to follow Him, Jesus assured them that all who had done so would receive one hundredfold in this present age and eternal life in the world to come. How much have we missed because of those three little terms—want, love, long for?

Jesus gave us a parable about these terms. "You fool!" said God to the farmer who concentrated on building and filling more and more barns with grain. "This very night your soul is required of you; and now who will own what you have prepared?" (12:20, NASB) Jesus summed up all the words with His stern admonition in Matthew 16:26: "For what is a man profited, if he shall *gain* the whole world, and *lose* his own soul?"

Many people think they were not only born with a silver spoon in their mouth, but that they will leave this earth with a gold one. But neither is true. Paul wrote:

For we have brought nothing into the world, so we cannot take anything out of it either (1 Tim. 6:7, NASB).

In this verse Paul is referring to Job's ancient cry of worship to the Lord. When it was reported to Job that all his material possessions (plus all his children) were gone, he fell to the ground and worshiped, saying:

Naked I came from my mother's womb and naked I shall return there (Job 1:21, NASB).

Whether the possessions of King Tut or those of an ancient peasant were buried with them, or the Cadillac with the owner propped up in it in our day, the soul has been separated from those possessions. And it will never be coming back to get them.

For many years my pastor-husband kept himself reminded of this fact by keeping on his desk a motto from the diary of martyred missionary Jim Elliot: "He is no fool who gives what he cannot keep to gain what he cannot lose."

## THE HAVES AND THE HAVE-NOTS

Paul, in continuing his teaching about worldly possessions in 1 Timothy 6, divides people and their riches into two categories: those who *want to* get rich (v. 9), and those who are *already* rich (v. 17). There are possible losses for

465

both in their seeming-gains. After giving instructions to those who want to become rich, Paul adds two warnings to those who are already rich:

> Instruct those who *are rich* in this present world not to be conceited or to fix their hope on the uncertainty of riches (1 Tim. 6:17, NASB).

First, Paul is saying, "You people with money, *don't be conceited.*" Pride is always spelled s-i-n in the Bible. The reason for not being conceited is as old as Moses, who in effect asked the Israelites, "Take a look at the source of your riches." He reminded them that God gave them water and manna in the wilderness. "Otherwise, you may say in your heart, 'My power and the strength of my hands made me this wealth.' But you shall remember the Lord your God, for it is He who is giving you power to make wealth" (Deut. 8:17–18, NASB). No room for conceit there!

Paul's second warning is directed to those who already have riches: "*Don't fix your hope on the uncertainty of riches*" (1 Tim. 6:17, NASB).

I lived through the Great Depression as a little girl and watched the devastating effect on people as the banks went broke. Everything was gone in an instant. My cousin, a bridegroom at the time, was ready to buy all the furniture for his new home, and the bank containing all his savings closed. My father was wiped clean overnight.

Now on the other end of life, I'm living through inflation. Security for retirement? It's like chasing an elusive bubble—always just a little out of reach. Carefully planned insurance and security programs are totally insufficient for those whose earning power has ceased. Missionaries are unable to live on their allotted support funds because of the high rate of inflation in the countries where they are serving. Citizens of other countries have had their currency and savings become instantly worthless as opposing political regimes have taken over the government.

We have no hope in riches. How our seeming-gains can so quickly evaporate—and turn to losses!

## GAINS FROM SEEMING-LOSSES

But there can also be gains from seeming-losses. God has recorded in His holy Word the *whys* of His instruction on seeming-losses of material possessions and money. He knew from eternity past that the *givers*, not the *takers*, would be the happy people. So He told us which pursuits, priorities, and principles would produce those qualities of life we all are seeking. Here are just a few of those eternal truths:

*Confidence.* The Bible gives a tremendous reason why we should be free from the love of (one of those three little terms—*want, love, long for*) money. Why? Because it produces confidence.

Let your way of life be free from the love of money, being content with what you have; for He Himself has said, "I will never desert you, nor will I ever forsake you," so that we *confidently* say, "The Lord is my Helper, I will not be afraid. What shall man do to me?" (Heb. 13:5–6, NASB)

This is a freedom which cannot be guaranteed by any country's constitution or bill of rights. It is freedom which only we can give ourselves. It produces confidence because of who our Helper is—Jesus Christ. Placing our trust in Him with the assurance that He, unlike uncertain riches, is "the same yesterday and today, *yes* and forever" (v. 8, NASB). One of God's eternal truths!

*Contentment.* This is one of life's most prized possessions. Paul in another Scripture portion gives us a peek into his secret of being free from another one of those little words—"want." *Being content.* Contentment comes from making do rather than always wanting more wealth. In explaining why his contentment is not dependent on the gifts of the Christians at Philippi, Paul reveals his philosophy of wealth:

> Not that I speak from want; for I have learned to be content in whatever circumstances I am. I know how to get along with humble means, and I also know how to live in prosperity; in any and every circumstance I have learned the secret of being filled and going hungry, both of having abundance and suffering need (Phil. 4:11–12, NASB).

*Contentment* in the Greek means self-sufficiency. Independent of changing circumstances. Detachment from reverses of fortune. Looking back, I realize how true this has been in my life.

There are two periods in my life which stand out as times of great contentment: during the Great Depression when as a small child I felt the enormity of the decision as to how to "invest" that rare nickel at the candy store; and while following my husband from post to post during his pilot training in World War II, trying to live on $50 a month. I was sometimes a little hungry, but never dissatisfied. Only contented. God's principles really have been a reality in my life.

Just before he gives us those three little terms of which to beware, Paul tells us that if we have food and covering—we should be *content* (see 1 Tim. 6:8). This is not an exhortation, but a statement, a dogmatic assertion of fact that the way to contentment is in *not wanting*. And an eternal fact.

*Life.* After all the warnings in the Bible about seeking riches, surprisingly we find that it also shows the gains for those who are rich. Paul instructs Timothy to tell these believers the way to have tremendous gain—real life:

> Instruct them [those who are rich] to do good, to be rich in good works, to be generous and ready to share, storing up for themselves the treasure of a good foundation for the future, so that they may take hold of that which is life indeed (1 Tim. 6:18–19, NASB).

How is this real life available to those who are rich? By being *rich in good works, generous,* and *ready to share!* My husband listened as a pastor lashed out at any Christian who owned a Cadillac—while sitting in front of him were two men who did. But together they were almost supporting a whole mission field.

A doctor's wife in my prayer group startled us with these words: "I'm praying for more money." Then laughing heartily as she saw our shocked expressions, she said, "Oh, not for *me*—so I can give it away!"

Another eternal principle: real life comes, not from having, but from sharing.

*Joy.* This is a much sought-after quality of life. One of the puzzling precepts shared by Jesus is that it is "more blessed to give than to receive" (Acts 20:35, NASB). Joy comes with giving away; losing—not gaining—money.

I hesitate to write this portion, for as I was reviewing the joys received when I have given, God flashed a Scripture verse across my mind. "Let not thy left hand know what thy right hand doeth" (Matt. 6:3). "Oh, oh," I said half aloud. "How then can I write this chapter?"

But an amazing thread has been running through this whole *Gaining Through Losing* manuscript—*joy.* So, how can I leave out money?

These joys do not come from expected or contrived reactions. No, I'm usually surprised by a spontaneous, unheralded outburst from within. When I was informed that my first book was to be translated into Chinese, the thrill of the potential was exhilarating. But the real joy came when I read that there would probably be little royalty payment. My heart soared at the thought. The *privilege* of being able to give the book was one of the greatest joys I have ever experienced. No twinges of "I wonder how much I'll be losing," or, "It's my book; they can't do that to me." No, only complete, engulfing joy!

The same reaction came when I received an inquiry about

teaching my prayer material to a large international missions organization. "Lord," I prayed, "give me the *privilege* of teaching them." And as I added, "No money, Lord," a great joy surged through me. Then spontaneously I prayed, "Lord, give me the *joy* of giving them all the books—free." Not negating the verse, "For the worker is worthy of his support" (Matt. 10:10, NASB), but affirming 2 Corinthians 9:7:

> Every man according as he purposeth in his heart, so let him give; not grudgingly, or of necessity; for God loveth a cheerful giver.

Just a secret of the source of joy!

This year I checked with my sister to see if her reaction had been the same as mine when I made a decision about our uncle's will. Our only brother had preceded our uncle in death. Because of the wording in the will, our brother's children were unintentionally left out. Legally, nothing was theirs. But when I made the phone call explaining that it was my wish to divide my share, I was surprised at the surge of engulfing joy that flooded my whole being.

"Oh, Evelyn," said Maxine, "that's exactly how I felt when I decided to share too."

My mother, the greatest giver I've ever known, joined in with her jubilant, "Me too" at sharing her part of that will. Not our loss—but our gain—from sharing! Again, God's principle from eternity past: "It is more blessed to give than to receive" (Acts 20:35, NASB).

But is there joy in giving for those *who have nothing to give?* Yes. To encourage those in Corinth to support the poor in Jerusalem, Paul relates to them the startling example set by the churches of Macedonia in their extreme poverty:

> That in a great ordeal of affliction their abundance of joy and their deep poverty overflowed in the wealth of their liberality. For I testify that according to their ability, and beyond their ability they gave of their own

accord, begging us with much entreaty for the favor of participation in the support of the saints (2 Cor. 8:2–4, NASB).

When my mother's oldest sister was ready to go away to school to study to become a teacher, she worked hard to buy the one new dress to take with her. Yet she didn't look on herself as being poor. She and her family always managed on their farm to produce enough food for the winter, livestock to butcher, and chickens to fry.

But from that frugal setting, prompting her little brother to comment to a dinner guest, "Go easy on the butter. Ma wants to sell some," my mother recalls the gaunt, undernourished appearance of a little school friend. One day while waiting for my mother to get ready for school, her friend left her dinner pail in my grandmother's kitchen. Grandma Wyatt peeked inside. Only dry soda crackers. From that day on, her little lunch bucket mysteriously contained a sandwich from their "abundance." Joy? Oh, yes! Just another one of those seeming-paradoxes of Jesus. It truly *is* "more blessed to give than to receive."

*No anxiety.* One of life's most precious endowments— freedom from worry. In exhorting us not to be anxious, Jesus contradicts the driving motivation of most people today.

> Do not be anxious then, saying, "What shall we eat?" or "What shall we drink?" or "With what shall we clothe ourselves?" . . . For your heavenly Father knows that you need all these things. But seek first His kingdom and His righteousness; and all these things shall be added to you (Matt. 6:31–33, NASB).

Jesus was speaking of needs, not wants, one of those three little terms of which Paul speaks. It is easy to confuse the two. A friend in the top social stratum of a large southern city told me that she decided to obey those words of Jesus and live on the basis of her needs, not her wants. "It was just like going through drug withdrawal," she confided.

As I was giving this chapter a final reading with my husband, I just finished the preceding paragraph when my phone rang. "You may not remember me, but I saw you in California last week. Evelyn, do you need $2,000?" Stunned, with needs versus wants so fresh on my mind, I stammered that I really didn't *need* $2,000. Then I suggested to her a couple of Christian organizations that desperately did need her money. When I hung up the phone, I felt trembly all over. I wondered if this was another one of God's tests. Had I passed? I realized that if she had said, "Do you want . . . ?" or, "Could you use . . . ?" my response might have been different. But *need*? Then I sighed with considerable relief as I realized that my response had been a spontaneous, truthful one. "No, I don't *need* $2,000." My real attitude surfaced under pressure. Is that all God wants?

Once we get *wants* versus *needs* straightened out, we can turn to the reason for our not being anxious—the Source of our supply. "And *my God* shall supply all your needs according to His riches in glory in Christ Jesus" (Phil. 4:19, NASB). When we set our eyes on the enormity of the wealth of our heavenly Father—who owns the whole universe— we can relax. God's pursuits, priorities, and principles produce that abundant life in Christ.

## YOUR BALANCE SHEET—PROFIT OR LOSS?

When God initiated these principles of profit and loss, for whose profit were they? His own? He, who owns all the land, oil, and other precious resources on earth? Whose balance sheet is it that tips heavily on the "profit" side through these principles? Ours! Paul said, "Not that I seek the gift itself, but I seek for the profit which increases *to your account*" (Phil. 4:17, NASB).

The Bible, in its instructions concerning money and material possessions, says, "All these things shall be added *unto you*" (Matt. 6:33); "For this is *to your* advantage"

(2 Cor. 8:10, NASB); "Give, and it will be given to you; good measure, pressed down, shaken together, running over, they will pour into your lap. For whatever measure you deal out to others, it will be dealt *to you* in return" (Luke 6:38, NASB). Filling the profit columns of our balance sheets!

## GAMBLERS FOR GOD

It seems that without the willingness to risk losing, there can be no great gains in God's economy. Retired bank president Chester Eggen said to me, "I'm thinking of doing some seminars on the spiritual application of 'There Is No Gain Without Pain.' As a bank president, I know we must let go of our profits in order that we can earn more profits."

A pastor-friend whose wife is in real estate commented, "I know I could make money in investing, but I'm too chicken!" And God's Word affirms this truth in the spiritual sense:

He who sows sparingly shall also reap sparingly; and he who sows bountifully shall also reap bountifully (2 Cor. 9:6, NASB).

Our nonprofit United Prayer Ministries organization decided to test that principle. From its inception, the love offerings had never quite paid the travel, publicity, and mailing expenses. So, after much prayer and with our treasury still in the red, we voted to launch a giving program— free books, tapes, and leaders' guides to missionaries and prisoners. To our surprise, at the end of that fiscal year, we had enough money left over to buy a typewriter and a desk—and the trend has never reversed itself. It works!

## JESUS' WORDS

God set in motion all the laws of cause and effect long before they were recorded in sacred Scripture for us. He wasn't surprised when He saw the principles working in His

473

human creatures on Planet Earth. He knew they were true all along.

Then Jesus, who in the beginning was with God and was God, came down to Planet Earth bringing with Him the words of the Father for us. And when He was ready to go back to His Father in heaven, He prayed in His high priestly prayer: "Father, I have given unto them the words which Thou gavest Me" (John 17:8).

Jesus, in order to bring words to us, temporarily gave up His godly prerogative as Possessor of the entire wealth of the universe, to be born in the poverty of a cattle stall:

> For you know the grace of our Lord Jesus Christ, that though He was rich, yet for your sake He became poor, that you through His poverty might become rich (2 Cor. 8:9, NASB).

He was willing to bid farewell to all His possessions so that we might become rich. Not as measured by the world's gold standard, but in God's infallible economy.

Now these words that God sent down for us about givers and takers were not just commands God decided arbitrarily to impose on His creatures. No, He knew from eternity past what would bring real gains. So He gave us the rules, not as a harsh taskmaster, but as an all-loving Father graciously explaining to His own how to get the end results of joy and happiness for which we all are longing. Thus, instead of demanding a poverty mindset through seemingly difficult scriptural principles, He actually opened the lid of a vast treasure chest—revealing to our shocked eyes the secrets of the ages. Gaining through losing!

"What shall it profit a man if he GAIN the whole world and LOSE his own soul?"                         —Jesus Christ

# 11

## *Losing My Right to Be an Unfit Christian*

"I'VE NEVER SEEN a happy jogger," a friend confided to me. I agreed, admitting that I frequently slow down the car to get a better look at a sweating, sometimes struggling, figure with the grimacing face. Exercising!

Because much of man's physical labor has been replaced by push buttons and elevators in our mechanical age, the need for exercising the body's muscles through various programs has become imperative. So wherever we look we see the puffing, panting beginner or the sleek, invincible expert valiantly striving to build up and tone down.

Contrived, organized and meticulously timed exercise programs—these are good. With today's emphasis on preventive medicine—precautionary measures—exercise is part of a lifestyle that helps keep us well. In addition to physical benefits, the experts tell us that exercise produces a whole array of good results—a pleasant mental state, an exhilarating lifestyle, an antidote to depression, the ability to respond to stress and pain and, if not years to one's life, certainly, life to one's years!

475

But there is another kind of exercise program—a spiritual one—which builds up our inner man. I find myself wondering why so much importance is placed on being in shape physically and so little on being spiritually fit. Also, since physical exercise is so exhilarating, producing such profound feelings of well-being, why are we so skeptical and apprehensive about spiritual exercise? Why do we try so hard to avoid it?

## GOD'S EXERCISE PROGRAM

Before the foundation of the world, God knew we would need spiritual as well as physical exercise. So He placed in the Bible His spiritual exercise program. Surprisingly, I have discovered that, as does physical exercise, it produces the same exhilarating lifestyle, pleasant mental state, an antidote to depression, the ability to respond to stress and pain, and adds life to one's years!

But what *is* spiritual exercise? Don't be surprised if you don't know. In the Book of Hebrews we are told that we have *all* forgotten God's method of exercising His children, as set forth in Proverbs 3:11–12, so the writer reminds us:

"My son, despise not thou the chastening of the Lord . . . for whom the Lord loveth He chasteneth . . . afterward it yieldeth the peaceable fruit of righteousness unto them which are EXERCISED thereby" (Heb. 12:5–11, Caps are mine).

Exercised by what? By an often misunderstood biblical word—*chastisement.*

Accepting this teaching is often difficult because of our negative concept of the chastisement—assuming it to mean "punishment." This causes us to think that all the hard things which come to us are God's form of retribution for our wrongdoing. But the accurate definition of that word is "discipline, training." How different! The purpose is just the opposite—not punishing, but perfecting. God assuring us that the things which come into our lives and the things which He sends will be used by Him to *exercise us*—to make us fit for the tasks and trials of life.

William E. Vine, in his *Expository Dictionary of New Testament Words* (Revell, p. 183), says that "the word *chastening* primarily denotes training children: suggesting the broad idea of education by (a) correcting with words, reproving, admonishing, or (b) by chastening by the infliction of evils and calamities; suggesting the *Christian discipline that regulates character.*" Back in Ecclesiastes 3:10 is recorded, "I have seen the travail, which God hath given to the sons of men to be *exercised* in it"—God's exercise program.

Strangely, the writer of the Book of Hebrews calls this forgotten process an *exhortation,* which means "encouragement or strengthening consolation." I should be encouraged or consoled by the infliction of evils and calamities? Adults, not just children? Strange reasoning by today's standards.

But trials are not to be resented nor do they represent unjust punishment from God. They are just a part of our moral training, designed for us, and used by our heavenly Father to further the education of His children.

At 18 years of age, I underlined in my Bible, in red, Deuteronomy 8:5, "Thou shalt also consider in thine heart, that, as a man chasteneth his son, so the Lord thy God chasteneth thee." But then I understood little of God's future spiritual exercise program for me.

## LOSING MY RIGHT TO BE FREE
## FROM GOD'S EXERCISE PROGRAM

Do I have a choice?

I do have the right to choose if I will engage in a bodily exercise program. But as a Christian, I have *lost the right* to choose whether or not I will be spiritually exercised.

For whom the Lord loveth He chasteneth, and scourgeth every son whom He receiveth. If you endure chastening, God dealeth with you as with sons; for what son is he whom the father chasteneth not? But if you be without chastisement, whereof all are partakers, then are you bastards, and not sons (Heb. 12:6–8).

If I am never exercised by God, then I am not truly a child of God. But when I am exercised by Him, I know I am His child. As such, I have lost my right to be a flabby, unfit, unexercised Christian. The choice is not mine.

And even more astonishing is the fact that it is the one whom God loves, that He chastens, disciplines, and trains. It was through our Judy, afflicted with spina bifida, that God's exercise plan for me was unfolded. (See *"Lord, Change Me!"*)

When the doctor told me that Judy (at that time just five months old) would not live, I didn't have any problem knowing that I was a real Christian—and one whom God loved. But God chastening the one He loves—like that? In our sorrow we sometimes become angry and blame someone. Frequently it is God. I have never blamed God, but I did become very angry with the pastor of my home church. After my mother told him about Judy, his immediate response was, "God must love Harold and Evelyn a lot to give them all that sorrow."

Those words stung and burned deeper and deeper as I knelt by my bed far into the night. Judy's temperature had soared to 105° in a couple of hours that morning. Later in the day, the doctor had said not even to stop at home after leaving his office, but to take her right to the hospital. Then came the awful void of my first night without her. For hours battling with God on my knees by my bed—becoming more and more angry with the man who had so abruptly said those shocking words.

"Sorrow!" How could *he* understand? Had he been there during the awful labor that produced the baby paralyzed from the waist down? Had he heard the head nurse say, "I thought you would like to know, you had the hardest kind of labor this hospital records"? Had he been there when my kind Christian doctor walked alongside my cart as I was being wheeled back to my room, holding my hand, trying to keep me from hurting too much as he explained, "Everything is not good with your baby. In fact, it looks pretty bad. Spina bifida, some paralysis. Tests tomorrow."

How could that pastor have known the ache in my heart, as a new mother, when everybody had gone home that first night, and the sympathetic head nurse, Miss Payne (how I smiled afterward at the appropriateness of that name for the labor room of that hospital), sat by my bed stroking my hair with her tender hands, and applying the cool wet cloth to my burning, tear-filled eyes and throbbing forehead. How could he know *that* sorrow?

But our pastor had said, "*All* that sorrow." In my anger, I relived the sorrow of my stillborn's birth. Of laboring—in vain. Two whole days in the final stage of labor, trying to deliver the baby I had known for 10 days was already dead. And the two miscarriages. My anger grew.

But deep down I knew that what he said was in accordance with Scripture. And I had never doubted God's Word. I never had been angry with the God of those Scriptures. So numbly, still on my knees, I reached for my Bible on the nightstand to read Hebrews 12 once again for myself—"For whom the Lord loveth He chasteneth" (v. 6).

Yes, it was all there. I had really known it all along. What that pastor had said was true. But in my crushing sorrow, there was a vague feeling of something being unfair—or at least beyond my understanding. The King James Version had used the word *chastisement*, and I bent lower and lower under it. I didn't doubt that God loved me, but *this* to express and prove His love? The thought swirled foggily through my befuddled, bowed head.

Suffering chastisement, the writer to the Hebrews said in essence, was a sign not of God's displeasure, but of His *love*. I knew that love was one of God's attributes. He is love, and

479

His actions cannot be inconsistent with who He is. The Bible clearly stated that *He* was the one doing the chastening.

So I learned about losing my right to be free from God's exercise program—because I knew I was one of those whom God—the God who *is* love—loved. *Losing my right* to be a flabby Christian!

## FOR MY PROFIT—GAINING THROUGH LOSING

But God didn't leave me wounded and broken under this puzzling proof of His love. This was the point at which He gently nudged me to read on.

I recall the words *exercised by it* just standing there, hazily, as if the printer should have used more ink—completely beyond my grasp. But the three words that seemed to be in the printer's bold type for me were in verse 10:

But He [chastens] FOR OUR PROFIT, that we might be partakers of His holiness (Heb. 12:10, Caps are mine).

When the frenzy of a current physical exercise program diminishes, there is sometimes the realization that all that was produced was not necessarily for the exerciser's profit—runner's shin splints; blisters; orthopedic problems with knees, back, and feet; tennis elbow, or even a rare exerciser's heart attack. But not in God's program. His is always *for our profit.*

What do I gain from spiritual exercise? The same results that are gained from a good physical exercise program! I'm amazed at the parallels I find. Identical!

George Blanda, who retired from the National Football League at the age of 48, indicated in his recent book, *Over Forty: Feeling Great and Looking Good* (with Mickey Herskowitz, S and S Enterprises), that the more the body is exercised, the better is its ability to respond to sudden stress and other work in general. It is also true that the more I am spiritually exercised, the more strength I have to cope with the sudden stresses brought about by adverse circumstances or attacks from the enemy. The more I have been disciplined, the more efficiently I am able to respond to day-by-day hard work for God.

While reading James Fixx' best-seller *The Complete Book of Running*, I kept smiling to myself as I saw the astounding parallels between the glowing results from physical exercise and the results of being spiritually exercised by God. "We don't guarantee to add years to your life," he writes, quoting Robert Glover, physical fitness director of the West Side YMCA, New York City, "but life to your years" (*Book of Running*, Random House, p. 9).

Are a zest for life, exhilarated feelings, sparkling eyes, a glow and radiance produced only by physical exercise? No. These are also a part of the abundant life that Jesus promised. And He has really produced this exciting lifestyle in me; but, surprisingly, it has come through a difficult spiritual exercise program.

At a Christian Booksellers' convention I sat looking at Joni, that quadriplegic author of two best-selling books, star of the movie of her own life, and founder of an organization to help others who are handicapped, and saw all of these qualities exuding from her. Because she had been swimming, diving, or hiking? Oh, no. While immobile in her wheelchair! What produced her glow, her radiance, and exuberance? Physical exercise? No—spiritual exercise! What God had produced in her *since* that devastating diving accident which left her paralyzed from the shoulders down.

"There's nothing quite like the feeling you get from knowing you are in good physical condition. You wake up alert and singing in the morning and really ready to go," writes Mr. Fixx, quoting a runner from Massachusetts (*Book of Running*, p. 9). Sounds familiar! That's just the way I feel after I've been spiritually firmed and built up by God's exercise program.

Again, writing about what people say physical exercise produces, Mr. Fixx says, "Such factors as willpower, ability to apply effort during extreme fatigue, and the acceptance of pain—have a radiating power that subtly influences one's life" (*Book of Running*, p. 14). Exactly what I experience as a result of being spiritually chastened and exercised. When we were discussing this, my former next-door neighbor, Betty, said emphatically, "It works. I watched it for almost 15 years."

James Fixx also noted, "Running (being exercised) is a powerful antidote to anxiety, depression, and other unpleasant mental states . . . an ideal antidepressant" (*Book of Running*, pp. 15–16). Yes, I too can assuredly face life without a worry or a hassle, being anxious for nothing. It is because of God's chastening program that I can know absolutely that God has prepared me for everything He will allow or send my way. I will never have to worry about overexercised spiritual muscles, knees, or feet. There will never be a spiritual heart attack from overexertion. All fear and apprehension about the future is gone. I will always be spiritually prepared!

At the time of Judy's final crisis, while there on my knees, God unfolded His spiritual exercise plan to me. I could hear Him saying so clearly, "*For your profit*, Evelyn." Then He said, "If you're going to be a pastor's wife, you will have to understand some of these things." Then I read the rest of Hebrews 12:10:

"But He for our profit, that we might be PARTAKERS OF HIS HOLINESS" (Caps are mine).

Mr. Fixx quoted a young editor who was working on *The New Yorker*: "A good run sort of makes you feel holy" (*Book of Running*, p. 15). The Bible says that a good exercising by God *does* make you holy. God chastens and exercises us spiritually that we might be *partakers of His holiness*. The process that makes us holy as He, the God of the universe, is holy. In fact, in the comparison of physical and spiritual exercise programs, Paul goes so far as to say, "Bodily exercise profiteth *little*, but godliness is profitable unto *all* things" (1 Tim. 4:8).

## WHEN?

So many people have asked me *when* they could expect these great results from being chastened and exercised by God. The very next verse in Hebrews 12 gives the answer:

Now no chastening for the present seemeth to be joyous, but grievous, nevertheless AFTERWARD it yieldeth the peaceable fruit of righteousness unto them which are exercised thereby (v. 11, Caps are mine).

But when is afterward?

In heaven? "It will be worth it all, when we see Jesus," serenely, assuredly, sang our close friend, Faye, with her teeth and jaw still wired in place after the accident. It was her first solo since an oncoming car, in an attempt to pass another in a blinding snowstorm, hit her car head-on. Her husband, her only child, and her mother were killed.

Were the words she was singing so confidently in her sorrow true? Absolutely. How thrilling to think of heaven, where all of God's reasons for and results of His exercise program will be unrolled like a scroll before our eyes. Not our sometimes-manufactured "whys" to satisfy our demands for answers or the inquisitiveness of others, but the real, the fabulous profits from His exercise program (see 2 Cor. 4:16–18).

But does *afterward* refer only to heaven? I remember the day God showed me that there is an "afterward" here on earth too. It was on a critical day of a very deep family trial. While I was studying for my Bible study in 1 Peter, I came to chapter 5, verse 10:

But the God of all grace, who hath called us unto His eternal glory by Christ Jesus, AFTER THAT YOU HAVE SUFFERED A WHILE, make you perfect, establish, strengthen, and settle you (Caps are mine).

483

I cried out in prayer, "O God, *when* is 'after awhile'?"

I recorded that cry to God in the margin of my Bible and dated it. Then almost four weeks later when I was to teach that verse again, I resignedly wrote in the margin, "When is God's after a while?" Then I answered my own question, "Not yet!"

It wasn't till a whole year later that I scrawled in large bold letters on that page, "NOW is God's after a while. Great joy again! I'm finally settled. To God be the glory!" Through the years, God has given me the privilege of experiencing countless "after a while" periods—after the exercising is done and the results can be measured—right here on earth.

Now while I was going through that time of chastening, the experience certainly didn't seem joyous. But a careful study of that verse in 1 Peter helped me understand what was happening *during* my trial. I discovered four things God was doing for me: (1) *Making me perfect.* Restoring a part which was lacking, repairing a weakness, and mending me. (2) *Establishing me.* Making me as firm as granite. Instead of collapsing under the weight of the trial, I was coming through it with spiritual muscles like tempered steel. (3) *Strengthening me.* Toning up my flabby inner man. (4) *Settling me.* Laying my foundation solidly on bedrock. Anchored on The Rock—Jesus. This produced in me the peaceable fruit of righteousness.

Chatting with me on an airplane, a woman returning from a trip to Japan remarked, "I had a $100 steak dinner there. The meat was so tender I cut it with my butter knife. The cattle had been kept so immobile that they could not develop any tough muscles. Then they were massaged by hand to further soften their flesh—until they could no longer even stand up."

*That*, I thought, *may make for a good steak dinner, but it won't produce great people.* When I am being matured by God, He doesn't only soothe and caress me, He gives me an exercise program that spiritually strengthens me.

484

## DURING

But does spiritual exercise mean I can never be happy *during* my trials? No. Paul told Timothy, "Exercise thyself rather unto godliness. For bodily exercise profiteth little, but godliness is profitable unto all things, *having promise of* the life that now is, and of that which is to come" (1 Tim. 4:7–8).

All joggers are not unhappy. Though they strain for more air in their lungs, they may be enjoying their exercise immensely. Tom, a young seminary student, came trotting in for breakfast like a young horse with his tail to the wind, having had a good run; his body glistening with sweat, his skin aglow. He explained to me the "high" he had reached that morning while jogging his 10 miles. At that point, his effort had turned into sheer joy.

Just as a jogger experiences the exhilaration of strain during exercise, the invigoration of blood racing through his veins, the euphoric "high" during a good run, can't we expect a "high" *while* being spiritually exercised? Perhaps others see only our sweating, our struggling, and our occasionally grimacing faces. But, if they slow down and take a closer look shouldn't they be able to see an inner exuberance as we spiritually strain against the wind? Yes, they should, because the challenge of being stretched, the rush of spiritual adrenaline for the struggle, can produce the same glow that results from physical exercise—not just afterward, but during the trial.

## BITTER OR BETTER

My husband and I missed the morning business session of a convention as we sat spellbound at the breakfast table listening to our surgeon-friend explain his views on "bitter or better" from Hebrews 12. His face glowed as he recalled the time when Chris had put him on a plane in Chicago and afterward when he arrived at home he had found his wife comatose, after suffering a severe stroke. Then he told us about his daughter, the wife of a young doctor, who, during pregnancy had become ill with polio. He told us how they struggled to save her and the child, and of the decision he made that the moment had come to try to save only the baby's life. Then of the death of both, recalling the casket with his daughter holding the tiny infant in her arms.

In the past we had so admired the exuberance and excitement of his full, well-rounded life—Sunday School superintendent of the largest church in our conference, highly esteemed surgeon, tennis champion. But the glow that morning was not the result of having just finished an exhilarating tennis match, or even the flush of one of his national tennis tournament victories. No, that glow was from God's exercise program—spiritual exercise.

"It all depends on how you respond to trials," he explained, eagerly leaning toward us, radiant and serene. "Bitter or better. And the only difference is one letter—I changed to E. And the E stands for 'Emmanuel—*God with us'*. The secret is when the *I* of me changes to the *E* of Emmanuel—Jesus!" Our Coach!

## KEEP YOUR EYES ON THE COACH

And the secret to victory during the exhausting training and the rugged athletic event is to keep your eyes on the coach!

Eric Heiden, winner of five Olympic gold medals for speedskating in the 1980 Winter Olympics, commented during a television interview that the crucial thing he did to win was to take his eyes off his human competition and *put them on his coach.*

We can look unto Jesus, who not only is our Coach, but also our Example:

And let us run with patience the race that is set before us, looking unto Jesus, the Author and Finisher of our

486

faith; who for the joy that was set before Him, endured the cross . . . lest you be wearied and faint in your minds" (Heb. 12:1–3).

Our Example shows us how He endured during His trials. The reviling, the nails, and the excruciating death were certainly not joyous to Jesus. But still He endured, looking forward to the joy of His after a while—sitting down at the right hand of the throne of God.

Eric Heiden must have remembered his day-after-day, year-after-year disciplining as President Carter, welcoming him and other 1980 Winter Olympic athletes to a White House luncheon, said:

"It's hard for [some people] to appreciate what it means to get up before dawn, year after year, when others are still asleep . . . to endure pain and exhaustion and disappointment. . . . To go through all that pain and sacrifice is indeed a great achievement" *(Minneapolis Tribune,* February 26,1980, p. 1A).

Eric had tangible evidence of his gain from that sacrificial training—five shining, first-place gold medals.

And so it is with us. Our great Coach—God—puts us through a tough training program—because He always goes for the gold!

And what do we profit? The seeming-losses turn into the same great *gains* that are only to be attained by the most grueling, sacrificial spiritual training possible. But the greatest gain of all is that we are fit for the Master's use!

Spiritual exercise. Some never let the Coach get started with the training. Others don't stay with it long enough to ever experience that possible high. Some just get bitter instead of better. And then there are those glowing, radiating participants—spiritually exercised!

Are you fit for the Master's use?

487

# 12

## Losing
## My Right to Be
## Free from Suffering

WHEN YOU RECEIVED Christ as your Saviour and Lord, were you informed of the rights you could expect to gain? They were myriad—the right to find life, abundant life; the right to have the power of Christ rest upon you; to have God fill all the voids left by human losses; the right to life after death in an eternity with Jesus; the right to expect God to come in proportion to your every need; the right to expect to bear fruit; the right to expect to have good mental health. These are but a partial list of the rights that were promised to you, that you could expect to gain when you took Christ as Lord of your life.

On the other hand, did someone also tell you that if you became a Christian, all the problems of your life would disappear? So you accepted Him, and felt you had the right to expect the bumps of life to smooth out. Now the gains you did have the right to expect when you became a Christian were fabulous—but the right to be free from suffering and difficulties was not one of them. In fact, according to

Scripture, that seems to be one of the rights you lost the moment you became Christ's.

In the Epistle of Philippians, Paul wrote these startling words:

> For unto you it is given in the behalf of Christ, *not only to believe* on Him, *but also to suffer* for His sake (Phil. 1:29).

Both? Doesn't it say, "If you believe, your suffering will be removed?" *Expect* to suffer?

To young Timothy, Paul reiterated the same thought by telling him "*all* that will live godly in Christ Jesus *shall* suffer persecution" (2 Tim. 3:12). Not even "may," but *expect* to?

Don't be surprised? That's exactly what Peter said: "Think it not *strange* concerning the fiery trial" (1 Peter 4:12). In this passage the word *strange* is best translated "surprising." Are you surprised? I have underlined these verses in all of my Bibles since I was 18 years old. Yet when I put them all together for this book, their impact surprised me.

There seems to be a progression of reactions to suffering that comes as we mature in Christ. *Reject* it . . . just *accept* it . . . then actually *expect* it.

By now are you questioning the wisdom of ever "signing up" for such a religion? But let's look more closely.

## GAINING T-H-R-O-U-G-H SUFFERING

The sufferings recorded in the Bible seem so frequently to be related to gaining. There is a little word—an important preposition that shows relationship—that is the key. *T h r o u g h.*

A speaker introducing Joyce Landorf at a convention said, "Every time I see Joyce, she has just come through a crisis." I suddenly saw what a compliment that was, and when I had an occasion to introduce her, I explained to the audience: "He did not say she was *in* a crisis, but had just come *through* a crisis—making her the successful author/singer/speaker that she is—giving her insight and answers for the people whom she is addressing.

But we cannot come *through* one without being *in* one. The Bible (and history) is full of examples of God's great ones who suffered in various ways—persecution, personal losses, physical suffering. But their suffering was not an end in itself, but just a *means to an end.* The victories, triumphs, and gains which came through these sufferings are astonishing. Gains by losing? Yes, *losing the right to be free from suffering.*

In this book we have looked at the suffering and difficulties of some of God's heroes and heroines. The spiritual giants in the Bible were not free from hardships. The list is endless. What terror Joseph must have experienced when he was sold into slavery by his brothers—but selected to be God's person to preserve His chosen people from famine. And Moses, snatched from his family in Pharaoh's slaughter of the male children, then living in obscurity for 40 years on the backside of the desert—being prepared to lead God's chosen people to their promised homeland. And Paul—through beatings, stonings, shipwrecks, hunger, cold, nakedness, imprisonment, and pain—reaching his world, and all following generations, for Christ. Then Peter suffering amidst persecution along with other first-generation Christians—equipped to encourage and buoy up "God's elect"—then—and now. And the beloved Apostle John, suffering isolation in his exile on the Isle of Patmos—but receiving from God the revelation of things to come—for all generations until Christ returns. Then, of course, the most important on the list of God's chosen ones, His own Son—who suffered so that He might bring fallen man to God. Gaining, through losing the right to be free from suffering!

## FELLOWSHIP OF HIS SUFFERING

For even hereunto were ye called, because Christ also suffered for us, leaving us an example, that ye should follow His steps (1 Peter 2:21).

These startling words were written by Peter. We are called to be like Christ—but even in His suffering?

Paul, in explaining his philosophy of *gaining through losing* all for Christ (Phil. 3:7–10), concludes with three *so thats* resulting from this process: "That I may (1) know Him, and (2) the power of His resurrection, and (3) the fellowship of His sufferings." But how common it is for us to want to know only the first two—just two-thirds of what Christianity is all about—Him and power. But the remaining third—the fellowship of His sufferings—we so frequently leave off our list of wants.

The chairman of the government arm of our thousand-member, city-wide telephone prayer chain just this morning said to me, "I took Philippians 3:10 as my life verse when I was a teenager. I meant it with all my heart, and was very sincere about it. And I've consciously worked at living according to it ever since. But as the years have passed, I've discovered I was only concentrating on the first part—that I may know Him and the power of His resurrection."

She shook her head and continued, "But it finally dawned on me that that was only part of the verse. The rest was 'and the fellowship of His sufferings'. . . ." It was so easy for me, also, to take just two-thirds of what Paul said—or even what the whole Bible says.

This is not to say that suffering is *never* removed. However, it is when I get past the idea that the *only* gain possible from suffering is to have it removed, that I mature into Christlikeness—what He was able to be in His sufferings. Not enjoying the suffering, but with Christ, willingly enduring all that is God's will.

But what did Christ suffer while here on earth? Only the cross? No. Sometimes we think that the crucifixion was Christ's only suffering Then we can feel secure in the remoteness of the possibility of our being martyred for Him. But Jesus' whole ministry was laced with suffering—many different kinds—while He was doing His Father's will.

Peter, who probably did not witness Christ's death on the cross, was yet able to say, "I who am also . . . *a witness of the sufferings of Christ*" (1 Peter 5:1). Therefore, Christ must have suffered in other ways and at other times. But how? Right after entering into His ministry, Jesus suffered alone under the temptation of Satan for 40 days. But from that time on, Peter was there. He saw the agony Jesus suffered when His former peer group tried to push Him off the cliff at Nazareth. And Peter saw the deep hurt in Christ's face when so many who had wanted to make Him king, turned and followed Him no more. He watched as Jesus wept over Jerusalem with a broken heart. And Peter, a member of Jesus' inner circle of three, was so near to the agony of Gethsemane as Jesus wrestled in prayer with the Father. But it was *only* Peter who saw the anguish in his Lord's eyes as He turned and looked on him, after he forsook and denied Him, just as Jesus was facing His greatest physical and spiritual suffering—crucifixion.

Is the tenderness that exudes from Peter's first letter, his suffering epistle, the result of his having experienced these sufferings with Jesus? Is that what sends me fleeing to that book when I am hurting? Is this the reason God so graciously led me to be teaching that book in my neighborhood Bible study when the deepest grief of our pastoring years occurred? Is this why I get the feeling that this is the book that understands me?

Early one Sunday morning in the midst of tunneling through 1 Peter for the writing of this chapter, I asked God not to let me just write. But I begged Him to make this chapter *real* to me. Then I slipped down to the living

492

room and, with my heart growing heavier and heavier, once again read through Paul's sufferings in the Book of Acts and 2 Corinthians. Then I sat in silence thinking through all of Jesus' sufferings. Overwhelmed, I prayed, "O God, I am not *worthy* to write this chapter!" Tears were straining to get out of my eyes. I wept. "I am not *worthy* to suffer—*even* to suffer!"

## REJOICE

I went back to reading 1 Peter 4:12–13: "Beloved, think it not strange concerning the fiery trial which is to try you, as though some strange thing happened unto you, but *rejoice."*

"O God," with tears still persisting, I cried out, "how can I rejoice when my heart is breaking?"

Then God gave me the answer from those verses.

"Rejoice because you are *sharing Christ's suffering."* I have a part in the suffering that broke His heart—and mine? I have that privilege? "Yes, it is Jesus—whom you love so much—whose sufferings you are sharing!" said God.

And there was more than just the *reason* for the joy. It actually said to rejoice *in proportion* to our sharing in the sufferings of Christ. "To the degree that you share the sufferings of Christ, keep on rejoicing" (v. 13, NASB). The more *I lose my right to have suffering removed, the* more *I gain* the ultimate privilege possible for any human being: not only being like Christ—but actually sharing His sufferings!

## REJOICE—THERE'S GLORY

While all the personal sufferings of my life seemed to be marching in shadowy review through my mind, God kept dealing with me. He said next, There is a *so that* to being partakers of Christ's sufferings: *"That, when His glory shall be revealed, you may be glad also with exceeding joy"* (v. 13).

Again my mind slipped back to the man, Peter. How uniquely qualified he was to write about future glory. I have often tried in vain to grasp the magnitude of the glory of the transfiguration. But Peter was a witness as Moses and Elijah "appeared in glory" and talked with Jesus—whose face was shining like the sun and whose raiment was radiating and glistening. When Peter awoke from his sleep, he "saw Jesus' glory" (Luke 9:30–32).

And through eyes still red with weeping after having forsaken and denied his Lord, Peter was the first apostle to see Jesus in His resurrected, glorified body that first Easter. The awe of that glory must have left him prostrate and trembling at Jesus' feet (See 1 Cor. 15:5 and Luke 24:34). Then between the resurrection and ascension, Peter's eyes were opened as Jesus explained the Old Testament prophets' predictions about Christ's sufferings and the glory which would follow (See 1 Peter 1:10–11). So Peter scattered throughout his writings the astounding association between suffering and glory—for me. And my tearfilled eyes, too, beheld Christ's glory!

How different was Peter's understanding from the time when his newfound Messiah had said the strange-sounding words so early in His ministry: "Blessed are ye, when men shall revile you, and persecute you, and shall say all manner of evil against you falsely, for My sake. Rejoice, and be exceeding glad; for great is your reward in heaven" (Matt. 5:11–12). Peter must have thought, "Master, wouldn't it make more sense to say that we should rejoice as our trials are removed?" It would have been natural for him to have questioned Jesus' logic very early in their relationship.

## FUTURE GLORY

Peter also used this same word *rejoice* in the first chapter of his first letter to explain that sufferings, although necessary, are only temporary—completely transcended by that which is to come. Rejoice because trials have a purpose—to prove the genuineness of our faith which is much more precious than gold—which also must be tried with fire. And then rejoice because *beyond the trials,* at the appearing of Jesus, there will be *praise and honor and glory!*

We can endure, and actually rejoice while enduring, if there is something great enough to look forward to. And that something is a Person—my Jesus. I have not seen Him either but, believing, I love, and rejoice with great joy too deep for words, transfigured beyond earthly bliss—my Jesus! (See 1 Peter 1:6–8.)

Paul summed it up writing:

And if children, then heirs; heirs of God, and joint-heirs with Christ; if so be that we *suffer with Him, that we may be also glorified together.* For I reckon that the sufferings of this present time are not worthy to be compared with the glory which shall be revealed in us (Rom. 8:17–18).

Christ's pathway to glory is also our pathway to glory.


## GLORY NOW TOO?

That Sunday morning as I continued to meditate on His Word, God kept adding more understanding about that glory. This verse I found hard to comprehend: "If you be reproached for the name of Christ, happy are you; for the spirit of glory and of God *resteth upon you"* (1 Peter 4:14). The spirit of glory glowing and radiating God's presence— on me? The glory of Christ that Peter remembered from the Mount of Transfiguration? Or the glory John said they had beheld in Jesus? (John 1:14) Or the glory Jesus had with the Father before the world was? (John 17:5) Or perhaps the visible brightness of the Shekinah glory as mentioned in the Old Testament, the luminous glowing of the presence of God among His people?

495

On me? That possibility seemed absolutely untenable, impossible. The best I could do was to look back to those whom I had remembered actually radiating during and after deep suffering.

While I was Corrie ten Boom's hostess in St. Paul for a week, I saw that glow on her face as she said to me, "Every day while I was in Holland during World War II, I prayed, 'Dear Father, don't send me to the concentration camp. Don't send me to the concentration camp!' But, Evelyn, He sent me to the concentration camp! But I now know why."

Her reason took me by surprise: "*So I could learn to suffer.* Evelyn, 60 percent of the Christians on earth are suffering active persecution today. And God has sent me to 63 countries to teach the Christians how to suffer. And Evelyn, God has said to me—it is coming to America. That's why I'm here." The radiance on her face transcended all the Nazi horror of World War II.

## GLORIFIED BY ME?

Then God unfolded to me a second reason for present rejoicing during trials. That one I couldn't handle. "But *on your part* He is glorified" (1 Peter 4:14). Then Peter adds, "Yet if any man suffer as a Christian, let him not be ashamed, but let him *glorify God on this behalf*" (v. 16). I, by my attitudes and reactions during suffering not only have His glory resting on me, but can actually glorify *God*?

Then a scene from 10 years ago flashed through my mind. The ache of having decided I was not worthy to serve Christ publicly because of a deep family crisis again engulfed me. But then I remembered my hostess showed me what her husband's mother had written in her Bible at what was to have been my last neighborhood Bible study:

The follower of Christ does not hang his head in shame as the difficulties of life come upon him. He trusts God;

and, by his poise and grace in the midst of difficult circumstances, declares to all the world that God is able to deliver, yes, *to glorify Himself* in that which has come to pass.

Then the memory of another Bible filled my thoughts. In it is the first recorded prayer for me—written after I found Christ at nine years of age. My mother bought me that first Bible, and in it wrote the prayer for her daughter:

Mother's Prayer
In life's great journey,
As you travel through,
May GOD BE GLORIFIED
In *all* you do.

Each year I pray a birthday prayer for myself for the coming year. On my last birthday, I prayed, "God, You be glorified in me this year. I want only You to get the glory all this year, not me. All the glory—not just 'You be glorified most and me a little less.'" What an exciting prospect! What a fantastic gain for me—the God of the universe glorified in *me*! And yet—what an overwhelming thought.

Then I hesitated and questioned. Was I being brazen, egotistical, too pushy? Who did I think I was? "In me"— an ordinary, everyday human being—the glory of the God of the universe? The Creator—and I only the creature? Was this a scriptural prayer? Yes it was. First Peter 4:14: "On your part He is glorified"!

As I write, this year is now 11 months old. Has it happened? God has certainly not removed all the suffering from this year, but it has been a year of unprecedented joy. Not that I had expected that prayer to produce joy. But God gave it while I consciously, one by one, gave all the things which could have brought *me* glory—to God—only for *His* glory.

But there is a warning here. All these examples of the connection between suffering and glory indicate that we are to rejoice *only* if we do not deserve the suffering. Christ's sufferings all occurred while He was doing good, and when no guile was found in His mouth (1 Peter 2:22). We rejoice when we suffer *wrongfully*—when innocent like Christ.

## GOD'S WILL?

All the old wounds of my Bible study class in 1 Peter opened up when I read verse 19 of chapter 4. It had been the capstone then, and became once again for me now—God's will. "Wherefore let them that suffer according to the will of God commit the keeping of their souls to Him in well-doing, as unto a faithful Creator." When? When I am in God's will.

This is God's plan. But it is much more than submitting to an inevitable destiny. It is being able, when in His will, to entrust myself completely to Him. In my prayer seminars, I teach how to pray in God's will. But before I ask people to entrust their souls to Him—in joy or sorrow, victory or defeat, healing or suffering—I point out that they must know *who God is.* He loves us so much that He has dedicated and consecrated Himself to work everything out for *our* good. He chastens for *our* profit. He intends every *loss* to be that through which we can *gain. The One who takes all our losses and turns them into gains.*

God is the faithful and powerful Creator of the universe. He has power over all creation—and all suffering. Enough power to do anything He chooses! To transcend suffering—to give grace to endure it, or comfort through it, or to remove it—the decision is His. We entrust it all to God and leave the results to Him.

To be sure, the results are not all the same. But they are always for our eventual gain. Sometimes it is the shock that a prisoner named Ralph experienced after giving his most precious possession, his family, to God. The next morning, Ralph learned that his daughter had been struck by a car and was not expected to live. Through much prayer and a series of miracles, he soon was on his way to her. In the midst of that horrible crisis, he found himself thanking and praising God—what better hands could his daughter be in?

Then there were the results God gave to Doris. Last Sunday I telephoned Dr. Doris Johnson, president of the Senate of the Bahamas, United Nations representative, author of their constitution's preamble guaranteeing religious freedom for her nation.

"How are you, Doris? I've been hearing some great things about you!"

"Oh, Evelyn, you will never believe how the Lord has worked this all out!" she exclaimed. "The mortgage on my house, the pain, all the burdens—gone—since I turned them all over to Him!"

What did she mean? Two years ago at a convention in the Bahamas, she came to me and said she wanted to bring her prayer partner to my room to pray. For almost three hours we sat in a tight circle, knees touching, her prayer partner and I praying intermittently as Doris rehearsed her problems. With her doctorate degree in educational administration, Doris had had a fine-paying job. Her present Senate position held lots of prestige, but not all that much money. Her husband had died. She couldn't keep up with the mortgage payments and was losing her home. She had a pain in her shoulders and neck that no doctor, nor a well-known faith healer, had been able to help. Should she give it all up and go back to making more money?

I finally said, "Doris, can *you* pray now?"

"What should I pray?"

I explained that she should *release it all to God.*

"What do you mean *release?*"

"It's the word *commit* in 1 Peter 4:19. When we suffer undeservedly, we are to turn ourselves over to God. It is the same word Christ used on the cross when He was suffering while absolutely innocent. Jesus, our example, who all through His life entrusted Himself to His Father's will. Even at the time of His supreme suffering, the crucifixion, He committed His soul to His Father. Doris, just give it all to God."

I slipped down on my knees and she dropped her head onto my shoulder. For 15 minutes, with deep emotion, one by one she gave each facet of her life to God—for His will. The next morning at the convention she delivered a beautiful, almost state-of-the-union address.

"That was terrific! How are you?" I bubbled.

"Oh, Evelyn, it's all gone—the pain, the burdens. I'm just great."

On the phone she brought me up-to-date through the two years of God's working out every single thing after she gave it all to Him.

"And," she exclaimed, "the last great thing that happened to me was in October. I was invited to Buckingham Palace and knighted by Queen Elizabeth—with the Dame Commander of the Most Distinguished Order of the British Empire!

"And as the Queen was pinning the star over my heart," she continued, "its hook fell to the floor. While all the attendants and guards stood frozen at attention, the Queen stooped down at my feet and picked it up. All I could think of was: 'AT THE NAME OF JESUS EVERY KNEE SHALL BOW'!"

Immediately I thought, *If we suffer, we shall also reign with Him* (2 Tim. 2:12). The final glory Peter mentions is *the crown of glory* (Cf. 1 Peter 5:4). A crown of exaltation—the victor's crown.

Reigning with Jesus of whom, *through* His crown of thorns, it could be written, "And a crown was given unto Him; and He went forth conquering, and to conquer" (Rev. 6:2). And, because I too have LOST my right to be free from suffering, I have GAINED the greatest of all gains: I will reign with Jesus!

But, until that time, while we are still here on earth, God is in the business of turning all our LOSSES—physical suffering, being forsaken, aloneness, bereavement, forfeited money, and relinquished rights—into GAINS. Maturing us, refining us, strengthening us, preparing us, enriching us— if we let Him.

Are you *gaining* through your losses—with God?

# Epilogue

PERHAPS YOU HAVE never experienced God's turning your losses into gains. First, you must be His child. How can you become a member of His family? Realize that "all have sinned and come short of the glory of God" (Rom. 3:23). But God has provided a way for you to come to Him. "For God so loved the world that He gave His only begotten Son, that whosoever believes in Him should not perish, but have everlasting life" (John 3:16). To become His child, you must receive Christ as your Saviour. "As many as received Him, to them gave He power to become the sons of God" (John 1:12).

If you desire this personal relationship with God, pray:

"God, I confess that I have sinned and thus am separated from You. Jesus, I believe that You are God's only provision for my sins, having paid for them by dying on the cross. I receive You, Jesus, into my life as my Saviour and my Lord. Thank You for making me one of Your own."

Pray this prayer sincerely and start a new life with God.

And, with Him in control, you will be eligible for God's intended plan for you—His taking your losses and bringing you great gains through them.

And for all of God's children, the secret of this life is in loving Him above all else, deeply desiring His will, and faithfully obeying all of His instructions. As you search for His leading in His Word and listen to Him in communing prayer daily, He is faithful and will reward you.

Write me (4265 Brigadoon Drive, St. Paul, MN 55126) and let our prayer chain pray for you.

Love in Christ,
Evelyn